# OREGON INDIANS

# OREGON INDIANS
## Culture, History & Current Affairs

An Atlas & Introduction

Written by

Jeff Zucker, Kay Hummel & Bob Høgfoss

Drawings by

Faun Rae Hosey

Cartography by

Jay Forest Penniman

**WESTERN IMPRINTS**
THE PRESS OF THE OREGON HISTORICAL SOCIETY
1983

Library of Congress Cataloging in Publication Data

Zucker, Jeff, 1949–
   Oregon Indians.

   Bibliography: p.
   Includes index.
   1. Indians of North America—Oregon. I. Hummel, Kay, 1954–      . II. Høgfoss,
Bob, 1952–      . III. Hosey, Faun Rae, 1950–      . IV. Penniman, Jay Forest,
1952–      . V. Title.
E78.O6Z8   1983      979.5'00497      80-84478
ISBN 0-87595-094-9
ISBN 0-87595-109-0 (pbk.)

Printed in the United States of America.

This volume was originally developed by the *Atlas of Oregon Indians Project*
through grants from the Yarg Foundation, the Oregon Episcopal School, and the
Multnomah-Washington CETA Consortium (under the Comprehensive Employment and Training Act of 1973). The content of the publication does not necessarily
reflect the view of these granting agencies, their staffs, or governing boards.

The production of *Oregon Indians* was supported by funds from the Oregon Historical Society's Western Imprints Fund.

This volume was designed and produced by Western Imprints.

# CONTENTS

PREFACE                                                      xi

ACKNOWLEDGEMENTS                                             xii

INTRODUCTION                                                 xiv

## PART ONE: TRADITIONAL

NATURAL AND CULTURAL AREAS                                   3
    DATING OF TRADITIONAL CULTURE            3
    ENVIRONMENT AND CULTURE                   4
    LOWER COLUMBIA AREA                       6
    COAST AREA                                6
    INLAND VALLEYS AREA                       6
    KLAMATH LAKES AREA                        6
    COLUMBIA PLATEAU AREA                     7
    GREAT BASIN AREA                          7
    CHANGING BASIN-PLATEAU BORDER             7
THE TRIBES OF TRADITIONAL OREGON                             8
    LOWER COLUMBIA AREA TRIBES                8
    COAST AREA TRIBES                         9
    INLAND VALLEYS AREA TRIBES                10
    KLAMATH LAKES AREA TRIBES                 11
    GREAT BASIN AREA TRIBES                   11
    PLATEAU AREA TRIBES                       11
    TRIBES ALONG THE BASIN-PLATEAU BORDER     12
    CHANGING TRIBAL ORGANIZATION              13
    TRIBAL TERRITORY AND LAND OWNERSHIP       14
FOOD RESOURCES                                               15
    FISHING                                   15

PLANT GATHERING 21
SEAFOOD AND SHELLFISH 25
HUNTING 26
SEASONAL CYCLES 29
WINTER 30
EARLY SPRING 31
LATE SPRING AND SUMMER 31
FALL 31
SETTLEMENT AND POPULATION PATTERNS 32
HOMES AND FAMILY ORGANIZATION 35
WESTERN OREGON WINTER DWELLINGS 35
EASTERN OREGON WINTER DWELLINGS 39
TEMPORARY SHELTERS AND SWEATLODGES 40
FAMILY ORGANIZATION 41
TRADE NETWORKS 42
TRANSPORTATION 45
OREGON INDIAN LANGUAGES 48
SOCIAL ORGANIZATION 54
LOWER COLUMBIA AREA 56
COAST AREA 56
INLAND VALLEYS AREA 56
KLAMATH LAKES AREA 56
PLATEAU AREA 57
GREAT BASIN AREA 57
FIRST CONTACTS WITH NON-INDIANS 58
EXPLORATION AND SETTLEMENT OF OREGON BY
EURO-AMERICANS 58
EPIDEMICS 60
MEETING OF CULTURES 60
ARMED STRUGGLES 62

# PART TWO: HISTORICAL

EARLY U.S. INDIAN POLICY IN OREGON 67
INTRODUCTION 67
SOVEREIGN INDIAN TRIBES 68
TREATY—MAKING WITH INDIAN NATIONS:
RESERVING PRE-EXISTING RIGHTS 69
IGNORING SOVEREIGNTY: REMOVAL POLICIES 70
TRUST RESPONSIBILITIES AND INDIAN LANDS 70
BUREAU OF INDIAN AFFAIRS (BIA) 72
EARLY RESERVATION PERIOD 73
ALLOTMENT OF RESERVATIONS 73
OTHER LAND LOSSES AND A SHRINKING TRUST
COMMITMENT 75
CITIZENSHIP AND THE INDIAN REORGANIZATION ACT 75
MORE ASSIMILATION: THE 1950S AND TERMINATION 77
SINCE THE 1950S 78

TREATY-MAKING IN OREGON: MORE THAN A QUESTION
    OF LAND    79
    WHAT IS A TREATY?    79
    OREGON INDIAN COUNTRY: THE CREATION OF
        RESERVATIONS    79
    HISTORY OF OREGON TREATIES    82
    UNRATIFIED TREATIES OF 1851    84
    WESTERN OREGON TREATIES: 1853-55    85
    1855 PLATEAU TREATIES    87
    TREATIES OF SOUTH-CENTRAL AND EASTERN OREGON  88
    TREATY NEGOTIATIONS: LAND, LANGUAGE AND
        MISINTERPRETATIONS    89
    TREATY PROMISES: AN ONGOING RELATIONSHIP    91
DISPLACEMENT OF OREGON INDIANS    93
SHRINKING INDIAN LANDS    95
    TRIBAL TRUST LAND    95
    ALLOTMENT    95
    SURPLUS LANDS    96
WARM SPRINGS INDIAN RESERVATION    97
UMATILLA INDIAN RESERVATION    101
MALHEUR AND BURNS PAIUTE INDIAN RESERVATIONS    103
KLAMATH INDIAN RESERVATION    107
GRAND RONDE AND SILETZ INDIAN RESERVATIONS    113
CLAIMS CASES    122

# PART THREE: CONTEMPORARY

RECENT U.S. INDIAN POLICY    129
    SOVEREIGNTY AND THE TRUST RELATIONSHIP    130
    FEDERAL RECOGNITION    131
    BUREAU OF INDIAN AFFAIRS TODAY    133
    IMPACT OF TERMINATION    134
    NEW POLICY DIRECTIONS    135
    SELF DETERMINATION IN OREGON    136
    ECONOMIC DEVELOPMENT    137
    RESTORATION OF INDIAN TRIBES    139
TRIBES OF CONTEMPORARY OREGON    140
    TRIBAL AFFILIATIONS    140
    ORGANIZED TRIBES    140
    OTHER TRIBES REPRESENTED IN OREGON    142
    INTERTRIBAL AND REGIONAL ORGANIZATIONS    143
URBAN INDIANS    144
    MIGRATIONS, TERMINATION AND RELOCATION    144
    URBAN ASSISTANCE PROGRAMS    146
    QUESTIONS FOR THE FUTURE    148
INDIAN POPULATION    149
    OREGON INDIAN POPULATION    149
    UNRELIABILITY OF U.S. CENSUS DATA    151

DIFFERING ESTIMATES OF OREGON'S INDIAN
    POPULATION        153
JURISDICTION OVER INDIAN COUNTRY    156
    TRIBAL POWERS IN INDIAN COUNTRY    156
    LIMITS TO TRIBAL AUTHORITY    157
    PUBLIC LAW 83-280    157
    JURISDICTION IN OREGON    158
HUNTING, FISHING AND GATHERING RIGHTS    160
    ON RESERVATION RIGHTS    160
    PROBLEMS DUE TO DIMINISHED RESERVATION
      LANDS    160
    EFFECTS OF TERMINATION    161
    OTHER ISSUES    162
    IMPORTANCE OF HUNTING TO KLAMATH PEOPLE    163
COLUMBIA RIVER FISHING CONTROVERSY    165
    BASIS FOR INDIAN FISHING RIGHTS    165
    DECLINING FISH RUNS    167
    DAMS ON THE COLUMBIA    167
    COURT DECISIONS AND MANAGEMENT    169
    THE "50 PERCENT ALLOCATION"    170
    FUTURE OF THE INDIAN FISHERY    170

CHRONOLOGY    173

BIBLIOGRAPHY    193

INDEX    223

PROFILES    inside
back cover

# ILLUSTRATIONS

## PART ONE: TRADITIONAL

| | | |
|---|---|---|
| Chart: | Tribes & Bands of Traditional Oregon | inside cover |
| Map: | Natural & Cultural Areas | 2 |
| Chart: | Summary of Cultural Areas | 5 |
| Map: | Tribes & Bands of Traditional Oregon | 9 |
| Drawing: | Transportation (Travois) | 14 |
| Map: | Major Food Resources | 16 |
| Drawing: | Fish Club | 17 |
| Drawing: | Fish Wier | 17 |
| Drawing: | Fish Hooks & Spears | 18 |
| Drawing: | Fish Nets & Traps | 19 |
| Drawing: | Fishing Platform | 20 |
| Drawing: | Food Gathering & Preparation Tools | 22, 23 |
| Drawing: | Food Gathering (Clam Basket, Diggers) | 25 |
| Drawing: | Hunting (Bola, Whistle, Quiver, Bow) | 27 |
| Drawing: | Hunting (Deadfalls, Snare) | 28 |
| Chart: | Seasonal Cycle of Plateau Tribes | 30 |
| Map: | Settlement Patterns: Aboriginal Pop. Density | 33 |
| Map: | Settlement Patterns: Village & Seasonal Movements | 33 |
| Drawing: | Western Oregon Winter Dwellings | 36, 37 |
| Drawing: | Eastern Oregon Winter Dwellings | 38 |
| Drawing: | Sweatlodges | 40 |
| Map: | Indian Trade Network at The Dalles & Celilo Falls | 43 |
| Drawing: | Transportation (Footwear) | 45 |
| Drawing: | Transportation (Canoes, Raft) | 46, 47 |
| Drawing: | Transportation (Burden Basket) | 47 |
| Chart: | Classification of Oregon Indian Languages | 49 |
| Map: | Indian Languages | 51 |

Chart:      Social Organization                                    55

# PART TWO: HISTORICAL

Photograph: Gathering at Old Chief Joseph's reburial              66
Photograph: Men at The Dalles, ca. 1920                           71
Map:        Ratified Treaties & Cessions                          80
Map:        Unratified Treaties                                   83
Map:        Temporary Western Oregon Reservations                86
Map:        Displacement of Oregon Indians                       92
Map:        Shrinking Indian Lands                               94
Map:        Warm Springs Indian Reservation                      99
Map:        Umatilla Indian Reservation                          100
Map:        Malheur & Burns Paiute Indian Reservations           104
Map:        Klamath Indian Reservation                           108
Photograph: Klamath families in dugout canoes                    109
Map:        Grand Ronde & Siletz Indian Reservations             112
Photograph: Coastal family gathering oysters                     115
Chart:      Indian Claims Commission Cases                      116-21
Map:        Claims Payments for the Taking of Indian Lands       124

# PART THREE: CONTEMPORARY

Photograph: Warm Springs representatives signing
            Celilo Fishing Rights Settlement, 1952               128
Photograph: Drummers at tribal gathering                         138
Photograph: Women at Grand Ronde celebration                     139
Chart:      Tribal Affiliations of Oregon's Indian Pop.          141
Map:        Other Tribes Represented in Oregon                   142
Map:        Tribes & Urban Indian Communities                    145
Chart:      Oregon Urban & Rural Population                      146
Chart:      U.S. Urban & Rural Population                        147
Chart:      Age Distribution of Indian & Total
            Populations, 1970                                    150
Chart:      Age Distribution of Indian Pop. in Selected
            Counties                                             151
Chart:      Projected Growth of Indian & Non-Indian Pop.         151
Chart:      Indian Population                                    152
Chart:      Differing Estimates of Indian Population             153
Map:        Indian Population by County, 1890-1970               154
Chart:      Annual Run Sizes of Anadramous Fish
            Entering Columbia River                              166
Chart:      Fishing Rights: Treaty Indian Catch in Relation
            to Other Fisheries                                   167
Map:        Declining Fish Runs in the Columbia Basin            168
Photograph: Indian fishing grounds at Celilo Falls               171

# PREFACE

Written materials about Oregon Indians have been accumulating on library shelves for over 200 years. These include tribal records, explorers' journals, legal documents, historical and anthropological writings, and endless government reports. Generally, these materials have been unavailable to either the people from whom they were gathered or the general public. Until recently most writing on Oregon Indians has either been technical in nature (with a limited distribution) or has been popularized to the point of stereotyping. In 1977 the "Atlas of Oregon Indians" Project was initiated by Jeff Zucker to compile information from these previously gathered sources and make it accessible in visual form. Indian educators, tribal planners and others encouraged the authors to expand the materials into a general reference book.

*Oregon Indians: Culture, History and Current Affairs* is the product of seven years of cumulative work carried on by many people. The original staff consisted of five non-Indians (those listed on this volume's title page) with backgrounds in ethnic studies, history, geography, anthropology and art. This group avoided a purely academic approach to the subject and consulted directly with the Oregon Indian communities.

In addition to this volume, the Atlas Project staff also compiled the *Oregon Directory of American Indian Resources*, which is now published bi-annually by the Oregon State Commission on Indian Services.

The Atlas Project staff felt it essential to set up a process of preview and review, whereby tribal organizations, Indian educators and others involved in Indian-related issues would have a chance to affect the outcome of the book. Suggestions were solicited on subject matter and approach, working drafts were circulated and over 300 copies of a rough draft were eventually distributed. This process was followed by rough-draft review sessions at schools and tribal headquarters throughout Oregon. Many suggestions received about content, tone and format were incorporated in this volume.

In the end, more time was spent on the review process than had been spent on the original library research and writing. Perhaps the most tangible evidence of this long process is the set of profiles and statements by persons directly involved in Indian issues.

This study is by no means the final word on Oregon Indians. There are undoubtedly many persons whose viewpoints the authors were not able to gather. No written document could ever compress all the years of lived experience which make up Indian history and current affairs. It is hoped that this book will provide background information which will raise a number of questions. Readers can seek the answers to these questions by exploring the reference materials listed in the resource notes, by following Indian-related issues in the news, and especially by asking those directly involved—the Indian people of Oregon.

# ACKNOWLEDGEMENTS

Many people helped in the preparation of this book. Concerned individuals donated hundreds of hours reviewing drafts. The list below includes only those who gave substantive criticism during preview and review sessions or in letters. Many others, too numerous to name, provided support and suggestions. In addition, we would like to thank the boards and staffs of the Oregon Indian Education Association and the Oregon State Commission on Indian Services, who hosted numerous review sessions. The Native American Rights Fund in Boulder, Colorado, provided much bibliographic support. We also thank the Multnomah-Washington CETA Consortium, the Oregon Episcopal School and the Yarg Foundation for their assistance.

The list is arranged alphabetically and includes organization affiliation at the time of writing. Many of those listed have moved on to other positions since 1979. None of the persons listed are responsible for any misrepresentations or errors. Neither they nor the organizations listed necessarily endorse this book.

Dorothy Ackerman (United Indian Women), Mike Adams (Migrant Indian Coalition), Lewis Alexander (Urban Indian Council), Linda Anderson (Klamath), Lynn Anderson (Klamath), Warner Austin (United Tribal People), Dean Azule (Oregon Indian Education Association), Clement Azure (Oregon Department of Education), Pat Badnin (Northwest Regional Education Lab), Kirk Beiningen (Oregon Department of Fish & Wildlife), Art Bensell (Siletz), Robert Benson, Bruce Bishop (Commission on Indian Services), Robert Bojorcas (Eugene Indian Center), William Brainard (Coos, Lower Umpqua, Siuslaw), Robert Buschman (Cow Creek), Gil Calac (Urban Indian Council), Jody Callica (Warm Springs), Marie Callica (North American Indian Women's Association), Rochelle Cashdan (University of Oregon), Ron Cihan (Portland State University), Robey Clark (Title

IV), Warren Rudy Clements (Warm Springs), Joseph Coburn (Klamath), Rob Collier, Jackie Colton (Grand Ronde), Dale Cornett (BIA), Mike Darcy (Title IV), Kay Davis, Annabelle Dement (Indian Economic Development, Inc.), Elen Deming, Dayton Densmore (Indian Program on Alcohol and Drug Awareness), Hetta Dines (Title IV), Trin Dumlao (Urban Indian Council), Ed Edmo (Urban Indian Council), Steve Engle (CETA), Barbara Farmer (Urban Indian Council), Judith Farmer, Mike Farrow (Umatilla), Catherine French, David French (Reed College), Elizabeth Furse (National Coalition to Support Indian Treaties), Leland Gilsen (Office of Historic Preservation), Kathleen Gordon (Umatilla), Dora Goudy (Warm Springs), Georgia Goudy (Fort Dalles Urban Indian Center), Kathy Greene (Commission on Indian Services), Verbena Greene (Warm Springs), Alan Hamm (Northwest Area Indian Health Board), Catherine Harrison (Lampa Mountain Sweathouse Lodge), Carmen Haug (Grand Ronde), Merle Holmes (Grand Ronde), Mike Houck (Oregon Episcopal School), John Hughes (Umatilla), Shirly Iman (Celilo Village), Charles Jackson (Cow Creek), Nathan Jim (Warm Springs), Ed Jones, Nick Kalama (Warm Springs), Vi Kalama (Warm Springs), Dennis Karnapp (Warm Springs), Marvin Kimsey (Grand Ronde), Art Kraiman (Indian Program on Alcohol and Drug Abuse), Richard La-Course (Umatilla), Victor LaCourse (Indian Health Service), Lucy Lamb (Title IV), Jim Lavadour (Umatilla), Nancy Levidow, Lavonne Lobert-Edmo (Oregon Indian Education Association), Steve Lowenstein, Karleen McKenzie (Tchinouck), Bill McLean (Indian Education Institute), Suzanne Mandiberg, Faith Mayhew (Urban Indian Council), Brian Mercer, Antone Minthorn (Umatilla), Dennis Mulvihill (Commission on Indian Services), Douglas Nash (Umatilla), David Parrella (University of Oregon), Woody Patawa (Umatilla), O. J. Pelland (Western Chinook), Helen Peterson (BIA), Evonne Pettijohn (Tututni-Tolowa), Jean Pierce (Indian Economic Development), Jane Pond (Umatilla), Ron Pond (Umatilla), Jackie Provost (Grand Ronde), Margaret Provost (Grand Ronde), Elmer Quinn (Warm Springs), Dick Rankin (Migrant and Indian Coalition), Bill Ray (Northwest Regional Education Lab), Bill Robinson (Department of Fish and Wildlife), Jim St. Martin (Burns/Paiute), Jack Schwartz, Sue Shaffer (Cow Creek), Gail Sharp (Commission on Indian Services), Amos Simtustus (Warm Springs), Peter Sipple (Oregon Episcopal School), Eleanor Smith (Title IV), Minerva Soucie (Burns/Paiute), Twila Souers (Title IV), Kay Steele (United Indian Women), Theodore Stern (University of Oregon), Esther Stutzman (Coos, Lower Umpqua, Siuslaw), Wayne Suttles (Portland State University), John Talley (KBOO), Robert Taylor, Richard Thierholf (Organization of Forgotten Americans), John Volkman, Nelson Wallulatum (Warm Springs), Wilfred Wasson, Don Wharton (Oregon Legal Services), Rick Wheelock (Title IV), David Whited (Southwest Oregon Indian Health Program), Charles Wilkinson (University of Oregon), Chuck Williams, Tessie Williams (Umatilla), Pat Woodside (North American Indian Women's Association), Hirohito Zakoji (BIA), Henry Zenk.

# INTRODUCTION

The Indians of Oregon have had a long and varied history and are active today throughout the state. There were originally over 100 tribes and bands in Oregon, each with its own pattern of social organization, political system and language. Each tribe had a different history of contact with non-Indians; some signed treaties and accepted reservations, others did not. Today there are many different elements in the Oregon Indian community, including reservation and landless tribes as well as a large group of Indian people who have moved to Oregon from other parts of North America. This book is intended to provide background information that can serve as a starting point for understanding the diversity and cultural richness of Oregon's Indian people.

Two hundred years ago there was no "state of Oregon." In a way, it is artificial to speak of the Indians of Oregon, yet there are several reasons why it is important to do so. In the first place, all Indian people currently living within the state boundaries are faced with similar concerns and have formed organizations (such as the Oregon State Commission on Indian Services and the Oregon Indian Education Association) based on the concept of the state of Oregon. Secondly, Oregon Indians have often been neglected in general works on Indians which have usually dealt with the more "glamorous" cultures of the Northwest Coast, the Plains and the Southwest. Thirdly, it is important to realize that Indian cultures were not all alike. Some readers may be surprised to learn that Oregon Indians had customs and experiences completely different from the more commonly known Indian cultures.

Oregon's Indian people are very much a part of today's society and play an important role in the state's culture. All too often, the history of Indian people is separated from current activities and achievements. Popular accounts focus only on events of the past, giving little indication that the Indian cultural heritage continues to be vital or that Indian people today participate in all sectors of American society.

Movies, television and even some textbooks lead us to associate Indians exclusively with the past. Preoccupation with Indian history leads many people to the conclusion that there are no "real Indians" left. This misconception is based on the idea that the only "real Indian" is one who dresses and acts as did the Indians of many centuries ago. But Indian cultures, as with all cultures, have changed and adapted to the times. Indian culture is not a museum culture—a frozen image of the past—it is a living tradition.

It is a mistake to judge the Indian people of today by yesterday's standards, but it is also a mistake to ignore the historical process that links the past with the present. Many of the issues that remain important in current Indian affairs have their basis in history. Legal and social conditions affecting Indians today are often rooted in traditional values and historical policies. In order to understand the process of change that has taken place in Oregon Indian societies for the past two centuries, it is necessary to see Indian history and current affairs as a continuity. For this reason, this book has been designed to include three parts dealing with the traditional, historical and contemporary Indian peoples of Oregon.

Part One describes the traditional Indian cultures of Oregon from the point of view of the people who lived in them. The early Euro-Americans who explored and settled Oregon were often unable to evaluate Indian cultures on their own terms. Instead, they used values relevant to their own societies to judge Indian societies. As a result, many people today have a mistaken impression of traditional Indian cultures. The Indians of Oregon were not the savages portrayed in Hollywood movies, nor were they living in a romanticized golden age.

The traditional Indian cultures of Oregon had values and customs quite different from those of present-day American culture. The relationship between people and the natural world, the concepts of territory and land ownership, and the settlement patterns of the various tribes were all unique. Instead of comparing these customs with American culture or with some arbitrary standard of civilization, it is more important to ask whether they benefited the people who followed them (the relevant question in comparing technologies, for example, is not whether the dugout canoe was as fast as an outboard motorboat, but whether the canoe served the needs of the people who used it).

The same principle holds true for other aspects of traditional culture and society. Indian economic and political systems were all uniquely adapted to the resources available, the methods of exploiting those resources and the population dependent on them. There is no way to directly compare the current American economic and political system with traditional Indian systems since each is based on a completely different balance between resources and needs.

Part One, rather than making comparisons, examines how traditional Indian societies operated and interacted before the coming of Euro-Americans.

Part Two examines the period of transition during which Euro-Americans settled Oregon and confronted the traditional Indian cultures. The conflicts and changes that occurred during the settling of Oregon were in a large part the result of these cultural differences. Indian economies based on hunting, fishing and gathering came into contact with an economy based on agriculture and industrial development. Indian political systems based on family ties and flexible affiliations confronted the less flexible American governmental system. The purpose of studying the sometimes painful history of these contacts is not to assign guilt or to bemoan the wrongs done, but to understand some of the events that had so much effect on Indian peoples. There were many unfortunate incidents involved in the settling of Oregon, and the disruption of traditional cultures was a great misfortune; yet, nothing is learned by blaming one side or the other. Questions must be asked about why these incidents occurred and what effect they had.

The treaty-making process in Oregon was an attempt to resolve the conflicts between the two types of societies. This solution was, however, rather one-sided. The once independent tribal organizations became islands within the dominant American society. Whether the Indian tribes could survive became the central question. The United States Constitution, early Supreme Court decisions and treaties recognized the principle of sovereignty—that Indian societies have a right to continue. Yet United States Indian policy has been like a see-saw of contrasting views on Indian survival. Policies such as removal, allotment of Indian lands and termination have seriously undermined the principle of sovereignty. Tribes without treaties and reservations have fought to remain united. In order to insure their survival, Indian tribes entered a special relationship with the United States government. Part Two chronicles the development of this relationship and outlines some of the changes that occurred in the various Oregon Indian communities.

Part Three examines the current situation of Indian people in Oregon. Contrary to the popular myth that Indians are a ''vanishing race,'' Oregon's Indian population is growing rapidly. Yet more than the population survives; Indian people are working to preserve their cultural heritage and to fuse old ways and new. Many concerns of the traditional and historical periods are still vital to Oregon Indians. Cultural values such as strong family ties and use of native languages remain important to many Indian people. Hunting and fishing continue to have economic, cultural and political relevance. The relationship between tribes and the United States developed in the last century is still very important and legal principles set down in treaties remain in effect. Yet there are also many completely new interests in the Indian community. Indian people have initiated new programs in such fields as health, education and employment. Economic enterprises have been developed both on and off the reservations. Oregon's Indian community continues to respect its past, but it is also actively planning its future.

No single statement can cover the wide range of Indian activities in Oregon today. Issues and concerns differ from one Indian community to the next. Urban Indians face different problems from Indians living in rural areas and there are wide differences between reservation and non-reservation tribes. Even on the reservations there are differences because legal and economic conditions vary considerably. No outsider can explain the unique concerns of the various Indian communities. Therefore, Part Three, as much as possible, allows the different communities to speak for themselves. The community profiles attached are statements by the major Oregon Indian organizations describing their own views on the role of Indian people in Oregon today.

The three parts of this book demonstrate that from the earliest recorded history until the present day the Oregon Indian community has been marked by diversity. During the traditional period, numerous languages, cultures and political systems existed side by side. Policies carried out during the historical period often attempted to reduce this diversity by assimilating Indian cultures into the dominant American culture. Recent policies such as self-determination and bicultural education are moving in the direction of recognizing the value of cultural diversity. Such policies are important for everyone, for Indians and non-Indians alike will benefit from the cultural and political diversity of a truly pluralistic society. In the final analysis, all Oregonians are enriched by having a strong and growing Indian community in the state.

# OREGON INDIANS

## PART ONE
## TRADITIONAL

# Natural & Cultural Areas of Oregon

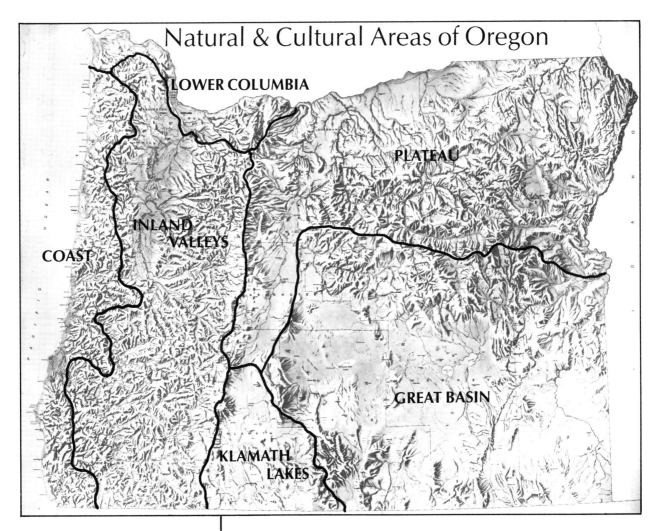

LOWER COLUMBIA

PLATEAU

INLAND VALLEYS

COAST

GREAT BASIN

KLAMATH LAKES

MAP: NATURAL AND
CULTURAL AREA
(Photographic base from USGS.)

Area borders drawn using drainage basin maps, data from tribal distribution sources (*see* pp. 8-12) and culture areas listed in this section.

Other culture area maps include Wissler; Driver (1961); Josephy (1968); Kroeber (1939); and Beckham (in Loy, 1976).

# NATURAL AND CULTURAL AREAS

DATING OF
TRADITIONAL CULTURE
Archaeology

Much information on pre-contact Indian societies can be found in works by Oregon archaeologists. Two recent works on Oregon's prehistory are by Cressman (1977); and Aikens (1975). Cressman's earlier books (especially 1962) provide general sources on Oregon archaeology. Johnson & Cole present a bibliography of prehistory in Oregon. Jennings' study is a comprehensive survey of North American prehistory.

Specific Oregon studies include Aiken's works on the Great Basin (1971) and the Willamette Valley (1975). Other important sources are the cultural resource surveys being prepared by the U.S. Forest Service, the BLM and the Corps of Engineers.

## DATING OF TRADITIONAL CULTURE

Indian people have been living on the land now called Oregon for more than 10,000 years. Throughout this long period, Indian cultures were changing and continually adapting to new situations. It is beyond the scope of this book to summarize the archaeological evidence of this Indian pre-history. Part One will pick up the story of Oregon Indians just prior to the arrival of Euro-American settlers.

This epoch is often called pre-contact or aboriginal, yet both of these terms refer to Indian history as "that which came before non-Indian history." The term used here to describe this period will be "traditional," referring to the time when knowledge was passed on through oral traditions whose origins stretch back to the beginning of human history in North America.

It is not easy to put a definite date on the traditional period since Euro-Americans arrived at different times in different parts of Oregon. Willamette Valley Indians, for example, were profoundly influenced by white settlement long before Indians of southeastern Oregon had even met their first Euro-American. Contact occurred roughly between the years 1790 and 1855 and, unless otherwise noted, all references to traditional culture refer to that time.

The use of culture areas has been popular in American anthropology since 1914, when Clark Wissler published his first maps using the concept (*see* Wissler, 1950). Oregon is usually seen as an intersection of culture areas although no two authors seem to agree on how the state should be divided. The six-area system presented here is meant to apply to Oregon itself and can be incorporated into any of the continent-wide culture area schemes.

# ENVIRONMENT AND CULTURE

During this long traditional period, the various tribes and bands developed their own customs and traditions suited to the particular environment they inhabited. The cultures of the local groups—their customs, beliefs and activities—shared much with other Indian cultures in North America, but were in many ways unique to this area. Even within Oregon, there was great variety in physical environments and in Indian cultures.

The geographic features of Oregon—mountains, rivers, deserts and shorelines—played an important part in traditional Indian life. The rivers were rich sources of food and provided easy travel by canoe. While mountains were often barriers that separated Indian cultural areas, they were also good places for hunting and berrypicking and may have been the home of some Oregon tribes. The ocean provided fish, seal and many kinds of shellfish, both edible and ornamental. Even the scrublands and deserts of eastern Oregon had their own attractions: edible roots, small game of all types and rocks for arrowheads and spearpoints.

In addition to the physical characteristics of the land, natural resources had (and continue to have) deep spiritual significance for Oregon Indians. Land and wildlife were viewed as being filled with power that gave them an importance far beyond the purely economic. Mountains and forests were seen as places where humans could contact the spirit world. Fish, plants and animals were regarded as spirit beings who assist the human race. In some cultures, the earth was seen as a mother who nurtures the human children who live on her.

In order to describe the importance of the natural environment and to discuss the diversity of Oregon Indian cultures, in this book the state is divided into six geographic regions. The map (p. 2) "Natural and Cultural Areas of Oregon" shows the boundaries of these six areas based largely on river drainage basins, mountain crests, major waterfalls and other features. These are natural boundaries in which terrain and resources are similar. They are also cultural areas, since the distinguishing features include not just the land itself, but also the way Indian people used the land.

Land was the basis for a way of life and differences in the land were reflected in the Indian cultures. The natural resources in the six areas were related to the methods of food gathering, the settlement patterns and the seasonal cycles of the Indian people who lived there. Even such aspects of culture as architecture, methods of transportation and political organization were linked to the physical environment and to the particular methods of adaptation to the environment.

Throughout Part One, these six natural and cultural areas will be used to describe the great differences and the similarities among Oregon Indian cultures.

The six areas should not, however, lead to too many generalizations. In actual fact, each tribe (often each family) had its own cus-

# Summary of Cultural Areas

| CATEGORY | LOWER COLUMBIA | COAST | INLAND VALLEYS | KLAMATH LAKES | PLATEAU | GREAT BASIN |
|---|---|---|---|---|---|---|
| MAJOR FOOD RESOURCE | Fish | Fish | Plants | None dominant | None dominant | Plants |
| POPULATION DENSITY* | Very high | High | Medium | Low | Low | Very low |
| DISTANCE OF SEASONAL MOVEMENT* | Short | Short | Medium | Medium | Long | Long |
| METHOD OF LONG DISTANCE TRAVEL | Canoe | Canoe | Canoe/Foot | Canoe/Foot | Horse | Foot (before 1840s) |
| WINTER DWELLING | Wood plank house | Wood plank house | Plank & bark house | Earth-covered lodge | Mat longhouse | Willow-frame house |
| SOCIAL ORGANIZATION | Stratified by wealth and heredity | Stratified by wealth | Partially stratified by wealth | Partially stratified by wealth & achievement | Partially stratified by achievement | Not stratified |
| FIRST NON-INDIAN CONTACT BY LAND | 1805 | 1810-30 | 1810-30 | 1810-30 | 1805 | 1840s |

(*These categories are relative and apply only to comparisons within Oregon)

toms, often dissimilar to those of other groups or individuals within the same culture area. The boundaries drawn are not absolute because Indian people moved around and shared cultures even across the lines marked on the map. Natural and cultural areas also extended into neighboring states, although only the Oregon portions will be considered in this book.

Following are brief descriptions of the six natural and cultural areas. Cultural features of these areas—tribal organization, languages, food resources, architecture, transportation and trade—are discussed more fully in the remaining sections of Part One. The chart (p. 5) summarizes the cultural features of the six areas.

The Lower Columbia Area is generally combined with the Coast Area in a large "Northwest Coast Culture Area" that also includes the coasts of Washington, British Columbia and southern Alaska. One exception is the easternmost Chinooks who are sometimes classfied as part of the Plateau (*see* Driver 1961). David H. French (personal communication) has proposed that the Wasco-Wishram be classed with either the Northwest Coast or the Plateau.

The Inland Valleys Area is often divided into sections. The Shasta and some Athapascan tribes are classed in the California culture area which includes most California tribes (Josephy 1968; Driver 1961). The Kalapuyans have been designated as both Northwest Coast (Kroeber 1939) and Plateau (Josephy 1968; Driver 1961).

The Klamath Lakes Area is another subject of controversy. Driver places it in the Plateau. Josephy and Kroeber place it in the Great Basin. Ray (1963) asserts that the Klamath were Plateau oriented while the Modoc were California oriented. Stern (1964, and personal communication) disagrees, claiming that both Klamath and Modoc were more related to the California and Basin areas than they were to the Plateau.

The Plateau and Great Basin areas are now usually treated as separate areas extending north to upper British Columbia and south to Nevada. Wissler divided the Basin between the Plains, the Plateau and California. Kroeber combined these three divisions into the "Intermontane Area." Lowie proposed a similar "Ultramontane Area." Ray (1939) argued that the Plateau was indeed an area unto itself, and not simply a mixture of Plains, Basin and Coast.

The six-area system used in this volume is meant to bypass these arguments. For example, the Klamath

## LOWER COLUMBIA AREA

The Lower Columbia Area includes the lower portions of the Columbia and Willamette rivers. These rivers were rich in salmon and were important in the Indian trade network. Major features within the area included several important rapids and falls and a major island. The rapids and falls were vital fishing spots that marked the boundaries of the area both in the east (at Fivemile Rapids, near The Dalles) and in the south (at Oregon Falls, near Oregon City). Sauvie Island contained abundant roots and edible plants. The Lower Columbia Area was the most densely populated in Oregon and was characterized by plank houses, long-prowed canoes and emphasis on rank.

## COAST AREA

The Coast Area includes the lower portions of the Rogue, Umpqua, Coquille and Nehalem rivers and all of the smaller coastal rivers. Bounded on the west by the Pacific Ocean and on the east by the summit of the Coast Range, this area had two major resources: salmon in the rivers and seafood along the shoreline. The Coast Range provided game and berries and served as a partial barrier between coastal and inland peoples. In the southern part of the area, where the Coast Range merges with the Siskiyous and Klamath Highlands, borders were less distinct and were marked by rapids such as the Scottsboro of the Umpqua. The Coast Area was also heavily populated and the Indians here built plank houses and canoes.

## INLAND VALLEYS AREA

This large and diverse area includes the upper portions of the Willamette, Rogue, Umpqua, Coquille and Nehalem drainages. The best fishing on these rivers occurred downstream in the territory of Coast and Lower Columbia tribes. Therefore, salmon was not as available to people of the Inland Valleys Area as it was to their neighbors. Nuts, roots and game were, on the other hand, fairly plentiful.

Within the Inland Valleys there were several types of environmental zones. The large valleys of the Willamette and Rogue provided a variety of natural resources. The smaller valleys along the Cascade and Siskiyou slopes were much less rich. Culturally, the area was marked by plank and brush houses, foot travel supplemented by canoe and a fairly low population.

## KLAMATH LAKES AREA

The major features of this area of south central Oregon are the Klamath lakes and the marsh country surrounding them. Upper and Lower Klamath lakes, Tule Lake and Agency Lake provided many edible plants and waterfowl. The rivers draining into these lakes

Lakes tribes have not been identified as Plateau or Basin Indians, but rather recognized as belonging to a unique area that shares some features with each of the larger areas but is basically a unit in itself. Likewise, the Inland Valleys Area tribes share certain identifying characteristics—medium population density, mixed food resources, foot and canoe travel and use of secondary and tertiary streams—that differentiate them from both the Coast and Inland tribes they are usually associated with.

The six-area system is based on cultural and environmental patterns, rather than on specific customs or "culture traits." Exhaustive studies have been made listing thousands of these traits, including everything from basketry styles to ceremonials. In Oregon, these trait lists have been compiled for the Coast (Barnett 1937), the Plateau (Ray 1942), the Great Basin (O.C. Stewart 1941) and portions of the Inland Valleys Area (Wheeler-Voegelin 1942; Driver 1939). Statistical surveys of these traits include Kroeber (1957); and Driver & Coffin. While such trait surveys are interesting when examining use of a particular technology, the statistical approach to the traits tends to overemphasize details and to view culture areas as absolute entities rather than as conceptual guides.

(especially the Williamson River and Lost River) had good fishing. Klamath and Sycan marshes were lush hunting and gathering spots. The Cascade Mountains to the west provided hunting and berry-picking sites.

The people of this area developed a culture that was adapted to the specialized lake and marsh environment. Population was fairly low, earth-covered lodges were used as winter dwellings, and shovel-nose canoes were the major form of transportation.

## COLUMBIA PLATEAU AREA

The Columbia Plateau Area includes the middle portion of the Columbia River and a number of smaller rivers (Deschutes, John Day, Umatilla, Grande Ronde). Except for the fishing site at Celilo Falls on the Columbia, none of these rivers provided as good fishing as did the rivers in the Lower Columbia and Coast areas. The hills and valleys offered abundant edible roots, and hunting was probably better in this area than anywhere else in Oregon.

Culturally, Columbia Plateau people were quite different from western Oregon tribes. Mat longhouses were the common winter dwelling, population density was low and (after 1730) horses were the main form of transport.

## GREAT BASIN AREA

This large and diverse area is high scrubland with few major rivers. Although some fishing was done on the Snake River (which formed the eastern border of this area) and along several smaller rivers, fish were not the most important food source. Lakes (including Malheur, Harney, Silver, Goose and Warner) were a source of plant products and waterfowl. The slopes of Steen, Hart and other mountains were well stocked with roots and seed plants.

Great Basin peoples had a very low population density, lived in small camps, wintered in willow-frame houses and traveled mostly on foot until horses were introduced in the mid-1800s.

## CHANGING BASIN-PLATEAU BORDER

The border between the Great Basin Area and the Plateau Area was even less rigid than other culture area borders. The country north of this line was fairly dry, and the rivers (upper portions of the John Day and Deschutes) were not abundantly stocked with fish. Mountain ranges such as the Ochocoes, Blues and Strawberries provided some game and plants, but food resources were relatively sparse in this northern and western boundary of the Great Basin.

The region between the North and Middle forks of the John Day River was used, at one time or another, by peoples from both the Plateau and the Basin. The region between the upper Deschutes and the Cascade Mountains was also used by these people as well as by Inland Valleys and Klamath Lakes tribes.

MAP: TRIBES OF
TRADITIONAL OREGON

Tribal locations and names are derived from the sources listed below by area. *See* page 4 for a description of land boundaries. Historical maps can be found in Thwaites (1904); and Wilkes (1845). Recent statewide maps include Beckham (in Loy, 1976); Benson; Berreman; and Schaeffer (1959). Local maps produced by ethnographers are in Dorsey (1890); Drucker (1936); Garth; Howe; M. Jacobs (1945); Kelly; Ray, Murdock & Blyth; Spier (1930); Stern (1966); O. C. Stewart (1941; 1966); Steward & Wheeler-Voegelin; and Whiting.

GENERAL SOURCES ON TRIBAL
DISTRIBUTION

Swanton summarizes information on tribal names, locations and distributions. Mooney (1928) provides a list of tribal names and subdivisions. Berreman's 1937 study, although somewhat dated, gives the most complete overview of Oregon Indian distribution. The 1910 *Handbook of North American Indians*, edited by Frederick W. Hodge, contains much material and the forthcoming new edition will be invaluable. Additional information on tribal distribution can be found in ethnographies, in ethnohistorical sources (*see* notes pp. 56-57) and in treaty records and Commissioner of Indian Affairs reports as well as in all Oregon ICC cases discussed in Part Two.

LOWER COLUMBIA AREA
TRIBAL DISTRIBUTION

*See* Suphan; H. C. Taylor, Jr. (1974); and ICC dockets 234 & 198.

# TRIBES OF TRADITIONAL OREGON

In traditional Oregon there were hundreds of small independent villages and mobile bands; each community had its own pattern of political and social organization. These local communities were linked together into larger units, commonly called tribes. Neighboring communities were linked by many kinds of bonds. Family relationships, shared language, political and economic alliances and common ethnic identity all served to unite groups. It is difficult to define the word tribe so that it applies to all Oregon Indians. In the following discussion, the word tribe will be used in its most general sense to refer to any group of people who shared one or more of these bonds.

The areal distribution within Oregon is shown on the map on page 9, "Tribes and Bands of Traditional Oregon," and discussed by culture area below. A more detailed list of tribes and bands can be found inside the front cover. It is important to study these local examples before examining the larger question of tribal organization. Changes brought about by non-Indian settlement, confusion over the meaning of tribal names and the unique Indian attitude toward land ownership are all involved in this complex issue.

## LOWER COLUMBIA AREA TRIBES

The people of the Lower Columbia Area are popularly referred to as Chinook Indians, although they were actually divided into a number of tribes and bands. The various tribes—Clatsop, Cathlamet, Skilloot, et cetera—were marked off from each other by differences in dialect and, in some cases, by cultural differences. Each tribe included several bands (listed in the chart on p. 49). At the basis of Chinookan social organization were large, permanent, independent villages strongly linked together by trade and marriage alliances.

There was virtually no distinction between Oregon's Chinooks and those living in Washington. The Columbia River was a highway, not a barrier. Washington groups such as the Shoalwater Chinook and the Wishram were closely allied to their southern neighbors.

There was greater diversity in the east-west division of tribes. The Wasco-Wishram, near The Dalles, lived in a different environment, spoke different dialects of the Chinookan language family and were separated by many miles from the Clatsop and Shoalwater Chinook, who lived near the mouth of the Columbia.

All of the people in this area shared a general cultural pattern based on fishing, which included emphasis on trade and rank. In a broad cultural sense, all the Lower Columbia people can be referred to as Chinook. The people all spoke dialects of the Chinookan language family, so they can also be called Chinookan-speaking peoples or Chinookans. Politically and socially, however, the Chinookan-speaking people belonged to many separate tribes. Today, some

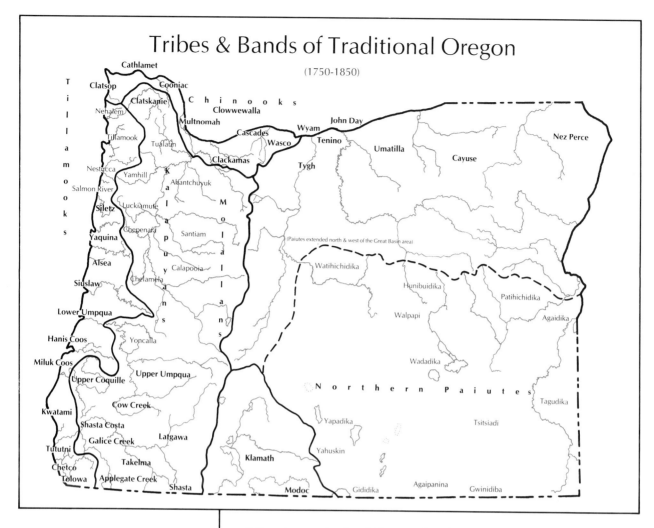

## Tribes & Bands of Traditional Oregon

(1750-1850)

Cathlamet

Clatsop
Cooniac

Clatskanie
C h i n o o k s

Nehalem
Clowwewalla

Multnomah

T
i
l
l
a
m
o
o
k
s

Tillamook
Tualatin
Cascades
Wyam
John Day

Nestucca

Salmon River

Siletz

Yamhill
Ahantchuyuk

Wasco
Tenino
Umatilla
Cayuse
Nez Perce

Tygh

Yaquina

Luckiamute
Clackamas

Chepenafa
Santiam

Alsea

Calapooia

Siuslaw
Chelamela

Lower Umpqua

Yoncalla

Hanis Coos

Miluk Coos

Upper Coquille
Upper Umpqua

Kwatami

Cow Creek

Shasta Costa

Galice Creek
Latgawa

Tututni

Takelma

Chetco

Tolowa
Applegate Creek
Shasta

K
a
l
a
p
u
y
a
n
s

M
o
l
a
l
l
a
n
s

(Paiutes extended north & west of the Great Basin area)

Watihichidika

Hunibuidika
Patihichidika

Walpapi
Agaidika

Wadadika

N o r t h e r n    P a i u t e s
Tagudika

Yapadika
Tsitsiadi

Yahuskin

Klamath

Gididika
Agaipanina
Gwinidiba

Modoc

---

COAST AREA TRIBAL DISTRIBUTION
J. Owen Dorsey (*see* especially 1884, 1889 & 1890) did extensive fieldwork on the Siletz Reservation, gathering information on tribal distribution. His notes and articles include long lists of village names and locations. No records exist to indicate when each of these villages was occupied, however, and information on their tribal affiliations is minimal. *See also* H. C. Taylor, Jr. (1974); and ICC Docket 234.

of the descendants of these tribes have confederated into one and call themselves the "Chinook Tribe."

## COAST AREA TRIBES

The people in the Coast Area belonged to many different tribes speaking a number of languages. They lived in large, permanent villages clustered along the coastal rivers. Since travel was easier up and down river than it was between valleys the people of each river system developed a local dialect and set of customs.

The northern coastal rivers were inhabited by bands who spoke related dialects and were known collectively as the Tillamook. The Siletz, who spoke a slightly more divergent dialect, were sometimes referred to as a band of the Tillamook. The central coast was occupied by the Yaquina, Alsea, Siuslaw and Lower Umpqua tribes. Each had a group of related villages along a major river. The Hanis Coos and Miluk Coos spoke related languages and lived in large villages along the shores of Coos Bay.

South of Coos Bay, the tribal divisions become somewhat arbitrary. There was a continuous series of villages and bands speaking Athapascan languages. Each village was somewhat independent and it is difficult to assign them to one tribe or another. The Tututni, especially, included a number of divergent bands and villages. The southernmost tribes—the Tolowa and Chetco—extended into California.

## INLAND VALLEYS AREA TRIBES

In terms of tribal organization this was perhaps the most diverse area in Oregon. Villages were often smaller and less permanent than in the Coast and Lower Columbia areas; individuals or families could easily change allegiance from one village to another.

The Willamette River's central valley (upriver from the falls at present-day Oregon City) and the lower parts of its tributaries were occupied by bands that spoke languages in the Kalapuyan sub-family. The Yoncalla Kalapuyans extended southward into portions of the Umpqua River drainage. Each of the Kalapuyan groups listed on the map was made up of smaller mobile bands with significant dialect and cultural differences.

Along the western slopes of the Cascades, from the Clackamas to the Rogue River, were the bands of the Molalla. These people ranged as far east as the Deschutes River in their seasonal food gathering rounds. The Molalla bands, isolated from early white settlement, were at one time thought to be an eastern Oregon tribe pushed into the Cascades by warfare. Evidence is accumulating, however, that the Molalla had been living in the western Cascades for a long time. They were divided into bands, although there is little evidence of their names and exact locations.

The Athapascan-speaking Clatskanie formed a cultural pocket along the upper Nehalem and Clatskanie rivers. Closely related to the Washington Kwalhioqua tribe, they may have entered Oregon in the not too distant past.

The Inland Valleys of southwestern Oregon were occupied by a variety of Athapascan-speaking tribes including the Upper Umpqua, the Upper Coquille and the Shasta Costa. Portions of the Rogue River drainage were inhabited by the Takelma and their upland relatives, the Latgawa. Two Athapascan tribes, the Galice Creek and Applegate Creek, lived along smaller rivers within Takelma territory. Several bands of the Shasta, a California tribe, extended into Bear Creek, a tributary of the Rogue. The Karok, another Californian tribe, probably made use of some southern Oregon lands.

Settlers called all southern Oregon tribes the Rogue River Indians. This is misleading since it implies that the diverse Athapascan, Takelman and other tribes were similar.

## INLAND VALLEYS AREA TRIBAL DISTRIBUTION

Early authors such as Melville Jacobs (1945) separated the Molalla geographically, into northern and southern groups divided by an area occupied by Kalapuyan bands. More recent authors (Rigsby 1966, 1969; Benson; and others) depict the Molalla bands as continuously inhabiting the upper tributaries of the Cascades. *See* the note on page 11 for the theory that Molalla Indians were recent migrants to western Oregon.

The Clatskanie are placed by some (e.g. Benson 1973) on the Columbia River. They may have occupied this area during historical times but were, apparently, basically an upland people who lived along secondary streams (like their Athapascan relatives to the north).

The Shasta may have occupied more Oregon territory than was once assumed. Dixon (1907) places them on Bear Creek, a southern Rogue River tributary. Spier (1927b) disputes this although most later authors support Dixon (*see* Heizer & Hester 1970; *also* Benson by personal communication).

*See also* Drucker (1936); Sapir (1907a); and Holt.

KLAMATH LAKES AREA
TRIBAL DISTRIBUTION

*See* Spier (1930); Ray (1963); Stern (1966); and ICC Docket 100.

PLATEAU AREA
TRIBAL DISTRIBUTION

Early beliefs that the Cayuse and Molalla languages were closely related led to several hypotheses about the original location of these tribes. George P. Murdock (1938); Thomas R. Garth; and others claim that both originally occupied a common area but disagree on its location and the cause of displacement. Murdock hypothesizes that the Molalla were driven westward, and eventually pushed over the Cascades, by the Tenino, while Garth suggests that the Molalla were driven westward and the Cayuse eastward by Paiutes. Other anthropologists such as Bruce J. Rigsby (who recently demonstrated that the two languages are not closely related) support the theory that the Molalla and Cayuse lived in the areas shown on the map on page 9 for a long time previous to non-Indian contact.

*See also* Anastasio; Aoki (1967); Chalfant; Ray (1936); Ray, Murdock & Blyth; Spinden; and Suphan. *See* below for discussion of Paiute use of Plateau lands.

GREAT BASIN AREA
TRIBAL DISTRIBUTION

Several issues have come up in regard to the nature and distribution of Paiute bands. Erminie Wheeler-Voegelin (1955) points out that the histories of two Paiute bands listed on treaties—the Walpapi and the Yahuskin—are clouded by poor record keeping. Army and reservation reports confuse the bands that signed the treaties with bands that are listed on early reservation records.

## KLAMATH LAKES AREA TRIBES

Two major tribes lived in this area, the Klamath and the Modoc. Although there were many differences between the two, they both spoke dialects of the same language and shared much culturally. Two Modoc bands lived in Oregon along Lost River. The majority of Modoc Indians lived in California, especially in the vicinity of Tule Lake. Several bands of the Klamath lived around Klamath Lake and in the vicinity of the present city of Klamath Falls; a large group lived near Klamath Marsh; and others lived near Agency Lake, along the Williamson River and in the hill country near present Bly. A third tribe, the Achomawi, lived in California but made occasional use of Klamath area lands.

## PLATEAU AREA TRIBES

The Nez Perce were divided into many bands in both Oregon and Idaho. In Oregon, the Joseph and Imnaha bands lived in the Wallowa Mountains.

The Cayuse roamed a wide area stretching from Washington south to the Blue Mountains. They were probably divided into bands although the exact divisions are unknown.

The Umatilla and Walla-Walla spoke dialects of the Sahaptian language family also spoken by the Nez Perce and the Warm Springs bands and by Washington tribes such as the Yakima. The Walla-Walla lived mostly in southeastern Washington, while the Umatilla ranged from present Arlington east to the Umatilla River.

Along the lower John Day and Deschutes rivers and in the Celilo Falls area of the Columbia lived four bands called the Tenino, the Wyam, the John Day and the Tygh. They spoke closely related dialects and shared many customs but were each independent. In treaty times, settlers lumped the bands together, calling them Walla-Wallas or Warm Springs. Today the four bands are known collectively as either the Warm Springs, the Wayampam or the Tenino.

Influenced by Plains Indians, the Nez Perce and Cayuse (and to a lesser extent other Plateau tribes) acted as tribal units more than other Oregon Indians. Individual leaders often came to have the respect of and influence with a number of villages and bands. Large-scale tribal and inter-tribal enterprises such as buffalo hunts were organized.

## GREAT BASIN AREA TRIBES

All of the bands in this area spoke the Paiute language and shared much culturally and socially. The Basin Area was diverse in terms of natural resources, and the individual Paiute bands developed a variety of lifestyles suited to the particular environmental zone they inhabited. The Paiutes were called Snake Indians by settlers, a confusing name because relatives of the Paiutes—the Shoshone, Ban-

Julian H. Steward (1939) claims that the names of Paiute bands refer only to temporary food gathering units and do not represent political groups (Wadadika, for example, is the name of a food and as a Paiute band name simply identifies a group who gathers it). Omer C. Stewart (1938, 1939, 1941, 1966) disputes this, claiming that Paiute bands were actual political entities. The fact that Stewart, Isabel T. Kelly and Beatrice Blyth all arrived at similar lists of the Paiute band names and locations gives credence to the idea that these names were part of a definite, flexible, political structure.

Arguments over the nature of Indian political organization, such as that between Steward and Stewart, took on a practical importance during the ICC cases, as lawyers utilized anthropological theories in court. *See also* discussion on tribal territories (p. 14); and on the ICC in Part Two.

TRIBES ALONG THE
BASIN-PLATEAU BORDER

Another question brought out in ICC cases is the extent of Paiute and Shoshonean Plateau land use. Paiutes may have been the primary users of the area between the north and middle forks of the John Day River, especially before the Plateau groups had horses. Paiutes may also have used the area west of the Deschutes River (including the land presently occupied by the Warm Springs Reservation). Blyth places Paiutes as far north as Gateway. Murdock (1938) claims that up to 1810 the Paiute occupied lands as far north as Simnasho. On the other hand, Steward & Wheeler-Voegelin locate the Paiute entirely east of the Deschutes. Suphan lists extensive Sahaptian and Cayuse use of campsites as far south as present Bend.

Early maps (such as Berreman's) locate a group called the Lohim on Willow Creek in Umatilla territory. The

nock and Southern Paiute of Idaho, Nevada and California—were also called Snakes.

In this area the only permanent social unit was the family foraging group. Families would join together to form temporary winter camps but membership in these camps varied from year to year. These changing groups of people who shared a common method of food gathering and who lived in a certain zone often named themselves after a popular food source. The Wadadika of Harney Basin, for example, were named after the wada plant whose seeds were an abundant food source near Harney and Malheur lakes.

The flexible Paiute band structure prevented overuse of any one resource. A drought or famine in one environment could be avoided by moving to a new area and joining another band.

TRIBES ALONG THE BASIN-PLATEAU BORDER

The northern and western extremes of the Great Basin was a region with relatively sparse resources, used by tribes from several culture areas. Small groups set up temporary hunting and gathering camps but there were probably few permanent settlements.

Paiute people from the Great Basin and Cayuse, John Day, Nez Perce and other Plateau Indians were the primary users of the region between the north and middle forks of the John Day River.

Molallas from the Inland Valleys Area and Klamaths from the Klamath Lakes Area traveled and hunted in the land between the upper Deschutes River and the Cascade Mountains.

When Plateau tribes obtained horses, they began exploiting this region more intensively. Later, in the mid-1800s, when Paiutes obtained horses, they too began more intensive use. Although this region was the scene of skirmishes between Paiutes and their northern neighbors, there was no full-scale war or conquest on either side.

Lohim are usually identified as Snake or Shoshone Indians; O. C. Stewart (1938); and Suphan, however, suggest that they were a group of mounted Bannocks or Shoshoneans who migrated to Oregon from Idaho in the 1800s.

Paiute use of Plateau lands, the possible existence of the Lohim, and Lewis & Clark's report of Shoshoneans on the Columbia River led to hypotheses about large-scale population shifts prior to non-Indian contact. Teit; and Berreman both hypothesize that the Sahaptian and Cayuse tribes originally lived far to the south of their historical locations and were pushed northward

by Paiutes around 1830. Murdock (1938) argues the opposite: Paiutes originally lived farther north and were pushed southward by Sahaptians.

Other authors see the southern Plateau and northern Great Basin as an area of mixed usage at various times (David H. French, personal communication). Some movement into this area from both north and south probably occurred, but major conquests or large-scale population migrations in the several hundred years prior to non-Indian contact appear unlikely.

## CHANGING TRIBAL ORGANIZATION

The organization of tribes and bands in Oregon, like all aspects of Indian culture, was constantly changing. In the 1700s, as horses became important in northeastern Oregon, many new ideas about tribal organization were imported from the Plains tribes. With the arrival of Euro-Americans in the 1800s, many tribes again changed their structures in order to deal with the newcomers. In some cases, loosely affiliated bands began to work together and confederate under a single leader for purposes of trading, treaty-making or protection of their homelands.

The later reservation period brought even larger confederations, as tribes from totally different culture areas were pressured into working together. The present-day Confederated Tribes of Warm Springs, for example, is made up of descendants of three traditional tribes: the Wasco, from the Lower Columbia Area; the Paiute from the Great Basin Area; and the Warm Springs (a tribe made up of four bands), from the Columbia Plateau area.

Another factor in the changing tribal organization was the Euro-Americans' misunderstanding of Indian tribes. Often they could not interpret the true complexity of the Indian political scene. Settlers, traders and government officials often indiscriminately lumped disparate tribes together. Popular use of names such as Rogue River Indians to refer to all southwestern Oregon tribes led these newcomers to ignore the fact that there were actually many independent tribes in that area. The same was true of the name Snake as a label for all Great Basin area people.

The settlers' practice of misnaming Indian tribes was complicated by the problem of spelling—the romanization of Indian names into French or English. Spelling of English was much less standardized in the 1800s than it is today and many settlers were poorly educated. Most settlers also lacked the ability to understand Indian names. For these reasons, tribal names were often incorrectly reported. The name Kalapuya, for example, has been spelled more than 30 ways. In some cases, settlers simply ignored the Indian names and invented their own in French (e.g. Nez Perce, which is French for pierced nose) or English (e.g. the Applegate Creek Indians—who called themselves the Dakubetede). These misspellings and invented names were not simply harmless mistakes; they led to years of confusion and were often incorporated into treaties.

Euro-Americans also misunderstood the kinds of bonds linking local communities into larger tribal units. The Nez Perce, for example, included over 70 local bands and villages in traditional times. They all shared a common language and common ethnic identity. They viewed themselves as belonging to the Nez Perce tribe, which they called Nimipu. Certain cultural patterns, customs, clothing styles, et cetera, marked them off as distinct from neighboring tribes. But politically and socially each local band was independent. Local leaders made decisions on seasonal routes and alliances with other bands. There was no overall leader who spoke for all of the

# Transportation

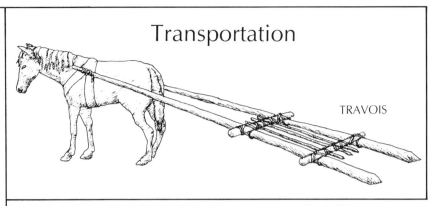

TRAVOIS

Nimipu. Euro-Americans, however, assumed that there was one Nez Perce tribe with a single chief who represented all Nez Perce people. This misunderstanding led to problems in treaty-making and eventually led to the Nez Perce War of 1877. Similar misunderstandings occurred with other Oregon tribes.

## TRIBAL TERRITORY AND LAND OWNERSHIP

**TRIBAL TERRITORY AND LAND OWNERSHIP**

The questions of land ownership, land use and land tenure have come up repeatedly in ICC cases and in the anthropological literature. Nancy O. Lurie; and Imre Sutton examine the ICC controversies over land use. Particularly destructive to tribal claims has been the Commission's application of Euro-American standards to Indian land practices, with its insistence on proof of exclusive use of all lands, and tendency to deny claims on areas of mutual use. Sue Whalen gives a Nez Perce viewpoint on land ownership and territoriality.

Indian cultures of Oregon had no strict territorial borders. This does not mean that the tribes had no concept of territory, as there is much evidence that Oregon tribes possessed lands they considered tribal territory. Village, hunting and berrypicking sites were usually "owned" in common by the tribe. Fishing spots were owned sometimes by families and sometimes by the whole tribe. But this "ownership" was very different from the concept of property and ownership in current American society.

In traditional Indian thought, land was sacred and was never actually owned, although rights for the use of a particular piece of land could reside in certain people. Thus, for example, lands around the lower Umatilla River were the tribal property of the Umatilla people; anyone fishing or hunting there would need the permission of the tribe, and this permission was usually granted freely except in the case of traditional enemies such as the Paiute. The Umatilla people saw themselves as guardians or custodians of the land, rather than as its owners in the Euro-American sense.

The map on page 9 has been drawn without tribal territory lines to emphasize this unique attitude toward land. The culture area borders on the map have been drawn using information about Indian winter villages and do not indicate territorial borders. Winter villages were fairly permanent and indicated generally the area actually occupied by a group of people. Settlement patterns at other times of the year were much more variable. Hunting, gathering and trading expeditions often brought people far from home into other culture areas. The border lines on the map should thus be thought of as generalized limits, not as absolute territorial divisions. The line along the Cascade crest, for example, indicates that the Molalla had the majority of their winter villages on the western slopes; the Molalla certainly ranged onto the eastern slopes for hunting or berrypicking, just as all tribes occasionally crossed the borders shown.

14

GENERAL SOURCES

The economic significance of food gathering in Indian societies has been discussed by Walker (1967a); Suttles (1968a); and Vayda. Food gathering implements and methods are discussed in H. Stewart and amply photographed in Wheat. Schoning; and Kroeber & Barrett deal specifically with fishing; plant poisons used for fishing are detailed by Meilleur. Most archaeological reports include lists of plant and animal species used for food. Culture Areas chart (p. 5) and ethnographies listed (pp. 56-57) also cover food resources.

# FOOD RESOURCES

While the Indians of Oregon used hundreds of wild plant and animal species for food, the dominant types varied according to culture area (see map, "Major Food Resources," p. 16). In order to maintain a balanced diet, Indians had to have a detailed knowledge of fish and animal habits (migration, nesting and mating behavior). They also needed to be able to identify food plants and to know exactly when and where they could be picked. Each area of the state had its own food specialties and there was great variation in the ease with which food materials could be gathered.

In Oregon Indian cultures, plants and animals had a special meaning beyond the economic. According to the Oregon Indian viewpoint, humans are privileged to be able to eat natural products and owe thanks to the spirits of the natural world for this bounty. In ceremonies and religious stories Indians honored the spirits of fish, deer and plants and passed on traditional knowledge about behavior and habitat.

Restrictions on certain kinds of hunting and fishing, seasonal movements to avoid overuse of resources, and ceremonial honor paid to plants and animals all point to how important is this respect of nature. Yet not all Indian people lived in total harmony with their environment; the use of intentional burning as a tool indicates that Indian people could often have a significant impact on their surroundings. This impact was mitigated by generations of accumulated botanical and zoological knowledge and by the fact that traditional Indian populations were relatively small.

## FISHING

The fish along Oregon's coastal rivers provided one of the richest food sources in all of North America. Fishing was a way of life along the coast, and was also important inland for ceremonial and economic reasons.

Salmon, the most important of Oregon's fish, held a place in western Oregon cultures similar to the place of buffalo in Plains Indian cultures. The unique life cycle of salmon—their regular migration upriver to spawn—provided Indians with both a plentiful food supply and a great symbolism; the upriver migrations were both a dependable means of catching fish and a symbol of the renewal of life. Each spring the return of the salmon was commemorated in first-salmon rites, and large fishing villages along major rivers were set up.

Indians built wooden platforms (see illustration p. 20) near the falls, rapids and narrows of the western Oregon rivers. The rapids not only slowed the fish down, they also increased the white water, making it difficult for the fish to detect the Indian nets. Standing on the wooden platforms, the Indian fishermen used long-poled dipnets or spears. Seine nets, weighted at the bottom edge, were ma-

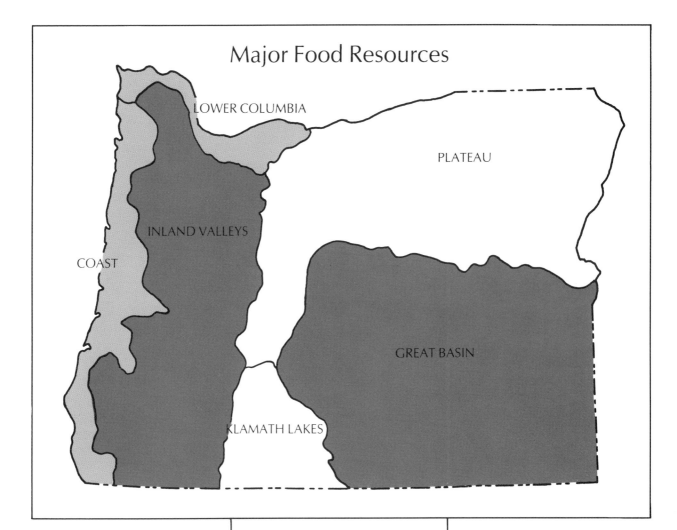

# Major Food Resources

LOWER COLUMBIA
salmon, wappato, game, berries

COAST
salmon, camas, seafoods, game, berries

INLAND VALLEYS
acorns, hazelnuts, camas, fish, game, berries

KLAMATH LAKES
wocas, mullet, waterfowl, game, berries

PLATEAU
camas, kouse, bitterroot, salmon, game, buffalo, berries

GREAT BASIN
epos, wada, other seeds & roots, antelope, small game, berries

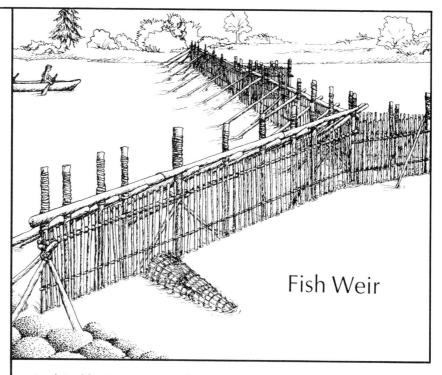

Fish Weir

Fish Club

nipulated by two or more fishermen. A variety of specialized points was used on the spears. On smaller streams Indians constructed log, rock or brush weirs, which channeled fish into a basketry trap or a shallow pool where they could easily be caught (see illustration). In eastern Oregon plant poisons were thrown into pools and streams to stupefy the fish. The more familiar technique of hook-and-line fishing was also common. Hooks were made from wood or bone, and lines were manufactured from sinew or plant fibers (see examples of fishing tools on following pages).

Salmon were a dependable food source, for they usually came into the rivers at the same time of year and could be "harvested" in large quantities. This dependability meant that permanent villages could be set up and long-lasting stable societies could develop similar to those based on agricultural harvests. The traditional salmon catch may have been in the neighborhood of 20 million pounds a year on the Columbia River alone. This catch apparently had little impact on the salmon population; the recent depletion of that population has been caused by dams and overuse of the salmon resource.

Indian men did most of the fishing while women helped prepare for fishing expeditions, and did the cooking, processing and preserving. Much of the salmon would be hung on racks and either dried in the sun or smoked over a fire. This preserved salmon was the main food in winter months and was a much sought-after trade item.

DRAWING: FISH HOOKS & SPEARS
Harpoon
(After sketches in Slickpoo; Ray 1963)
Harpoons, fishing spears attached to a hemp line, were thrown from a fishing platform or canoe; when the point lodged in a fish it could be hauled in. Harpoons were used for salmon, sturgeon, seal and sea lion.

Leister
(After sketches in Slickpoo; H. Stewart; and Spinden)
This three-pronged fishing spear was sometimes used for night fishing, thrust into the water from torchlighted canoes.

Harpoon (gig or spear)
(After sketches in Slickpoo; H. Stewart; and Ray 1963)
A multi-pronged spear (4-10 points) was used in shallow water to pin fish to the bottom until they were dead.

Spear with Detachable Points
(After sketches in Ray 1963; H. Stewart; Underhill; and a photograph in Sauter & Johnson)
Similarly to the harpoon, after one or both spear points lodged in a fish the fisherman holding the spear shaft could shore his catch. The first point illustrated here is typical of that used in the Klamath Lakes Area; the other two were common in the Coast, Lower Columbia and Plateau areas.

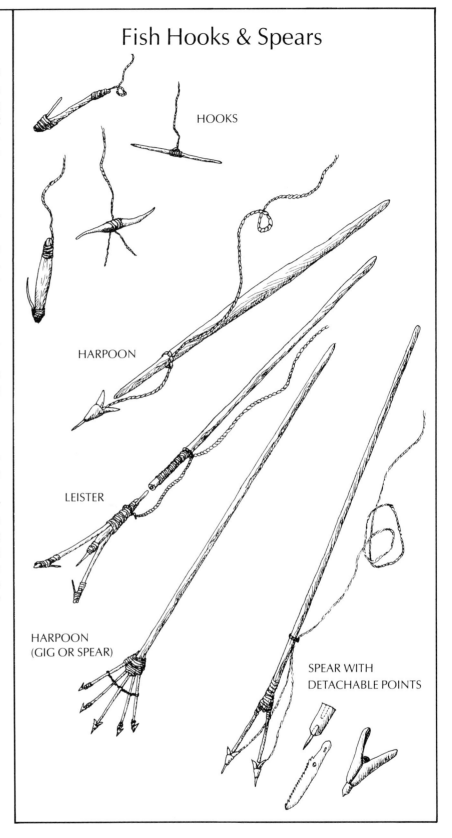

# Fish Hooks & Spears

HOOKS

HARPOON

LEISTER

HARPOON
(GIG OR SPEAR)

SPEAR WITH
DETACHABLE POINTS

DRAWING: FISH NETS & TRAPS
Fishing Nets
(After sketches in Underhill; H. Stewart; and Spinden text)
A knotting technique was used to construct nets from Indian hemp or nettle fiber. In addition to those illustrated, many other types of nets were used, including seine and gill nets. Nets were cast from riverbanks, fishing platforms and canoes; the shape of each and their mesh size were designed for specific fishing conditions (falls, deep hole, weir trap, et cetera), as well as size of fish to be netted. Fish caught in this manner included minnows, smelt, trout and salmon.

Fish Trap used with Weir
(After photograph in Barrett)
Placed at the end of a weir, this woven trap's wide funnel encouraged fish to enter but made it difficult for them to swim back out.

Fish Traps
(After photograph in Barrett)
The traps pictured here are constructed of willow and/or roots in a basketry technique called twining, and used in shallow streams or with a weir. The long, narrow trap prevented fish from turning around to exit.

# Fish Nets & Traps

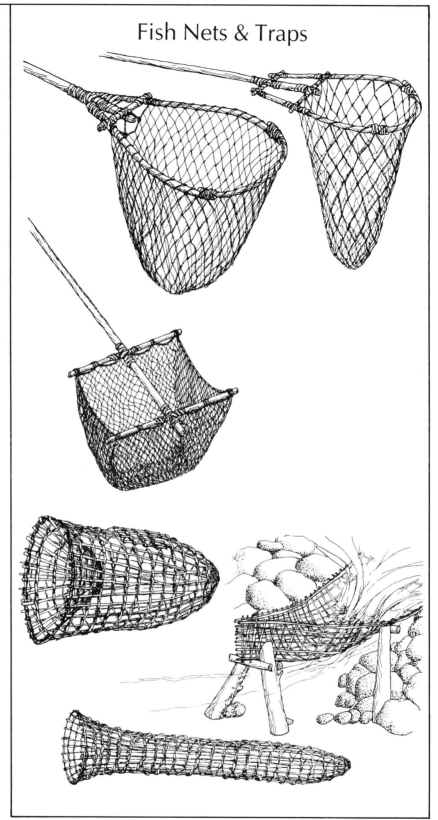

DRAWING
Fishing Platform
(After photographs in Underhill; Billard; and Curtis)
At particularly lucrative fishing sites (especially falls), platforms were constructed from cedar planks and poles lashed together. Extending out over the water, they were supported and braced by piers sunk into the river bottom. These platforms facilitated net, harpoon and spear fishing. Sometimes a weir downstream channeled the fish nearer to shore and the platform.

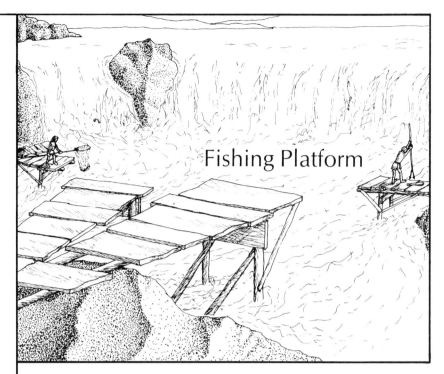

Fishing Platform

Salmon were not the only fish used by Oregon Indians; steelhead, suckers, sturgeon and flatfish were among the secondary fish resources, and Coastal Indians caught large numbers of smelt. Inland Valleys people, deprived of large salmon runs by the steep falls at Oregon City, fished also for eels. In the streams surrounding Klamath Lakes, the Klamath and Modoc Indians fished for mullet and other freshwater species.

Fish were the primary food source in the Lower Columbia and Coast areas. They were a secondary food in the Plateau and Klamath Lakes areas and a supplemental food in the Inland Valleys and the Great Basin. Although the economic value of fishing has decreased somewhat in recent years, the social and ceremonial importance of fish continues for many Oregon Indian communities.

Plant Use

As David H. French (1979) points out, foods that a society considers "staples" have both nutritional and cultural value. Coming from cultures that place a much greater emphasis on meat, Euro-American observers have tended to overlook the importance of plants as staple foods in Indian societies. French (1965) provides the most complete survey of plant use in Oregon and the Northwest. Gunther's 1945 study applies mostly to Washington, but details cultural implications of plant foods and medicines. A forthcoming book by Marilyn Couture will examine Paiute plant usage. Ratcliff discussed the depletion of food sources resulting from non-Indian settlement in the Willamette Valley. *See also* French (1956, 1960); and Colville (1897, 1902). O. C. Stewart (1955); and H. T. Lewis discuss the practice of Indian forest and grass burning as related to food gathering.

PLANT GATHERING

Wild plants were a staple food in several areas of Oregon and were an important food supplement for all Indian cultures. Rich in many vitamins and minerals, plant materials formed an indispensable part of Indian nutrition. Roots, nuts, seeds and berries were gathered from many kinds of plant and tree species.

Most plant gathering was done by women, although men often helped out. The women collected roots with special bone and wood digging sticks. They used a basketry seed beater or comb to knock small berries and seeds into baskets and a loosely woven winnowing tray to separate seed kernels from hulls (various food gathering baskets are illustrated on pp. 22-23, 25, "Food Gathering and Preparation Tools"). Once they had gathered the seeds, the women used grinding stones and a variety of mortars to pulverize them into meal for puddings or breads.

The Indian women were expert botanists. They knew exactly which parts of a plant to use and which time of year to gather them. Often, each part of a plant would be important for different purposes—roots, stalks, flowers and seeds each had their own use. Plants were not only food sources, they were also used as dyes, teas, medicines, even insect repellents, and for their fibers.

Wild plants were plentiful enough in Oregon that widespread agriculture was unneccessary, although Oregon Indians did use several agricultural techniques. The Inland Valleys people burned forests and prairies to encourage the growth of favored plant species such as berries. On the southwest coast, and in some other areas of Oregon, the Indian people cultivated tobacco, proving that they were aware of agricultural methods.

The importance of specific plants differed from season to season and from area to area. Root plants and tubers were much used because of their large size and nutritional value. Camas, the bulb of a wild lily, was widely used, especially in the Inland Valleys Area, and was often baked as bread in special earthen ovens. Wappato, called Indian potato or arrowhead, was a root plant that was abundant on Sauvie Island. Due to environmental changes resulting from recent settlement, this once plentiful plant is now close to extinction. Other roots included bitterroot, used in the Plateau Area, and several species related to wild celery (the most common of which is called kouse).

Nuts and seeds were additional major wild food sources, especially in the Inland Valleys and Great Basin areas. Acorns, which contain bitter tannic acid, had to be carefully prepared by leaching before they could be eaten. Hazelnuts, a wild relative of the filbert, were gathered in the Willamette Valley. The seeds of the water lily were used by Klamath Indians who called the plant wocas, and who prepared enough for home use and trade. In the Great Basin, Paiute Indians gathered seeds from plants such as wada and a variety of sunflower relatives.

DRAWING: FOOD GATHERING AND
PREPARATION TOOLS
Twined Berry Basket
(After photograph in Sauter & Johnson)
Berrypickers used tightly woven, relatively small baskets so that the tiniest berries would not be lost and those on the bottom would not be crushed. With the carrying strap, the baskets could be hung from the neck or tied around the waist. Some of the smaller berries were gathered by ''combing'' them from their branches; in this case, a larger basket was used.

Mortar and Pestle
(After photograph in Mackey 1974)
Stone grinding implements, used largely for grinding seeds and nuts, were most commonly carved from lava. The Kalapuya type mortar, with an 8-12 inch diameter, was used throughout most of western Oregon; in the Lower Columbia Area it was often decoratively carved. With a 6-19 inch diameter, the Klamath type mortar was proportionately deeper. The largest of these weighed nearly 100 pounds, and were partially buried in the ground to steady them during use.

Wooden Mortar
(After photograph in Curtis vol. 8)
This mortar, common in the Lower Columbia Area, was usually carved from a hardwood burl, and was used primarily for mashing berries or grinding salmon to be dried for storage.

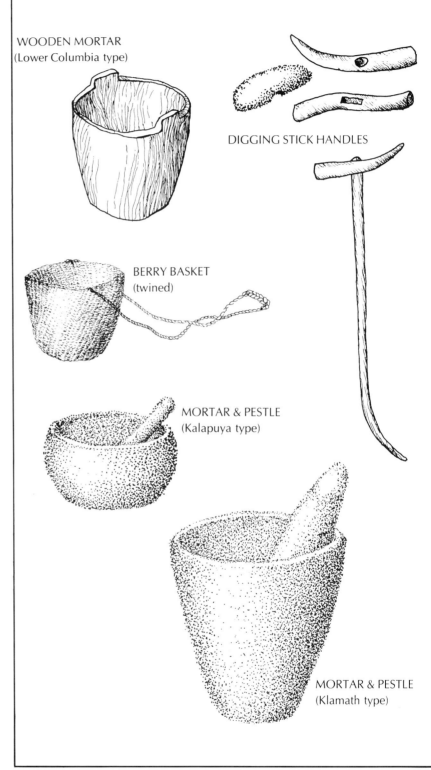

WOODEN MORTAR
(Lower Columbia type)

DIGGING STICK HANDLES

BERRY BASKET
(twined)

MORTAR & PESTLE
(Kalapuya type)

MORTAR & PESTLE
(Klamath type)

22

# Food Gathering & Preparation Tools

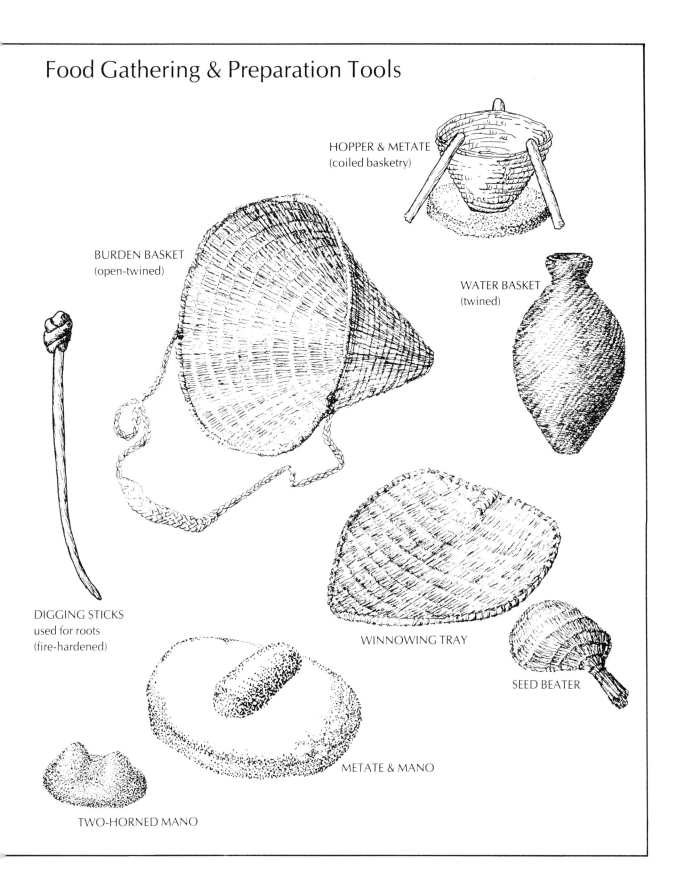

HOPPER & METATE
(coiled basketry)

BURDEN BASKET
(open-twined)

WATER BASKET
(twined)

DIGGING STICKS
used for roots
(fire-hardened)

WINNOWING TRAY

SEED BEATER

METATE & MANO

TWO-HORNED MANO

23

Digging Sticks and Handles
(After photographs in Howe; Curtis vols. 8, 13; Sauter & Johnson; Mackey 1974)
Used in all areas of Oregon for root gathering, the digging stick was fashioned out of spruce or other strong wood, and was pointed and hardened over a fire. The handles, of stone, antler or fire-hardened wood (or, in the Great Basin Area, a wrapping of buckskin), were notched or pierced so they could be lashed to the end of the digging stick.

Coiled Basketry Hopper with Metate
(After sketch in Slickpoo)
The metate (Spanish for "flat stone") was most common in eastern Oregon although it was not unknown along the Coast. With the basketry hopper the metate could be used with a pestle in place of a mortar. The coiled hopper pictured here was used in the Plateau Area, while a similar twined hopper was used in the Coast Area's southern end.

Metate and Mano
(After photographs in Wheat; Howe; Sauter & Johnson)
The metate and mano (Spanish for "hand"), a stone grinding tool, were fashioned from lava stone. This round, flat metate was used throughout Oregon. Great Basin and Klamath Lakes tribes also used another version, an elongated stone with three raised edges; the fourth unraised edge was positioned over a tray onto which crushed seeds were pushed.

Two-honed Mano
(After photograph in Howe)
This specialized grinder appeared only in the Klamath Lakes Area, where wocas (water lily seeds) were an important resource.

Berries and fruits of all kinds were collected by all Oregon Indians to eat raw or to preserve. Blackberries, thimbleberries, salmonberries, crabapples, choke cherries and many others were gathered in the fall from the Cascade slopes and other mountainous regions. Berries were often dried into cakes and were sometimes mixed with salmon in a pemmican-like loaf that was a major winter food.

Minor plant resources included a number of foods used in times of famine. Cacti, fungi and lichen were all used occasionally. In the Great Basin, the Paiute people gathered the inner bark of sugar pines as a supplemental food.

In addition to food-related uses, plants were important as materials for construction. Digging sticks were made from oak, bows from yew, houses and canoes from red cedar. Indian hemp, bear grass and a variety of willows were used in basketry. Reeds such as tule and cattail provided excellent mat-making materials so important for housing and clothing. Knowledge of plant properties was essential for all aspects of Indian life.

Burden Basket
(After photograph in Wheat)
Designed in a variety of shapes and weaves, most burden baskets were carried on a woman's back and attached to a "tumpline" or strap around her forehead. Flat-bottomed burden baskets sometimes doubled as storage containers.

Winnowing Tray
(After photograph in Wheat)
Coarsely woven and often-repaired, the winnowing tray was employed for tossing roasted seeds in the wind, to separate the hulls from the kernels. These basket trays were also useful for catching minnows.

Seed Beater
(After photograph in Wheat)
Rather than hand-picking small seeds and berries, Indians knocked them off the plant into a fine-woven basket with a comb or beater such as the one pictured above. (Larger berries and wocas were picked by hand.)

Water Basket
(After photograph in Wheat)
This tightly woven basket, designed to hold water, was used mostly in Eastern Oregon (the Lower Columbia and Coast Area tribes, in particular, used wood containers for this purpose.)

Stirring Stick
(After photograph in Wheat)
Stirring sticks were used when cooking food in baskets.

Digging Sticks for Shellfish
(After sketch in Underhill)
Carved from wood, these had tapered points and cupped blades, and varied in length from two to more than four feet. Digging sticks were used primarily for extracting clams from sandy beaches.

Twined Clam Basket
(After photograph in Sauter & Johnson)
Several types of baskets were used for clam gathering, all constructed in an open weave so that the sand could be washed out.

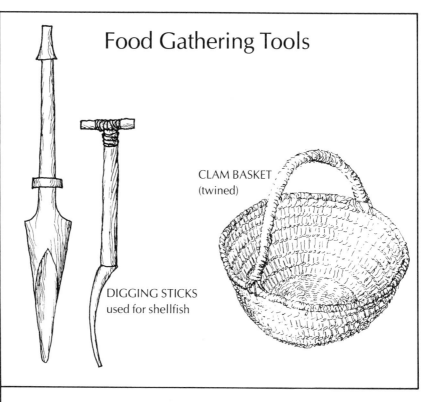

# Food Gathering Tools

CLAM BASKET
(twined)

DIGGING STICKS
used for shellfish

## SEAFOOD AND SHELLFISH

Indians along the coast gathered many kinds of foods from tidal pools, estuaries and offshore islands. Mussels, clams and other shellfish were Coast Area foods. (Freshwater mussels were eaten inland.) Several kinds of shells were widely traded as ornaments (the thin, white, crescent-shaped dentalium, found further north near Vancouver Island, was especially prized). As the coastal Indians gathered shellfish they also took advantage of the large nesting colonies of gulls, cormorants and pelicans. All of these birds provided edible eggs easily collected on beaches and offshore rocks.

Seals and sea lions made their homes along the Oregon coastline and provided Indians with sport and food. The Indians clubbed the seal cubs and used harpoons and canoes to chase the adults. While sea-going hunts probably did not yield as much food as salmon fishing, they were hard and dangerous and thus brought much prestige to the seal and sea lion hunters.

In Oregon, Indian people apparently did not hunt whales as did the Indians of British Columbia and Alaska. Whales often washed ashore, however, and were used for food, oil and their bone for tools.

## HUNTING

Although hunting was practiced in all Oregon Indian cultures, it was never as important as fishing and plant gathering in terms of the amount of food provided. Nevertheless, a wide variety of game was hunted.

Men did most of the large-game hunting while women participated in group hunts, did much of the processing and hunted some smaller game. The principal weapon was the bow and arrow, which superseded the spear thrower or atlatl. Hundreds of the specialized arrow and spear points were made from obsidian or jasper, each point suited to a particular kind of game. Oregon Indians also used a variety of traps including snares made from bent saplings, deadfalls made from logs or stones attached to twine mechanisms (see illustration) and covered pitfalls. They also used dogs to track and chase game animals. Some Indians participated in group hunts called drives or surrounds. They would chase, for example, rabbits or antelope into an enclosure where they could be easily killed. Klamath Indians also used nets for drives to catch coots and other waterfowl.

Whatever the method of hunting, the Indian hunters always used their knowledge of animal behavior and habitat to increase their hunting efficiency. When hunting ducks, they used decoys made of whole duck skins stuffed with tule. They also used deer and elkhide disguises in order to move close to game. The Paiute Indians used their knowledge of bird mating habits to catch sage grouse on Steens Mountain: they knew that in the spring the grouse gathered for a mating dance, and that it was easy to club the birds when they were preoccupied with their ritual.

Deer and elk were the principal large game in Oregon. They provided food, skins for clothing and antlers for tools. Antelope were also important, especially in the Great Basin and Klamath Lakes areas. Bears were not a major food source and were restricted in some areas; occasionally an Indian hunter would track one down for fur, claws, or for the honor of having killed such a mighty animal. Indians from the Plateau, once they had horses, crossed the Rocky Mountains into Montana to hunt buffalo. Buffalo hunting expeditions lasted many months, and often included several hundred individuals from various plateau tribes.

Small game animals were hunted by all Oregon Indians and were especially important for those of the Inland Valleys and Great Basin. The latter hunted waterfowl, marsh birds and grouse, for food, eggs, ornamental feathers and bones to make whistles. Squirrels and groundhogs (marmots) were also hunted, and rabbits were very important to the Paiute who used them for food and for their fur.

Lizards and insects such as grasshoppers were a dietary supplement in several areas of the state.

## DRAWING: HUNTING

**Bola**

(After photograph in Howe; Cressman text)

When thrown properly, two grooved stones tied at each end of a length of sinew or rawhide cord would wrap around the legs of a small animal or bird. The hunter then clubbed the hobbled animal to death.

**Bird Whistle**

(After photographs in Howe; Sauter & Johnson)

A hollow bone with holes carved in one side could be played to imitate bird calls and attract game birds.

**Quiver**

(After photograph in Wheat; sketch in Mackey)

To carry bow and arrows, quivers were used. They were constructed from the whole skin of an animal (such as a bobcat, otter, wolf, fox or coyote). Sometimes hunters carried a club or tomahawk suspended from the quiver by a sinew string.

**Bow and Arrow**

(After photographs in Curtis; Cressman; and Sauter & Johnson; sketch in Collins; O. Stewart 1941; and Kelly texts)

Made of oak, juniper or yew and backed with sinew (the string was twisted sinew), bows were on average 30 inches long and 2 inches wide, tapering at the ends; sometimes they were decoratively painted. Arrows of oak, mahogany or other hardwood were meticulously straightened with heat and a grooved or pierced stone. The arrowpoint, of stone, was attached at one end with pitch-covered sinew; feathers were attached at the other end in the same manner. Spears, though larger and used for larger prey, were fashioned similarly. The atlatl, superseded by the bow and arrow,

# Hunting

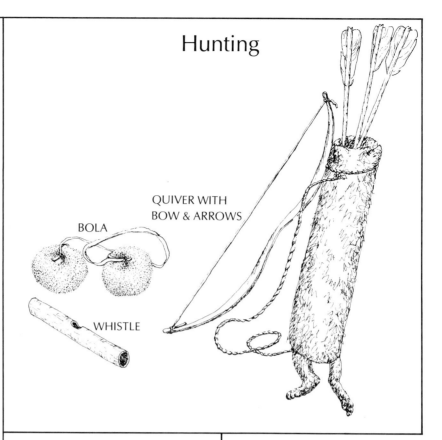

BOLA

QUIVER WITH BOW & ARROWS

WHISTLE

was a sort of harpoon used to hunt animals. These weapons were used throughout Oregon.

**Decoys and Disguises**

(not illustrated)

Duckskins stuffed with tules were floated on lakes; they were moved by the wind or by the hunter with an attached string. Hunters in some areas would wear deer or elkhide (including the head and antlers) as a disguise.

# Hunting

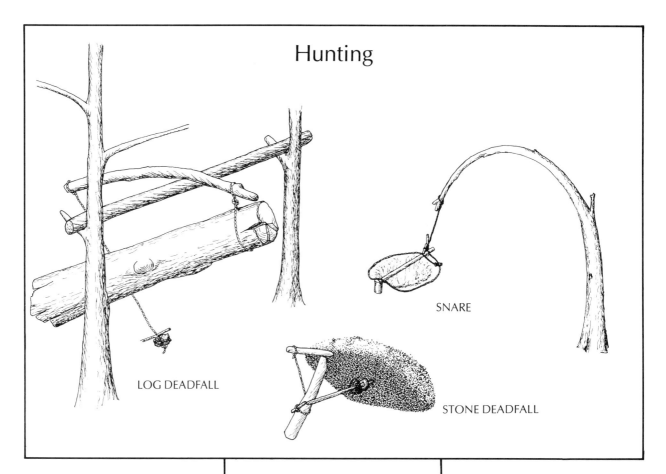

LOG DEADFALL

SNARE

STONE DEADFALL

**Deadfall**
(After photograph in Wheat; sketch in Sauter & Johnson)
A deadfall was a heavy log or flat rock delicately balanced overhead and attached to a piece of bait on the ground. When an animal disturbed the bait, the deadfall was released and fell on top of its victim.

**Pitfall**
(not illustrated)
Hunters dug a large hole in an animal trail, then camouflaged it with sticks and grass. Animals that stumbled into the pit were trapped.

**Snare**
(After sketches in Underhill; Kelly; and Mackey)
The spring power of a bent sapling was effective in catching both large and small game. A noose tied to the sapling's tip was pulled to the ground over a pit and held there by another easily sprung twig. When a passing animal stumpled into the pit, it released the sapling spring and was caught by foot or neck in the noose. Snares were used throughout Oregon.

**Hunting Net**
(not illustrated)
Sagebrush nets up to 100 feet long proved effective in the Great Basin Area for capturing rabbits and some birds. Several people were required to handle each net.

**"Surround" or Corral**
(not illustrated)
A barrier (such as a fence, net or brush) was constructed in a large U shape. Many people then participated in a hunt, covering a large area and driving animals into the corral where they could be shot with bow and arrow. This method was particularly effective for capturing antelope in the Great Basin Area.

GENERAL SOURCES

Anastasio details seasonal activities in the Plateau. Aikens (1975) examines Kalapuyan seasonal movements, which were related to elevation differences among plant and animal resources. The most detailed summary of Paiute annual rounds is by Whiting. Details on other tribes can be found in most ethnographies (*see* p. 57 for listing). Of relevance to this topic are Euro-American attitudes toward nomadic peoples (discussed by Lattimore).

# SEASONAL CYCLES

Food resources, terrain and climate varied so much in Oregon that each culture had a different seasonal pattern of travel and food gathering. Food resources changed with the seasons, creating a pattern of alternating scarcity and abundance. Likewise, the tribes alternated between large gatherings during times of plenty and dispersed smaller groups during times of scarcity. The activities of both men and women also changed with the seasons, creating a yearly cycle of social events.

The Plateau Area's seasonal cycle was fairly regular (*see* p. 30). In other parts of the state, especially the Great Basin and Inland Valleys areas, the seasonal round was different from year to year. Heavy rain, snow, shortage of useful plants or animals, or social gatherings might affect the timetable of tribal movements. The village and band leaders carefully studied the weather and wildlife conditions before they suggested moving camp.

Early settlers, who observed the seasonal movements of the Indians, often could not understand why the tribes moved so often. They labeled the Indians roving nomads and claimed that they wandered aimlessly and had no fixed abode. It is true that most Indians in Oregon moved camp several times a year, but these movements were far from aimless. Indian seasonal movements were carefully planned to make optimum use of the environment and were based on years of observation of local conditions.

The purpose of seasonal movements was to be in the right place at the right time of year. For fishing peoples this meant being on the river when the salmon runs were heaviest. Coastal people went upriver to fish in the spring, came back to the coast for seafoods in the summer, and returned upriver in the fall. For Inland Valleys people, seasonal movements were often related to food sources at various elevations. The low-lying Willamette floodplain provided camas, wappato and marsh birds. Higher portions of the valley offered stands of acorn oaks and some mammals. The valley margins, above 500 feet in elevation, provided abundant mammals and upland bird species such as grouse and quail. The Kalapuyan bands, for example, visited each of these elevation zones at the appropriate season.

Indian ceremonies and religious practices were often closely linked to seasonal cycles. Stories and myths included information on seasonal changes. One Alsea story, for example, mentions that swallows regularly return to the central coast just before the spring salmon run hits its peak. Some myths could only be told during the appropriate season. Ceremonial celebrations were also tied to the seasonal cycle. Rites such as the first-salmon ceremonies and the various root feasts were carefully timed and marked the changing seasons. These seasonal ceremonies are still carried out in many Oregon Indian communities and the summer pow-wow circuit continues the ancient traditions of summertime inter-tribal socializing.

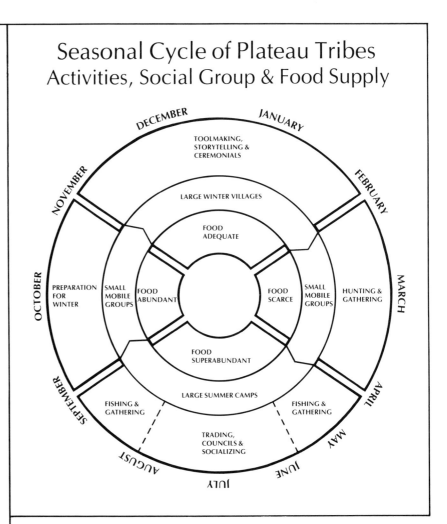

## Seasonal Cycle of Plateau Tribes
### Activities, Social Group & Food Supply

DECEMBER
JANUARY

TOOLMAKING,
STORYTELLING &
CEREMONIALS

NOVEMBER

LARGE WINTER VILLAGES

FEBRUARY

FOOD
ADEQUATE

OCTOBER

PREPARATION
FOR
WINTER

SMALL
MOBILE
GROUPS

FOOD
ABUNDANT

FOOD
SCARCE

SMALL
MOBILE
GROUPS

HUNTING &
GATHERING

MARCH

FOOD
SUPERABUNDANT

SEPTEMBER

FISHING &
GATHERING

LARGE SUMMER CAMPS

FISHING &
GATHERING

APRIL

TRADING,
COUNCILS &
SOCIALIZING

AUGUST

JULY

JUNE

MAY

CHART: SEASONAL CYCLE OF
PLATEAU TRIBES

The times on this chart are approximate. In any given year at any given locale, transition times depended on when the seasons actually changed; when plants matured, when fish ran, when cold weather arrived, et cetera.

## WINTER

Winter was the time of year when there was the least movement and food-gathering activity. Indians ate mostly stored foods (dried fish, roots and berries) supplemented by an occasional deer or elk driven into the lowlands by snowfall.

In most areas there were permanent winter village sites occupied for generations. In the Great Basin, where stores of food were smaller, people might move camp several times during the winter to use caches of dried food or to get to a better hunting area.

Manufacture and repair of tools and clothing occupied much of the winter. Storytelling and ceremonials also took place, making it a sacred season in some areas.

EARLY SPRING

When stored foods were running out and before late spring fishing and gathering could begin in earnest, Oregon Indians faced the time of greatest food scarcity. In some years this meant actual famine, although often it only meant that the large winter camps had to be broken into smaller groups; small family groups went off in different directions to hunt and to gather the few plant shoots appearing above ground. These smaller groups had a better chance of finding foods and would be less likely to overhunt or overpick an area, thus protecting both themselves and their environment.

LATE SPRING AND SUMMER

In mid-April or May food became more abundant. The fish runs increased and root crops began to ripen. First-salmon ceremonies and root feasts marked the beginning of this season of plenty. Large groups of people, sometimes from several different tribes, would gather at accustomed fishing spots along the major rivers and streams. While men fished, women went to the marshes, flatlands and hillsides to gather roots. As the summer progressed, various foods became available. On the shores of Klamath Lake, seeds of the wocas (water lily) were gathered; Paiute people went in large numbers to collect crickets; and Inland Valleys peoples harvested camas.

The middle of summer was marked by a slowdown in food gathering and more emphasis on social events. Dancing, gambling and trading brought Indians from many tribes together and often led to intermarriages that created more permanent alliances between tribes.

FALL

After the last big migrations of salmon, most tribes split into smaller groups and headed for favorite spots in the hills and mountains. The women gathered berries while the men hunted. This was the last chance to gather fresh foods and much time was spent in preparing for winter. Hides were readied for tanning, wood and mats were gathered for house repair and the last game and berries were dried. As the first snows began to fall, the scattered groups gathered together in winter villages where they began preparations for the coming spring.

GENERAL SOURCES

Data sources include the 1910 and 1928 studies by Mooney; and Kroeber's of 1939. (Mooney's estimates for most Oregon tribes also appear in Swanton.)

Oregon Indian Population Figures

Original estimates were by Lewis and Clark (*see* Twaites 1904, vol. 6, p. 114). Various commissioners of Indian Affairs and Hudson's Bay Company officials (*see* H. C. Taylor, Jr., 1969a, b) provide figures for Oregon's Indian population (*see also* Minto). More recent interpretations are found in Cook (1956); Lee; Anastasio; and H. C. Taylor, Jr. (1962).

Lewis and Clark's estimates are generally accepted, although Taylor (1969a) claims that their figures for Chinook and Clatskanie are high. (Wayne Suttles, in personal communication, has pointed out that Taylor's figures are based on Hudson's Bay Company records, which include only Chinooks living "to the head of the tide," thus disregarding the heavy Chinook population near The Dalles.)

# SETTLEMENT AND POPULATION PATTERNS

The population of traditional Oregon was small compared to present-day figures, perhaps as low as 45,000 for the whole state. Nevertheless, it was important that the population be balanced with the resouces available. Too many people crowded into one region could result in overuse of food sources and possible starvation for some. Yet, too sparse a population could lead to isolation and absence of trade. The people in each culture area achieved a different balance between population and resources by varying the size and location of villages and camps.

The seasonal cycles chart on page 30 shows that the times of heaviest concentrations of people occurred in summer and winter. During winter months, when people were living on stored foods, there was less danger of overusing the local resources. In all of Oregon, except for the Great Basin, winter villages were usually permanent. This meant that they held a common core of inhabitants and were located on or near the same site year after year. Individuals or families might move, but the community remained fairly stable. New villages were sometimes formed when family feuds, population growth or depletion of resources changed the needs of the villagers.

In the Great Basin, where resources were scarce, winter villages were less permanent. Here the village sites and populations would vary from year to year depending on the availability of resources. Camps might even move several times during a single winter season. Some people of the Inland Valleys Area who lived in similarly sparse environments probably also had a flexible settlement pattern to match supply with demand.

Oregon Indian winter villages might hold as few as 20 or as many as 500 people. During the summer, visiting between tribes could raise village populations to several thousand people, especially along the Columbia River. These summer gatherings were possible because fish and wild plants were plentiful. Such summer encampments were less permanent than winter villages. They would usually be held at the same place—a favorite fishing spot or open meadow—but might be formed by different groups of people each year.

During the spring, fall and parts of the summer, Indian people dispersed into much smaller groups. A family or group of friends would travel on their own to gather and hunt. The map, "Village and Seasonal Movements" (p. 33), shows that there was great variation in the distances traveled during these seasonal movements.

The Wasco Indians of the Lower Columbia Area, for example, wintered at sites inland from the Columbia, traveled five to ten miles to the river for fishing and trading in the summer, and ranged over the slopes of Mount Hood (30 miles away) to gather and hunt. Contrast this with the pattern of the Wadadika Paiutes, who win-

KEY
Persons/100 sq. miles

KEY
Persons/100 sq. miles

400    150    50    10    5

## MAP: SETTLEMENT PATTERNS

These population density figures are based on estimates by Mooney (1928) as interpreted by Kroeber in 1939; they have been adjusted to fit Oregon's natural and cultural areas. For other population density maps, *see* Kroeber (1939); Farmer & Holmes; and Walker (1978).

KEY
　　Seasonal Movements
Permanent Villages
　☐ Short Distance
　☐ Medium Distance
　☐ Long Distance
No Permanent Villages
　■ Long Distance

# Settlement Patterns
## Aboriginal Population Density
(Estimated for 1780)

# Settlement Patterns
## Village & Seasonal Movements

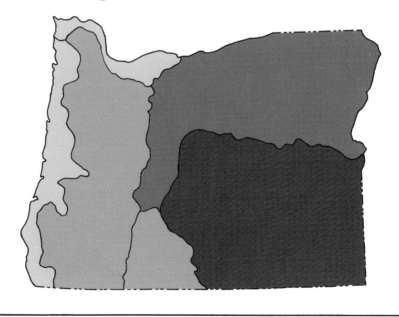

Problems of Population Estimates

Most records of pre-contact Indian population are based on early explorers' educated guesses. Poor recording methods and ignorance of Indian social organization often led to haphazard figures. Most of these estimates are probably low, since many Indian communities had been depopulated by epidemics before they were made. Henry F. Dobyns, for example, after reviewing population estimates for North America, concludes that Mooney's earlier figures are far too low; he suggests use of depopulation ratios to calculate losses due to epidemics. *See* page 60 on epidemics and Part Three for discussion of current population estimates.

Cultural Implications of Population Patterns

Shirley Lee has related population figures to cultural changes in some Northwest Indian societies. Madge Schwede has linked Nez Perce population figures and settlement patterns. Martin Baumhoff discusses ecological factors in population growth.

Alfred L. Kroeber (1939), correlating population density, natural and cultural borders, and social organization, observed that coastal densities are usually higher than those inland. In this study he also identifies assumptions commonly made by researchers that influenced the population figures they arrived at.

tered at various sites near Harney Lake and their seasonal round brought them as far as the present-day sites of Drewsey (50 miles away) and Canyonville (80 miles away). The Wadadika were obviously dispersed over a wider area than were the Wascos.

In general, areas where resources were the most scarce required the longest seasonal travels, but length of these movements was also influenced by the type of transportation available. When Plateau people obtained horses, their seasonal movement extended considerably. Before horses, they probably stayed in the vicinity of rivers and streams. After horses, they ranged throughout the Blue Mountains in seach of game and wild plants.

The map, "Aboriginal Population" (p. 33), illustrates Indian population density. As just explained, populations varied through the seasons and also ranged over differing territories. The population density figures show averages of both season and geography. For example, the average density of the Coast Area was approximately 150 people per 100 square miles. Actual densities would have been higher or lower at certain times and places.

The population density figures point out how great a variation there was in Oregon. Parts of the Lower Columbia Area contained populations 100 times more dense than the population of the Great Basin Area. Such differences in settlement pattern were associated with many aspects of Indian culture including availability of food, transportation methods, housing styles and social organization. The extent of crowding or isolation obviously affected the lifestyles of people in the various areas of Oregon.

# HOMES AND FAMILY ORGANIZATION

The architecture of traditional Oregon reflected both the physical and the cultural needs of the Indian people. Several styles of buildings were used, including permanent winter dwellings, smaller temporary shelters and two types of sweatlodges. Housing styles varied from area to area because of differing settlement and population patterns, because family organization was different in each area and because of the availability of natural construction materials. Family households usually worked communally as an economic and social unit within the village. In this sense, house styles were an important indicator of village organization.

## WESTERN OREGON WINTER DWELLINGS

The Indian people west of the Cascade Mountains made their winter dwellings from wood. These rectangular plank houses looked somewhat similar to early Euro-American settlers' houses but were used centuries before the latter arrived in Oregon. Several styles of plank houses were used, including a bark and plank house common in parts of the Inland Valleys and Lower Columbia areas (*see* p. 37).

The basic plank house was a long, large house that held a number of related families. The average size was about 40 by 80 feet although some ranged to as long as several hundred feet. Corner posts (and sometimes a central ridgepole) supported the walls and roof (which could be formed of either horizontal or vertical boards, depending on the custom of the local house-builders). Roof styles included a two-pitch roof and also a shed-style roof used by the Tillamook Indians of the northern coast. Eaves occasionally went all the way to the ground. The doorway was usually circular and placed at one end of the house, and was covered with either mat, hide or wood.

The interiors of plank houses were often excavated from one to five feet below ground. Along the sides of the house, sleeping quarters and storage benches were built from wood or packed earth. The center of the house was occupied by a series of fireplaces, each with its cooking utensils and drying rack. Each married couple or family unit would have its own sleeping and storage area near their fireplace. Such sleeping quarters were sometimes made private by wood or mat partitions.

The large plank houses were important in the village social organization. Members of a household were usually related by birth or marriage, thus making the household a cohesive group with shared interests. Each household had a chosen leader and acted in common for purposes of fishing, gathering and childcare. The house itself and some of the utensils and tools were owned communally. The size and quality of the house indicated the family's social importance. Larger houses were sometimes named to emphasize their status.

## DRAWING: WESTERN OREGON WINTER DWELLINGS

These illustrations portray representative dwellings—construction details varied extensively. Roof planks generally ran parallel to the rafters, except in Tillamook housing, where they paralleled the eaves (Boas 1923; Ray 1938; Vastokas 1967; and A. B. Lewis 1906). Wall planks were generally set on end except, again, among the Tillamook. (Poorer Tillamook groups used mats, not planks, to cover their houses.) The planks were held in place not by nails or pegs but by hold binders, tied through holes drilled in the planks.

Sometimes houses were partially or entirely dismantled in order to use the planks at the summer camp location, or store them, or when moving to a new winter location. While household groups were cohesive, they weren't necessarily permanent. It was possible for part of a household to break from the group and take some of the house planks with them (Drucker 1937; Ray 1938; Underhill; and Beckham 1977).

In the Inland Valleys Area, one exception to the generalized winter dwelling illustrated here was that of the Molalla Indians, who live in shelters more closely resembling the Klamath or Plateau earth-covered lodge shown on page 38 (Minor & Pecor).

Photographs of these dwellings can be found in Curtis (vols. 8, 13); Sauter & Johnson; and Billard. Additional illustrations are in Swan and Vaughan (Paul Kane). *See also* Beckham (1977); and Underhill.

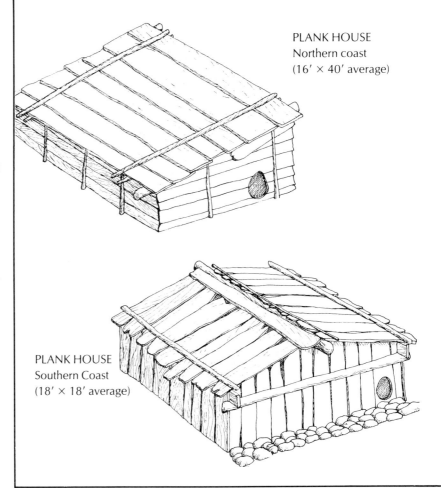

PLANK HOUSE
Northern coast
(16′ × 40′ average)

PLANK HOUSE
Southern Coast
(18′ × 18′ average)

The bark-and-brush plank houses used in the Inland Valleys and the eastern part of the Lower Columbia were less elaborate than the houses of the Coast and western Lower Columbia, but were similarly constructed. A powerful family with adequate resources could build an all-plank house; however, the shifting settlement patterns and smaller population density of the Inland Valleys Area usually called for less permanent housing. Cedar trees were less plentiful, while brush, mats and bark were all readily available without long hours of woodworking.

# Western Oregon Winter Dwellings

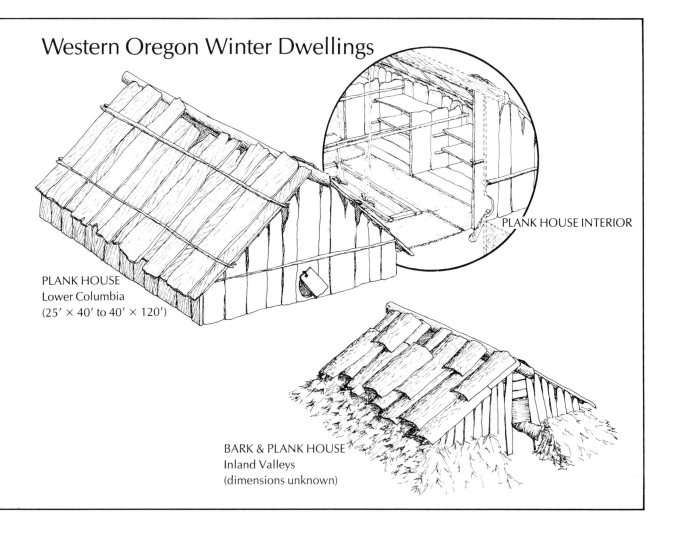

PLANK HOUSE INTERIOR

PLANK HOUSE
Lower Columbia
(25' × 40' to 40' × 120')

BARK & PLANK HOUSE
Inland Valleys
(dimensions unknown)

# Eastern Oregon Winter Dwellings

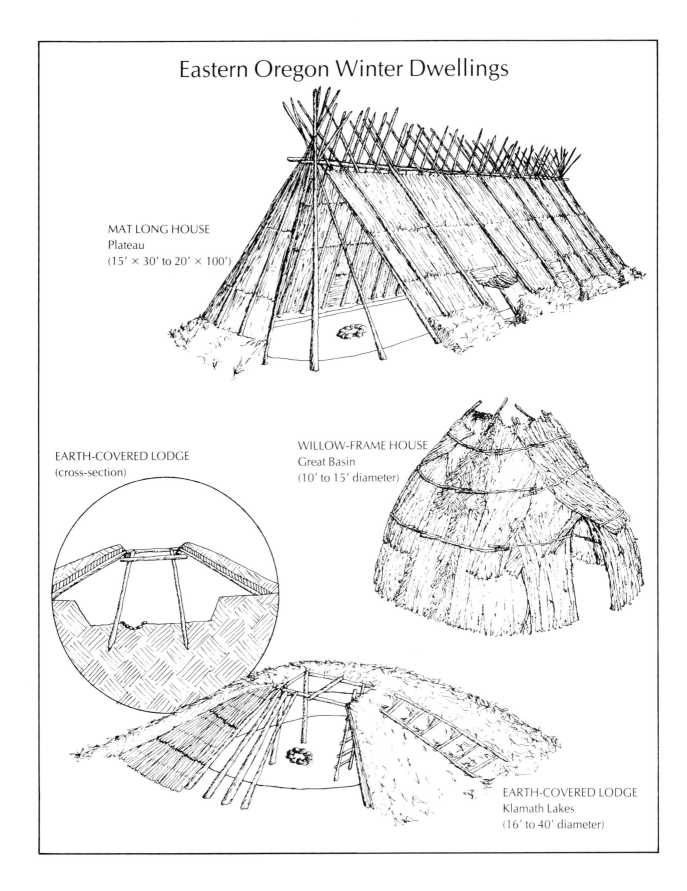

MAT LONG HOUSE
Plateau
(15′ × 30′ to 20′ × 100′)

EARTH-COVERED LODGE
(cross-section)

WILLOW-FRAME HOUSE
Great Basin
(10′ to 15′ diameter)

EARTH-COVERED LODGE
Klamath Lakes
(16′ to 40′ diameter)

DRAWING: EASTERN OREGON
WINTER DWELLINGS

Variations on the Plateau Area mat longhouse include the smaller (and less common, in early times) circular mat lodge, and the skin longhouse, used for celebrations. The circular lodges, which held only one or two families, were about 25 feet in diameter, while the longhouses always measured about 15 feet wide and up to 80 feet (eight fires) long (any longer and they would get too smoky).

Another kind of housing found in all Plateau settlements was the circular semi-underground shelter. Separate structures were built for men and pubescent girls (Spinden). Although smaller, these shelters were not unlike the Klamath winter dwellings. Plateau dwellings are described by Slickpoo; and by Walker (1978).

The Klamath winter dwellings had storage space at ground level under the eaves. Poorer Klamath Area groups had only circular, above-ground tule mat lodges, similar to the circular mat lodge of the Plateau tribes. Further details can be found in Ray (1968); Stern (1966); and Curtis.

Information on the Great Basin willow-frame houses (also known as wickiups) is in O. C. Stewart (1941); Kelly; and Whiting. *See also* photographs in Curtis; and in Wheat.

# EASTERN OREGON WINTER DWELLINGS

In the Klamath Lakes Area, the major winter dwelling style was the earth-covered lodge (see p. 38). The circular lodge was built over an excavation two to six feet deep. Poles and mats covered the excavation and a layer of packed earth formed an insulating cover. Persons entered these lodges by a ladder that protruded through a hatchway in the roof. Earth lodges held from one to eight families. Sleeping quarters were arranged around the perimeter and there was a single, central fireplace. Cooking and most storage was done in smaller structures near the main dwelling.

The mat longhouse, used in the Columbia Plateau Area, was constructed similarly to a tipi. A series of pole tripods were set up with double ridgepoles stretched between them. More poles were leaned against the ridgepole and the whole structure was then covered with mats. Earth was piled along the bottom for insulation. There were often several doorways along the length of the house. The longhouses were as long as the plank houses of western Oregon and held a number of families who chose a leader and acted as a group. Family fireplaces were lined down the center of the house eight to ten feet apart.

In the Great Basin, the most common winter dwelling was the conical or domed willow-frame house. This house was built on a frame of bent willow branches and covered with brush or mats. Willow-frame houses were smaller (usually large enough to hold only one or two families) and more temporary than other Oregon Indian houses. This was a result of the temporary nature of Paiute winter camps and the fact that the flexible Paiute political organization was based on small family units that could join together and disperse as resources required. Each winter the Paiute Indians would build a new house from willow, cottonwood, tule reeds, sagebrush and other readily available material. Construction of a willow-frame house was relatively simple and a good builder could make it totally water- and wind-proof.

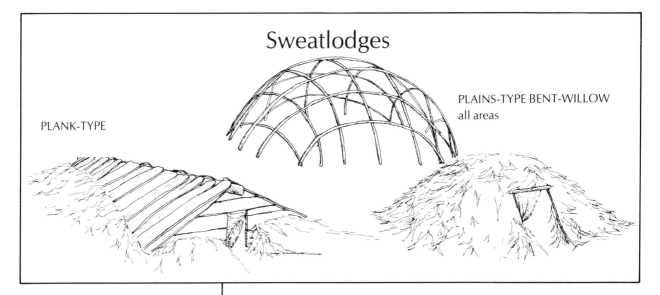

# Sweatlodges

PLANK-TYPE

PLAINS-TYPE BENT-WILLOW
all areas

## DRAWING: SWEATLODGES

In plank sweatlodges, a single ridgepole supported roof planks; the eaves rested on the ground. The floor was excavated at a slant to make the back deeper than the front. Floors were either of planks or dirt. *See* Curtis; Barnett (1937); and A. B. Lewis (1906).

Bent-willow sweatlodges varied in appearance. They could accommodate as few as one person or as many as ten, and depending on their size and permanence might be covered simply by the user's blanket or with mats and sod. *See* Boas (1923); Curtis; Barnett (1937); Slickpoo; Spinden; O. C. Stewart (1941); and Minor & Pecor.

Rocks were heated outside the sweatlodge and then thrown in and splashed with water to create steam. Users could cool themselves off in the nearby river or lake. Sweatlodges in the Plateau Area, the Klamath Area and the south coast received widespread and frequent use while the sweatlodges in other parts of the state were used primarily for medicinal purposes or prayer. *See* Beckham (1977); and Ray (1938).

## TEMPORARY SHELTERS AND SWEATLODGES

All Oregon Indians used temporary shelters during their seasonal travels. Brush, bark and mats were used to construct a variety of lean-tos and sheds. Along the mid-Columbia, mats were used to make a tipi-like house. Skin tipis came into use when horses allowed more hunting and greater contact with Plains Indians. Tipis were traditionally used in Oregon only by some Plateau peoples, although they have come to be common among many Oregon Indians today. Temporary shelters permitted Indian people to travel long distances in their search for food. Mats could be easily carried and brush or bark could be found almost anywhere.

The sweatlodge was an important feature of Oregon Indian architecture. Two major styles were constructed, a plank-type sweatlodge in the Coast and Klamath Lakes areas, and a Plains-type willow-frame sweatlodge used elsewhere in Oregon (*see* p. 40). Sweatbaths were an essential part of Oregon Indian hygiene and religion. Water was poured over heated rocks causing steam that was considered a physical and spiritual purifier.

Sweatlodges were used both daily and for special ceremonies connected with healing or religion. In parts of the state, the sweatlodge was used as an informal clubhouse where people could go to relax, talk over village politics or just get away from their families.

The spiritual and social importance of sweatlodges to Oregon Indians continues today. Several alcohol and drug abuse programs use the sweatlodge as a means of introducing young Indians to their culture and purifying them from the ill effects of alcohol and drugs. Some of these sweatlodge programs have their roots in Oregon Indian traditions, while others derive from Plains Indian traditions brought to Oregon by other tribes.

## FAMILY ORGANIZATION

Most ethnographies contain information on kinship, marriage and family life (*see* p. 57 for listing). A number of articles discuss technical details of kinship terminology: *see* Aoki (1966, 1970); Lundsgaarde; and M. Jacobs (1932) on Sahaptian kin terms; and Kroeber (1937) on Athapascan terminology. The Takelma kinship example in the text is from Sapir (1907a).

Studies of Oregon Indian marriage and family organization include Park. Brideprice is discussed in DuBois (1936); Drucker (1936); and Gould.

Although there are a number of articles on Indian child-raising practices and family relationships, many, unfortunately, attempt to apply Euro-American theories of psychology to native American societies irrespective of cultural differences. Discussions of child training are included in articles on the Paiute (Brink); and Klamath (Pearsall). Erickson compares Yurok child rearing to that of other world cultures.

## FAMILY ORGANIZATION

Household and family groups were basic to Oregon Indian social organization. Families lived and worked together and formed social alliances as a unit. Most Oregon households were extended families. Kinship ties could be traced through either the mother or father or both—each culture had its own method of defining relationships and setting rules about marriage. Ties could be traced through many generations and the kinship networks were complex.

The Takelma kinship system indicates how complex and precise Oregon Indian kinship systems really were. The Takelma people had many terms that can only be translated as cousin in English. The English word cousin describes either a boy or a girl, makes no distinction between a cousin on the father's side and the mother's side, and tells nothing about age. The Takelma, however, had separate terms to describe each of these relationships. The Takelma word *wa* meant mother's younger sister's son while at least ten other terms were used to refer to other kinds of relationships. These precise terms were necessary to describe the mutual familial obligations.

Marriage in Oregon Indian societies was seen as an alliance between two families. In-laws had certain rights and responsibilities to each other. If a household leader wanted to form a large seal-hunting expedition or a slave-raiding party, he called on his in-laws and relatives to join in the activity. The importance of village leaders was in proportion to the number of people they could mobilize in such undertakings. Marrying into a powerful family brought status and meant a definite source of recruits for political or economic ventures.

One aspect of Oregon Indian marriage that is much misunderstood is the practice usually called brideprice. In southwestern Oregon, when a couple was to be married, their families would negotiate a sum of goods to be given to the bride's relatives, as a sign of the alliance between the two families, and not meaning that the man bought the woman in the way a slave could be bought. The so-called brideprice was the first in a series of exchanges that helped create economic and social bonds. In other parts of the state, in-law obligations were not as formal but were important nevertheless.

The raising and education of children were very important and were shared by various members of the family. Fathers and uncles taught sons the basics of hunting, fishing and toolmaking. A boy's first catch was usually marked with a ceremony and distribution of the game. Girls began helping their mothers at an early age and were often put in charge of infants and younger children. They accompanied their mothers and aunts on gathering expeditions, learning the intricacies of plant identification.

Elders played a major role in educating children. They passed on traditional knowledge through stories and proverbs. Respect for elders was extremely important. Children were often cared for by a variety of relatives and friends, which helped develop strong kinship ties. The communal approach to child raising, the respect for elders and the importance of kinship ties all continue today.

GENERAL SOURCES

James T. Davis provides an overview of California and southern Oregon trade networks, detailing the complex exchanges between neighboring tribes. Angelo Anastasio examines trade goods and relationships in the Plateau, discussing the system of "task groupings" that tribes of this area developed for buffalo expeditions, trade fairs and raids against Basin and Plains tribes. Task groups included members of several different Plateau tribes, usually led by those in whose homeland the activity occurred. Celilo Falls task groups, for example, were hosted by the Wyam but included most other Plateau tribes.

Local details of trade can be found in ethnographies (listed on p. 57), especially French (1961); and Spier & Sapir.

# TRADE NETWORKS

Intertribal cooperation and communication were extremely important in traditional Oregon. Raw materials such as bone, stone and animal skin were traded everywhere as were finished products such as basketry and ornaments. Just as important was the trade in ideas. Stories, religious ideas and social and political concepts were all passed from one culture to the next.

Communication was important. Navigable rivers and trails made access fairly easy, even over mountain passes. Oregon Indians were well aware that they differed from their neighbors and kept abreast of development in nearby cultures. Before Euro-Americans first arrived in Oregon, most Oregon Indians had heard about the conflicts between settlers and eastern Indian groups. Such knowledge was a result of the well-maintained trade network.

While all tribes traded with their immediate neighbors, there were also certain places where huge trade fairs would be held each year. At sites near The Dalles and Celilo Falls, the Wasco and Wyam Indians hosted large gatherings every summer. Indians from all over the Northwest came to these large trading centers, bringing with them the specialties of their own region. Objects were often traded several times and might end up hundreds of miles away from their place of origin. Trade goods from The Dalles and Celilo Falls have been found as far away as Alaska, southern California and Missouri. The Chinookan-speaking Indians of the Lower Columbia utilized their central position, their control of the Columbia River transportation route and their abundant source of salmon to become one of the most important trading peoples of the West Coast. Wealthy traders came to occupy a high position in Chinookan society as trade took on a social and ceremonial importance.

The trade fairs at Celilo Falls and The Dalles and smaller trade gatherings throughout Oregon always involved more than trading. There were dances and ceremonial displays, and both children and adults participated in races, games and gambling matches. Persons from various tribes had an opportunity to socialize and share their experiences with each other. Marriages were often formed at such trade fairs, thus creating permanent links between tribes.

Two products stood above all others in importance at the trade fairs: salmon and slaves. Indians with access to the Columbia River were able to trade huge amounts of preserved salmon to people with poor fishing resources. Many tons of salmon were dried and traded each year. Slaves, captured in war raids or traded from other tribes, were also common at the large trade fairs. Indian people preferred to own slaves from faraway places, since there was less chance that the slave would try to return home. Pit River and Shasta Indians from California were frequently slaves in Oregon. Klamath and Modoc people would bring large numbers of the California slaves to the Columbia River markets where Chinookans would trade them even further north (*see note on pp. 56-57 for details*).

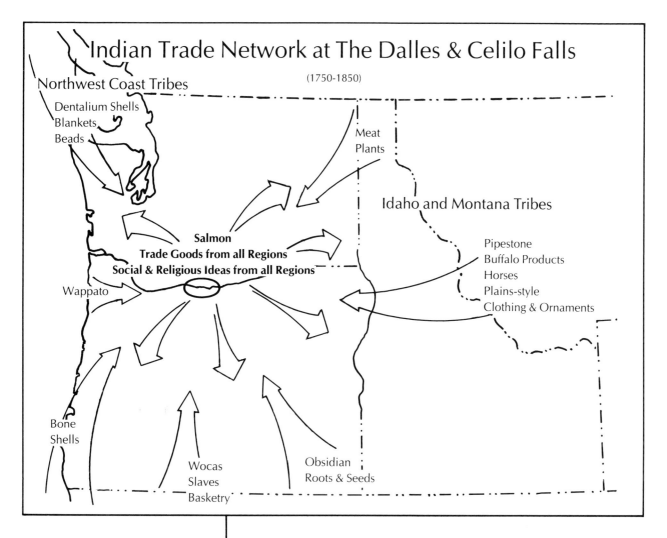

## Indian Trade Network at The Dalles & Celilo Falls
### (1750-1850)

**Northwest Coast Tribes**

Dentalium Shells
Blankets
Beads

Meat
Plants

**Idaho and Montana Tribes**

**Salmon**
**Trade Goods from all Regions**
**Social & Religious Ideas from all Regions**

Pipestone
Buffalo Products
Horses
Plains-style
Clothing & Ornaments

Wappato

Bone
Shells

Wocas
Slaves
Basketry

Obsidian
Roots & Seeds

MAP: INDIAN TRADE NETWORK AT
THE DALLES & CELILO FALLS

This general map does not list all of
the goods traded at the mid-Columbia, nor does it delineate the actual
trade routes. It should also be noted
that a number of other trade centers
existed in Oregon.

Many of the goods traded at the large gatherings did not originate on the Columbia but came from throughout the Northwest.
Oregon's complex trade network insured that goods would be distributed over a large area. Whale and seal bone and ornamental
shells came from the Coast. Obsidian and other stones useful in
toolmaking came from the Great Basin. Buffalo and deer skins came
from the Plateau. Klamath and Modoc Indians carried finished baskets to The Dalles. There was also a lively trade in plant products
—tribes of each area trading their own specialty for rarer foods.
Wappato, camas, acorns and bitterroot were all traded. Special ceremonial objects were also widely exchanged. Feathers, pipestone
and ornaments came from across the Plains. Dentalia, the much-val-
ued crescent-shaped shells, were traded from the Northwest Coast.

43

## Ceremonial Wealth

DuBois (1936); Drucker (1936); and Gould examine the use of wealth by southwestern Oregon Indian societies, whose unique legal and economic system was related to the wealth and potlatch system of more northerly tribes. In Oregon, display of wealth was more important than the gift-giving and destruction of goods reported from British Columbia and Alaska.

Dentalium shells, red woodpecker scalps, large obsidian blades and various other items were used as ceremonial wealth in western Oregon. They were a means of indicating wealth and social importance rather than a medium for buying food, shelter or clothing. These ceremonial wealth goods were also used in a system of social payments—they were symbols of alliances and obligations. The bride price (discussed on p. 41) and the blood-money compensation for injury or death were paid in dentalium and other such mediums of exchange. Because dentalia had a symbolic value and because they were not used to buy everyday items, they cannot be considered in the same manner as cash. Wealth, in Oregon Indian terms, was thus a measure of social and ceremonial importance.

Euro-Americans affected the Indian trade network long before these outsiders set foot in Oregon. Wasco Indians, for example, traded guns they had received from trading ships to the Lewis and Clark Expedition in 1805. Horses, guns, glass beads, wool blankets and brass kettles were commonly introduced trade items. For many decades these new goods were exchanged in the Indian markets without changing the traditional trading style. The Indians took those foreign goods that interested them and ignored the rest, much as they had always done with goods from other cultures. In the late 1700s and the early 1800s, European and American ships tapped the native trade network and established trade routes to the Orient.

Eventually, the Euro-American traders began flooding the Indian markets with new items, and inflation set in. The introduced goods increased the importance of slave and horse trading as new wealth made prestige possessions easier to obtain. Unscrupulous traders also introduced alcohol, thus making a profit for themselves while weakening traditional culture. Alcohol was completely unknown to Oregon Indians before contact.

The greatest single impact of Euro-Americans on the Indian trade network was the introduction of a cash economy. Wealth and trade goods had been important before contact; after contact goods became important solely for their economic value. Cash gradually replaced barter and ceremonial wealth as a medium of exchange.

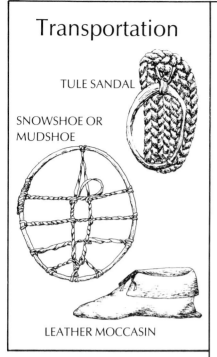

TULE SANDAL

SNOWSHOE OR
MUDSHOE

LEATHER MOCCASIN

DRAWING: TRANSPORTATION

Moccasin: after sketches in Kelly
(1963). Tule Sandal: after photographs in Cressman; Mason. Mudshoe (snowshoe): after sketches in
Mason; Slickpoo.

Canoes: after photographs in Curtis
(vols. 8, 13); Colville. Raft: after
sketch in Ray (1963). Tule boat: after
photograph in Wheat. Paddles: after
sketches in Underhill. Poles: after photographs in Curtis; Colville. Travois:
after photograph in Ballard.

Burden basket, tumpline and basketry hat: after sketch in Mason; photographs in James; Curtis (vols. 8, 13).

*See also* Barnett (1937); Drucker
(1937); Gunther (1945); Howe; A. B.
Lewis; Minor & Pecor; Olson; Ray
(1963); Sauter & Johnson; Spinden;
H. Stewart; and O. C. Stewart (1948).

Foot Travel

Moccasin and sandal construction
utilized a variety of techniques. One
type of leather moccasin was a shaped
piece of buckskin, folded and sewn up
the front and back. A second piece
could be added at the ankle and

# TRANSPORTATION

The Indian people of Oregon transported themselves and their
goods by canoe, raft, dog, horse and on foot (*see* illustrations pp.
14, 45-47). Each tribe used a combination of methods, choosing the
mode of transportation best suited to the terrain, the type of load
and the desired speed. Since each band and local group had a different pattern of settlement and seasonal movement, the mixture of
transportation methods differed from group to group and from season to season.

Long-distance travel by foot was, of course, common all over
Oregon. In rougher parts of the Inland Valleys Area and in eastern
Oregon prior to the arrival of the horse, it was the principal mode of
long-distance travel. Foot trails wound across most mountain passes
and were important in maintaining the vast Indian trade network.
Leather moccasins and tule sandals were worn for long hikes and for
protection against cold, rather than for everyday use. In winter,
snowshoes were used for hunting expeditions. In the Klamath Area,
where lakes were well stocked with waterfowl and plant products,
Indians used mudshoes (built similarly to snowshoes) to keep from
sinking in the mud.

Canoes and rafts were used by Indians in all parts of Oregon,
although they were not a major method of travel in eastern Oregon.
The boats were used on lakes and rivers for fishing, gathering water
plants, bird hunting and travel. Oregon Indians occasionally ven-
tured to sea for seal hunts or slave raids, but long sea voyages were
much less common than they were further north among the Nootka, Kwakiutl and Haida. The use of canoes along the Columbia River
contributed to the development of trading and continued communication among neighboring tribes.

Most Oregon canoes were made by hollowing logs—no birch-
bark type canoes were used. The wooden dugout was uniquely suited to western Oregon's plentiful supply of timber. The canoes were
expertly carved in a variety of shapes and sizes to insure a smooth
and quiet voyage even in rough waters. Skill in canoe carving was
widely appreciated and ownership of a well-carved canoe was a
mark of prestige.

Cedar was the most common tree for canoe construction, although redwood was used on the southern coast. Drift logs on
beaches were often used for canoes. The logs were hollowed with
controlled fire and carved with stone, bone or shell adzes. Paddles
and poles were made in a variety of styles, including a pointed paddle used as a stake for tying up canoes and a two-pronged pole,
used for particularly muddy lakes.

Along the Lower Columbia River, the long-prowed Chinook-style
canoe was popular. Larger Chinook canoes had an added wooden
prow and stern, could hold twenty or more people and were similar
to the large war canoes used by the Nootka and other Northwest
Coast tribes. Elsewhere in Oregon, the shovel-nose canoe was most

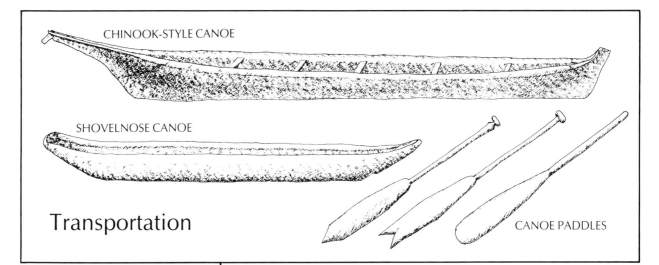

CHINOOK-STYLE CANOE

SHOVELNOSE CANOE

# Transportation

CANOE PADDLES

folded over the thong tie to protect the ankle from friction. Cushioning inner soles were made from shredded tule. Worn outer soles could be replaced simply by sewing new ones on.

### Water Travel

The swift Chinook-type canoe averaged 20-30 feet in length (although some were as long as 50 feet), its prow providing a vantage point for the spear or harpoon thrower while the narrowed bow served as an excellent cutwater. The shovelnose canoe, 10-25 feet long, was used in all areas of northern and western Oregon.

Tule boats, 8-12 feet long and accommodating three or four people, could be constructed quickly but also wore out quickly.

Paddles (4½-5 feet long) were made from yew, ash, cedar, maple, alder and fire-hardened fir. The paddle picture at left is the most common type. The notched end of the center paddle could fit over a tow rope and was also useful in hazardous streams, to push the canoe away from rocks or snags. The paddle shown at right is noiseless, and was therefore preferred on hunting trips. Rafts and tule boats were always propelled by poles, also used with canoes in areas such as shallow streams and dense marshes, where a paddle was impractical.

common. In the Great Basin, where wood was in short supply, a more temporary canoe was made from tule. Rafts, which could be constructed quickly, were often used on lakes or slow-moving rivers.

During most of Oregon's history, no horses were available. When horses were introduced, about 300 years ago, they became important only to some Oregon tribes. By about 1700, the Shoshone Indians, living in the Rocky Mountains, had obtained horses from the Spanish settlements in New Mexico and had begun trading them to Oregon tribes; the Nez Perce and Cayuse received horses by about 1730. During the next century horses slowly spread to other tribes in Oregon.

The Nez Perce, Cayuse and (to a lesser extent) other Plateau tribes accumulated huge herds of horses and utilized techniques such as gelding and cross-breeding to improve their stock. Horses came to play a central role in their culture. Wealth began to be measured almost exclusively by the number of horses owned. Travel to distant places (such as the buffalo hunting grounds of Montana) became much more common. The importance of large-game hunting increased. Contact with surrounding tribes also increased (this included both friendly contacts with tribes such as the Yakima, Coeur d'Alene and Flathead, and hostile contacts with tribes such as the Blackfoot and Paiute). Increased contact meant more trade and an increased flow of ideas and customs. In less than a century, the tribes of northeastern Oregon adapted to horse culture and became some of the world's most proficient horse riders and trainers.

The Paiute peoples of southeastern Oregon apparently owned a small number of horses in the early 1800s, and they used their horses primarily for carrying burdens and as food in times of famine. By about 1850, Paiutes became a mounted culture, a dramatic shift. Paiute bands increased in size and band leaders took a more prominent role. Within just a few decades, the Paiutes had almost totally adjusted to this new method of transportation and the social changes that it brought.

# Transportation

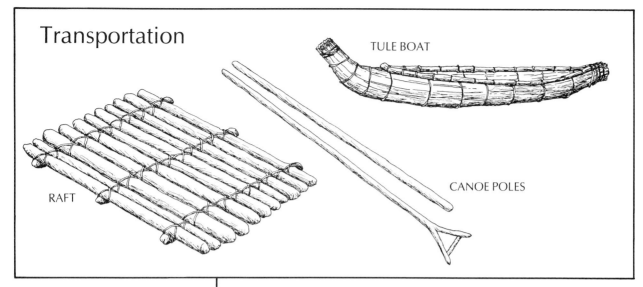

TULE BOAT

CANOE POLES

RAFT

## Horses

Francis Haines, who has traced the history of horses in western America (*see* 1938a, b, 1963), claims that the 1690 New Mexico revolt against the Spanish by Pueblo Indians led to the general availability of horses west of the Rocky Mountains. Charting the diffusion of horses northward into the Plains and northwestward up the Rockies, he claims that the Nez Perce and Cayuse acquired them before the northernmost Plains tribes such as the Blackfoot. Frank G. Roe examines the cultural importance of horses.

## Transporting Burdens

The travois (*see* p. 14), used in the Plateau Area, was made by tying tipi or mat-lodge poles to a strap at the horse's shoulder, then lashing them to shorter crosspieces nearer the ground. The burden basket, used in all areas of Oregon (and carried most often by women), was made of willow, conifer root or tule, depending on local resources.

Indian people in other portions of Oregon also used horses, but in a much more limited fashion. In western Oregon, the various tribes used horses as beasts of burden and as items of trade. Horses were few enough in number that owning one brought a certain amount of prestige. No western Oregon tribe became a fully mounted culture like the Nez Perce, Cayuse or Paiute. Horses never completely replaced the canoe as the major method of transportation in western Oregon and never became as culturally important there as they did in the east.

Indians used many methods for carrying heavy loads. The Nez Perce used dogs (and later horses) for carrying packs and pulling a special sled, called the travois (*see* p. 14). In other parts of the state, burdens were carried in large baskets or in skin bags. The usual method of carrying was the tumpline—a line passed around the forehead supporting the basket or bag on the back. Basketry hats were worn to protect the forehead from chafing. Tumplines were also used with cradleboards, the Oregon Indian version of a baby pack.

# Transportation

BASKETRY HAT,
TUMPLINE &
BURDEN BASKET

GENERAL SOURCES

The best overview of linguistic research in the Pacific Northwest is L. C. Thompson's 1970 article. This includes many grammars, dictionaries and technical studies of Oregon languages, beyond those cited in the notes below. Pierce (1964a) provides a more technical summary for Oregon. Earlier research is summarized by M. Jacobs (1941).

Much of the discussion in this section was influenced by commentary prepared by Robert Benson, David and Katherine French, Theodore Stern, Wayne Suttles and Henry Zenk.

CHART: CLASSIFICATION OF
OREGON INDIAN LANGUAGES

The phylum level of classification is questioned by many linguists and is particularly hypothetical for Penutian. Language families which contain only a single language are now called language isolates; their former family names (e.g. Waiilatpuan & Lutuamian) are included here for convenience. This chart omits sub-family divisions and lists only major dialects. Each village probably had its own dialect—a language area may be seen as a continuous chain of related dialects.

# OREGON INDIAN LANGUAGES

Traditional Oregon was one of the world's richest areas in linguistic diversity. More distinct native languages existed in Oregon than in all of present-day Europe. Of the eight major Indian language groupings in the United States, five had representatives in Oregon. A total of 21 languages were spoken in Oregon, including some 40 dialects. Each Oregon Indian language was organized differently and had its own vocabulary and grammar. Methods of expression were in some cases similar to English and in other cases were so different that literal English translations lose much of the original meaning.

Each of the Oregon Indian languages was a fully developed, sophisticated system of communication capable of transmitting any kind of information, from day-to-day pragmatic details to philosophical abstractions. Many persons are aware that the Indian languages made use of a wide variety of metaphors, puns and idioms in the beautiful poetry and prose of traditional oral communication. Less well known, however, is the fact that the Indian languages were also fully able to communicate technical details about the fields of knowledge important to native life. Special terminologies were developed for describing kinship, botanical and zoological classification and many other areas of interest. Even the adjectives for colors, numbers and geographical directions showed great variety in Oregon languages.

The language map on page 51 shows that the distribution of Oregon languages was quite complex. Linguists assume that this pattern was caused by numerous migrations into Oregon over thousands of years, each succeeding wave bringing a new language. Although it will probably be impossible to discover exactly how these migrations occurred, much can be learned by comparing Oregon languages to related Indian languages in other parts of North America. By comparing vocabulary, grammar and the sounds used in various languages, linguists are able to form theories about their relationships and history.

The Athapascan family of languages includes languages from Alaska (Haida), from New Mexico (Navaho) and from Oregon (Tututni, Clatskanie, Umpqua and others). The similarities between these languages are so consistent that linguists conclude they all once shared a single parent language or cluster of languages. According to one estimate, the original proto-Athapascan language was spoken in Alaska some 5,000 years ago. Some of the speakers of the language presumably moved south to Oregon, while others traveled to the southwestern United States. As centuries passed with little or no communication between these different groups of Athapascan speakers, the languages grew more and more different. Today, only a fraction of the vocabularies of the various languages within the family is similar.

# Classification Of Oregon Indian Languages

| PHYLUM | FAMILY | LANGUAGE | DIALECT |
|---|---|---|---|
| Salishan | Salishan | Tillamook | Tillamook |
| | | | Siletz |
| Hokan (?) | Shastan | Shasta | Shasta |
| | | | Klamath River |
| Aztec-Tanoan | Uto-Aztecan | Northern Paiute | Northern Paiute |
| Na-Dene | Athapascan | Clatskanie | Clatskanie |
| | | Umpqua | Umpqua |
| | | | Cow Creek |
| | | Coquille-Tolowa | Galice-Applegate |
| | | | Coquille |
| | | | Tututni |
| | | | Tolowa-Chetco |
| | | | Kwatami |
| Penutian (?) | Chinookan | Coastal Chinook | Clatsop |
| | | Upper Chinook | Cathlamet |
| | | | Clackamas |
| | | | Cascades |
| | | | Wasco |
| | Kalapuyan-Takelman | Tualatin Kalapuyan | Tualatin |
| | | | Yamhill |
| | | Santiam Kalapuyan | Santiam |
| | | | Mary's River |
| | | | McKenzie |
| | | Yoncalla Kalapuyan | Yoncalla |
| | | Takelma | Takelma |
| | | | Latgawa |
| | Sahaptian | Sahaptin | Umatilla |
| | | | Warm Springs |
| | | Nez Perce | Nez Perce |
| | Lutuamian | Klamath | Klamath |
| | | | Modoc |
| | Molallan | Molalla | Molalla |
| | Waiilatpuan | Cayuse | Cayuse |
| | Yakonan | Alsea | Yaquina |
| | | | Alsea |
| | Siuslawan | Siuslaw | Siuslaw |
| | | | Kuitch |
| | Coosan | Milluk | Miluk |
| | | Hanis | Hanis |

## Classification of Languages

Complete classification of a language is based on its phonetics, grammar and vocabulary. Early classification of Oregon languages is largely educated guesswork based on vocabulary, the Hokan and Penutian phyla in particular.

Sources consulted are Driver (1961); Trager & Harber; Voegelin & Wheeler-Voegelin; L. C. Thompson; Suttles (n.d.); Henry Zenk; and Robert Benson (the last two by personal communication).

(Note on spellings: the suffix "-an" is used to distinguish a family from a language. Thus the Takelma language is a member of the Takelman family.)

### Athapascan

This language family is also spelled Athabascan. The summary presented in the text (pp. 48, 52) is simplified; proto-Athapascan may have been a cluster of dialects rather than a single parent language.

The Coquille-Tolowa dialects have no standard classification. Scholars speak of a variety of dialects or lump them with Umpqua in a single language called "Oregon Athapascan." Galice-Applegate was probably the most divergent of the dialects.

### Salishan

The Tillamook language is closely related to the coastal Salishan languages of western Washington and British Columbia, and more distantly related to the interior Salishan languages of eastern Washington and Idaho. The Siletz dialect is only slightly divergent from Tillamook proper.

### Shastan

The Shasta language may be related to languages grouped in the Hokan phylum, and so is tentatively placed there. Other members of Hokan include Karok and Achomawi, both spoken by Indians living near Oregon's borders. A number of Shastan dialects were spoken in California.

### Uto-Aztecan

The Northern Paiute language is closely related to the languages of various Shoshonean peoples who bordered on Oregon (Bannock, Shoshoni, Utes) and more distantly related to languages of Mexico (including Nahuatl, the Aztec language). It is presumed that Northern Paiute was divided into dialects but so far none have been positively identified.

### Penutian

The Penutian phylum of languages is highly arbitrary. A number of California languages are also called Penutian but a firm connection between them and Oregon Penutian languages has not been established. Even within Oregon, relationships are unclear. General articles on the Penutian problem include those by Hymes (1957, 1964); Sapir (1921); and Swadesh (1954).

Coastal and Upper Chinook languages include several dialects in Washington. Upper Chinook is sometimes called Kiksht and divided into downriver (Cathlamet) and upriver (Clackamas, Cascades, Wasco) dialects.

The Takelman family is composed on two sub-families—Kalapuyan and Takelman—formerly believed to be distinct. Swadesh (1965) proposes a 2,400-year divergence between the two sub-families and a 1,200-year divergence among the various Kalapuyan languages.

The Sahaptian family includes the Nez Perce language and the Sahaptin language (formerly called the Walla Walla language). Both Sahaptin and Nez Perce include dialects spoken outside of Oregon.

The Klamath language may be related to Sahaptian or to California Penutian although no firm relationships have been documented. Modoc is a slightly divergent dialect of Klamath.

The Molalla and Cayuse languages were once lumped together in a hypothetical Waiilatpuan family. In recent work, Rigsby (especially 1969) has shown them to be distinct. Molalla probably included several dialects, although their exact boundaries are uncertain.

Yakonan and Siuslawan were at one time thought to constitute a family but are now separated. *See* Hymes (1966). The Hanis and Miluk languages were formerly thought to be dialects of a single Coos language. Recent work by Pierce (1965, 1966) shows they are more distinct. Aoki (cited in L. C. Thompson) suggests that divergence between the two languages may be the result of prolonged Athapascan influence on Miluk.

### Chinook Jargon

Chinook Jargon was initially not considered a language, but rather a *lingua franca*, or trade language, made up of portions of other languages. Recent work has shown that Jargon was a first language for many during the historical period. Hymes & Hymes hypothesize that Jargon was frequently used by children of multilingual marriages. They also report that Jargon was very important on the multilingual reservations such as Siletz, Grand Ronde and Warm Springs. Michael Silverstein has shown that the grammar of Jargon varied depending on the original languages of the speakers.

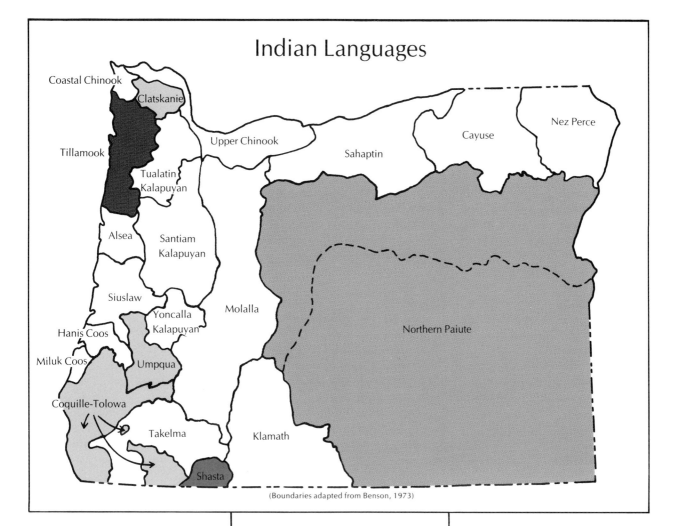

# Indian Languages

Coastal Chinook

Clatskanie

Tillamook

Upper Chinook

Tualatin
Kalapuyan

Sahaptin

Cayuse

Nez Perce

Alsea

Santiam
Kalapuyan

Siuslaw

Yoncalla
Kalapuyan

Molalla

Hanis Coos

Northern Paiute

Miluk Coos

Umpqua

Coquille-Tolowa

Takelma

Klamath

Shasta

(Boundaries adapted from Benson, 1973)

KEY
Language Groups
■ Salishan Family
■ Shastan Family
■ Uto-Aztecan Family
■ Athapascan Family
□ Penutian Phylum
   (Various families)

MAP: CLASSIFICATION AND
DISTRIBUTION OF LANGUAGES

Boundary lines adapted from Benson. Classification follows sources listed below for each language family.

Other linguistic maps consulted are
Beckham (1977); Suttles (1973);
Schaeffer; Driver (1961); Berreman;
and Voegelin & Wheeler-Voegelin.
Benson is in the process of preparing a
color-coded linguistic map of North
America.

### Language and Thought

Every language has a system for organizing fields of knowledge. The categories, and even the definition of "fields of knowledge," vary from language to language. Ethnoscience, the study of the relationship between classification systems and culture, has found rich material in Oregon Indian languages. Various studies have covered Nez Perce kinship terms (Aoki 1966), Wasco botanical terms (French 1956) and numerical systems of the Klamath (Gatschet 1880) and the Tillamook (Elmendorf 1962). Other articles on the connection between language and culture in Oregon include Haas (1967); French (1958); Rumberger; and Spier & Sapir.

### Language Change and Diffusion

There is no generally accepted theory explaining migrations and the diffusion of languages in Oregon. In 1937 and 1954 M. Jacobs published various theories including one according to which new languages entered Oregon not as a result of conquest but by gradual replacement of pre-existing languages. See Haas (1969) for technical overview.

The theory of language change, known as glottochronology or lexicostatistics, is based on the idea that language modification occurs at a steady rate, which can be measured by examining changes in basic vocabulary. By looking at vocabulary differences between two languages, linguists can estimate the period when the languages diverged. This theory is not universally accepted and the accuracy of time-depth estimates has been seriously challenged. Sources on Oregon glottochronology include Swadesh (1949 and 1965 in particular); Hymes (1960a, b); Hoijer; Miller; Tanner & Foley; Krauss; and N. A. Hopkins.

Even within one language, geographic separation often resulted in change. Tututni (an Athapascan language) for example, was divided into many dialects. The Indians living in various villages in southwestern Oregon each spoke slightly different dialects of Tututni. There were no rigid boundaries within the language group, yet the further from home a person traveled, the harder it would be to understand the local speech. Dialectal differences included minor changes in vocabulary and pronunciation such as occur between American and Australian dialects of the English language. When speakers of two dialects can no longer understand one another, linguists label the two dialects as separate languages.

The language classification chart on page 49 represents the most recent theories about the relationship among Oregon Indian languages. Yet language classification is by no means standardized, especially in reference to dialects. There is wide disagreement over theories of language change and migration. Classification of Oregon Indian languages is especially difficult due to their great variety and the fact that many of them are no longer spoken. A further confusion is caused by the massive borrowing that apparently occurred in Oregon. The Miluk Coos language (spoken on the lower Coquille River) shared many words and phrases with the Coquille language (spoken on the upper portions of the same river); though Coquille and Miluk Coos are historically unrelated and belong to different language families (Athapascan and Coos, respectively), their physical proximity caused much borrowing.

Because there were so many different languages in Oregon the ability to translate was a valuable skill. Each tribe had several members capable of understanding neighboring tongues. Intermarriage, trade and slavery meant that people from various areas would mix and learn each other's language. Along the Columbia River and the Coast, a special international common language developed called Chinook Jargon. Originally derived from the Coastal Chinook language, Jargon began to be used for trade and interaction in many parts of Oregon and the Northwest. Eventually Jargon incorporated many words from various Indian languages and from French, Russian and English. Sign language, although used to a limited extent, was never as important in Oregon as it was on the Plains, partly because Chinook Jargon was so widely used.

Translators and Jargon were common enough that members of different language groups could communicate easily. This meant that language boundaries were sometimes different from political or cultural boundaries. In some cases, a tribe would be allied to a people speaking a foreign tongue and be enemies of a tribe that spoke their own language. In southwestern Oregon, the Galice Creek Indians spoke an Athapascan language but were surrounded by people who spoke a Penutian language called Takelma. The Galice Creek tribe probably shared customs with their Takelma-speaking neighbors as often as they did with other tribes who spoke their own Athapascan language.

It is difficult to find accurate information on the extinction of languages. L. C. Thompson's list of extinct languages in the Northwest is the most extensive.

Local curriculum programs have produced word lists and other language tools for Klamath, for Chinook Jargon and for Nez Perce. Indian-related geographic names have been compiled by H. S. Lyman (1900); and Lewis A. McArthur (1974).

The nineteenth century saw the demise of many native languages. People were grouped on reservations without regard to the diversity of their languages. The Warm Springs, Klamath and Umatilla reservations each had three major dialects. Siletz and Grand Ronde reservations were even more diverse: their early inhabitants spoke 30 different dialects in addition to Chinook Jargon, English and probably some French. In these multilingual communities, the common languages such as Jargon and English increased in use and the local languages decreased. Non-Indian educators speeded up this destructive process by punishing Indian children for speaking their native languages.

Of the 21 original Indian languages in Oregon, about one-third are still spoken. Chinook Jargon and some dialects of Sahaptin, Nez Perce, Upper Chinook and Northern Paiute are currently being used in Oregon. Klamath, Shasta, Tillamook and some of the Athapascan dialects are remembered by only a few persons. The other languages are only partially remembered and can be considered extinct. To say that a language is extinct does not necessarily mean that the tribe or culture associated with the language is also gone. The Cayuse language, for example, is no longer spoken fluently, yet the Cayuse people continue to thrive, speaking either Nez Perce or English as a first language.

Recently there have been a number of efforts to revitalize the study of Indian languages. Sahaptin, Klamath, Chinook Jargon, Wasco and others are being taught to Indians in various parts of the state. The Burns-Paiute Reservation presents an interesting picture: 90 percent of the people over age 30 on the reservation speak Paiute, yet only a few of those under that age speak it. To keep the language alive, tribal educators have begun teaching it to children and are working with linguists to develop a written alphabet.

Indian languages and their preservation will also continue to affect non-Indians as they have so significantly in the past. Nine Oregon counties have names of Indian origin, and there are also innumerable roads, towns, rivers and mountains in the state, whose names have come from native languages.

Social Ranking and Leadership

For further information on chieftainship, social ranking and wealth *see* Drucker (1939); Elmendorf (1971); Gould; DuBois (1936); Ray (1960); and McFeat.

Shamanism, Religion and Myth

World view in Indian cultures, as reflected by spirituality, philosophy, healing and ritual, is a subject many contemporary Indians consider inappropriate for academic articles. Many traditional Indian religions are currently being practiced and the best source of information is the practitioners. There are, however, a number of written sources on both traditional world view and contemporary revival movements in Oregon.

Indian traditional world view has been studied for the Chinook (Franz Boas 1893; M. Jacobs 1955), the Klamath (Spencer), the Paiute (Whiting), northeastern Oregon tribes (Coale; Walker 1967b; and Murdock 1965) and southwestern Oregon tribes (Sapir 1907b; Cutsforth & Young).

Special rituals have also been studied. Ray (1937) discusses the Plateau Spirit Dance. Goldschmidt has explored the White Deerskin Dance of southwestern Oregon tribes. Gunther (1926, 1928) discussed the First Salmon Ceremony.

Indian revivalist movements of 19th and 20th century Oregon include the Dreamer religion, the Feather Cult and the Ghost Dance, as well as a number of smaller spiritual movements. *See* DuBois (1938); Nash; Spier (1927a, 1935); Stern (1960); Walker (1969); and Relander, the last of which contains some excellent photographs.

# SOCIAL ORGANIZATION

In general, Oregon Indian societies had few rigid social distinctions, and allowed all tribal members a voice in decision making. There were, however, major differences between the culture areas. The charts on page 55 are generalized. It is not meant to sum up Indian societies, rather it emphasizes that even within Oregon there were differences between tribal organizations.

Political leadership varied a great deal both in methods of choosing leaders and in the amount of authority granted to them. The word "chief" cannot be used in any strict sense for Oregon tribes, since leaders had no absolute power and were not usually formally elected. Leaders acted as advisors to the tribe and were chosen for personal qualities such as wisdom, speaking ability and fairness in settling disputes. In western Oregon, wealth was a major factor in leadership, since only a wealthy person could afford the lavish hospitality expected of the leader. Family background was important, especially in the Lower Columbia Area. Relationship to a former leader, however, did not necessarily guarantee leadership.

In each tribe or band there was an informal council that aided leaders in making decisions, chose new leaders and served as a public forum for the discussion of subjects important to the group. The council usually consisted of all adult members of the tribe, but might be limited to elders or persons who were held in high regard. Certain persons whose advice was valued might have more influence, but decision making was usually a process of consensus. This process emphasized communal decisions rather than elections or individual leadership.

The shaman (or priest/doctor/psychiatrist) often held some power in addition to religious duties. Spirituality played such a major role in Indian cultures that the shaman was influential in all aspects of society. Anyone who had spirit power, even a slave, could become a shaman. In the charts on page 55, shamans have been placed in a separate box from other social classes to emphasize their special role. These charts also show that shamans rose to leadership in a manner different from others. In the Klamath Lakes and Great Basin areas, shamans often had more power than the political leaders and some disputes were settled through a spiritual rather than a directly political process.

Women played an important role in Oregon Indian societies. In all tribes, especially those relying heavily on vegetable foods, women were central in the economy. Women shamans were common; along the southern coast they were in the majority. Often the opinions of mothers and grandmothers would be the deciding factor in a marriage alliance. The importance of marriages made this role very significant. Women were also important in the political sphere, as rank and social standing applied to women as much as to men. Although men were more likely to hold overt power, there were times when women acted as leaders. Women had much to say in

# Social Organization

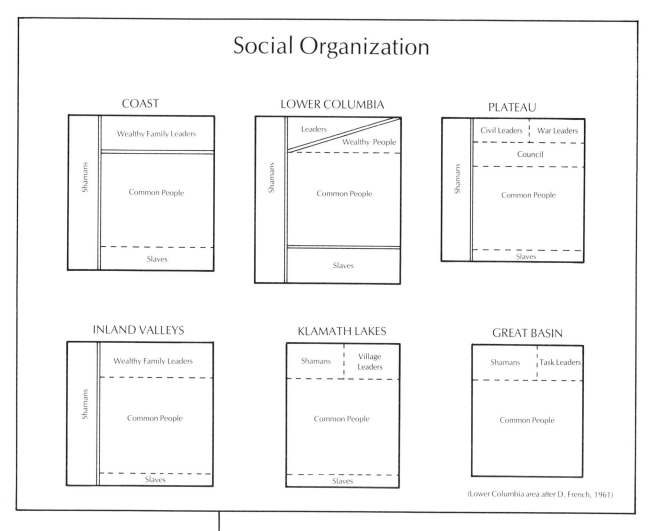

(Lower Columbia area after D. French, 1961)

KEY

– – – – – – – – –

Easily crossed social boundaries

===========

Infrequently crossed social boundaries

council meetings either directly or indirectly through their male relatives.

The practice of slavery in Oregon Indian societies was different from slavery in the American South. Slaves were uncommon in Oregon except for those kept in the Lower Columbia Area. Slavery sometimes was a temporary situation: people could purchase freedom or have their relatives do so. In most cases persons became slaves through capture, but some became slaves through debt or as punishment for a crime. The slave usually was treated as a poor relative. Prestige, rather than economic gain, was the major motive for owning slaves. Along the Lower Columbia, however, where slavery was more common, slaves did become an important economic commodity.

The most popular Indian revivalist movement in Oregon continues to be the Shaker Church (unrelated to the furniture-making Shakers). *See* Barnett (1957); Gunther (1949); Harmon; Sackett; and Ruby.

Oregon Indian oral literature was collected by a number of early ethnographers such as Franz Boas; Edward Sapir; Livingston Farrand; Leo J. Frachtenberg; and Melville & Elizabeth Jacobs. Jarold Ramsey provides many examples of their translations and gives an excellent bibliography including interpretations by Melville Jacobs, Dell H. Hymes and others who studied the structure of Indian myths. A more popularized work containing Oregon Indian traditional literature is provided by Ella E. Clark.

Recently, the Northwest Regional Education Laboratory's Indian Reading and Development Program has worked with tribal authors from Oregon and other Northwest states to produce a series of tales. This excellent series is entirely written and illustrated by members of the tribes who originally told the stories. To date, the lab has produced materials for grades one through six and is expanding its program.

Women

There are no comprehensive books or articles on the role of women in Oregon Indian cultures. Partial treatments of the subject may be found in M. Jacobs (1958); Mead; and Scott (1941).

Slavery

Elsie F. Dennis provides a partial study of Oregon Indian slave practices. More details may be found in the ethnographies listed below by culture area.

## LOWER COLUMBIA AREA

Chiefs were chosen because of their position within a family, their degree of wealth and respect for their advice and dispute-settling ability. They were fairly powerful because of their wealth and backing from large families, but they had no absolute authority. Trade was so important that a separate wealthy class evolved. These people might exert much influence and power but rarely held official positions (unless they belonged to a chief's family). Common people could raise their social standing by gaining wealth or by marrying into more prestigious families. Slaves were distinctly set off from other social classes; only an exceptional slave had the chance to rise in society. Shamans were separate from the political system; they had a respect and power of their own no matter their social background.

## COAST AREA

With a few exceptions, the social situation here was similar to that of the Lower Columbia Area. But rather than actual chiefs, family and village leaders had powers that only occasionally were as strong as those of Lower Columbia leaders. The leaders formed a sort of class in themselves based on their wealth and personal qualities rather than on any hereditary basis. Leaders presided over a judicial system of payments for insult and injury that formed the legal basis of coast society. Slaves were less numerous here and their position more like that of a poor commoner.

## INLAND VALLEYS AREA

The family and village leader system of the coast prevailed here, although there was no major gap between leaders and commoners. Slaves were rare and were not treated much differently than other society members. In general, Inland Valleys groups had fewer class differences than other western Oregon peoples, and mobility between classes was easier.

## KLAMATH LAKE AREA

Leadership was less formal than in western Oregon and shamans played a more decisive role in the political structure. Leaders were selected for their personal qualities although wealth was important. There were few slaves until horses and inflation increased their trade value at The Dalles market (*see* p. 42). Movement from one social position to another was not difficult for a person with special qualifications.

Ethnographies & General Studies
of Social Organization

"Ethnography" is a term used to denote a study of a particular tribe written by someone who had first-hand knowledge of the culture. The sources listed below vary widely—some are attempts at comprehensive ethnography, while others cover only individual aspects or report on secondary sources. Some popularized works and older studies which may contain inaccuracies are included here because, in some cases, these are the only sources.

*Lower Columbia Area*: French 1961; Spier & Sapir; Ray 1938; H. C. Taylor, Jr. 1974; Suphan 1974; Jones; Ruby & Brown 1976.
*Coast Area*: Beckham 1977.
  *Tillamook*: Boas 1898, 1923; Sauter & Johnson.
  *Alsea*: Drucker 1936; Farrand 1901.
  *Coos*: M. Jacobs 1939; Frachtenberg & St. Clair.
  *South Coast Athapascans*: Drucker 1937; DuBois 1932, 1936; Gould.
*Inland Valleys Area*: Beckham 1971, 1976.
  *Kalapuyan*: Lloyd Collins; M. Jacobs 1945; Frachtenberg; Minor & Pecor; Ratcliff; Mackey 1974.
  *Molalla*: Mackey 1972; Rigsby 1966, 1969; Minor & Pecor.
  *Umpqua*: Riddle; Bakken; Jensen.
  *Shasta*: Dixon 1905, 1907; Holt; Heizer & Hester.
  *Takelma*: Sapir 1907.
  *Rogue River Athapascans*: Drucker 1937; DuBois 1932, 1936.
*Klamath Lakes Area*: Stern 1964, 1966; Spier 1930; Ray 1963; Gatschet 1890; Howe; Mohammed & Barker.

## PLATEAU AREA

Leadership was almost entirely based on achievement and respect; wealth and heredity were of less significance here than in western Oregon. The chiefs had no absolute power but often came to be respected among several bands. The everyday leader rarely took leadership in war raids or major hunting expeditions. This role was left to another, often temporary, leader who was chosen for war or hunting skills. Slavery was rare.

## GREAT BASIN AREA

Bands were so small that there was little formal leadership. Most decisions were made by consensus or by consulting the shaman or another respected elder. Individuals with particular skills (such as directing an antelope drive) were chosen to lead in those tasks. They were called the boss of that task (e.g. antelope boss) but had no authority beyond the immediate undertaking. There were probably no slaves and little differentiation between society members except for shamans.

*Plateau Area*: Bailey; Farrand 1921; Haines 1955; Murdock 1938, 1958; Ray 1936, 1939; Spinden; Anastasio; Suphan; Schwede; Chalfant; Ruby & Brown 1965, 1972.
*Great Basin Area*: Blyth; Whiting; Kelly; Steward 1934, 1938, 1966; Steward & Wheeler-Voegelin; O. C. Stewart 1938, 1939, 1941; Winnemucca; S. W. Hopkins; Aikens; D'Azevedo.

GENERAL RESOURCES

General histories of Oregon include those by Johansen & Gates; Carey; and Dodds. *See also* Corning's *Dictionary of Oregon History;* and Farmer & Holmes *Historical Atlas of Oregon.* For the history of the Willamette Valley, *see* R. C. Clark; and Bowen. The Northwest fur trade is covered in numerous books and articles, notably those by Chittenden; Merk; and Gunther (1972). The journals, diaries, letters, government records and newspaper stories on which these secondary works draw (and are refered to as ethnohistorical documents), comprise a revealing picture of non-Indian views of Indians.

Journals and Ethnohistorical Material

Ethnohistorical writings relevant to the history of Oregon reservations, treaties, et cetera are cited in Part Two. Listed here is a small selection of the journals and writings documenting early Euro-American exploration and settlement.

One of the most important ethnohistorical records is that left by the Lewis and Clark Expedition. Although many abridgements of Lewis and Clark's journals and letters have also been published, R. G. Thwaite's seven-volume work (1904) is complete, and includes other coverage of the expedition.

Other important explorers and traders who kept journals include Ross Cox; Alexander Ross (1923, 1924); John C. Frémont; John McLoughlin (*see also* E. E. Rich, 1941-44); Peter Skene Ogden (*see also* K. G. Davis; and E. E. Rich 1950); James G. Swan; John Work; and Nathaniel J. Wyeth. The writings of the botanist-explorer David Douglas have been collected by

# FIRST CONTACTS WITH NON-INDIANS

The Indians of Oregon had for centuries been adopting new tools, lifestyles and values from neighboring cultures. When the first Euro-Americans arrived, many Oregon Indians treated them as if they were simply visitors from any other tribe. Although there were many peaceful and sharing contacts between Indians and Euro-Americans, the overall effect of contact was a disruption of native life. The different attitudes of Indians and Euro-Americans toward wildlife and land caused friction. White missionaries, though well-meaning, created problems by attempting to change native religions and lifestyles. Army officials, traders and settlers were usually convinced that their way of life was best and paid little attention to the rich Indian cultures.

The non-Indian settlement of Oregon was accomplished in three major stages: trade and exploration (from the 1770s to the 1830s), initial settlement (1830s to 1850s) and final displacement (1850s to 1880s). The major effect of the first period on Indian people was epidemics; in the second, it was cultural clash and reduction of native resources; in the third, it was armed struggles and displacement. The closing sections of Part One give sketches of settlement, epidemics, the cultural clash and armed struggles. The questions of what became of Indian lands and governments in the reservation period are left for Part Two.

## EXPLORATION AND SETTLEMENT OF OREGON BY EURO-AMERICANS

Oregon Indians began receiving Euro-American trade goods and hearing stories of newcomers by 1700. Coastal tribes, from the Tututni to the Tillamook, first met these explorers during the 1770s and 80s when British, Spanish and American ships coursed along the Oregon shoreline in search of sea otter furs and ports of trade.

Contact between the original inhabitants and the newcomers remained sporadic until the Euro-American "discovery" of the Columbia River in 1792. Trading ships began making the Columbia a regular port of call in a global network, which included Europe, the eastern American seaboard, the Pacific Northwest, Hawaii and China. Furs traded from Chinook and other Oregon Indian peoples brought a considerable profit to Euro-Americans and provided the financial base for later exploration.

The first Euro-American land exploration of Oregon was carried out by the Lewis and Clark Expedition sent west by President Thomas Jefferson to map the newly acquired Louisiana Purchase. Lewis and Clark and their party were the guests of the Nez Perce in the fall of 1805. They traded with Wasco, Wyam and other Indians on their way to the coast and spent the winter of 1805–06 among the Clatsop.

Lavender; those of the voyager Gabriel Franchere were reprinted by H. C. Franchere. Vaughan has reconstructed the artist Paul Kane's mid-19th century travels in the Northwest. Dale has edited materials from the Jedediah Smith Expedition.

Mid-19th century students of Oregon Indian history include Slacum; Gibbs; Wilkes; and Hale.

Other early land exploration of Oregon was carried out by employees of the Canadian Northwest Company and the American J. J. Astor's Pacific Fur Company. Fort Astoria was established in 1811 and an overland party of Astorians traveled through Nez Perce, Umatilla, Warm Springs and Cayuse territory later that year. Astorians traded with Chinook and Tillamook people and explored the territory of the northernmost Kalapuyans.

The Northwest Company took over Fort Astoria in 1813 and in 1821 merged with the Hudson's Bay Company which became the primary non-Indian influence in the Northwest. During the 1820s, the company's brigades, under leaders like Peter Ogden, traveled into the interior of Oregon to trade for furs with previously uncontacted tribes such as the Upper Umpqua, the Paiute and the Klamath.

During the 1830s and 40s the Euro-Americans shifted from exploration and trade to settlement. Communities based on farming and cattle raising sprang up near the present-day sites of Oregon City, Salem, The Dalles and Astoria. A group of French Canadians retired from the Hudson's Bay Company and moved to French Prairie in the fertile Willamette Valley. They were later joined by members of a party led by Nathaniel Wyeth, an American entrepreneur who hoped to set up canneries and trading posts. A third group of settlers was made up of American mountain men such as Joe Meek and Ewing Young who were forced out of the Rockies by the declining fur trade.

The most influential members of the new settlements were the missionaries. Methodists under Jason Lee and Elijah White set up missions near present-day Oregon City, The Dalles and Astoria. Congregationalists, Presbyterians and Lutherans funded Marcus and Narcissa Whitman and Henry and Eliza Spalding. The Whitmans and Spaldings founded the first missions near Walla Walla and Lapwai, and were the first overland party to include white women. Father Blanchet and other Catholics were active at The Dalles and in the Willamette Valley, especially among the French Canadian communities.

The missionaries organized and set the moral tone of the new settlements, and did much to encourage emigration to Oregon. Elijah White led a party of 114 settlers into the Willamette Valley in 1842, almost doubling the existing non-Indian population. Glowing reports by explorers and missionaries and rumors of free land led thousands of Americans (mostly from the Midwest) to take the long wagon road to Oregon during the 1840s. The main route of travel was the Oregon Trail, which passed directly through the lands of Plateau and Lower Columbia tribes. Pioneers such as Jesse Applegate blazed new routes that eventually crossed Paiute, Klamath, Takelman and Athapascan territories.

After the 1850s, 60s and 70s even more Euro-Americans came to Oregon. Gold strikes in Athapascan and Nez Perce territories brought a new breed of immigrants whose lawlessness caused problems for Indians and settlers alike. Ranchers and farmers began at

EPIDEMICS

Works on Oregon epidemics include Cook; Taylor & Hoaglin; Farmer & Karnes; and Boyd. Leslie Scott's 1928 article demonstrates the callousness of non-Indians regarding diseases that decimated American Indian populations.

MEETING OF CULTURES:
Missionaries

The role of missionaries in Oregon was far more complex than indicated by the brief sketch. An excellent bibliography of primary accounts and later studies published on this subject is found in the *Indian Historian* 5 (1975) No. 2: 46-48. Important references include Blanchet; De Smet; J. Lee; Lee & Frost; and Spaulding. Later studies include Bischoff; and Drury (1936a, b).

this time to move into remoter regions of Oregon, displacing Indian societies along the coast, in the Wallowas and in the Harney Basin.

## EPIDEMICS

Throughout the early period of exploration and settlement, epidemics formed a deadly backdrop to the events of first contact. Prior to Euro-American settlement, Oregon Indians developed biological resistance to and medical treatment for many diseases. However, certain illnesses such as smallpox, influenza, measles, malaria and venereal disease were apparently non-existent in the traditional period and the Indian population was thus unprepared for their introduction. When Euro-American ships brought these diseases from the East Coast of America, from Europe and from the tropics, Indian people fell ill and died in large numbers. Without a natural biological immunity (built up over years of exposure) even diseases such as measles could be fatal.

Epidemics occurred along the Oregon Coast in 1782–83, along the Lower Columbia and Willamette rivers, and in the Klamath Lakes Area during 1830–33, and in northeastern Oregon in the mid-1840s. Indian people in all other areas of the state also suffered losses due to foreign diseases. The death toll in western Oregon was incredibly high. Estimates of the loss of life range from 75 to 90 percent. Whole villages and tribes were wiped out.

It is impossible to calculate the extent of destruction caused by these epidemics. Depopulated villages were abandoned and survivors were forced to confederate into new political groups. Indian societies were thus faced with drastic changes just at the time they also had to deal with the question of Euro-American settlement.

Epidemics also affected the Euro-Americans' relations with Indian cultures. Many Euro-Americans got their first view of Oregon Indian cultures at a time when Indian communities were disorganized and demoralized by disease and a massive death rate. Most early settlers' accounts of the poor conditions in Indian villages should be interpreted as a reflection on the effects of disease rather than as an accurate picture of traditional life. The failure of settlers to understand the devastation of epidemics led to many misunderstandings in later years.

## MEETING OF CULTURES

The period of exploration and trade was on the whole marked by cooperation between original inhabitants and newcomers. Explorers followed Indian trails and often depended on Indian guides. In several cases Indian food and assistance saved the lives of explorers. The Nez Perce, for example, extended help to the Lewis and Clark Expedition at a crucial point when the expedition members were weak from hunger and exhaustion after their long climb and descent over the Rocky Mountains.

The fur trade that brought inflation to the traditional Indian economic systems and was the means of introduction of epidemics, otherwise had little effect on Indian cultures. There was no direct competition for resources and traders had a vested interest in maintaining good relations with Indians. The Hudson's Bay Company had a firm policy of non-interference with the internal affairs of tribes. The American explorers, lacking such a code, came into conflict more frequently.

The period of initial white settlement brought Indians and newcomers into direct competition, although violence was still minimal. Whereas the fur trade encouraged Indians to maintain their traditional lifestyles, settlement required them to assimilate or be pushed out of the way. The Hudson's Bay Company's hands-off policy toward Indian internal affairs was reversed by the American missionaries who wanted to change Indian culture.

The use of resources by early settlers was in direct contrast to traditional Indian land use. Farmers plowed up the camas and wappato beds to plant corn and wheat. Ranchers built fences that interfered with seasonal movements. The use of guns and the influx of settlers greatly reduced the number of deer and elk. Domestic animals like pigs and cattle destroyed many traditional gathering areas. In later years, mining and logging were even more destructive to traditional food resources. The overall effect was that traditional styles of food gathering became less and less possible.

At the same time Indian economic resources were being destroyed by settlers, Indian culture was being attacked by missionaries. Missionaries were often the buffer between settlers and Indians and provided medical and other assistance to Indian people. But the main result of their efforts was to weaken traditional cultures. Because missionaries rarely took the time to study Indian philosophy, they dismissed Indian religion as superstition. They discouraged the use of Indian languages and declared communal housing immoral. They also attacked traditional Indian family systems by forcing Indians to adopt Euro-American styles of living.

Many of the conflicts between missionaries and Indians were centered around the difference between the Indians' hunting-fishing-gathering economy and the farming-ranching economy of the settlers. The missionaries saw farming and ranching as the only civilized pursuits. The settled lifestyle was seen as morally superior to the "aimless wandering" of traditional seasonal rounds. Tilling the earth was somehow supposed to be morally superior to the less productive pattern of gathering. Missionaries were unaware of the careful planning and environmental soundness behind the nomadic lifestyles that they were so quick to condemn. The attitude of Gustavus Hines, a Methodist minister, was unfortunately all too prevalent. Hines wrote in 1840 about the epidemic-ridden Kalapuyans: "The hand of Providence is removing them to give place to a people more worthy of this beautiful and fertile country." Hines and other mis-

ARMED STRUGGLES

Northwest Indian "wars" have been surveyed by Glassley; and by J. P. Dunn. Although both authors incorporate a number of stereotypes, they provide valuable information on the events of the various conflicts. Each of the following references covering the major struggles contains a bibliography.

Cayuse War: Jessett; E. N. Thompson 1973; Ruby & Brown 1972.

Modoc War: Murray; Riddle; E. N. Thompson 1971.

Nez Perce War: Slickpoo; Beal; Haines 1955; Wasson; Josephy 1971; Ray 1974. Original accounts include Chief Joseph the Younger (1879, 1968); and Howard.

Paiute Campaigns & Bannock War: Brimlow 1938; Egan; S. W. Hopkins; Winnemucca; Steward & Wheeler-Voegelin; Wheeler-Voegelin 1955.

Rogue River Wars: Beckham 1971 (this excellent survey provides a full bibliography).

Yakima War: Relander 1956; Ruby & Brown 1965.

sionaries rarely questioned their assumption that Euro-American culture was more worthy than the Indian cultures.

During the period of initial settlement, Indian people continued to contribute to the emerging Euro-American community. Mountain men and pioneers often married Indian women. Indian people worked as hired hands on farms and at trading posts. Indian trails were the basis of most pioneer routes and Indians often assisted the travel-weary newcomers. Nez Perce and Cayuse, for example, traded horses to immigrants on the Oregon Trail whose herds had been depleted by the rough journey.

ARMED STRUGGLES

By the late 1840s many Oregon Indian communities were depopulated by epidemics, impoverished by destruction of traditional food sources and culturally weakened by the influence of missionaries, the introduction of the cash economy and alcohol. Yet incidents of violence were still fairly isolated. There was no prolonged fighting during the first 75 years of contact. From the late 1840s onward, as non-Indian emphasis shifted from trade to settlement, conflicts increased. The cooperation of the fur-trade era and the limited conflict over resources during initial settlement gave way to outright fighting over the occupancy of Oregon's land.

There had been isolated violence by both settlers and Indians from the beginning of the contact period, the result of cultural misunderstandings and racial prejudices. Settlers complained of unprovoked thefts and attacks while Indians were angered by pioneer mistreatment of Indian women, the unequal justice meted to Indians in the courts and the continuing trespass on Indian lands.

Many settlers lived peacefully with their Indian neighbors and sought to protect their rights. Others, especially those with financial interests in Indian land and resources, called for the extermination of all Indians. Vigilante groups were formed in several areas to kill Indians and the U.S. Army often found itself trying to keep the settlers in check.

Indian leaders were faced with many difficult decisions during this period. Not only did they have to decide how to negotiate with settlers, soldiers and Indian agents, but they also had to maintain peace within their own groups. Non-Indian settlement had driven deep wedges into Indian societies which threatened to tear tribes apart. Distinctions were introduced between treaty and non-treaty Indians, between Christian and heathen, and between those who wanted to assimilate and those who wanted to maintain traditional values. Some leaders, such as Halhaltlossot ("Lawyer") of the Nez Perce, Winnemucca and Sarah Winemucca of the Paiute and Old Schonchin of the Modoc, thought it wiser not to fight. Others, such as Toohoolhoolzote of the Nez Perce and Schonchin John of the Modoc, wanted to resist non-Indian encroachments. Hinmahtoo-yahlatkekht (Chief Joseph the Younger) of the Nez Perce and Kientapoos (Captain Jack) of the Modoc believed in the moral right of resistance, but felt sure that war could not be successful. Both Chief Joseph and Captain Jack were eventually forced by circumstances to fight.

The major Indian struggles in Oregon—the Cayuse War, the Rogue River wars, the Modoc War, the Nez Perce War and the Paiute campaigns—were touched off by a variety of incidents perpetrated by both sides. The underlying causes however were similar: settlers' hunger for land and gold, treaty misunderstandings and problems caused by poorly administered reservations. One of the most basic mistakes of the era was the 1850 Oregon Land Donation Act which opened Indian country to settlement but made no provisions for purchase or compensation for the stolen lands.

The Cayuse War of 1848, the Rogue River wars of 1853–56 and the Paiute campaigns of 1850–68 were all related to frustration over Euro-American trespass on Indian homelands. The Cayuse people had welcomed the establishment of the Whitman Mission in their territory but came to regret their decision. By the late 1840s thousands of immigrants had passed through the Cayuse homelands and used the Whitman Mission as a stopover. The wagon trains trampled the Cayuse grazing lands, depleted Cayuse game and firewood and brought epidemics that decimated the Cayuse population. Similar problems were caused by wagon trains crossing Paiute lands in southeastern Oregon. Likewise, in the Rogue River country the discovery of gold brought an influx of settlers and led to the destruction of many native resources. Mining tore up the earth and native plant foods. Mining debris also killed fish in many streams.

The Modoc War of 1872–73 and the Nez Perce War of 1877 occurred after treaty negotiations. Both the Nez Perce and the Modoc were split between those who wanted to sign the treaties and accept reservations and those who refused to be moved from their homelands. The Wallowa bands of the Nez Perce were told to move to the Lapwai Reservation in Idaho, although an earlier treaty guaranteed them use of the Wallowas. The Modoc were lumped with Klamath and Paiute people on the Klamath Reservation, far north of their traditional homelands on Lost River and Tule Lake.

Several other armed struggles involved Oregon Indians. The Yakima War of 1855–56 affected the Warm Springs bands, the Cayuse and the Cascade Chinook. The Bannock War of 1878 started in Idaho but eventually involved some Oregon Paiutes. In both of these struggles innocent Indian people who had remained neutral or sided with non-Indians were punished indiscriminantly along with those who had taken a stand against the army.

The conception that all Indians were warlike is proved false by the many Oregon tribes who never fought against non-Indians. On the other hand, when Oregon Indians decided to fight, they did it well. Chief Joseph's band of Nez Perce fought many battles over a period of months without being defeated; Captain Jack and his handful of Modocs held off 1,000 soldiers for months; and different Paiute bands, under leaders such as Panina, frustrated settlers and soldiers for more than 15 years. Indian use of resources and terrain was superior to their opponents' tactics in the field. In fact, the army relied heavily on friendly Indians as scouts in several Oregon wars.

Indian tactical superiority could not prevent the inevitable conquest by the U.S. Army. The army was far better supplied, and had a much larger number of men, with howitzers and cannon to back them up. Military defeat, however, did not mean the end of Indian societies.

Wars, along with epidemics and Euro-American settlement completely changed the face of traditional Oregon. The central questions became: What form would Indian societies take within the dominant American society, and what would happen to the Indian lands? Parts Two and Three examine these questions and show that, fortunately for all of us, many aspects of traditional culture remain viable and dynamic today.

# OREGON INDIANS

## PART TWO

## HISTORICAL

PHOTOGRAPH:
Gathering at Old Chief Joseph's reburial in Nez Perce cemetery near Wallowa Mountains, 1926. (OHS neg. 65570)

*The earth was created by the assistance of the sun, and it should be left as it was . . . the country was made without lines of demarcation, and it is no man's business to divide it. . . . I see the whites all over the country gaining wealth, and see their desire to give us lands which are worthless . . . the earth and myself are of one mind. The measure of the land and the measure of our bodies are the same. Say to us if you can say it, that you were sent by the Creative power to talk to us. Perhaps you think the Creator sent you here to dispose of us as you see fit. If I thought you were sent by the Creator I might be induced to think you had a right to dispose of me. Do not misunderstand me, but understand me fully with reference to my affection for the land. I never said the land was mine to do with it as I choose. The one who has the right to dispose of it is the one who has created it. I claim a right to live on my land, and accord you the privilege to live on yours.*

*Hinmahtooyahlatkekht*
*(Chief Joseph, the Younger)*

# EARLY U.S. INDIAN POLICY
# IN OREGON

GENERAL SOURCES

A comprehensive overview of the federal-Indian relationship was prepared by Kickingbird & Kickingbird in 1977. Tyler and Prucha (1962) both have surveyed U.S. Indian policy. Sources on federal Indian law include Cohen's 1971 study (rev. ed.); and Getches, Rosenfelt & Wilkinson. L. P. Dunn's 1975 high school curriculum guide contains useful material on American Indians. Essays on Indian land tenure have been compiled by Sutton; and by Kickingbird & Ducheneaux. Since Peterson's 1934 survey, few writers have examined Indian policies in Oregon—recent works by Beckham; and Deloria (1977) begin to fill that gap. (All of Deloria's works are highly recommended.)

## INTRODUCTION

When Europeans and Americans entered the lands of the Indian peoples of Oregon, they encountered many independent Indian nations. The cultures and histories of these tribes reflected centuries of intimate interaction with the land and its resources. A new, but far from final, chapter of Indian history began after the arrival of the Euro-American traders, missionaries and settlers. Although the foreigners succeeded in imposing many of their ways during the last 200 years, it is important to understand that Indian life did not end when these changes occurred. Most Oregon Indian nations survived, adapting to the invading elements while continuing to preserve their own vital traditions. They fought to retain their land bases and continue to claim a cultural and political separateness from the rest of American society.

Many of the newcomers did not respect the land or the people who inhabited it. The Euro-Americans had the idea that they were discovering this land, and, in so doing, had exclusive rights to it. Believing that money could be exchanged for land, they necessarily thought that individuals could personally own land, erect fences on it and keep others from sharing its resources. These ideas contrasted greatly with traditional Indian values. For thousands of years, a sacred relationship between the people and the earth had provided the Oregon tribes with an enduring, communally based way of life. Individual ownership of land surely was a strange idea to these Indian peoples. They had never coveted the land for itself, but had valued and nurtured its life-giving benefits.

## SOVEREIGN INDIAN TRIBES

The best short appraisal of Indian sovereignty is Kickingbird, Kickingbird, Chibitty & Berkey (this provided the definition on p. 68). Major federal documents, laws such as the Trade and Intercourse acts of 1790, 1793, 1796 and 1802, and nearly all Indian treaties up to the 1860s recognized the sovereign status of Indian nations. But as the expanding United States surrounded eastern tribes, this sovereignty was challenged.

*Worcester* v. *State of Georgia* (1832) arose from the conflict between tribal sovereignty and state power: officials attempted to enforce state laws over two white missionaries who resided on Cherokee lands with the tribe's permission. Chief Justice John Marshall rejected Georgia's argument that the Cherokees were ''conquered subjects.'' He declined to view the tribes as foreign nations but did interpret the Indian Trade and Intercourse acts to ''manifestly consider the several Indian nations as distinct, political communities within which their authority is exclusive, and having a right to all the lands within those boundaries, which is not only acknowledged, but guaranteed by the United States.'' *31 U.S. (6 Pet.) 515, 557* (1832). The controlling cases on sovereignty and tribal powers are described in articles by Green & Work; F. Martone; and Getches, Rosenfelt & Wilkinson. Prucha (1962, pp. 5-25); and Washburn (1971, pp. 1-58) cover early European attitudes and policies.

As the number of Euro-American settlers in the Oregon Territory increased, friction developed between Indians who had always lived on the land and newcomers who were claiming it as their own. For the most part, the newcomers were United States citizens and their government attempted to resolve some of the conflicts that ensued. The Oregon tribes were many independent nations, each of whom had various contact with the early traders and explorers of the Northwest. Often the Indian nations and the United States government signed treaties that recognized that these tribes would retain certain lands and autonomy. Treaties created smaller land units and new political groupings among the Indian nations. In some cases, however, Oregon tribes had to settle on the reduced land bases of other tribal groups.

Besides causing many shifts in Indian land ownership, the treaties also initiated a special relationship between the tribes and the federal government. The Indian nations bargained for and retained a unique status for themselves when concluding these legal agreements. But often the unique position of Indian tribes was not protected as the expanding United States often acted contrary to the established rights of Indian people. Programs to divide Indian lands, end tribal customs and legislate Indians out of existence were part of a fluctuating history of United States Indian affairs. A review of major policies that have so greatly affected Indian nations illustrates how the past influences today's Native American situation and why Indian people continue to assert their rights as both citizens of their tribes and citizens of this country.

*Sovereignty is not an easy concept to describe but it is defined by Kickingbird & Kickingbird (1977, p. 1) as: "The supreme power from which all specific political powers are derived. Sovereignty is inherent; it comes from within a people or culture. It *cannot be given* to one group by another."

## TREATY MAKING WITH INDIAN NATIONS
### Reserving Pre-Existing Rights

The reserved rights doctrine is, according to Cohen (1971, p. 122) the "most basic principle of Indian law." When Indian leaders signed treaties, they typically relinquished something: millions of acres of their native lands. What they did not specifically relinquish, they reserved. Cohen (1971, pp. 122-49); and Kickingbird, Kickingbird, Chibitty & Berkey (pp. 7-13) outline reserved tribal powers. Important Supreme Court cases on reserved rights include *Winans* v. *United States* (1906); and *Winters* v. *United States* (1908).

## SOVEREIGN INDIAN TRIBES

Before the Thirteen American Colonies came into existence, Great Britain, France and Spain had recognized various Indian governments as sovereign and independent nations.* The United States Constitution and early U.S.-Indian treaties continued to acknowledge the sovereign rights of Indian peoples.

Yet the interpretation of Indian sovereignty seemed to change as the American nation expanded. While tribes were sovereign, their governments were not accorded the same status as that of states or foreign nations. Chief Justice John Marshall most clearly defined the tribes' special relationship to the central government in an 1832 Supreme Court case involving the Cherokee Nation. In that case (*Worcester* v. *Georgia*), Marshall ruled that Indian tribes were "distinct, independent, political communities" having the right to govern their own affairs. This important decision has been the basis of all federal-Indian relations for nearly 150 years, and implies that the United States recognizes tribal rights of continuing self-government. The federal government has willfully disregarded Indian sovereignty at times, usually through later treaties or specific acts of Congress limiting tribal powers. The Marshall ruling on internal sovereignty was repeatedly upheld by the courts, however. Though some tribes had been defeated in military actions, Indian nations continued to legally control their own concerns and remaining lands.

## TREATY-MAKING WITH INDIAN NATIONS: RESERVING PRE-EXISTING RIGHTS

Treaties are binding legal agreements. Between 1778 and 1871, North American Indian tribes and the United States negotiated and signed 371 treaties.

In many treaties the tribes exchanged large portions of their native lands for payments, goods and certain services; in many of these agreements they also retained portions of their long-occupied homelands as reservations. Treaties could not give sovereignty and reservations to the Indian tribes. They could only recognize these things as preexisting (inherent) rights.

Because some treaties were signed by tribes under threat of force and others were soon violated, it is sometimes mistakenly thought that Indian treaties have no meaning in today's world—but they are not curious scraps of historical paper. They are ongoing agreements on which the tribes base their own distinct governments, for the United States Constitution holds that all treaties "shall be the supreme law of the land."

IGNORING SOVEREIGNTY
Removal Policies

The 1832 decision in *Worcester* v. *Georgia* protecting tribal sovereignty was blatantly ignored by President Andrew Jackson, by the state of Georgia and by an expansionist Congress. New treaties, such as that of New Echota in 1835, and several Indian "removal" bills forced the Cherokees and other tribes to exchange their homelands for unfamiliar midwestern territories. In the same period (1816-46), Indian self-government and treaty provisions were frequently disregarded. Forced Indian removals are discussed by Foreman. Prucha (1962, pp. 224-49) covers the migration of the Five Civilized Tribes. *See* McNickle; and W. R. Jacobs for the displacement of other Indian tribes.

TRUST RESPONSIBILITY AND
INDIAN LANDS
Trust Relationship

The federal-Indian relationship is a political—not a racial—tie between tribal governments and the government of the United States. This relationship arose from specific contracts, treaties, that are still in effect today. For background, *see* Gilbert L. Hall's *The Federal-Indian Trust Relationship* (1979).

Confusion over the nature of this relationship may stem from the numerous uses (and misuses) of the term "wardship." Reviewing the contexts in which the term had previously been used, Felix Cohen came up with 1,023 possible meanings, but observed that "in its original and most precise signification [in 1831, in the case of *Cherokee Nation* v. *Georgia*], the term 'ward' was applied (a) to tribes rather than individuals; (b) as a suggestive analogy rather than an exact description; and (c) to distinguish an Indian tribe from a foreign state" (1971, p. 170).

## IGNORING SOVEREIGNTY: REMOVAL POLICIES

Indian nations and the federal government dealt with each other as substantial equals in the early treaties. Especially in its first years, the United States needed the alliance of powerful Indian nations against foreign claims in North America. However, with the United States victory over the British in the War of 1812, treaty-making policies and tactics changed. Indian sovereign rights were ignored as the growing nation demanded the removal of entire tribes from their homelands. In the southeastern states, for example, the Five Civilized Tribes (Creek, Cherokee, Choctaw, Seminole and Chicasaw) were forced to walk a "trail of tears" to the Indian Territory, which was to become the state of Oklahoma. This sort of displacement occurred time and again throughout the last century. Oregon Indian tribes experienced removal to small land bases within their own regions as well as displacement to reservations far from their native homes. These disruptive movements are mapped and discussed on pages 92-94.

## TRUST RESPONSIBILITIES AND INDIAN LANDS

Treaty-making also began a contractual or "trust" relationship between Indians and the United States. In exchange for native lands ceded in treaties, the United States promised certain supplies, services and cash payments to the tribes. The federal government became a manager or trustee over remaining Indian lands by holding the unceded reservation areas in trust for tribal use and benefit.

Like the concept of sovereignty, the trust relationship was defined by the Supreme Court in another Marshall decision. In *Cherokee Nation* v. *Georgia* (1831), Marshall said that the continuing relationship between the United States and Indian people resembled that of a guardian and a ward; again referring to the idea that tribes were different from foreign nations and that the federal government should assist them while still recognizing their sovereign rights.

The ideas of trust and wardship have often been misunderstood. In Oregon, as elsewhere, the trust commitment generally meant that the United States agreed to aid Indian survival by providing technical assistance. The tribes accepted federal authority over them; all matters on the new reservations were strictly tribal or federal concerns, free from any state or local interference.

Indian trust lands are sometimes called "restricted lands" because they cannot be sold or leased without federal government approval. These lands are exempt from federal, state and local taxes since tribes are sovereign governments on their reservations. Indian peoples are entitled to the benefits of this special trust relationship, not because of their race, but because their tribes made unique legal and political agreements with the United States.

Some writers, such as Coulter, have objected to the paternalistic implications of the trust doctrine. Others have analyzed the dual nature of the federal protectorate role: Chambers (1975); Wilkinson & Biggs; and Getches, Rosenfelt & Wilkinson (pp. 157-204).

Indian Lands and Federal Obligations

Despite the leading role land transactions played in early federal-Indian relations, the government's responsibilities are to the tribes, not to the land, and continued fulfillment of trust obligations is not contingent on possession of trust land. This has been upheld in the courts, where various rulings have determined certain laws to be applicable even in the absence of reserved lands. (See *United States* v. *Sandoval*, 1913; *see also* notes on the definition of "Indian Country," p. 79, 81)

The federal government's right to participate in Indian affairs is based not on the land protection it has provided, but on U.S.-Indian treaties and Congress's plenary power (derived from the constitutional clause stipulating that only the federal government can "regulate commerce" with Indian nations) (Art. 1, sec. 8, clause 3). While courts have set a noble standard for governmental dealings with Indian tribes, there have been frequent lapses or outright disregard for the basic principles of Indian law. *See* Deloria (1969); Kickingbird & Ducheneaux; Wilkinson & Volkman; Josephy (1971); and *NYU Law Review* (1972).

PHOTOGRAPH:
Men at The Dalles, ca. 1920 (OHS neg. 15117)

Besides specific items mentioned in treaties, Indian tribes also reserved ownership rights to the water and other natural resources on their reserved lands. The United States had committed itself to "helping Indians make the best use of their lands" but its policies frequently did not reflect the ideals of the federal trust relationship; removal was the earliest example of policies contradictory to the established legal rights of Indian people. In Oregon, both federal oversight and legislation promoting assimilation reduced tribal autonomy. ("Assimilation" refers to deliberate attempts to replace tribal cultural values with Euro-American cultural values and modes of behavior.) Some Oregon Indian treaties were never ratified by Congress—in these cases native lands were simply taken rather than purchased (*see* "Treaty-Making in Oregon," pp. 79-91). Tribes repeatedly lost more of their lands as reservations were reduced in size, some of them disappearing completely. Through all these changes, however, the courts always reaffirmed the trust relationship as one of the basic concepts underlying all federal-Indian affairs. Even when Congress stopped making treaties with Indian nations in 1871, all the terms of these legal agreements remained in effect.

## BUREAU OF INDIAN AFFAIRS (BIA)

L. F. Schmeckebier wrote a general history of the BIA in 1927. More recent accounts of the conflicting responsibilities of the BIA include McNickle & Fey (pp. 61-90); Cohen (1953); and Hagan. The War Department did not create a separate office for Indian matters until 1824, and it took ten more years before an act of Congress actually set up the bureau's internal organization. Transfer of the bureau to the civilian-controlled Department of the Interior in 1849 was met with widespread criticism, which continued as subsequent Indian wars spread upheaval throughout the West and whenever corruption involving politically appointed Indian agents was exposed. However, Congress never voted on the matter of returning Indian affairs to the military. Oliphant; Burns (1966); Josephy (1965); and Haines (1950) provide different perspectives on the nineteenth century situation in the Northwest.

### Oregon Superintendency of Indian Affairs

Edward E. Hill (1974) provides a short outline of Oregon's many Indian agencies and subagencies. Commissioner of Indian Affairs annual reports (hereinafter cited as CIA) contain the most detailed information, however: individual summations by Indian agents and superintendents (filed 1848-73 under "Oregon Superintendency" and thereafter separately reported by agency). CIA annual reports also are filed in the annual reports of the Department of the Interior. The National Archives and Records Service (NARS) has 28 rolls of microfilm containing textual records of the Oregon superintendency; these may be viewed at the NARS Research Center in Seattle or at the Oregon Historical Society in Portland. All records of the

## BUREAU OF INDIAN AFFAIRS (BIA)

According to the United States Constitution, Congress has the ultimate authority over Indian matters, but day-to-day trust responsibilities of the federal government are carried out by the Bureau of Indian Affairs (BIA). Originally known as the Office of Indian Affairs, the agency first belonged to the War Department and was transferred to the newly created Department of the Interior in 1849. The year before, the Oregon Territory had been organized and an Oregon superintendency of Indian affairs was set up with three subagents in various districts (the region then included both of the present-day states of Washington and Oregon).

The first Oregon territorial governor, Joseph Lane, acted as *ex officio* Indian superintendent until a separate official was appointed in 1851. The early superintendents traveled around the territory making treaties and trying to prevent hostilities between Indians and newcomers. Keeping the peace was not an easy matter as these officials grappled with land-hungry settlers and a diverse number of Indian cultures (*see* "Armed Struggles," pp. 62-64). Getting the U.S. Senate to ratify all of their treaties, and afterwards, keeping the promises in those treaties proved to be a nearly impossible task for the superintendents.

Continual pressure from interest groups both in and out of government often conflicted with the federal duty to protect Indian rights and land. The BIA was also dependent on the honesty of its field agents and the cooperation of local people in operating the reservation system.

Oregon reservations are being inventoried by NARS. Thus far, David W. Owens has prepared a guide to records for Grand Ronde-Siletz; John S. Ferrell for Umatilla; and Kenneth F. Hirst for Warm Springs and Burns.

Another helpful guide is the pamphlet from NARS (Washington, D.C., 20005), *National Archives Microfilm Publications Pamphlet Describing M2, Records of the Oregon Superintendency of Indian Affairs, 1848-1873. Also see* Hobbs's Seattle NARS guide; the manuscript holdings of the Oregon Historical Society; and the source note on "Locating Treaties," pp. 79, 81.

## EARLY RESERVATION PERIOD

In the early reservation period, the role of the Indian agent changed markedly. Originally a commercial agent negotiating with foreign nations, he became a military supervisor, and later, the "civilizing" agent and regulator of tribal business affairs. *See* Cohen (1953, pp. 352-53); and Hagan. Assimilationist philosophy has been analyzed by Blinderman; the writings of late nineteenth century Indian reformers were compiled by Prucha in 1973.

Information on the numerous agencies dealing with the Coos, Lower Umpqua and Siuslaw tribes came by personal communication from Esther Stutzman, Coos Bay, Oregon. Consult CIA reports; and O'Callaghan (1960) for documentation of the early reservation years.

## EARLY RESERVATION PERIOD

With the westward expansion, the old Indian frontier had broken down and numerous settlers intermixed with Indian tribes in the new territories and states. By the 1850s, the early-nineteenth-century idea of an unorganized and separate Indian country gave way to a reservation policy to isolate Indians on lands surrounded by non-Indians. Reservations in California and the Northwest, first established in the 1850s, became the models for nearly all other Indian reservations west of the Mississippi.

The Indian Office organized the reservations into a system of agencies or districts, each with one or more agents and teachers assigned to the tribes of that region. During its first decades, the Oregon superintendency had a changing set of districts and personnel. Federal orders for treaty-making and removal, as well as several Indian wars caused much bureaucratic confusion in these years. Some Coos Bay Indians recall that their tribe was associated with more than ten different Indian agencies over the ensuing years.

All congressional and BIA policy was based on the idea that Indians should be assimilated (integrated) into non-Indian society. The fundamental goal was to make Indians leave their tribal ways behind and become farmers and ranchers. While authorities used the separatist method of isolating tribes in remote areas, supposedly free from lawless frontier influences, they actively encouraged Indians to adopt non-Indian ways. Missionaries and teachers sought to have the Indians develop agriculture, accept Christianity and other new values. Sending children to distant boarding schools, such as the Chemawa Indian School near Salem (first established in 1880 in Forest Grove) was typical of the deliberate attempts to break down the Indian family and traditions. Indian dress and languages often were forbidden and sometimes the Indian agents removed traditional leaders from power.

## ALLOTMENT OF RESERVATIONS

In the late 1880s, there were six Indian reservations (Malheur, Klamath, Grand Ronde, Siletz, Warm Springs and Umatilla) in Oregon. The tribes who owned these last Indian lands faced further troubles from outsiders who disliked the continuation of separate Indian communities. Congress and many Americans thought that Indian people should enter the dominant society at a faster rate. This belief culminated in a plan to divide tribal lands into individually owned parcels (allotments) for farming. The remaining Indian lands were to be declared surplus and opened to non-Indian settlement.

In 1887 Congress passed the General Allotment Act (Dawes Act), allowing Indian reservations to be divided into 160-acre (or smaller) allotments for assignment to tribal members. The allotments remained in trust status for 25 years, after which time the secretary of the Interior could issue a fee patent on the tract (thereby removing sales restrictions) if the Indian owner was declared competent.

## ALLOTMENT OF RESERVATIONS

Oregon's land allotments are detailed in the source notes to each reservation. For the consequences of national allotment policy, *see* Holford; and Kinney. The piecemeal amendments to the Dawes Act and problems arising from it are summarized by Cohen (1971, pp. 78-87, 202-33, 320-35); and by Getches, Rosenfelt & Wilkinson (pp. 69-77, 560-85). Problems related to the last century's allotment policies have persisted, as described by Umatilla Chairman Leslie Minthorn at a recent U.S. Senate Indian Affairs Subcommittee hearing in Pendleton (U.S. Senate 1977). Sutton (pp. 60-64) includes an essay on allotment as a "failed resource scheme."

In the late nineteenth century Euro-American settlers influenced allotment policy, as observed by Deloria (1969, pp. 52-54); Washburn (1971, pp. 143-49); and Prucha (1976), who comment on the pressure for Indian lands development to benefit adjacent landholders. For example, responding to this pressure, officials sometimes deemed Indian timber and grazing lands unsuitable for agriculture in order to justify assigning less valuable tracts as allotments to Indians. Most reservation land was remote and of inferior quality (settlers usually obtained the choice lands); as a result Indian allotments tended to be smaller and less productive than the lands homesteaded by non-Indians (Indian allotments usually were 160 acres or less whereas settlers could obtain 320- or 640-acre tracts under public land and homestead laws).

Behind the allotment policy was the assumption that private land ownership would somehow cause Indians to accept the outsiders' ways and abandon communal land practices. But tribal people rarely were provided the technical skills necessary to effectively compete with more-experienced farmers. Additionally, not all Indians wanted this new lifestyle. Consequently much Indian land was leased to neighboring ranchers and farmers.

When the 25-year trust periods expired on Indian allotments, many persons were still unaccustomed to private property ownership, refusing to drop their tribal loyalties and adopt agricultural ways. Increasingly impoverished, many Indians had to sell their allotments to non-Indians in order to survive. Often they were unaware that their individual tracts were now subject to taxation and so lost their lands through tax sales. As non-Indians began moving inside reservation boundaries, the allotments they purchased were removed from trust status and passed onto the tax rolls of the localities where the reservations were situated. In a very short time the allotted reservations came to resemble checkerboards of Indian and non-Indian ownership. (For an example of such subdivided lands, see the Umatilla Reservation map, p. 100.)

Land losses continued as later amendments to the Dawes Act facilitated the leasing and sales of allotments to non-Indians. In addition, the act declared that Indian lands left over after allotments had been made were surplus lands open to sale and settlement. After the initial assignment of tracts to tribal members, allotment rolls were closed, dictating that future generations could be landless. These younger Indians could inherit only fractional interests in a relative's allotment after his or her death. The repeated division of allotments through inheritances led to as many as 100 or more persons sharing a tract as small as 80 acres. This inefficient division of land benefitted none of the Indian owners. Often, the only solution was to sell or lease these shared allotments to non-Indians.

Very few officials questioned the wisdom of allowing the large non-allotted surplus tracts to leave tribal ownership, arguing that since native populations had been declining (as a result of disease, war and displacement) Indians did not need so much land. Furthermore, landowners on adjacent property were pressuring Congress to open up reservations for development. However, about this time the decline in the Indian population began to reverse, and in the twentieth century the growing number of Indian people found it difficult to support themselves and their children on the fixed amounts of land. (*See* Indian population chart on p. 152.)

Allotment policy did not accomplish the goal of assimilating Indians into American society but it hastened the loss of 90 million more acres from the national Indian land base. Although the Klamath and Warm Springs managed to keep their large tribal reserves, the disastrous effects of allotment were felt at every reservation in Oregon. Grand Ronde and Siletz surplus lands were sold at extremely low prices. Land sales at Umatilla resulted in fractional ownership which continues to adversely affect tribal development today.

OTHER LAND LOSSES AND
SHRINKING TRUST COMMITMENT

For details refer to the source notes to each Oregon reservation. *See also* Oliphant; Kickingbird & Ducheneaux (pp. 196-219); and Holford (1975).

## CITIZENSHIP AND THE INDIAN REORGANIZATION ACT

Brophy & Aberle; and Washburn (1971, pp. 75-98) summarize twentieth century federal Indian policies. Since 1934, as a result of the Indian Reorganization Act (IRA), the secretary of the Interior has had the authority to restore any remaining surplus lands to tribal ownership, provided that no one's private property rights are affected. But exercise of this authority is not mandatory, and funds are seldom appropriated for this purpose. *See* the Act of June 18, 1934, *25 USC 461*. Although the IRA prohibited allotment, it did not end further losses, which continued through land sales to non-Indians. *See 25 USC 349*. The IRA's legislative weakness, and the tendency of officials to disregard it are examined by Kickingbird & Ducheneaux; and Deloria (1974, pp. 187-206). As Wilkinson & Biggs (pp. 144-45) observed, the IRA was a positive reform, yet it still supposed assimilation to be desirable.

In the Northwest, tribal opposition to the IRA sprang from the belief that the program was tainted by communism and anti-religious sentiment (charges also leveled at other programs in the 1930s). For discussion of the IRA in Oregon, *see* Beckham (1977, pp. 182-85); and Harvison (1970). Also consult the Brookings Institution's massive *Meriam Report*. The 1933 National Industrial Recovery

# OTHER LAND LOSSES AND A SHRINKING TRUST COMMITMENT

Even before the allotment period, Oregon Indians struggled to hold onto their reservation lands while stockmen and various public and private agencies clamored for more Indian lands. Illegal stock grazing occurred on most reservations, and federal authorities could do little to stop it. Some land losses stemmed from discrepancies in the actual reservation boundaries first outlined in the treaties. Both the Warm Springs and Klamath Indians had prolonged disputes over lands taken from them because of delayed and faulty boundary surveys. Congressional land-grants to build roads and provide utility rights-of-way across reservations also contributed to the shrinking land base.

Sometimes Congress responded to pressure from settlers by passing legislation removing sizable parcels of land without reimbursing the tribes; this occurred at Siletz reservation in 1865 and 1875. All land losses affected tribal life by slicing into Indian autonomy and forcing many people to leave their reservations. In the cases of the Malheur Paiute, Coos, Lower Umpqua and Siuslaw peoples, such actions completely dispossessed them. Without any trust lands, some returned to their old homelands. The BIA did little to assist them in the following years.

A few landless groups managed to relocate to distant reservations while some Indians in southern Oregon obtained small land allotments from the public domain during the 1890s. But these people lived far from established reservation centers, and gradually became forgotten tribes with an uncertain federal status. Shrinking Indian lands coincided with a shrinking trust commitment toward ensuring the survival of Indian cultures. Certain Tillamook and Chinook bands (who had never settled on reservations) experienced the same lack of federal recognition as those forced to leave the reservations, which meant the loss of most, if not all, federal assistance. (*See* pp. 131-32 for the consequences of federal recognition.)

## CITIZENSHIP AND THE INDIAN REORGANIZATION ACT

Public demand for reforms in federal Indian policy increased after the turn of the century. Congress granted United States citizenship to all American Indians in 1924, largely as a result of their distinguished military service in World War I. The citizenship act recognized that Indians were still citizens of their tribes and their U.S. citizenship did not diminish treaty rights.

Some other positive changes occurred in the 1920s. The huge loss of trust lands, poor health and economic conditions on reservations, and the inefficient services to tribes were well documented in a famous 1928 study, *The Problems of Indian Administration* (also known as the Meriam Report).

(NIRA) and Federal Emergency Relief (FERA) acts both included land provisions for homeless Indian bands. *See* the source notes to the Malheur and Burns reservations, pages 103, 105-106.

During Franklin Roosevelt's administration some of the Meriam Report's suggestions were implemented. John Collier became the new Commissioner of Indian affairs and he spearheaded the passage of the Indian Reorganization Act (IRA) in 1934. This legislation ended the allotting of Indian lands and unrestricted sale of trust property. It also included provisions for tribes to recover remaining surplus lands not sold to outsiders. Under the IRA, tribes could form corporations for their own economic development and the BIA was to prefer Indians in its hiring practices. Stronger self-government, new credit and technical assistance were promised to the Indian tribes accepting the IRA.

Other important reforms also began at this time. Congress passed the Johnson-O'Malley Act in 1934, to provide needed educational assistance to Indian children in public schools. Other new laws authorized the secretary of the Interior to acquire lands for homeless Indian bands.

Unfortunately this "Indian New Deal" was inconsistently applied and underfunded. Only two Oregon reservations, Grand Ronde and Warm Springs, accepted the IRA. Other tribal groups showed little enthusiasm for yet another federal program and they rejected the act's provisions. At Grand Ronde, the benefits of the IRA were meager; only a few hundred acres were restored to the tribe and other assistance never materialized. Warm Springs fared better by tribal incorporation, and was later able to consolidate many lands and develop ongoing tribal enterprises.

The IRA and other New Deal legislation contained provisions to help homeless Oregon Indian bands organize and obtain land, but federal officials largely failed to use these measures to assist non-reservation Indians. A tribal hall was built on donated lands at Coos Bay in the late 1930s. The Paiute people at Burns received 642 acres of land of dubious value in 1935; this effort seemed half-hearted when Congress did not transfer the trust title of these lands to the tribe itself. The Paiutes waited 37 long years to become the rightful owners of their land. In the meantime they, along with all Indian tribes, felt federal services wane as Congress failed to uphold all of its trust responsibilities.

Termination Era

In the early 1940s John Collier's IRA reforms drew increasing fire from a budget-minded Congress, and in 1943 and 1944 investigators began to call for the BIA's abolition. Protesting this opposition to his programs, Collier resigned in 1945; four years later the Hoover Commission recommended termination as a "firm and continuing policy." The 1950 appointment of Dillon Myer (formerly director of the controversial War Relocation Authority) as Indian commissioner brought total integrationist policy to the BIA, a "voluntary relocation program" to move Indians to the cities, and an increasing absence of consultation with tribal people. Ironically, although Myer proposed the transfer of BIA functions to Indians themselves or to local and state agencies as a cost-cutting measure, BIA appropriations doubled between 1950 and 1953.

The general resolution calling for termination (HCR 108) was adopted only two weeks before PL 83-280 transferred civil and criminal jurisdiction over reservations in six states from the federal government to local authorities.

The repudiation of IRA philosophy and Indian rights in this era is summarized by Cohen (1953). Wilkinson & Biggs (1977); and Steffon have written excellent background reports on the development of termination legislation. *See also* the AIPRC *Final Report of Task Force Ten: Terminated and Non-Federally Recognized Indians* (1976).

Criteria for Termination

In 1948 Congress compelled Assistant Indian Commissioner William Zimmerman to set guidelines for legislated federal withdrawal of services to Indi-

## MORE ASSIMILATION: THE 1950S AND TERMINATION

Before any other positive features of the IRA could be put into effect, World War II broke out, and by the end of the war a new Indian policy had evolved. Congress again reviewed the different problems confronting Indian people, but this time it decided that the easiest solution would be to end all services and relationships with Indian tribes.

With an eye toward the expenses of maintaining its trust responsibilities, Congress made all Oregon tribes except Warm Springs subject to the state's civil and criminal laws in 1953. This withdrawal of federal jurisdiction was linked to a final and more destructive blow to Indian lands and sovereignty. On August 1, 1953, House Concurrent Resolution 108 declared that Congress wished to officially terminate its special relationship with all tribes. Lawmakers once again contended that Indians should be brought into the mainstream of American society. The adoption of the termination policy meant that Congress would withdraw from its historic responsibilities by removing the restrictions of federal supervision over Indians.

Specific termination bills followed; between 1954 and 1958, thirteen different acts ended the federal Indian status of more than 12,000 people in eight states. The BIA was given the task of naming the tribes most eligible for termination by judging which groups had already assimilated non-Indian ways. Of course, this sort of criteria was very difficult to judge and was poorly applied.

In 1954, Congress passed two termination bills, which affected the Klamath tribe and all western Oregon Indians (regardless of whether or not they lived on a reservation). All federal services to these groups ended and any remaining tribal lands were sold. The

an tribes. Under subpoena from the Senate Civil Service Committee, Zimmerman cited the following provisions for determining reductions: (1) degree of acculturation; (2) economic resources and condition of the tribe; (3) willingness of the tribe to be relieved of federal control; and (4) willingness of the state to assume jurisdiction (Wilkinson & Biggs, p. 146). In practice, however, these criteria often were misapplied or simply ignored. *See* Zimmerman on "The Role of the Bureau of Indian Affairs Since 1933."

Termination of Oregon Tribes

At the time of termination, 2,133 Klamath people and at least 2,081 In-

dians at Grand Ronde and Siletz were affected by the closure of their reservations and withdrawal of services. In western Oregon, the count is probably much higher since the act named 41 tribes and bands from that region, many of whose members lived far from reservations, already long overlooked by most federal agencies. Confusion resulting from hazy explanations of termination legislation, suspicion of the circumstances in which tribal approval of the act was obtained, and misunderstanding about remuneration for tribal lands persist among Oregon Indians, and is evident in their testimony in the AIPRC *Final Report of Task Force Ten*;

House and Senate hearings and reports on the termination bills (U.S. House 1954; U.S. Senate 1954) should also be consulted.

Secondary sources on Klamath termination and its effects include Stern (1966, pp. 236-66); McNickle & Fey (pp. 138-47); Hood; Kickingbird & Ducheneaux (pp. 160-78); Trulove; and the U.S. Federal Trade Commission's 1974 report on Consumer Problems of the Klamath Indians. *See also* Kimball v. Callaghan (1979), concerning the Klamath's unextinguished tribal rights to fish and hunt on their former reservation.

Information on termination in western Oregon is found in Beckham (1977); Confederated Tribes of Siletz (1977); the hearings for Siletz restoration (U.S. Senate 1976); and Coos, Lower Umpqua and Siuslaw Tribe (n.d.). For reactions of other Oregon tribes during the termination era, *see* the Commission on Rights and Responsibilities, *Rights and Liberties of the American Indian. See also* the discussion recent U.S. Indian Policy in Part Three, and that section's source notes.

SINCE THE 1950S

Records of the House and Senate hearings on Menominee and Siletz restorations (1973, 1976) are highly recommended reading. Further details on recent policy are in Part Three.

Grand Ronde and Siletz reservations were officially closed in 1956 and the Klamath Reservation was shut down in 1961. All of the tribes affected by termination lost their legal status and trust ties with the federal government. They were not fully consulted about this decision and its consequences were poorly explained.

The termination acts rushed through by a budget-cutting Congress in the 1950s sprang from the old assimilationist policy that in previous decades had forced removal and allotment on Indian tribes. With these actions, the United States tried to invalidate its agreements with, and end its responsibilities to, the sovereign people it had displaced. Indian lands were sold, leaving tribes with little over which to exert their sovereignty. By removing the land and many services, the termination policy created great hardships for many Indian people. Their reservations were closed, their tribes had no legal standing with the federal government, and many suffered discrimination and psychological injuries as a result.

SINCE THE 1950S

The termination era was a discouraging time for Oregon Indians, who felt the government was attempting to legislate them out of existence. Twenty years later, a new direction for federal-Indian relations is emerging. This new policy supports Indian self-sufficiency without demanding the forced change of assimilation. The discussion of recent policies in Part Three (pp. 129-39) details other consequences of twentieth-century events and the continuing sovereignty of Indian tribes. Many vital steps have been taken to overcome the consequences of allotment and termination—and nearly all of these developments have been Indian-initiated and directed.

Perhaps the clearest reversal of past policies came when two terminated tribes, the Menominees of Wisconsin (in 1973) and the western Oregon Siletz (in 1977), sought and obtained congressional restoration of their federal status and trust relationship. With positive changes at the federal level and a renewed tribalism locally, Oregon Indians may finally enjoy all their rights as both citizens of their tribes and of the United States.*

*For more references to national and Oregon Indian history, *see* the Chronology.

National treaty-making policies are discussed on pages 67ff of "Early U.S. Indian Policy in Oregon." Recommended supplemental reading includes Deloria (1974, pp. 85-186); National Coalition to Support Indian Treaties; Wilkinson & Volkman; and Hall. Royce; and Hilliard discuss westward land cessions. Standard views on the treaties in Oregon are found in Coan (1921, 1922); Peterson; Haines (1950); and Johansen & Gates. More recent sources reflecting Indian viewpoints are Deloria (1977); and Robbins.

### OREGON INDIAN COUNTRY: THE CREATION OF RESERVATIONS

Defining "Indian Country"

In the last 300 years, the physical boundaries and legal definition of "Indian Country" have changed. Before European settlement, Indian territory encompassed the entire continent; tribes were autonomous and they also had jurisdiction over most foreigners. Today, however, "Indian Country," a statutory term (18 USC 1151), refers specifically to the "country within which Indian laws and customs and federal laws relating to Indians are generally applicable" (Cohen 1971, p. 5).

The important question, when assessing the integrity of this determination, is not the method by which land was reserved for tribal use (by treaty, statute, agreement, land withdrawal or executive order) but whether a "distinctly Indian community"—recognized by the federal government—does indeed exist. *See* cases and commentary in Getches, Rosenfelt & Wilkinson (pp. 348-57); Cohen (1971, pp. 5-8); and the works of Vine Deloria, Jr.

# TREATY-MAKING IN OREGON: MORE THAN A QUESTION OF LAND

## WHAT IS A TREATY?

The United States Constitution holds treaties to be the "supreme law of the land." By reserving portions of their lands and other rights in treaties (binding legal agreements in which Indian nations and the United States recognized each other's sovereign government), the tribes sought to ensure the survival of their centuries-old way of life. Treaties never gave any reservations or special rights to Indian nations. Rather, the United States acknowledged the distinct political status of the tribes while attempting to resolve some of the larger conflicts that arose as newcomers invaded Indian lands. Although treaty-making frequently did not succeed in acting as a buffer between Indian and non-Indian ways of life, the treaties did establish a lasting federal-Indian relationship.

## OREGON INDIAN COUNTRY: THE CREATION OF RESERVATIONS

A number of Oregon tribes signed treaties exchanging large portions of their land for payments, goods and certain services. Thus, they granted settlers the right to occupy native lands. Indians retained parts of their homelands as reservations in these agreements.

Many believe that Indian lands were reserved only by treaties, but several other procedures set aside Indian lands as well. Acts of Congress, executive orders of the president and withdrawal of lands by the secretary of the Interior established Indian reservations. In Oregon there are two treaty-created reservations (Umatilla and Warm Springs) and two statutory reservations (Burns/Paiute and Siletz).

Locating Treaties

*Ratified* treaties are available in several sources, including *Statutes At Large of the United States* (*see* introductory text of Chronology for legal citation forms); and 2 Kappler. The Institute for the Development of Indian Law (IDIL) has published a Northwest volume of Indian treaties. Copies of the original documents may also be obtained from the Oregon tribes as well as from "Documents Re Negotiation of Indian Treaties, 1801-69," NARS RG-75, Microcopy T-494. Also, this microfilm may be viewed at the Oregon Historical Society, Portland; or photostatic reproductions may be purchased from NARS, Washington, D.C., 20005.

Many of Oregon's *unratified* treaties are recorded on "Unratified Treaties, 1821-65," NARS RG-75, Microcopy T-494, reel 8. Mackey (1974, pp. 75-86) has transcribed parts of the six 1851 Champoeg treaties. The unratified Coast Treaty of 1855 is in U.S. Senate (1893). Coan's 1921 article reprints four of the ten Tansey Point treaties (pp. 75-86). Further negotiation details can be found in "Letters

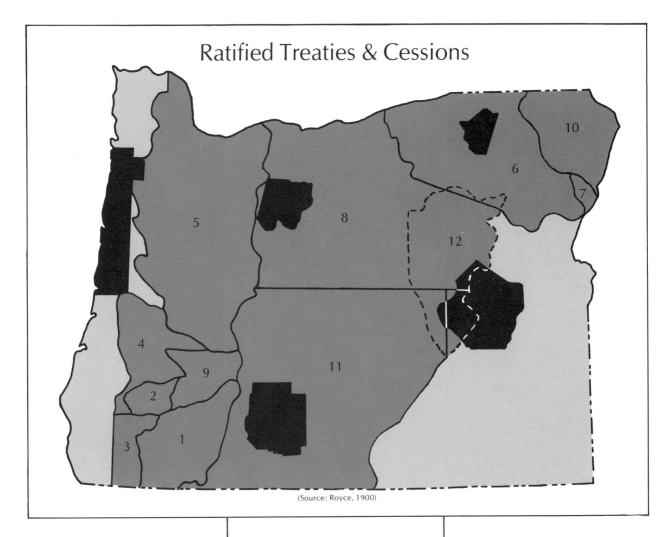

# Ratified Treaties & Cessions

(Source: Royce, 1900)

KEY

■ Ratified Treaties
□ No Ratified Treaties
■ Original Reservations

1  *Treaty with the Rogue River*
   Table Rock, 10 September 1853

2  *Treaty with the Umpqua Cow Creek Band*
   Cow Creek, Umpqua Valley,
   19 September 1853

3  *Treaty with the Chastas, Scotons & Grave Creek Band of Umpquas*
   Mouth of Applegate Creek on
   Rogue River, 18 November 1854

4  *Treaty with the Umpqua & Kalapuya*
   Calapooia Creek, Douglas County,
   29 November 1854

5  *Treaty with the Kalapuya & Confederated Bands of the Willamette Valley*
   Dayton, 22 January 1855

6  *Treaty with Walla-Wallas, Cayuses & Umatillas*
   Camp Stevens, 9 June 1855

7  *Treaty with the Nez Perces*
   Camp Stevens, 11 June 1855

8  *Treaty with the Tribes of Middle Oregon*
   Wasco, 25 June 1855

9  *Treaty with the Molala or Mollels*
   21 December 1855

10  *Treaty with the Nez Perces*
    Lapwai, 9 June 1863

11  *Treaty with the Klamaths, Modocs & Yahooskin Band of Snakes*
    Klamath Lake, 14 October 1864

12  *Treaty with the Woll-Pah-Pe Snakes* (also covered by 6, 8 &11)
    Sprague River, 12 August 1865

80

Received, 1824-80, Office of Indian Affairs," NARS RG-75, Microcopy 234. Helpful guides to other Indian-related materials at NARS include Hobbs (1977); Hill (1972); and Kelsay.

## MAP: RATIFIED TREATIES AND CESSIONS

All land cessions are from Royce. Not shown are the temporary western Oregon reservations: Table Rock Reserve within Cession 1; Cow Creek-Umpqua Reserve in Cession 2; and the reserve for the Umpqua and Kalapuya of Cession 4. Also not shown are two other ratified Oregon treaties which did not cede any lands: Treaty with the Rogue River (November 18, 1854) in which the Takelmas consented to the settlement of other Indians on their Table Rock reservation; and the second treaty with the Middle Oregon Tribes (November 15, 1865) that unfairly restricted off-reservation hunting and fishing. See page 97 for discussions of this latter treaty affecting residents of the Warm Springs Reservation.

Although not all reservations were created by treaties, the nineteenth century treaty-making process was extremely crucial as friction over Indian and non-Indian use of Oregon land increased.

Some treaties followed armed conflicts while others were more peacefully initiated. The erratic treaty purchases of Oregon Indian lands took place between 1851 and 1868, a period marked by wars, gold rushes and growing non-Indian settlement.

Two maps show the history of these different treaties. On the "Ratified Treaties and Cessions" map (facing page), the numbered areas indicate cessions, the lands ceded by tribes who retained the smaller black areas as reservations. All land cessions on this map were ratified by Congress.

Another map, "Unratified Treaties" (p. 83), shows the Oregon Indian treaties that were not ratified by Congress. The absence of ratification generally meant that these tribes were not paid for their lands and important federal protections were not extended at a time when many non-Indians had little respect for Indian rights. Some of these tribes eventually obtained ratified treaties and a more secure legal standing with the federal government. Others vainly awaited approval while outsiders kept moving into their lands.

The Indian reservations on lands ceded in unratified treaties were created by executive orders of the president. Today there are few distinctions between treaty and executive-order reservations, since the trust relationship extends equally to all recognized tribes. Sovereignty and resource rights are the same in all parts, but the failure to ratify certain treaties resulted in unequal treatment for many Oregon Indians in the decades following the creation of the first reservations.

## HISTORY OF OREGON TREATIES
Indian Land Title

When vying for supremacy in the New World, European states employed doctrines of "discovery" and natural law to claim Indian lands. They justified the displacement of "uncivilized" Indians by claiming for Christian and agriculturally based societies superior moral rights to land not already held by other whites (see Emmerich de Vattel, 1758). After 1776, the United States continued to use "discovery" as the basis of its claim to exclusive negotiation and land purchase rights—avoiding the moral question surrounding imposition of a Euro-American property system on North America's indigenous peoples. Discussion of the ramifications of "discovery" philosophy on Indian land title are by Kickingbird & Ducheneaux (pp. xix-19); and by Washburn (1971, pp. 1-123). Eventually, the Supreme Court did accord Indians the rights of "aboriginal use and occupancy" (*Johnson* v. *McIntosh*, 1823), ruling that Indian land title had to be formally recognized by treaty or statute, and only the federal government (not individuals or states) could purchase and convey Indian lands.

A common misconception of United States' expansionism is that most of the nation was acquired either by treaty from foreign powers (such as the 1803 Louisiana Purchase from France) or was taken from the Indians (as in the unratified Oregon and California treaties). Instances of the latter were relatively rare, however; generally treaty purchases were legitimate, albeit providing tribes with unconventional and notoriously low payment. Cohen (1947); and Getches, Rosenfelt & Wilkinson (pp. 143-52) provide other details on Indian lands acquisition.

### Ignoring Indian Title in Oregon Territory

Creation of the Oregon Territory in 1848 not only extended Indian-related federal laws to the region, it also voided earlier land claims by non-Indians. Ironically, Oregon's territorial status had been granted largely to reward the volunteers who had fought the Cayuse Indians following the 1847 Whitman massacre (Holman, p. 137; Johansen & Gates 1967, pp. 228-31). Provisional Indian Superintendent Henry A. G. Lee had proclaimed in 1847 that the Cayuse would immediately forfeit all their lands "because of their misdeeds" (Ferrell 1973, p. 32). It should be noted that Lee had no authority to extinguish Indian land title at this time, since only Congress (or its duly appointed agents) could negotiate and purchase Indian lands; the same disregard of Indian property rights occurred in a more serious manner when the Donation Land Act of September 27, 1850 permitted the taking of about 2.5 million acres of Indian lands prior to any treaty ratification. William G. Robbins provides the best critical summary of this situation. Other sources include Bergquist; Head (1969, 1971); and O'Callaghan (1951a, 1960).

## HISTORY OF OREGON TREATIES

In 1832 the United States Supreme Court ruled in *Johnson* v. *McIntosh* that Indian nations held aboriginal use and occupancy rights in their lands. This meant that tribes could continue living in their lands as they always had unless or until those lands were purchased by the United States government. Settlers were not supposed to enter the native lands until Congress had first recognized and purchased the Indian title in treaties. The intent was to prevent conflict by moving Indians from the land before opening it to non-Indians. The many years of expansion affected this concept of Indian title. Settlers often prematurely established claims on Indian lands, confident that the U.S. government would follow and force purchases from the tribes. The period between first non-Indian settlement and later treaty-making significantly disrupted Indian life as outsiders appropriated choice lands and harmed important plant and animal resources. This was the situation in Oregon from the early 1840s to 1868, while a treaty-making process was haphazardly carried out.

Both the United States and Great Britain seemed to tacitly assume that their discoveries in the Northwest gave them absolute claim to all the land. These claims of course ignored the original owners of the land: the Indian tribes and bands who had resided in the region for thousands of years. In 1846, the Americans and the British negotiated an end to the Northwest boundary question, with a treaty giving the United States control over the area between the 42nd and 49th parallels, and Britain over what is today British Columbia.

No provisions were made for Indian people in the Oregon Treaty of 1846, but two years later, when Congress created the Oregon Territory, Indian legal rights became a pressing issue. The territorial act recognized Indian rights to the land and extended federal laws to the new region, which included the present-day states of Washington, Idaho and Oregon. (Washington Territory was separately organized in 1853 and the Territory of Idaho was created in 1863.) Among the United States laws now applicable in Oregon was the important Northwest Ordinance of 1787, which said:

> The utmost good faith shall always be observed toward the Indians; their lands and properties shall never be taken from them without their consent; and in their property, rights and liberty, they shall never be invaded or disturbed, unless in just and lawful wars authorized by Congress; but laws founded in justice and humanity shall from time to time be made for preventing wrongs being done to them, and for preserving peace and friendship with them.

Both the Northwest Ordinance and the Organic Act creating the territory clearly obligated federal authorities to purchase native lands before allowing any more settlement. But this principle was disregarded two years later when Congress passed the Donation Land Act, designed to encourage more immigration from the east by awarding early Oregon settlers free land. No treaties had been

## KEY

A  Willamette Valley Treaties (6)
   with Santiam, Twalaty, Yamhill,
   Luckamiute Bands of Kalapuyas;
   Moolalle & Santiam Bands of
   Moolalle Indians, Champoeg
   Council, April-May 1851

B  Tansey Point Treaties (10)
   with Clatsop Tribe, Nucquecl-
   ahwemuck, Waukikum,
   Konniack, Wheelappa, Kathlamet,
   Klatskania & Lower Bands of
   Chinooks; Naalem & Tillamook
   Bands of "Chinooks", August 1851

C  Port Orford Treaties (2)
   with Yototan, Youqueechee,
   Quatonway & Yasuchah Bands of
   Indians, 20 September 1851

D  Treaty with the Clackamas Tribe,
   Autumn 1851

E  Treaty with the Tualatins,
   25 March 1854

F  Coast Treaty (cedes entire Oregon
   coast and overlaps cessions B & C)
   with Alcea, Yaquonah, Seletsa,
   Neachesna Bands of "Tillamooks";
   Siuslaw, Umpqua, Kowes Bay &
   Nasomah or Coquille Tribes;
   Too-too-to-nev Bands (13); Chetco
   Tribe; Coquille Bands (4) of
   Indians, 8 September 1855

G  Paiute Treaty (a treaty of "peace
   and friendship"; no lands ceded)
   with Weyouwewa, Gshanee,
   Egan, Ponee,
   ChowWaWaNatNee, Owits &
   Tashego, Fort Harney, 10
   December 1868

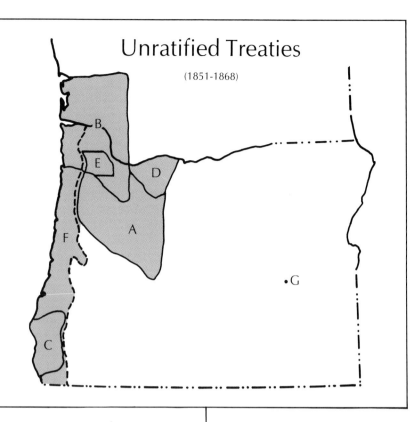

# Unratified Treaties

(1851-1868)

MAP: UNRATIFIED TREATIES,
1851-1868

Cessions A, B, C and D are based on
Coan (1921, p. 89); and Mackey
(1974). (Mackey reproduced some of
the six 1851 Champoeg treaties and
major portions of the 1851 Gibbs-
Starling map depicting the Willamette
Valley cessions shown here.) Cession
E, the unratified 1854 Tualatin treaty,
is based on the description in "Unratified Treaties, 1821-65," (NARS RG-
75, Microcopy T-494, roll 8); and personal communications of Henry Zenk
and Robert Benson, Portland. The
Coast Treaty of Cession F is from
Royce, while G represents the 1868
Paiute peace treaty at Fort Harney.

UNRATIFIED TREATIES OF 1851

The first Indian policy in Oregon mentioned in the text refers to the first explicit instructions to negotiate treaties under the act of June 5, 1850. As early as 1842, the first Oregon Indian agent, Dr. Elijah White, had managed to convince certain Nez Perce bands to accept his code of laws for insuring the safety of immigrants. But, because United States jurisdiction did not then apply to the Oregon Country, White lacked the authority to make treaties. Details on the first agents and policies are found in E. White; Ferrell (1973a); and Rivers.

Oregon's first territorial governor, Joseph Lane, had been doubling as *ex officio* Indian superintendent until the June 5, 1850 act established a separate office for that position. This act also created a three-member commission and appropriated $20,000 for treaty-making. Of the 19 unratified treaties in 1851, 6 were made at Champoeg by the three commissioners. They valued most of the land at about three cents an acre, believing that settlers would make better use of the land than the Indians residing there. They then pressured the tribes to leave; the Kalapuyan bands would not comply. The commission finally settled on a plan in which the bands retained two small reservations, one on each side of the Willamette River. Justifying its action, the commission's final report stated, "that these reservations will cause any considerable annoyance to the whites we do not believe. They consist for the most part, of ground unfitted for cultivation, but suited to the peculiar habits of the Indians" (Schmeckebier, p. 60). For the six Champoeg treaties, *see* Hussey; Mackey (1974); and "A Copy of the Journal of the Proceedings of the negotiation duties to the new Indian superintendent, Anson Dart, on February 27, 1851. Dart concluded his 13

signed, yet many of the settlers who emigrated to Oregon made claims on Indian lands.

UNRATIFIED TREATIES OF 1851

An 1850 federal law put forth the first Indian policy in Oregon by providing for a separate superintendent of Indian affairs and a treaty commission. The three-member commission was charged with purchasing western Oregon Indian lands and removing the native inhabitants to the east side of the Cascade Mountains. Anson Dart became Superintendent of Indian Affairs in 1851, and he made 19 treaties that year with bands in the Willamette Valley and along parts of the Pacific coast. However, none of these groups consented to move to lands in eastern Oregon. They insisted on agreements to sell most of their lands and keep small portions for their own use.

Eastern Oregon tribes were opposed to having western Indians settle on their lands. They feared exposure to foreign diseases that had proved so lethal along the coast and western rivers, and were unfamiliar with the customs of Willamette Valley tribes. Dart had little alternative but to agree to the Indians' demands. Although his treaties did not conform to the mandate for removal, Dart was sympathetic to the western tribes and he sent his treaty agreements to Washington, D.C. with a strong plea for their approval.

Congress refused to ratify the 1851 treaties (*see* map, p. 83; cessions A, B, C, D contain the different treaty parties) mainly because political leaders wanted the complete removal of western Oregon Indians to east of the Cascades. In addition, some senators felt that the payments for the native lands were too high. Having made many promises which could not be kept, Anson Dart resigned in 1853. This left the Coastal and Willamette Valley Indians in a precarious position as the land crisis worsened. Some of them had been willing to sell their lands, but now they had neither protection from a treaty nor any compensation as foreigners continued to intrude on their land. Violence broke out in northern California, and the 1852 discovery of gold in southern Oregon brought miners who cared little about the fate of the Takelma, Chetco and Tututni.

Board of Commissioners, Appointed to Treat With the Indian Tribes West of the Cascade Mountains, In the Territory of Oregon," NARS RG-75, Microcopy T-494, roll 8.

Before the Champoeg treaties could be ratified, Congress abolished the three-man commission and transferred treaties (cessions B, C, D, p.83) during summer and fall, 1851, and requested approval by the commissioner of Indian Affairs on November 7. The letter

of request is reprinted in Coan (1921, pp. 65-75); and in U.S. Senate (1893, pp. 16-20). These treaties covered about six million acres at two cents an acre (O'Callaghan 1960, p. 23). It should be noted that the Chinook groups at Tansey Point had been severely decimated by epidemics; one band had only three surviving adult males to sign the Konnack treaty. Also, two of the ten Tansey groups were actually Tillamook bands, not Chinooks as Dart reported. Besides the detailed Coan article on early Oregon treaties, other sources are Beckham (1977); and Deloria (1977, pp. 49-55). Various western Oregon tribes who lacked ratified treaties found themselves in a legalistic limbo, without clear relationships to the federal government, and usually defenseless against further invasion. Tribes north of the Columbia experienced similar dilemmas; without ratified treaties they eventually lost their lands with no payments. *See* Washington State (pp. 8-21).

## WESTERN OREGON TREATIES, 1853-1855

This period is best described by Beckham (1971, 1977). Coan (1922); and Spaid (1950, 1954) are also recommended. Information on southwestern Oregon is also found in Peterson; Bakken; Heckert; and Coos, Lower Umpqua, Siuslaw Tribe.

By 1854, incidents between settlers and Indians on the Tualatin Plains had become frequent, and, largely as a result of the Donation Land Act and the territorial legislature's prohibition against selling arms and ammunition to the Indians, native food resources were severely depleted. Tualatins approached Commissioner Joel Palmer with these and other grievances. The resultant March 25, 1854 treaty was a stop-gap measure. It was the second unratified treaty for the Tualatins, who had signed one of the earlier Champoeg treaties in 1851. *See* NARS RG-75, Microcopy T-494, roll 8; and the 1854 CIA annual report (pp. 260-61).

Other primary sources on the western Oregon situation include Joel Palmer's letters ("Letters Received," NARS RG-75, Microcopy 234); and the writing of Indian rights defender John Beeson (1858). Data on the unratified 1855 Coast Treaty is in Confederated Tribes of Siletz (1977); U.S.

## WESTERN OREGON TREATIES, 1853-55

In this tense setting, the first Oregon treaties to be confirmed by Congress were concluded. In the period 1853-55, the next superintendent of Indian affairs, General Joel Palmer, obtained treaties from western Oregon and Plateau Indian tribes (*see* cessions 1-9, p. 80). Because more settlers and American commerce were arriving, Palmer tried to isolate Indian people away from the paths of new railroads and immigration.

Some of these agreements were emergency treaties to halt the massacres of Indians by gold miners taking place in southwestern Oregon. Two of Palmer's treaties were never ratified by Congress, however. One was the 1854 agreement with the Tualatins (cession E, p. 83). This treaty tried to resolve some of the tensions between the Tualatins and Willamette Valley settlers. Although Palmer had received no explicit treaty instructions, he quickly negotiated this agreement to provide immediate relief to the Tualatins, whose essential plant foods were being destroyed by the newcomers' cattle and swine. Generally, this and other western Oregon treaties (cessions 1, 2, 3, 4, 5, 9, p. 80) allowed most tribes to temporarily remain on small reserves in their own lands. The map on page 86 shows these areas, reservations that seldom prevented further encroachments from non-Indians in southwestern Oregon. Palmer's main intention was to buy the lands of Coastal Area Indians and create one large reservation far from the growing American population of the Willamette and Rogue valleys.

Only after the end of the Rogue River wars did Palmer relocate the different tribes who had managed to survive diseases and the hostilities. Massive military roundups in 1856 sent Indians to the Grand Ronde and Siletz (Coast) reservations, although a few people escaped the authorities and some bands peacefully remained in their coastal villages.

For unknown reasons, Congress failed to ratify Palmer's most important treaty, the extensive 1855 Coast Treaty concluded with numerous bands and tribes from the area between the Columbia River and California. This treaty included lands where the Siletz Reservation was established by executive order. (*See* cession F, p. 83; the many different tribes signed the coast agreement during a series of

Senate (1893); and in two court cases, *Alcea et al* v. *United States* (1945) and *Coos et al* v. *United States* (1938). Evidently Palmer had more latitude in treaty-making than did his predecessors. In 1853, for example, he negotiated treaties with the Takelma and with the Cow Creeks, although Congress did not authorize negotiations until July 31, 1854 (and

then with an act that specified little in the way of policy but appropriated $45,000). As Rogue River conflicts intensified, Palmer developed a plan of mass removal to the coast reserve.

KEY

I Treaty with the Umpqua &
  Kalapuya
  Calapooia Creek, Douglas
  County, 29 November 1854

II Treaty with the Umpqua, Cow
  Creek Band
  Cow Creek, Umpqua Valley, 19
  September 1853

III Treaty with the Rogue River
  Table Rock (Takelma)
  Reservation, 10 September 1853

MAP: TEMPORARY WESTERN
OREGON RESERVATIONS,
1853-1856

The legal description of the Umpqua and Kalapuya Treaty, November
29, 1854, *10 Stat. 1125*; and Bakken
were used to locate reserve I. The Cow
Creek Reservation (II) was located
from the treaty description, September 19, 1854, *10 Stat. 1027*. The Table
Rock Reservation (III) is based on
Royce; and the September 10, 1853
Treaty with the Rogue River, *10 Stat.
1018*.

# Temporary
# Western Oregon Reservations

(1853-1856)

*Columbia River*

*Willamette River*

*Umpqua River*

I  • Sutherlin

• Coos Bay

 • Roseburg

II

*Cow Creek*

*Evans Creek*

III

*Rogue River*

 • Medford

86

In the mid-nineteenth century, the combination of expanding non-Indian settlement, gold discoveries in the area and the impending railroad route to the Pacific pressed treaty-making on the Plateau tribes. Pressure intensified in 1863, when rumors of a united Indian stand agains the newcomers alarmed Willamette Valley settlers and their representatives in Washington, D.C.

The Walla Walla Council (also referred to as the Camp Stevens Council) lasted from May 29 to June 11, 1855. Josephy (1965, pp. 277-323) provides an excellent account; another is by Kip, who was present at the negotiations. Slickpoo (this source includes the council minutes); LaCourse; and Relander (1956) provide tribal viewpoints. Other evaluations include Coan (1922); Day (1975b); and Ruby & Brown (1972, pp. 189-223). Twelve days after the council concluded, U.S. negotiator Isaac I. Stevens violated the terms of these treaties by opening the ceded lands to immediate non-Indian settlement, further alienating Kamiakin, Peopeomoxmox and other tribal leaders (especially those who had not participated in the council and its treaties). The ensuing Yakima War (1855-59) also gave rise to conflicts with the Coeur d'Alenes and Spokanes and incidents in the Puget Sound area. *See* J. P. Dunn; Burns; Ruby & Brown (1965); and Relander (1956).

Even before consulting the Wasco and Warm Springs bands at the Wasco Council of late June, Palmer had selected the lands they would sell. He instructed Agent R. R. Thompson: "You will proceed without delay to the Dalles of the Columbia and collect all the Indians inhabiting the country between Willow Creek and the Cascade Falls, and between the Columbia River and the 44th parallel of North Lati-

visits by Palmer in August and September, 1855.) Indians at Siletz and Grand Ronde thus faced a difficult legal situation: all of them had agreed to give up their lands in return for payments and government protection, but only a few had congressionally approved treaties. The majority were never paid for the lands they had sorrowfully left and would experience further hardships in the coming years.

## 1855 PLATEAU TREATIES

Treaties with interior Indian tribes (cessions 6, 7, 8, p. 80) resulted from two famous Columbia River councils held in June of 1855. The Walla Walla Council produced three important treaties ceding millions of acres of Indian lands. One treaty with the Yakima created a reservation in Washington; the treaty with the Nez Perce reserved lands in both Idaho and Oregon; and the agreement with the Umatilla, Cayuse and Walla Walla tribes established a reservation in Oregon. These groups reluctantly signed the agreements with Palmer and Washington Governor Isaac I. Stevens, after insisting on reservations in their own territories. Among other things, they retained the rights to fish, hunt and gather berries at traditional places. All groups strongly resisted the idea of giving up any of the lands of their ancestors and they especially resented what they perceived to be condescending attitudes of the United States officials. As at many treaty councils, certain Indians affected by the treaties did not attend; but the negotiators overlooked their absence, demanding that other Indians present sign for the missing participants.

Later, troubles arose because negotiators had used threats and had ignored many Indian questions, such as their moral dilemma about selling the land. Dissatisfactions among some Plateau tribes soon led to the Yakima War, causing Congress to delay ratification of all the 1855 treaties four years. Another serious mistake occurred with the signing of a second Nez Perce treaty eight years later. United States officials made this treaty with Nez Perce leaders in Idaho; it

tude" (quoted in Suphan, p. 36). This is the area that would be described in the Middle Oregon Treaty of June 25, 1855. Details of this council and treaty are found in Confederated Tribes of the Warm Springs Reservation (1972); Stowell (1978); French (1962, pp. 272-73); Courts; and Docket 198 of the Indian Claims Commission (hereafter, ICC). The Yakima War caused Congress to delay ratification of this treaty until March 8, 1859, though the Wascos and Warm Springs remained peaceful during the hostilities to the east.

## TREATIES OF SOUTH-CENTRAL AND EASTERN OREGON

### 1864 Klamath Treaty

In 1864, after the Oregon legislature's repeated requests for land purchases to insure the safety of increasingly traveled routes to California and southern Idaho, Congress authorized federal agents to deal with southern Oregon Indians. The October 14, 1864 Klamath treaty was actually preceded earlier that year by an unauthorized agreement, never ratified, with the Modocs at Yreka, California. The first agreement allowed the Modocs to retain Tule Lake; the Klamath treaty did not. Disregarding the history of intertribal warfare, it forced the Modocs to live on what was traditionally Klamath territory.

Dissension also arose among a group of Paiutes, led by Panaina, who refused to participate in the Klamath treaty, but who did sign the Walpapi treaty a year later. Like many Modocs, these Paiutes lived apart from other groups on the reservation, and most did not reside permanently at Klamath. Stern (1956); and Riddle provide the best accounts of the treaty period. Other details on Klamath and Walpapi negotiations are found in Gatschet (1890); Wheeler-Voegelin (1955); and Day (1975a).

### Unratified Northern Paiute Treaty, 1868

After the Klamath and Walpapi councils, little remained of the appropriation for southern Oregon treaties. In the 1860s Congress began to balk at the expenses incurred by the numerous treaties ratified since the 1850s. An 1868 Peace Commission was attempting to end conflicts in other parts of the West, so, often the fair purchase of Indian lands became secondary to the goal of ending hostilities. Acting Commissioner of Indian Affairs Mix directed Oregon Superin-

eliminated the last tribal lands in Oregon, which had been retained as part of their original reservation in the first Nez Perce treaty of 1855. (See cession 10, p. 80.)

From the Walla Walla Council, General Palmer proceeded downriver to meet with the Warm Springs and Wasco bands in late June. The resulting "Treaty with the Tribes of Middle Oregon" (cession 8, p. 80) gave the United States about 10 million acres of Indian lands, while the tribes kept a reservation lying far south of their valuable Columbia River fishing sites. Although peaceably signed, this treaty was hardly a welcome event in the history of these peoples. The idea of fairly negotiating with the tribes seemed false, for Palmer had arrived with a predetermined plan about which lands would be sold to the United States. Complaints were many and the Indians firmly stipulated that they would continue to fish and hunt (along with the newcomers) at their usual places. They were accommodating themselves to the outsiders, but later disputes over their reservation's boundaries and fishing rights were heavy sacrifices they had not bargained for in their 1855 treaty.

## TREATIES OF SOUTH-CENTRAL AND EASTERN OREGON

Oregon settlement in the 1850s did not markedly affect the Indian tribes and bands of south central and eastern Oregon. Pressures from military campaigns and the construction of forts and wagon roads brought the treaty-making process to them in the following decade. Klamath, Modoc and a few Paiute (Yahooskin Snake) tribes agreed to an 1864 treaty (cession 11, p. 80) that created the Klamath Reservation. (Many Modocs, however, had wanted to keep their native Tule Lake region in northern California and eventually fought a war on this principle.) A year later, a small band of Paiute (Woll-Pah-Pe or Walpapi Snake) Indians reluctantly agreed to settle at Klamath but gave lands to the United States that other groups had already ceded in previous treaties (see cession 12). Such an overlap situation was due to government and military ignorance about the different Paiute bands at the time. In addition, treaty policy always required that the United States negotiators obtain the largest land cessions possible without regard to whether an area actually conformed to a particular tribe's territory.

Seven Paiute bands were the last Indian people to sign a treaty in Oregon, after defying the military and raiding the Klamath and Warm Springs reservations for many years. Only after their defeat in 1868 did these bands sign a "peace and friendship" treaty at Fort Harney. By this time the U.S. Indian policy was to avoid paying Indians for their lands. Instead, officials received orders to obtain treaties ending hostilities, with assurances that the government would later find homes for these Indian people.

The map on page 80 indicates that a large corner of southeastern Oregon was not acquired through any treaty. Even the 1868 Paiute peace treaty went unratified when Congress ended all treaty-making in 1871. Most Paiutes were adamantly against forced removal

tendent J.W.P. Huntington to avoid actual purchase of Snake (Paiute) lands, preferring simply to secure assurances of good behavior, rights-of-way and grazing benefits for non-Indian ranchers. (*Snake or Paiute Indians* v. *United States*, 112 F Supp. 543, 557, 1953).

When it became apparent that most Paiute bands would not consent to relocation, local authorities and the secretary of the Interior recommended that the Malheur Reservation be established near Fort Harney. President Grant signed the order creating this 1.8 million-acre reservation on September 12, 1872. No comprehensive account of the unratified 1868 treaty exists, but pertinent details are found in the CIA annual report of that year; and in the "Findings of Fact" of Docket 17, ICC. The treaty is reproduced at 4 ICC 571a, pp. 568-88; a copy of the original is in "Unratified Treaties, 1868-69" (NARS RG-75, Microcopy T-494, roll 10). *See also* S. W. Hopkins (the only contemporary Indian account); Peterson; Wheeler-Voegelin (1955); and O. C. Stewart (1966).

## TREATY NEGOTIATIONS
### Land

Owhi's quote on page 89 is from Josephy (1965, p. 317); and the Peopeomoxmox statement on same page is from Kennedy (p. 54). Oregon's treaty council records effectively convey the contrasting Euro-American and Indian views of land ownership, a difference that could not be resolved. There is little doubt that to Indians personal ownership of land seemed immoral as well as impractical. Tribes made numerous attempts to circumvent or hamper land taking, sometimes planning their strategies in pre-treaty councils. For example, Plateau tribes (Anastasio, p. 192); and Klamath/Modoc bands (Stern 1966, pp. 40-41) attempted to reserve *all* of

when officials tried to send them to Klamath or Siletz. They demanded a reservation in their own lands, and an 1872 presidential order finally created the Malheur Reservation from Indian lands that had been designated the public domain.

## TREATY NEGOTIATIONS:
## LAND, LANGUAGE AND MISINTERPRETATIONS

The treaties brought about the most dramatic changes in Oregon Indian life between 1851 and 1868. Treaties were signed for a variety of reasons and in a multitude of circumstances. In a few cases Indians faced extinction through disease or extermination if they did not agree to drastically limit their use of the land and its resources. However, most tribes were strong nations who, noting the increasing number of newcomers, chose to adapt to some of the foreigners' needs rather than prolong the land crisis.

Of course the treaty-making process was not easy. Forced to negotiate and confederate at the treaty councils, Indians were confronted by foreign legal concepts about land and its ownership. The very idea of selling land was to many incomprehensible. Said one leader: "God made our bodies from the earth.... What shall I do? Shall I give the lands that are a part of my body?" Peopeomoxmox of the Walla Wallas declared that "goods and the earth are not equal; goods are for using on the earth. I do not know where they have given land for goods."

The treaty negotiations revealed the tribes' fervent desire to retain their homelands. The western Oregon bands claimed that they would rather die than leave their lands in 1851. Likewise, the Cayuse, Umatilla and Walla Walla people demanded a reservation of their own after learning that the United States authorities had planned to place them on one reservation with the Nez Perce. At more than one council, when asked which lands they wished to reserve, united tribal leaders proceeded to outline their entire territories and exasperate the federal officials.

The non-Indian attitude in making treaties not only favored a policy of removing entire groups to remote areas, it also reflected a basic misunderstanding of native cultures and Indian land tenure. Indian leaders usually spoke only for their respective bands or villages, but negotiators were determined to amalgamate these bands and deal with only a few leaders. Federal agents failed to notify Nez Perce Chief Joseph (the elder) and other Indian leaders about the 1863 Lapwai Council held in Idaho, where the ensuing treaty took all of their Wallowa Valley land in Oregon (cession 10). More than once such apparently fraudulent tactics caused divisions among Indian tribes and non-Indians were quick to exploit these situations. The drive to acquire Indian lands seldom slowed, and the United States accepted many treaties with questionable ethical consideration or regard for native politics.

Eager to obtain cessions covering immense areas, government agents often drew boundary lines that satisfied their orders from

their territories, thereby avoiding any land cession. Commentary on Indian land tenure is found in Large; Sutton; Washburn (pp. 143-49); Slickpoo (pp. 57-63); Josephy (1968, pp. 277-84).

Language

Language barriers, circumstance and, sometimes, dishonesty of federal negotiators resulted in several manifestly fraudulent treaties and others that incorrectly described the lands reserved and ceded by tribes. *See* Schmeckebier (pp. 59-60). Federal-Indian boundary disputes based on different interpretations of treaty language include the McQuinn Strip exclusion at Warm Springs (*see* p. 97); and the Klamath controversy (discussed on p. 107). For the limitations of Chinook Jargon in conveying treaty concepts, *see Duwamish et al Indians v. United States*, 79 Ct. Cl. 530, 578-79 (1934); and *United States v. Washington* 384 F.Supp. 312 (1974).

The repeated confusion of identities and names of the Northern Paiute bands (also collectively called Snakes, Shoshoni, Bannock or Paviotso) is discussed by O. C. Stewart (1966, pp. 1183-94); and by Wheeler-Voegelin (1955).

Washington, but did not reflect the actual land usage of individual bands. Comparison of two maps, "Ratified Treaties and Cessions" (p. 80) and "Tribes and Bands of Traditional Oregon" (p. 9), shows how the treaties forced tribes to move, resulting in significant changes in Indian life. First, it is apparent that treaties fundamentally disrupted native cultures by cutting heavily into their seasonal use of all the land. In addition, later information about Indian people was often rendered inaccurate because treaties created artificial areal distributions that often did not reflect traditional ownership. Treaty documents also confederated many independent tribes on the new land units (e.g. "Confederated Tribes of the Willamette Valley"), although no such Indian nations had ever existed.

Confusing interpretations and sometimes deliberate manipulation of language were additional problems at some treaty councils. Treaties were written only in English. Translators usually had to explain the proposals, first in Chinook Jargon (a trade language with a limited vocabulary for some of the complicated treaty issues), and again in the languages of the different tribes present. Agents also tended to anglicize tribal names or invent new ones (such as Snake or Rogue), since they typically lacked a detailed knowledge of native languages and political organization. Misnaming and other false assumptions about Indian people dating from the treaty period (perpetuated in documents until the present) caused more difficulties during the reservation period and in later claims settlements with the federal government.*

*It should nevertheless be emphasized that despite the notoriety surrounding treaty negotiations and ratification, the fact remains that these treaties were legal agreements between the United States and Indian nations, and that they are still in effect today.

90

Wilkinson & Biggs (1976) contains a concise review of Indian treaty law. Sources on the relevance of treaties today include M. Thompson; AIPRC *Final Report of Task Force One* (1976); Deloria (1974); and Hall.

Recognizing the unequal bargaining position of tribes and the implications of the trust relationship, the courts maintain three major principles for interpreting Indian treaties: (1) that ambiguities are settled in favor of the Indian parties involved (*Winters* v. *United States*, 1908), (2) that treaties must be interpreted as the Indians themselves understood them (*Choctow Nation* v. *Oklahoma*, 1970), and (3) that treaties must be liberally construed in favor of the Indian parties (*United States* v. *Walker River Irrigation District*, 1939). Wilkinson & Volkman (pp. 615-21) summarize the definitive cases regarding treaty interpretation; while Chambers (1975) discusses the enforcement of the trust responsibility. *See also* Cohen (1971, pp. 33-38).

# TREATY PROMISES: AN ONGOING RELATIONSHIP

Indians ceded non-Indians over 90 percent of the lands of the current state of Oregon. In return, the United States promised certain protections and services to the tribes. Treaty promises became the basis for a reservation policy in the Northwest and underlie the continuing legal and moral obligations of the nation to the first Americans.

Oregon treaties were not all alike. Some involved temporary reservations and a few agreements did not cede any lands at all. However, the majority of the treaties contain similar provisions, including:

> The United States would provide services in the form of doctors, educators and other personnel; it would construct buildings, mills and schools, and generally assist Indian people.
>
> Oregon tribes were to be free from outside interferences on their reservations.
>
> Indians would receive payments and beneficial goods for their ceded lands over a 20-year period.
>
> Tribes agreed to settle on reservations within a year of treaty ratification.
>
> Tribes acknowledged federal authority over them.
>
> Compensation from the federal government for any future roads and railroads passing through their lands was promised.
>
> Unpaid debts against Indian tribes from any wars would be subtracted from treaty annuities (payments).
>
> In some cases, tribes reserved their rights to continue traveling to hunting, fishing and berrying grounds off the reservations.

Through executive orders and treaties, Oregon tribes became self-governed islands on their reduced land bases.

Unlike any other minority group in the state, Oregon Indians have a unique relationship with the federal government. Treaties are a lasting part of Oregon and American history, which guarantee the political, cultural and economic survival of Indian communities despite non-Indian settlement on their lands.

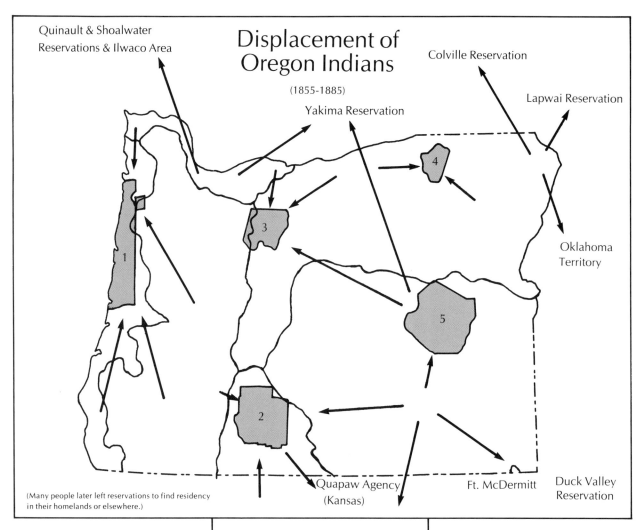

# Displacement of Oregon Indians

(1855-1885)

Quinault & Shoalwater
Reservations & Ilwaco Area

Colville Reservation

Lapwai Reservation

Yakima Reservation

1

3

4

5

2

Oklahoma
Territory

Quapaw Agency
(Kansas)

Ft. McDermitt

Duck Valley
Reservation

(Many people later left reservations to find residency
in their homelands or elsewhere.)

---

**KEY**
Arrows indicate major displacements, not actual routes of travel.

**OREGON RESERVATIONS**
1 SILETZ & GRAND RONDE
  RESERVATIONS
  Shasta, Takelma, Molalla,
  Tututni, Chetco, Yaquina, Siletz,
  Alsea, Tillamook, Coquille,
  Kalapuyans, Upper Umpqua,
  Some Chinooks & other Western
  Oregon tribes, Yachats
  subagency (Siuslaw, Coos, Lower
  Umpqua)
2 KLAMATH RESERVATION
  Klamath, Modoc, Paiute, Some
  Shasta, Pit River, Molalla,
  Chinook

3 WARM SPRINGS RESERVATION
  Wasco, Warm Springs Bands,
  Paiute
4 UMATILLA RESERVATION
  Walla Walla, Cayuse, Umatilla,
  Some Nez Perce, Yakima
5 MALHEUR RESERVATION
  (1872-1879)
  Some Paiute Bands, Tchinouck

**RESERVATIONS IN OTHER
STATES**
  YAKIMA: Wishram, Chinooks,
  Paiutes
  QUINAULT & SHOALWATER:
  Chinooks
  LAPWAI, OKLAHOMA
  TERRITORY & COLVILLE: Nez
  Perce

McDERMITT, DUCK VALLEY,
OTHER NEVADA &
CALIFORNIA
RESERVATIONS: Paiutes
QUAPAW AGENCY: Modocs

It should be noted that not all
displaced Indians went to
reservations. Other important
places of relocation were:
CELILO FALLS: Wyam & other
Mid-Columbia tribes
WESTERN OREGON &
WASHINGTON: Chinooks
SOUTHWESTERN OREGON:
Coos, Lower Umpqua, Siuslaw &
others
SOUTHEASTERN OREGON,
BURNS AREA: Paiutes

Four types of sources aided in compiling the map on page 97: (1) secondary sources (listed in the source notes for "Early Reservation Period" accompanying the text for each Oregon reservation); (2) CIA annual reports from the Oregon Superintendency and separate Indian agencies; (3) compilations by McChesney and by Swanton; and (4) most importantly, many Oregon Indian people reviewed drafts of this displacement map.

## DISPLACEMENT OF OREGON INDIANS

### National Removal Policies

Removal of entire southeastern U.S. Indian tribes, a major controversy of the 1820s and '30s, set the precedent and pattern for many other displacements. Major histories of these upheavals include Foreman (1932, 1946); McNickle; and W. R. Jacobs. Sutton comments on changes in livelihood and locus of tribalism.

### Oregon Removals

The best single account of military removal in Oregon, Stephen D. Beckham's (1971), paints the confusion and conflicts of this destructive experience in southwestern Oregon during the early 1850s. The only known Indian historian of southeastern Paiute bands, Sarah W. Hopkins, relates events concerning these Indians; and Jeff Riddle describes the 1873 Modoc War. Although a few historians (such as Josephy, 1965) have assiduously traced the repeated displacements of some tribal groups, it is extremely difficult to account for all the movements and residential changes of Oregon tribes. The major obstacles are the contemporary sources—newspapers, military reports and early reservation censuses—many of which misidentify

# DISPLACEMENT OF OREGON INDIANS

One consequence of treaty-making and armed conflicts was the displacement of many Oregon Indians from their original homelands. Whether the tribes were sent thousands of miles away or were allowed to remain closer to their homes, this relocation caused major upheavals in Indian life. Besides the physical hardships of long forced marches, displacement often separated persons from their families and land base, thereby weakening cultural ties. Indian people were denied access to burial sites and spirit quest locations, which had ages-old meaning. Tribal groups often were split apart and moved to reservations where they had to make a new life among strangers.

Paiute bands, the younger Joseph's Nez Perce followers and Modoc people all experienced forced military removal to distant reservations. In the late 1800s some of these groups were removed to Indian agencies as far away as Oklahoma and Kansas. The Indians of southwestern Oregon were marched hundreds of miles to the coastal reservations of northern Oregon. Many elderly, injured and ill persons did not survive these trips.

Displacement of Indian people often meant that traditional cultural groups were split apart. The various Northern Paiute bands, for example, were sent to more than five reservations. Chinookan-speaking Indians of the lower Columbia were similarly displaced to many reservations, including Grand Ronde, Siletz, Warm Springs, Yakima, Shoalwater and Quinault (the latter three in Washington). These arbitrary divisions disrupted families and villages, making the continuance of cultural traditions difficult. Indian languages were affected by displacement, since the dispersal of tribal groups left fewer and fewer speakers of each language in one location.

Another consequence of removal was the crowding together of very different tribes at reservations. The Grand Ronde and Siletz reservations, for example, held over 20 tribes each. While it is commonly believed that the term Warm Springs Indians describes a single tribe, in actuality members of several different tribes (see map listing, on facing page) live on the reservation and refer to themselves as the *Confederated Tribes* of the Warm Springs Reservation. The creation of the Umatilla and Klamath reservations also required different peoples to confederate, to act as one political group. Sometimes this process of confederation was difficult since it meant that tribes whose languages and cultures were different had to learn to live together. In some cases, former enemies were placed together.

The map opposite shows some of the displacements of Oregon Indian people during the last century. Many relocations are hard to trace or portray. In every area of Oregon there were Indians who refused to move to the reservations. Others moved but later returned to their homelands. Many Coos, Lower Umpqua and Siuslaw people, for example, left the Lower Siletz Reservation (Yachats)

# Shrinking Indian Lands

(1492-1979)

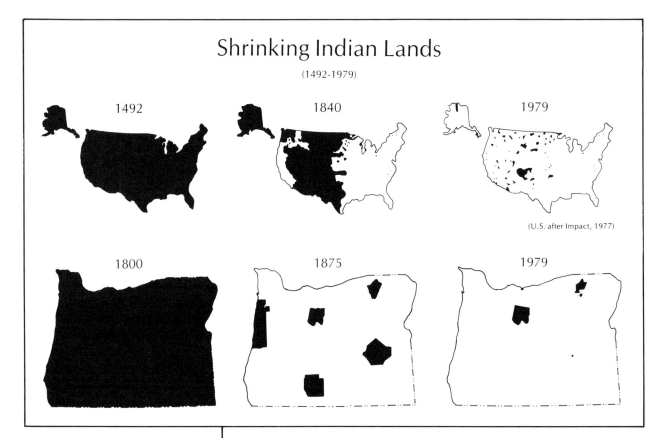

1492

1840

1979

(U.S. after Impact, 1977)

1800

1875

1979

tribes and their territories due to the writers' insufficient knowledge of complex native cultures, Indian languages, and even the tribes' proper names. Wheeler-Voegelin (1955) has described in detail the confused documentation of the many Northern Paiute bands in the period 1860-80. *See* the source note on page 90 for problems of treaty negotiation and interpretation due to language barriers and misnaming.

in the 1870s and returned to the Coos Bay region. Similarly, Chinookan and Paiute people often made their homes away from reservations. Other groups moved from one reservation to another. Some Paiutes who settled on the Malheur Reservation in 1872, were marched to Yakima after the 1879 Bannock War, and moved again to other reservations in later years.

Today, the effects of displacement can still be seen. There remain many distinct tribal groups on each reservation. The original diversity caused by displacement has sometimes increased, since there is much visiting and intermarriage between Indian communities. Each tribe has attempted to preserve its own traditions, but the sharing of different traditions has also become significant. Off the reservations, many smaller tribes have reorganized to meet the needs of the Indian people who were forgotten during the upheavals of displacement.

# SHRINKING INDIAN LANDS

Today Oregon Indian tribes own 1.2 percent of the land in the state. Settlement by newcomers and the creation of reservations in the nineteenth century initiated the dramatic reduction of native lands. When forming the trust partnership between Indian nations and the United States, a negotiator told one tribe: "If we make a treaty with you . . . you can rely on all of its provisions being carried out strictly." Treaty promises were not always upheld and Indian lands and autonomy shrank even further.

The following pages contain brief sketches of the Oregon Indian reservations. The maps show many changes (both losses and additions) that took place at the Warm Springs, Umatilla, Malheur-Burns, Paiute, Klamath, Grand Ronde and Siletz reservations. The accompanying descriptions focus mainly on the struggles to retain these reserved Indian lands; they are by no means complete histories of the peoples who own the land.

Past and present ownership of Indian land can be very confusing. Treaties and executive orders first created new geographical units for and among tribes. Later events caused more land losses and frustrating divisions of land. Today, reservation properties are generally classified in four ways.

TRIBAL TRUST LAND

Title is shared by the tribe and the United States. The United States manages the land for the benefit of the tribe. "Restricted" tribal land, "beneficial title" and "federal Indian land" all refer to the trust idea where the U.S. government is trustee on behalf of Indian people. Not only does the federal government protect the land base, it also must care for timber, mineral and water resources on reserved trust lands.

ALLOTMENT

Allotments are tracts of land owned by individual Indians (rather than whole tribes), which are held in trust status and protected by the United States. Usually allotments are inside reservation boundaries but sometimes public lands in other regions have been allotted to individual Indians.

FEE-PATENT ALLOTMENTS

Allotted tracts no longer held in trust by the United States. No restrictions apply and these lands may be owned by either Indians or non-Indians.

## SURPLUS LANDS

"Surplus Lands" are usually those adjacent to present-day reservations, and formerly belonging to the tribe. In the allotment period (*see* p. 95) these lands were opened for sale to non-Indians after tribes ceded the so-called "surplus" to the United States.

The United States and Oregon maps (p. 94) graphically portray massive changes in the Indian land base. Although much of their land disappeared, most Indian nations did not simply vanish.

Indian Country today is not a simple geographic designation. In addition to federal trust land on reservations, some Indian people live on state reservations. There are also corporately-held tribal lands, owned in fee-simple (having no restrictions) rather than in trust. And there are lands on which Indian people still retain certain of their ancient rights (such as hunting in federal forests or fishing in traditional waterways). Indians who reside in cities have often formed centers to assist one another and share their heritages. In many places there are the landless tribes, many of whom own only a school, meeting hall or their ancestral cemeteries (as in parts of western Oregon). The tenacity with which Indian communities hold on to their last tribal properties indicates the primacy of land in their cultures.

Frequently the protection of the Indian land base from encroachment has been difficult. An Indian tribe is a self-governing unit that needs a sound landbase and resources to sustain its people. But much misunderstanding about the income from tribal lands and Indian legal rights has occurred. The allotment period especially blurred the separateness of Indian territories when many non-Indians were permitted to buy surplus lands or individual allotments from Indians. Outsiders began to profit from tribal lands through direct purchase or lease agreements. This subdivision of Indian property was contrary to the treaty purpose of setting aside Indian lands for Indians. Sovereign tribal governments lost income and control over their own affairs each time their lands were taken.

The shrinking of the Indian land base is significant not only for economic reasons; continued losses also signify, as C. Wilkinson states, a "closing of the ring by a foreign culture." Many Indian people continue to regard as sacred the land that became Oregon. Indian defense of the land is directly related to the cultural and political continuance of Indian tribes. American courts have always acknowledged that Indian nations retained certain sovereign rights and powers. Whether future policies will support this central concept will be measured by the stability and growth of the Indian land base in coming years.

Early Reservation Years

For the negotiation of the June 25, 1855 Middle Oregon Treaty, *see* references in the source notes to "1855 Plateau Treaties" (pp. 87-88). For the taking of Indian land before the treaty's ratification, *see* Courts; Oliphant; and the 1854 CIA Annual Report. Details concerning the transition to reservation life are found in French (1961); Suphan; and the Findings of Fact in ICC Dockets 17 and 198.

1865 Supplemental Treaty

The November 15, 1865 "Treaty with the Middle Oregon Tribes," ratified on March 2, 1867, is recorded in 2 Kappler (p. 908). Courts and Confederated Tribes of Warm Springs (n.d.) discuss this controversial agreement, which gave rise to the tribes' claim recorded in Docket 198-A of the Indian Claims Commission. The tribes have never relinquished their off-reservation hunting, fishing and berrying rights and the Docket 198-A claim was dismissed without prejudice in 1970 (23 ICC 314). *See also Sohappy* v. *Smith* (1966); and *United States* v. *Oregon* (1969) for court cases relating to off-reservation reserved rights.

McQuinn Strip

Confederated Tribes of the Warm Springs Indian Reservation (1972); and Kickingbird & Ducheneaux (pp. 104-27) best describe the struggle to regain the McQuinn Strip, which began with the 1941 and 1945 *Warm Springs* v. *United States* cases. These cases were disappointing to the tribes, who received a favorable ruling over unjust taking of the McQuinn Strip but no actual remuneration, since government deductions ("offsets") for past services to the tribes exceeded the money due them. Next, in 1946, Senate Bill 845 attempted unsuccess-

# WARM SPRINGS INDIAN RESERVATION

The Tygh, Tenino, Wyam and John Day Indians (collectively the Warm Springs bands) and Wasco Chinookans, who signed the June 25, 1855 treaty, settled on their reservation even before Congress ratified their treaty in 1859. A third tribal group joined them in the 1880s when some of the Paiute people held prisoner at Yakima and the Fort Vancouver barracks made their way back to Oregon. Today the Confederated Tribes consists of the Warm Springs, Wasco and Paiute tribal groups, each with their own hereditary chiefs in addition to the modern tribal council.

It was hard for Wasco and Warm Springs people to leave their Columbia River homes for the more arid southern part of their country when settlers took the Indians' best lands near Celilo Falls. In fact, some people stayed along the river for years afterwards and many of those who accepted the reservation alternative often returned to fish and visit with friends and relatives on the Columbia.

Their 1855 treaty guaranteed the right to continue using traditional hunting and fishing spots off the reservation, but the federal policy of imposing a farming lifestyle on Indians attempted to curtail this right in an 1865 supplemental treaty. However, the people never really accepted the 1865 treaty and it was later abandoned. Adjusting to the reservation was not easy. Subsistence farming combined with livestock and traditional food gathering enabled the people to survive the many lean years until timber production became a significant tribal resource in this century.

Although the reservation area was less than 10 percent of the Confederated Tribes' 1855 treaty cession to the United States, they had difficulty retaining even this amount of land. Faulty surveys, conflicting studies and neighboring landholders' opposition kept the "McQuinn Strip" from tribal ownership for over 100 years. This 78,000-acre tract of timber and grazing land along the north and west boundaries of the reservation was incorrectly surveyed in 1871 (*see* map, p. 99). Court cases, several congressional bills and the Confederated Tribes' persistent efforts finally restored 61,360 acres of the McQuinn Strip to the tribes in 1972. The Indians made many concessions to regain these lands, and the tribe reaffirmed its commitment to the land by buying back 11,145 acres of privately held lands within the restored area.

The reservation today contains 639,898 acres, almost 90 percent of which is tribally-owned. Because the allotment policy was implemented late at Warm Springs and since the tribes have consistently tried to buy back lost lands, very little of the original reservation land is currently owned by non-Indians.

The tribes accepted the Indian Reorganization Act and incorporated in 1938. Their tribal powers are much like those of any local government, and include land management control, a court system and several human welfare and business departments. Throughout the detribalization efforts of the 1950s the tribes also lobbied and

fully to return the strip to the tribes. Two years later they were granted, as "economic justice," profits from timber in the excluded area, but not the land itself (Act of July 3, 1948). Finally, on September 21, 1972 Congress legislated the return of most of the McQuinn Strip. *See* Courts; U.S. Senate (1972). Acreage data for lands bought back by the tribes since 1972 came from Warm Springs Indian Agency (1977).

Allotment at Warm Springs

Hunt has written a good analysis of land tenure at Warm Springs since 1855. Land allotted into individual tracts totalled 144,122 acres but allotment never achieved the goal of creating individualistic Indian farmers who were competitive with non-Indian agriculturists. Repeatedly the trust periods on Warm Springs allotments had to be extended. Ultimately, the Indian New Deal Legislation of the 1930s halted all allotments on the reservation. Between 1960 and 1974, Warm Springs tribes bought back lands lost through allotment sales, reducing the land owned by non-Indians within reservation boundaries from 9,192 to 7,581 acres (Warm Springs Indian Agency, 1977).

Protecting Resources and
Tribal Development

The 1958 "Celilo Settlement Contract" awarded the tribes some $4 million for the loss of their valuable salmon fisheries after The Dalles Dam inundated Celilo Falls. Most of these funds went to a 1960 Oregon State College study of reservation development needs, business ventures and a $500 per capita payment to tribal members.

Other resource management schemes furthering Warm Springs Reservation development include sustained-yield forestry on tribal timber-

obtained their exclusion from Public Law 83-280 (*see* p. 157-58), thereby retaining federal and tribal jurisdiction over their lands.

Small per-capita payments (similar to stock dividends) from Warm Springs timber sales began in 1943 and have gradually increased. The tribes have many resources under their management and must often make careful decisions to protect and sustain these tribal assets. One decision was to spend most of their compensation for destruction of native fisheries at Celilo Falls (by construction of The Dalles Dam) for a thorough study of their assets and needs. From the findings of this study, Warm Springs made further decisions to develop tribal and individual opportunities on the reservation.

The tribes have promoted land consolidation through their own land assignment program. A 1972 federal inheritance bill facilitated the preservation of allotted lands in trust status for their members. Range management and sustained-yield timber harvesting also aid in insuring the tribal future.

In 1964, the Confederated Tribes opened Kah-Nee-Tah recreational resort (on lands once lost but purchased back from an outsider) near one of their scenic valley hot springs. Three years later they began operating their own sawmill on the Warm Springs River, enabling the tribes to process and market the timber from their own lands. The tribe is also helping preserve the anadromous fish runs in Oregon through the work of their own fisheries experts at their new fish hatchery. Development of tribal enterprises at Warm Springs is based on the tribes' continued commitment to the land and its proper use. These vital activities enable this traditional community to renew itself, grow with the modern world and continue as a separate Indian nation.

lands, construction of Pelton Dam in the late 1950s (*see Federal Power Commission* v. *United States*, 1955) and a new fish hatchery on the reservation (completed in 1978). For information on recent programs and resource issues, *see* Confederated Tribes of the Warm Springs Reservation annual corporate reports; and the biweekly tribal newspaper *Spilyay Tymoo*. Developments since the 1930s are outlined by French & French (1955). *See also* G. R. Miller; and the Warm Springs profile.

The tribal land-assignment program is designed to maintain Indian land in trust status, a goal also furthered by the Warm Springs inheritance bill, passed in 1972 (*see* U.S. Senate 1972, S.R. report 92-998 on H.R. 5721).

# Warm Springs Indian Reservation

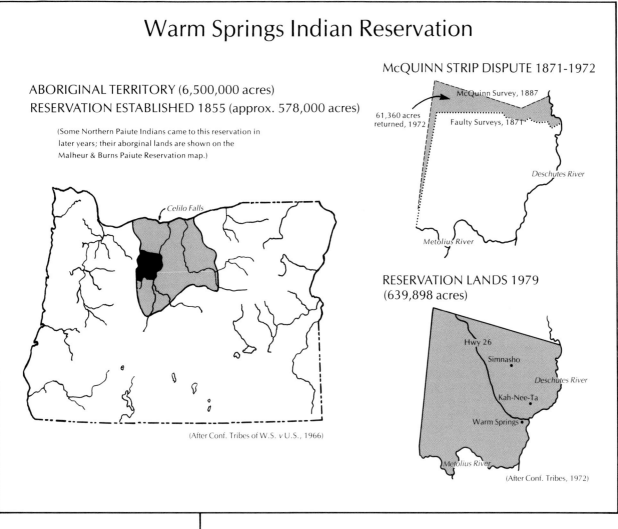

ABORIGINAL TERRITORY (6,500,000 acres)

RESERVATION ESTABLISHED 1855 (approx. 578,000 acres)

(Some Northern Paiute Indians came to this reservation in
later years; their aborginal lands are shown on the
Malheur & Burns Paiute Reservation map.)

Celilo Falls

(After Conf. Tribes of W.S. v U.S., 1966)

McQUINN STRIP DISPUTE 1871-1972

McQuinn Survey, 1887

61,360 acres
returned, 1972

Faulty Surveys, 1871

Deschutes River

Metolius River

RESERVATION LANDS 1979
(639,898 acres)

Hwy 26

Simnasho

Deschutes River

Kah-Nee-Ta

Warm Springs

Metolius River

(After Conf. Tribes, 1972)

MAP: WARM SPRINGS INDIAN
RESERVATION

Aboriginal territory and 1855 reservation are from the Appelant's Brief in
*Confederated Tribes of Warm Springs*
v. *United States* (1966). The modern
reservation and McQuinn Strip maps
are from Confederated Tribes of
Warm Springs (1972). Several sources
contributed acreage data: *Confederated Tribes of Warm Springs* v. *United
States* (1941, 1966); Oregon State
College; and Warm Springs Indian
Agency (1977).

# Umatilla Indian Reservation

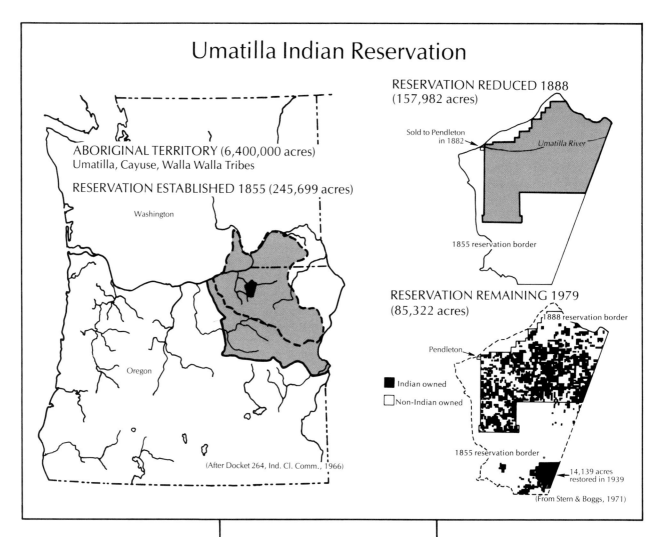

ABORIGINAL TERRITORY (6,400,000 acres)
Umatilla, Cayuse, Walla Walla Tribes

RESERVATION ESTABLISHED 1855 (245,699 acres)

Washington

Oregon

(After Docket 264, Ind. Cl. Comm., 1966)

RESERVATION REDUCED 1888
(157,982 acres)

Sold to Pendleton
in 1882

Umatilla River

1855 reservation border

RESERVATION REMAINING 1979
(85,322 acres)

1888 reservation border

Pendleton

■ Indian owned

□ Non-Indian owned

1855 reservation border

14,139 acres
restored in 1939

(From Stern & Boggs, 1971)

KEY
Broken line on aboriginal territory
map indicates 1855 Treaty cession
to U.S. (3,804,000 acres).

MAP: UMATILLA INDIAN
RESERVATION

Aboriginal territory and the 1855
treaty area are from information in
dockets 264, 264-A and 264-B of the
ICC. Map figure is taken from the Appelant's Brief in *Confederated Tribes
of Warm Springs Indian Reservation* v.
*United States* (1966). The Indian and
non-Indian land ownership map
(1979) is from Stern & Boggs (this map
is also reproduced in Ernst & Ernst; and
by Kennedy). Other maps are found in
Ruby & Brown (1972).

UMATILLA INDIAN RESERVATION
Early Reservation Years

For negotiation of the June 9, 1855
treaty with the Walla Walla, Cayuse
and Umatilla, *see* pages 88-89 of
"Treaty-Making in Oregon" and accompanying source notes.

Indian sources on the early reserva-
tion period are LaCourse (1976); and
Confederated Tribes of the Umatilla
Indian Reservation (1977). *See also*
Ruby & Brown (1977, pp. 265-96);
Burns (pp. 4-82); Relander (1956);
and Ferrell (1973b).

Resisting Outsiders

One of the earliest attempts to acquire Umatilla reserved lands was federally initiated: on July 1, 1870 Con-

gress resolved to commence land
negotiations with the tribes. Meetings
occurred at Umatilla in August of
1871, but the tribes refused to move
to another reservation. Attempts at
treaty abrogation also occurred at the
local level. For example, in 1874 the
Oregon Senate passed a joint memo-
rial petitioning for a land sale from the
tribes in order to develop the town of
Pendleton. In 1881 the tribes consented and the Act of August 5, 1882
ratified the sale of 640 acres. For documentation of outsiders' use of Umatilla reserved lands, *see* Oliphant;
Kennedy; and Sutherland (p. 28).

## Allotment at Umatilla

Three different commissions visited the Umatilla reservation before the tribes consented to allotment in 1885 (contingent on retention of certain timber and grazing lands on the eastern side of the reservation). In 1888, the Slater Act that legislated allotment was amended, and reservation land was further reduced, to 157,982 acres. An order of the secretary of the Interior (Dec. 4, 1888) specified the amended boundaries (1 Kappler, p. 891).

After the 1888 reduction, surplus lands totalled 87,717 acres. Sale of these lands began on April 1, 1891 and issuance of allotments started that summer, continuing until December, 1892. Multiple problems ensued from the allotment policy. Allegedly, some non-members received allotments; squatters were using tribal lands without permission; and the surplus lands were underpriced. Tribal people refused to disperse onto single allotments and adopt European agricultural ways. Frequently, when trust periods expired, they were forced to sell or lease their lands to non-Indian farmers and ranchers, which increased the reservation's grid or checkerboard appearance (see map on p. 100), as well as increasing the growing tribal population's already heavy demands on shrinking timber and grazing lands. Various amendments to the Slater and Dawes Allotment Acts (summarized by Cohen 1971, pp. 217-33) facilitated sales to non-Indians. See the analysis of land ownership and leasing relationships by Stern & Boggs. Kennedy's study of the land changes and legislation affecting reservation development includes socio-historical factors and outlines the losses due to taking of lands for roads, utility rights-of-way and other governmental purposes.

Umatilla, Cayuse and Walla Walla people reluctantly began moving to their northeastern Oregon reservation in 1860. Their 1855 treaty designated an area of 245,699 acres for their exclusive use —but the reservation did not remain free from outside influences for very long. Increasing numbers of settlers soon closed in on the reservation as the Umatilla region became a grain-producing wonderland.

The newcomers and their cattle and roads cut severely into native resources and the seasonal use of land. The people subsisted, using their aboriginal methods, farming some garden plots and raising cattle; yet they grew poorer as their land became more and more valuable to non-Indian farmers. The late arrival of promised treaty goods added to their problems as did the shifting Indian affairs bureaucracy of agents and rules. There were also certain adjustments to be made because the three tribes were now confederated on lands that had originally been Cayuse territory.

In 1871 the tribes resisted outside pressure by refusing to exchange their reserved lands and move elsewhere. Unfortunately, the famous Oregon Trail crossed their reservation and the settlers' desire for more Indian land did not abate. In 1882 the tribes sold 640 acres to the town of Pendleton, but the biggest diminution of the tribal land base came three years later when Congress passed the Slater Act: legislation ordering the reduction and allotment of the Umatilla Reservation. By 1888, tribal lands were reduced to 157,982 acres and the first allotments and surplus land sales soon followed.

Even before the assignment of individual land parcels to tribal members, the reservation had suffered from trespassers who used the Indians' timber and rangeland extensively. Allotment was a misguided policy for transforming Indian people into individual, self-supporting farmers. Although intended to make agriculture the dominant livelihood, the necessary technical assistance was seldom available for developing Indian lands. At Umatilla, the major consequence of allotment was the opening of the reservation to leasing by non-Indians, homesteading and further land loss. Various federal laws promoted this leasing and in time the Umatilla Reservation resembled a checkerboard of Indian and non-Indian ownership (see map, opposite). Deriving an adequate livelihood from the scattered land parcels was extemely difficult, with multiple ownership of the small allotted tracts (through inheritance rules governing the descent of allotments) and low rental fees from non-Indian tenants further complicating the situation.

In 1939 a special act of Congress restored 14,139 acres to the tribes from lands taken in 1888. These lands are important as a tribal timber resource and the recently opened Indian Lake campground is located on them. However, the main thrust of land usage lies in the effort to conserve and consolidate the total Umatilla land base. The people seek a sustained income from their lands as tribal needs for

## Land Consolidation

Between 1960 and 1977, 1,012 acres were returned to the Umatilla tribes. In the same period, however, due to complicated heirship factors and further land sales, 10,964 acres left trust status. Present trust acreage for both tribal and individual holdings totals 85,322 acres (personal communication of Tribal Development Office, May 1978).

Within its 1888 boundaries, non-Indians own approximately 55 percent of the reservation. Although the Act of August 10, 1939 returned about 14,000 acres of the Johnson Creek area to the tribes (from surplus lands taken in 1888), this legislation did not set up any mandatory procedures to enable further federal purchases for tribal benefit. Since mortgages on trust lands are not permitted, capital financing for more tribal lands is difficult. More information on this critical situation is in U.S. Senate 1977; and in 25 USC 463 D-G. The land consolidation bill of 1977 (S.470) proposed a wider variety of means for purchasing land and returning it to trust status. Controversy over reservation boundaries stalled the passage of this bill. Meanwhile, progress has been made on another front: on April 18, 1978, Congress passed a Umatilla inheritance bill, which facilitated retention of trust status on allotments.

## Contemporary Affairs

*See* the Umatilla Reservation profile. The tribal newspaper, *Confederated Umatilla Journal*; and planning materials published by the tribes are informative sources on current programs. *Also see* the tribal constitution and bylaws (Confederated Tribes of the Umatilla Indian Reservation 1957). Other sources on reservation events include Suphan; ICC Dockets 264, 264-A, 264-B (*see* chart, pp. 116-21); Stern (1953); and court cases such as *Maison* v. *Confederated Tribes of the Umatilla Reservation* (1963) and *Confederated Tribes of the Umatilla Indian Reservation* v. *Alexander* (1977).

housing, farming and business projects grow. Improving the lands they do own, combining scattered parcels into more usable tracts, and buying back lost lands (when available) will help finance other tribal projects and enable more people to live and work on their reservation.

The tribes adopted a constitution and bylaws in 1949. That year they also obtained better leasing terms for their rental farmlands. Previously, rental returns had yielded as little as fifty cents an acre, so that Umatilla people often lost money while their non-Indian tenants profited. The next decade saw more hardships, however. In 1953, the passage of Public Law 83-280 abolished their tribal police force (which had functioned since 1881) and transferred civil and criminal jurisdiction over the reservation from the tribe and federal government to the state of Oregon. Umatilla fishermen, like people from other Plateau tribes, saw their ancient native fishery at Celilo Falls destroyed when The Dalles Dam was completed in 1958. Although a monetary award was given to the tribes for this loss, the damage was irreparable; the tribes did establish a minors' trust fund with part of these monies and set aside some of the settlement for tribal business projects in addition to issuing individual payments to their members.

Although fractional ownership of reservation land is still a major problem, Umatilla people have worked hard to build their community facilities and services. Yellowhawk Medical Clinic was completed in 1972 and has since been expanded. In 1974 the Nicht Yow Way Village Community Center opened and in 1978 the tribes rebuilt their longhouse after a fire destroyed the old one.

Since 1964 the land purchase program and the tribal farm enterprise have been part of the current efforts to improve reservation conditions. Today the tribes have their own range and forest committees, as well as zoning control (in cooperation with Umatilla County), to oversee land management and prevent uncontrolled development. A federal inheritance bill, passed in 1978, is helping keep allotted lands in tribal ownership (trust status) while the Confederated Tribes have proposed other legislative reforms to make their reservation a more viable economic unit.

Land is not the only factor in a people's history, of course, but at Umatilla it has been of vital concern for a very long time. Rebuilding a sound land base is part of the Confederate Tribes' commitment to maintain and strengthen their Indian community.

Northern Paiutes Resist Invaders

Paiute efforts to retain their lands in Oregon, Nevada and California are described by Movius; Egan; and Colley; *see also* plaintiff testimony in Dockets 17 and 87 of the Indian Claims Commission. Colonel C. S. Drew; and Wheeler-Voegelin (1955) describe location and movements of Paiute bands between 1820 and 1870. It is difficult to correctly identify the names and territories of the many Paiute bands since historical records often contain misinformation about the culture and land tenure of Great Basin groups. (*See also* "Treaty-Making in Oregon" and "Tribes of Traditional Oregon.") During the period of serious hostilities in southeastern Oregon (1849-68), Paiutes advantageously used their knowledge of the immense and rough terrain against emigrant wagon trains and the U.S. military. Called "Diggers" by early invaders (who considered this a degrading term), with the acquisition of firearms and horses, the Paiutes succeeded in routing their enemies for a number of years.

Early Reservation Years

The Paiute lands were never purchased through formal agreement. The leaders Weyouwewa, Gshanee, Ehagant (Egan), Ponee, Chowwatnanee, Owits (Oits, Oitz) and Tashego signed the unratified 1868 peace treaty at Camp Harney. At this time Congress was balking at the expenses of treaty-making; formal treaty-making ended three years later. The September 12, 1872 executive order creating the Malheur Reservation and all other executive orders affecting it are reviewed in Kappler. *See also* pages 88-89, "Treaties of South-Central and Eastern Oregon."

# MALHEUR AND BURNS PAIUTE INDIAN RESERVATIONS

The Northern Paiute people successfully resisted settlers and the United States Army much longer than any Oregon Indian group. Most Paiute bands in Oregon surrendered to General George Crook in the summer of 1868, after a hard winter campaign. Seven of their leaders then signed a treaty in which they agreed to end their raids and settle on a reservation as soon as it could be established.

The 1868 peace treaty was never ratified by the Senate, but the Paiute bands continued to insist on having a reservation in their own territory rather than face displacement to distant reservations. By the time President Grant created the Malheur Reservation in 1872, some Paiutes were living elsewhere: on the Klamath Reservation, or camping near various southern Idaho, northern Nevada and California forts and reservations (*see* displacement map, p. 92). Thus the Malheur Reservation never was the home of all Paiute bands and many people continued to visit back and forth over the four-state area.

Pressure from settlers who eyed Malheur's fine grazing lands twice led to reservation boundary changes between 1872 and 1876. Some stockmen even built houses and ran cattle on the Indian lands, intentionally ignoring government orders against such trespassing. The 1877 Nez Perce War to the north and the Bannock tribe's loss of their Big Camas Prairie in southern Idaho added to the Paiutes' growing uneasiness over the maintenance of their lands. Inconsistent treatment by different Indian agents also angered them. They did not agree that they should abandon their seasonal movements and adopt non-Indian ways.

The Paiutes lost their reservation of almost 1.8 million acres after some of their people joined the 1878 Bannock uprising. All people, even those who did not participate in the conflict, suffered the consequences of the war and its aftermath. Most Paiutes were punished with forced removal to the Yakima Reservation in central Washington. Over 500 people had to walk north in the dead of winter and many of them did not survive the march. Others escaped to forts and reservations in Nevada and could not be induced to return to the Malheur area, fearing the hostilities of settlers who assumed the Indians were all unfriendly. Meanwhile, squatters quickly settled on their reservation, even before it was officially closed by executive orders in 1883 and 1889. The dispossessed Paiutes never received any of the monies from the sale of their reservation lands, despite one official's recommendation for compensation. Some of their descendants received belated economic justice in the form of a small Indian Claims Commission award in 1964.

A small group of Paiute people returned from Yakima and settled outside the town of Burns during the 1880s. Some of them obtained 160-acre allotments from the public domain in 1896–97, but these

# Malheur & Burns Paiute Indian Reservations

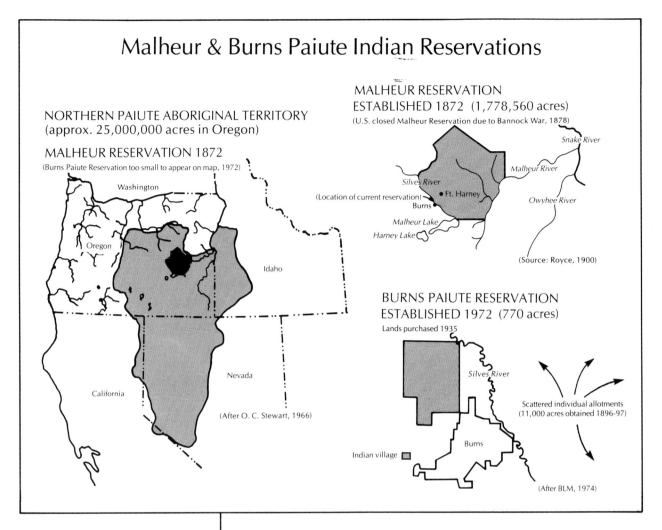

NORTHERN PAIUTE ABORIGINAL TERRITORY
(approx. 25,000,000 acres in Oregon)

MALHEUR RESERVATION 1872

(Burns Paiute Reservation too small to appear on map, 1972)

Washington

Oregon

Idaho

California

Nevada

(After O. C. Stewart, 1966)

MALHEUR RESERVATION
ESTABLISHED 1872  (1,778,560 acres)

(U.S. closed Malheur Reservation due to Bannock War, 1878)

Snake River

Malheur River

Silves River

(Location of current reservation)  • Ft. Harney
Burns

Owyhee River

Malheur Lake

Harney Lake

(Source: Royce, 1900)

BURNS PAIUTE RESERVATION
ESTABLISHED 1972 (770 acres)

Lands purchased 1935

Silves River

Scattered individual allotments
(11,000 acres obtained 1896-97)

Burns

Indian village ▣

(After BLM, 1974)

MAP: MALHEUR AND BURNS
PAIUTE INDIAN RESERVATIONS

Northern Paiute Aboriginal Territory Map is based on O. C. Stewart (1966). The 1872 Malheur Reservation Map is from Royce. A 1974 BLM map was used to locate the present Burns Paiute Reservation.

There is no accurate list of the bands that came to live at the Malheur Reservation; presumably, most of the seven groups whose leaders signed the 1868 unratified treaty with J.W.P. Huntington settled there, continuing their seasonal subsistence movements, with intermittent periods of "work" as directed by the Malheur Indian agents. At an 1869 post-treaty council, two bands (led by Chocktote and Ocheo) agreed to live at Klamath. Old Winnemucca's 200 followers, who resided alternately at Pyramid Lake, Camp Alvord, Fort McDermitt and Malheur, agreed to a treaty negotiated by Winnemucca's son, Natches, in August, 1868 at Fort McDermitt. *See* S. W. Hopkins; 4 ICC 571a (pp. 587-93); Brimlow (1938); and Wheeler-Voegelin (1955).

were arid tracts and provided little income. Consequently, many Paiutes sold or leased these lands and lived at the "Indian Village," a 10-acre tract donated to them in 1925 (*see* map, opposite).

In 1935, 762 acres of land northwest of Burns were transferred back to the Paiutes as a result of federal New Deal policies. Providing land to neglected tribes was part of the national Indian policy of the 1930s, a policy that attempted to bolster tribal governments and encourage Indian economic development. However, at Burns the intended progress was severely hindered because Congress failed to transfer the title of these new lands in trust to the Paiute people. Without the proper title to their lands, mortgages were difficult to obtain and the tribe had no means of financing any development projects. They actually ended up paying rent to the federal government on the very land they were supposed to own. Their school and community center burned in 1938 and were never rebuilt. Health problems and overcrowded housing were other hardships in these years. The BIA occasionally sent personnel to assist the Burns people, but most services were located at the Warm Springs Agency, a full day of travel away.

In 1968, the Department of the Interior finally recognized the Burns Paiutes as a tribe with full federal standing, and the people wrote a new constitution and bylaws that year. Since the early 1960s they had been working to secure their legal status and obtain the title to their lands. The overdue action transferred the beneficial (trust) title to the tribe in 1972, ending long years of uncertainty and formally creating the Burns Paiute Indian Reservation.

The 320 Burns members have begun long-range planning and other important activities for enhancing their tribal life. Recently they completed their new community center, and they are initiating other improvements. Major goals include new housing, improvement of agricultural lands and diversification of the economic base to enable members to live and work on the reservation. Labeled as one of the landless or "forgotten" Indian tribes for many years, the Burns Paiutes are continuing their own traditions with new optimism in modern-day Oregon.

## Pressure from Outsiders

Responding to pressure from settlers in adjacent areas, executive orders of May 15, 1875 and January 28, 1876 changed Malheur Reservation boundaries (Royce depicts these changes on a color map). Although settlers desired the Silvies River Valley inside the reservation, they were able to obtain only parts of the reservation's eastern boundary lands (Brimlow 1951, pp. 97-98). Both Brimlow and Oliphant (1950) discuss the rampant trespassing on Indian lands. Farming on the reservation was uncommon, as Paiutes preferred their traditional subsistence methods and only some 12,000 acres were tillable.

Oliphant, whose study relies heavily on CIA annual reports, did not question the abilities of the second Malheur Indian agent, W. V. Rinehart, but other sources (S. W. Hopkins; Brimlow 1938, 1951; Peterson) report chaos surrounding his administration. Rinehart withheld rations, favored non-Indian neighbors and, "worst of all, he told the Indians their crops as well as their land belonged only to the government" (Brimlow 1938, p. 49). Unrest was manifested in the emergence of the "Dreamer" movement among some tribal members and in the unsettling Nez Perce War of 1877.

## Bannock War and the Closure of Malheur Reservation

For accounts of the Bannock War, *see* S. W. Hopkins; Brimlow (1938, 1967); and Victor. Paiutes, not well received at the Yakima Reservation, soon began escaping south (they eventually were permitted to leave). Paddy Cap's band went to Duck Valley Reservation (Idaho-Nevada border) and others headed to Burns and to McDermitt and other Nevada towns. Winnemucca and others who had not participated in the Bannock War refused to return to Malheur because of the non-Indian hostility there in the first months after the war. *See* 4 ICC 571a (p. 605); and Peterson.

Two executive orders closed Malheur in stages. On May 21, 1883 all lands, excepting the 320 acres containing Fort Harney, were put into the public domain. Then on March 2, 1889 the last two sections of Indian land were also removed. Settlers moved onto the best parts of the reservation even before these official orders, however. Some were prosecuted for encroachment but the light penalties did not halt the trespassing. *See* Oliphant; Eggleston; and Brimlow (1951). Although the commissioner of Indian Affiars recommended that proceeds from the sale of Malheur's lands benefit the tribe, this proposal was not acted on (4 ICC 571a, p. 605). The 1964 ICC award for the taking of the Malheur Reservation, issued to descendants of the seven bands of the 1868 unratified treaty, came to only $743.20 per person. *See* Proceedings of Docket 17; and the chart on pp. 116-21.

## 1890-1935

Published information on the Paiute colony at Burns in this period is sparse; Warm Springs Agency records are one primary source (*see* Hirst). Brief mention of the Indian situation is also made by Whiting; Brimlow (1951); and the Bureau of Indian Affairs Planning and Support Group (1974).

## Indian New Deal at Burns

*See* page 77 on the Indian Reorganization Act (IRA). The submarginal lands for Burns Paiutes were purchased under the authority of the 1933 National Industrial Recovery Act and the 1933 Federal Emergency Relief Act. These lands consisted of a 605.67-acre tract and a 156.26-acre subsistence homestead tract. Although national Indian policy tried to increase Indian land ownership during this era and some 20 projects nationwide bought lands for homeless Indian tribes, the benefits and revenues from these purchases did not go to the tribes. Instead, land title was simply transferred between federal agencies. The Burns acreage, for example, had been purchased for $14,620. By August, 1968 the government had recovered $13,740 in permit fees charged to the Burns Paiutes (U.S. Senate 1972:2).

Although the Indians accepted the IRA and had formed a tribal business committee to oversee leases, lack of a trust title to their lands impeded community development between 1936 and the mid-1960s. Since most funding regulations required 50-year or longer leases on property, the Paiutes could not obtain financing for projects. The BIA did build 24 houses on the 1935 homestead tract but incentive to improve these homes was lacking so long as the Paiutes did not hold a secure land title. One incisive review of this situation is by Kickingbird & Ducheneaux (pp. 65-89, 196-210).

## Recent Developments

*See* Burns community profile for more details on current tribal activities. Conveyance of the trust title for the 660 acres purchased in the 1930s was effected on October 13, 1972, with an act that formally created the Burns Paiute Reservation. For its legislative history, *see* U.S. Senate (1972); U.S. House (1972). Other information is in McGreehan; Bureau of Indian Affairs Planning Support Group (1974); and Burns Paiute Reservation.

# KLAMATH INDIAN RESERVATION

Early Reservation Years

For details on the October 14, 1864 Klamath Treaty negotiation, *see* page 88 of "Treaty-Making in Oregon"; Stern (1956); Riddle; and Day (1975). Adjustments to reservation life are discussed by Stern (1966); and Zakoji (1953). *See also* Gatschet (1890); Wheeler-Voegelin (1955); Stern (1972); Martin; and Spier (1935). Further information on the numerous tribal groups residing at Klamath was provided by tribal informants and by Theodore Stern. *See also* McChesney; Swanton; and CIA Annual Report 1902-1903 (p. 286).

Klamath Boundary Questions

For more detail on Klamath boundary questions than appears in Map II (p. 108), *see* U.S. Senate (1897). When the reservation was first surveyed in 1871, certain lands were omitted that the tribe had understood their 1864 treaty to have reserved (some of these excluded lands were highly valued for grazing by nearby ranchers). Soon discovering the exclusion, the Klamaths complained to federal officials. On July 4, 1884 Congress appropriated funds for a second survey, completed four years later by William Thiel; Thiel also excluded most of the disputed lands on the eastern side of the reservation. The disagreement continued unresolved until 1896, when a congressionally designated boundary commission made a new study. The government then suggested that the tribe, which had rights to all the land reserved by the 1864 treaty, should cede the difference between the treaty and 1888 survey lines to the United States. In 1901 the tribes agreed, reluctantly. This agreement, ratified by the Act of June 21, 1906, compensated the tribe with $537,007 for the 621,824-acre difference, or 86 cents an acre. In the

The people who settled on the Klamath Reservation were mostly members of Klamath, Modoc, Pit River, Shasta and Northern Paiute bands of southern Oregon and northern California. A few Mollale and Chinook people from the north and west later came to reside at Klamath as well. As indicated by agent reports, the general atmosphere during the early reservation years was unsettled, when certain Paiute groups would leave for seasonal food gathering and still other militant Paiutes raided the reservation. The political amalgamation of so many different people was not easy; the Modocs were especially bitter at being forced to live on what was traditionally Klamath territory. The rebellion of Captain Jack and his Modoc followers in the 1872–73 war clearly demonstrated the Indians' resistance to reservation policy. By 1875, however, all of the Indian peoples on the reservation were commonly known as the "Klamath Tribe."

Adjusting to reservation life brought many new elements into Klamath life. Government agents tried to outlaw certain native practices and broke up families by requiring Klamath children to attend far-away federal boarding schools. Many older leaders were replaced by younger, more acculturated people. Although the Indians continued to rely heavily on hunting, fishing and gathering for their livelihood, they gradually entered the American "money economy" and acquired many new goods and skills. Slowly the tribe was transforming its economic base into thriving stock and timber enterprises.

In their 1864 treaty, the tribe had retained about 1.1 million acres for their reservation while ceding over 13 million acres to the United States (*see* map I, p. 108). Many invasions of this land base took place in the following decades, and each struggle to regain their lands helped unify the large Klamath tribe.

One long battle was based on the Klamath's understanding that reservation treaty boundaries ran from "peak to peak to peak," while different government surveyors excluded treaty lands by adopting straight lines between certain points (*see* map II, p. 108). This was resolved only when the tribe accepted the smaller boundaries of an 1888 survey and received a payment for the excluded 621,824-acre difference in 1906 (map II shows this lost land in black). The 1906 payment for this large area amounted to only 86 cents an acre, however, and more fair compensation was not paid until the Indian Claims Commission granted the tribe an award in 1969.

Another land exclusion occurred within the reservation itself. Beginning with an 1864 congressional land-grant for the construction of the Oregon Central Military Road, the tribe lost substantial lands in the heart of the reservation as parts of this road were constructed. Fraudulent land patents on the road's right-of-way lands by a land company followed. The United States twice tried to stop this in court, but did not succeed. Settlers purchasing the road's right-of-

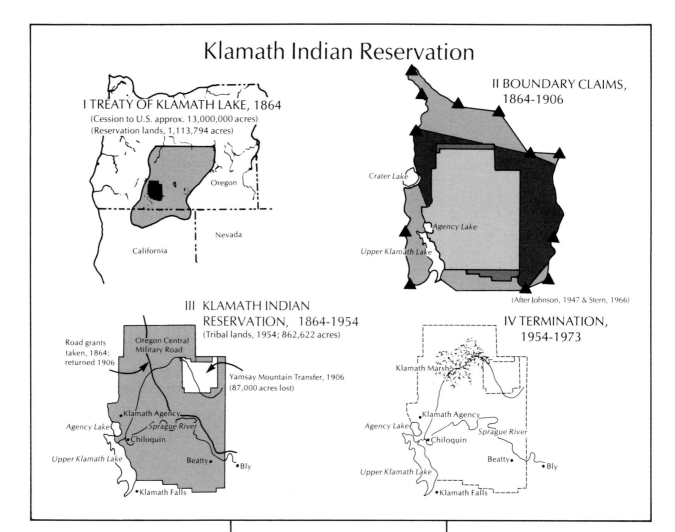

# Klamath Indian Reservation

## I TREATY OF KLAMATH LAKE, 1864
(Cession to U.S. approx. 13,000,000 acres)
(Reservation lands, 1,113,794 acres)

Oregon

Nevada

California

## II BOUNDARY CLAIMS, 1864-1906

Crater Lake

Agency Lake

Upper Klamath Lake

(After Johnson, 1947 & Stern, 1966)

## III KLAMATH INDIAN RESERVATION, 1864-1954
(Tribal lands, 1954; 862,622 acres)

Road grants taken, 1864; returned 1906

Oregon Central Military Road

Yamsay Mountain Transfer, 1906 (87,000 acres lost)

Klamath Agency
Agency Lake
Sprague River
Chiloquin
Upper Klamath Lake
Beatty
Bly
Klamath Falls

## IV TERMINATION, 1954-1973

Klamath Marsh

Klamath Agency
Agency Lake
Chiloquin
Sprague River
Beatty
Bly
Upper Klamath Lake
Klamath Falls

---

KEY

II BOUNDARY CLAIMS

☐ Survey, 1871

☐ Additional area claimed by tribes (Understanding of 1864 treaty: "From peak to peak to peak")

☐ Added by 1888 survey

■ Cession 1906: loss of 621,824 acres

IV TERMINATION

Federal Termination Act, 1954
End of federal services to 2,113 people, 1961
U.S. buys most tribal lands for Winema National Forest & Klamath Forest Wildlife Preserve, 1961/1973 (hunting & fishing rights retained)

MAP: KLAMATH INDIAN RESERVATION

Map I is from Royce; O. H. Johnson's; and Stern's (1966) maps were used to compile map II. Maps III and IV were derived from Stern (1966).

Reservation acreage data is from U.S. Senate (1897); *Klamath and Moadoc Tribes et al* v. *United States* (1935, 1938); U.S. House (1954); and O. H. Johnson.

Note: acreage figures will show discrepancies if Maps I, II and III are compared. All published Klamath acreage figures are, at best, approximate and are derived from fairly dated sources such as the 1897 U.S. Senate committee report.

PHOTOGRAPH:
Klamath families in dugout canoes. (OHS neg. 35789)

following years the tribes attempted to obtain a more equitable payment. They lost their 1938 case (86 Ct.Cl. 614) because of jurisdictional problems. The issue was heard again under the provisions of the ICC in Docket 100-A (*see* chart, pp. 116-21); and in 1969 a judgement for $4,162,992 (less $374,669 for legal fees) was awarded for the unconscionable 1906 payment (21 ICC 343). *See Klamath & Moadoc Tribes & Yahooskin Band of Snakes* v. *United States* (1938); U.S.Senate (1897); Stern (1966); and O. H. Johnson.

### Yamsay Mountain Case

As with the boundary disputes, this exceedingly complex case took years to resolve. The Klamaths agreed to their treaty in 1864. In a separate action that year, Congress authorized construction of the Oregon Central Military Road from Eugene to eastern Oregon's Owyhee district, granting the state some 800,000 acres (in alternate sections) for this purpose. The proposed road passed through the heart of reserved Klamath lands.

The land-grant rights soon passed from the state of Oregon to California and Oregon Land Company, and in the 1870s homesteaders began to settle on the proposed road's right-of-way lands. Not only were these lands ideal for tribal stock pasturage, later they were designated for allotment to individual Indians and so the land title problems worsened. The federal government stepped into the conflict by bringing a suit against the land company, alleging that the road was not actually being built and that the government certificates authorizing issuance of property patents had been fraudulently obtained. But the Supreme Court ruled that regardless of possible earlier fraud, the land com-

way lands in the Sprague River Valley threatened the tribe's winter stock pasturage and delayed allotment for several years. When Congress finally returned the road acreage to the tribe in 1906, it righted its wrong with another wrong, giving the land company who last owned the road acreage an 87,000-acre "transfer" of prime forest land from the reservation's northeast corner (map III, p. 108). Again the tribe was paid too little for land that was confiscated and another series of lawsuits ensued (known as the Yamsay Mountain Case) until the Supreme Court awarded compensation to the tribe in 1938.

Allotment occurred mainly in the period 1908–10 at Klamath, but the tribal surplus (unallotted) lands were not opened to outsiders, and the tribe was able to hold onto one of the finest stands of ponderosa (yellow) pine in the western United States. The BIA later began commercial harvests of this tribal resource, and by the 1950s, members were receiving up to $800 per capita annually from their timber sales.

The timber receipts and allotment policy had many profound effects at Klamath. Ranching declined as many people leased or sold their allotments. They, along with absentee members and those people born after the closure of allotment rolls (1910), comprised a landless group increasingly dependent on the timber as a major source of income. Additionally, the tribal government had to deal with some factional problems and membership questions at a time when it was already at odds with the federal government over reservation management issues. Outsiders often misperceived the Klamath people and their supposed wealth. Although there were great disparities in education, skills and income among tribal members, pany had purchased the titles in "good faith" and dismissed the case. See U.S. v. *California and Oregon Land Co.* (1904), 192 U.S.325.

The secretary of the Interior then investigated the controversy and recommended compensation to the tribe. The Act of June 21, 1906 authorized return of the land-grants (inside the reservation) to the tribe but at the same time it gave 87,000 unallotted acres near Yamsay Mountain as compensation to the land company for its loss. This transfer, made without knowledge or consent of the Indians, outraged the tribe. Two years later the Act of April 30, 1908 awarded them $108,750; they were pressured into accepting a release for this small amount in 1909. Of course the 87,000 acres had a much higher value and so the tribe continued to seek fair settlement. In 1920 they were granted jurisdiction to sue in the Court of Claims, but their first suit was dismissed on jurisdictional grounds. See *Klamath & Moadoc Tribes et al* v. *U.S.* (81 Ct.Cl. 79, 1935). On May 15, 1936 a new congressional act allowed them to file suit again, irrespective of any prior release or settlement. This time the Yamsay Mountain case was decided in favor of the tribe; the fair value of the 87,000 acres was assessed at $2,980,000, less the 1908 payment and government offsets. See *U.S.* v. *Klamath & Moadoc Tribes et al* (304 U.S. 119, 1938).

For more detail, see the court cases listed above, O. H. Johnson (pp. 185-86); and Stern (1966). The settlement was divided between some individual payments for tribal members, a special payment to unallotted members and the establishment of a tribal loan fund.

non-Indian society tended to focus only on their progress as alleged timber barons.

Then, in 1954, Congress terminated the Klamath Tribe's federal status. The lawmakers' decision to end trust responsibilities to Indians capitalized on certain political differences in the tribe at this time. The termination legislation was rushed through, and was faulty; it had to be amended twice before it became effective in 1961. (More details on national termination policy are on pp. 134-35 of "Recent U.S. Indian Policy.")

Under the termination law, Klamath people were required to choose whether to remain in the tribe as wards of a private bank or withdraw and receive payment for their share of the tribal lands. Termination affected 2,133 people and their remaining 862,622 acres of reservation land. Worn out by the wrangling and misled about the ultimate effects of termination, 78 percent of the members withdrew. Private companies bought some of their lands but most of the reservation became the Winema National Forest (map IV). The payments these people received were for the sale of their tribal lands, not a pay-off for the end of federal services.

The 474 persons who remained under the trusteeship of the U.S. National Bank of Oregon became dissatisfied with this arrangement. In 1965 and 1969, balloting by these persons moved them toward the eventual dissolution of this trust. Some requested their shares of the remaining tribal forest in land, rather than receiving only money payments from a forced sale of these last lands. Yet this option was not allowed and the federal government purchased most of the lands in 1973.

Obviously, no federal law can tell an individual that he or she is no longer an Indian. Many Klamath organizations have worked to maintain tribal goals and have considered seeking a restoration of federal tribal status. In the furor over the monetary aspects of the termination period, the social and economic problems that hit many people after the withdrawal of federal services in 1961 were ignored. Termination did not end the tribe's hunting and fishing rights on their former lands (*Kimball* v. *Callahan*, 1969) nor did it bar any legitimate claims settlements from the Indian Claims Commission. As they overcome much of the damage caused by termination in the 1960s, the Klamath Tribal Council and several other community groups continue to promote Indian education, health and traditional values in the 1980s.

Allotment, Tribal Timber and Klamath Economy

Although there was a timber boom in the first part of this century, tribal timber profits slumped during the Depression years. The difference in the wealth of those able to retain their allotments and those more reliant on the timber sales for income increased. While development programs and Klamath helped the tribe's economic standing, questionable BIA timber management occurred and prompted the tribe to file a timber mismanagement claim with the Indian Claims Commission (*see* Docket 100-B-2, in chart pp. 120-21). For more details, *see* Stern (1966, pp. 183-235); Zakoji (1953, pp. 153-55); Bunting & Trulove (1970); Trulove; and Kephart.

Termination

National termination policy is discussed on pages 134-35 and in accompanying source notes. *See also* Kickingbird & Ducheneaux (pp. 160-78); Hood; Stern (1966, pp. 236-66); McNickle & Fey (pp. 138-47); Oregon State Dept. of Education (1961); Marchington; Egerton; and OHS MSS 779. The original bill for Klamath termination, S. 2745, was passed on August 13, 1954 (PL 586, ch.732, 68 Stat. 718); it was amended on August 14, 1957 and again on August 23, 1958.

Congress had decreed that a management plan be effected for the Klamaths remaining in the tribe, without BIA supervision, after 1964. These remaining members' assets were put into a trust managed by the U.S. National Bank of Oregon, which continued until a majority of the members, unhappy with the bank's performance, voted to dissolve the trust in 1969. Dissatisfactions from termination also arose from the questionable way in which tribal approval of ter-

mination had been obtained and from the inadequacies of training programs mandated by the termination act. *See* the various hearings and House and Senate reports on termination legislation as summarized in Hood; and AIPRC *Final Report of Task Force Ten* (1976).

Recent Developments

Local Klamath programs have tackled issues and problems on several fronts, including improved education of children and adults, social services and health. Information is best obtained from tribal members or through publications such as *Mukluks Hemcunga* ("Indian Talk"), a newspaper published in Klamath Falls. Parents investigating discrimination and the Indian drop-out rate in Klamath and Chiloquin high schools in 1961 formed a group called the "Para-Board," a forerunner of later Indian organizations (personal communication, Annabelle Bates, Fort Bidwell).

*Also see* U.S. Federal Trade Commission (1974) for a report on consumer problems and discrimination. The tribe litigated its right to hunt and fish on the former reservation lands (*see Kimball* v. *Callaghan*, 1974, 1979; "Hunting, Fishing & Gathering Rights," Part Three, pp. 160-64). The Southern Oregon Indian Research Group was formed in May 1978. Many other local groups working on issues important to Indians exist in the Klamath region. Refer to the profiles included in this volume. *Also see* the Act of August 16, 1973; and hearings on the federal purchase of the Klamath forest.

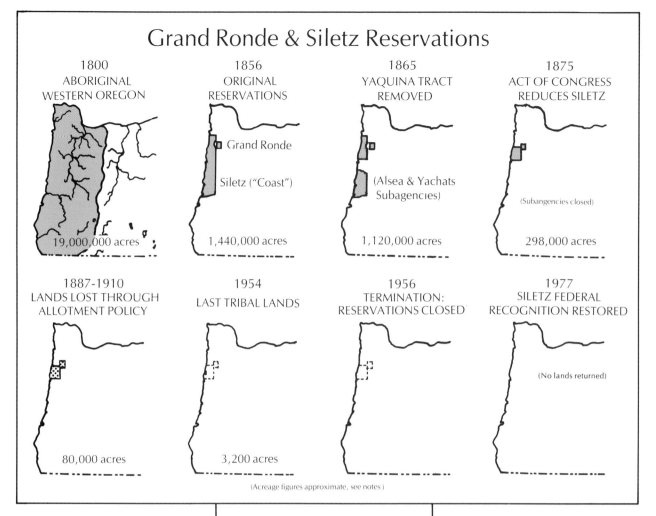

# Grand Ronde & Siletz Reservations

**1800**
ABORIGINAL
WESTERN OREGON

19,000,000 acres

**1856**
ORIGINAL
RESERVATIONS

Grand Ronde

Siletz ("Coast")

1,440,000 acres

**1865**
YAQUINA TRACT
REMOVED

(Alsea & Yachats
Subagencies)

1,120,000 acres

**1875**
ACT OF CONGRESS
REDUCES SILETZ

(Subangencies closed)

298,000 acres

**1887-1910**
LANDS LOST THROUGH
ALLOTMENT POLICY

80,000 acres

**1954**
LAST TRIBAL LANDS

3,200 acres

**1956**
TERMINATION:
RESERVATIONS CLOSED

**1977**
SILETZ FEDERAL
RECOGNITION RESTORED

(No lands returned)

(Acreage figures approximate, see notes)

MAP: GRAND RONDE AND SILETZ INDIAN RESERVATIONS

The information on these maps is based on Royce; Plummer; Work; Barth; U.S. Senate (1976); and CIA annual reports. Since acreage figures vary from source to source, those presented here involve some guesswork.

Acreage figures for Aboriginal Western Oregon map comes from Loy. Originally, Grand Ronde had 59,759 acres, and Siletz, 1,382,400 (U.S. Senate 1954). The opening of the Yaquina tract for Willamette Valley commerce and oyster production at Newport in 1865 measured some 25 miles north-south and 20 east-west (*Alcea v. U.S.*, 59 F. Supp. 934, 952, 1945). After Congress closed the Alsea subagency and removed lands on the northern and southern ends of Siletz in 1875, the remaining reservation comprised, according to different sources, either 225,000 acres (CIA 1893, p. 607), 225,280 acres (Beckham 1977), or 239,462 acres (Plummer). Following allotment, Siletz surplus lands, ceded to the government in 1892 and confirmed by Congress on August 15, 1894, constituted a loss of 191,798 acres (ICC Docket 239). Grand Ronde's surplus lands, taken in 1901 and confirmed by the Act of April 21, 1904, consisted of 26,111 acres (U.S. Senate 1954). By 1954, remaining Siletz tribal lands totaled 2,598 acres. The reservation's agency, cemetery and school were on 39.23 acres at Government Hill, deeded to the town of Siletz in 1956. At Grand Ronde, 597 acres remained by 1954. Individual allotments still in trust just before termination totaled 5,390 acres at Siletz and 800 at Grand Ronde (U.S. Senate 1954). Beckham (1977, pp. 171-87) chronicles most land issues; while *Alcea v. U.S.* (1945) and testimony in ICC 239 outline the legislation affecting these reservation lands.

Unratified Treaties

While some of the tribes at Siletz and Grand Ronde had ratified treaties, others did not; this caused a number of problems (see "Treaty-Making in Oregon"; and the maps on p. 112). The following tribes signed the unratified 1851 treaties but did not later obtain ratified agreements: Clatsop, Nehalem, Tillamook, NucQueeChahWe-Muck Chinook, Kathlamet, Waukikum and Wheelappa Chinook. Coastal groups signing the unratified 1855 treaty included various Tututni bands, Chetco, Coquille, Coos, Umpqua, Siuslaw, Salmon River, Siletz, Yaquina and Alsea bands or tribes. Various congressional acts and court decisions later granted limited reimbursement—which many tribes considered inadequate—for native lands taken in unratified treaties (payments made between 1894 and 1912 averaged between $1,500 and $10,500 per tribe). See Chronology (1861, 1875, 1894, 1912); and the ICC Cases chart on pages 116-21 for Dockets 234, 238, 239 and 240 concerning western Oregon tribes. The Coos, Lower Umpqua and Siuslaw tribes were never paid for their lands (see Coos et al v. U.S., 1938).

Early Reservation Years

The diversity of Indians at Grand Ronde and Siletz reservations is best described by Beckham (1971b, 1977); other sources include Harger; Heckert; and Kent. For a guide to agency records see David W. Owens; see also manuscript records at the Oregon Historical Society (OHS/MSS 442); and the many agency reports in CIA annual reports.

# GRAND RONDE AND SILETZ INDIAN RESERVATIONS

Most tribes and bands of the inland valleys and south coast were isolated on the Grand Ronde and Siletz reservations by late 1856. A few people eluded the military roundups following the last of the Rogue River wars in southwestern Oregon, but even the groups who remained peaceful had to leave their native lands for the unfamiliar northern reserves. Only Clatsop, Tillamook and Penutian-speaking groups of the central coast still lived in their old villages after the Coos and Lower Umpqua were forced to move to the southern part of the Siletz Reservation (or Alsea/Yachats Subagency) in 1859.

There were many hardships during the early reservation years when the diverse populations spoke many languages and shared limited food resources. Although the original Coast (Siletz) Reservation was sizable, its mountainous terrain and the cool marine climate precluded almost all farming. Agriculture was a little more successful on the other side of the Coast Range at Grand Ronde, but the same early problems existed: serious diseases, forced labor and poor or non-existent farming tools. Hunger and death were common and the Indian agents recorded many escapes from the reservations.

Nearly three-fourths of the people at Siletz were highly dissatisfied, and for a significant reason: the U.S. Senate failed to ratify the 1855 Coast Treaty that had ceded more than 11 million acres of their lands to the United States. While the few groups with ratified treaties received the small payments and supplies that had been promised, the majority anxiously waited to have their uncertain federal status resolved. But the treaty ratification never occurred, and these Indians were never paid for their lands.

Siletz originally contained 1,382,400 acres while Grand Ronde covered an area of almost 60,000 acres. Three-quarters of this land base was lost between 1865 and 1910 (see maps, opposite), causing further economic hardships and displacement within and away from the reservations.

As their land base shrank, some people left the reservations for their original homelands, joining others who had either escaped earlier or who had never gone to the reservations. Thus scattered groups of western Oregon Indians receiving little or no federal recognition and assistance increased yearly. The large 1875 reduction of Siletz lands uprooted even more people; many from Tillamook and Nehalem bays remained on the coast while others moved to Grand Ronde for government services. Some Indians from the south moved up to the crowded Siletz Agency while others tried to homestead among the incoming non-Indians at Newport. Most Coos, Lower Umpqua and Siuslaw families simply returned to their old homes around Coos Bay and on the Siuslaw River—but their homes

Several military forts were established on or near the reservations, serving to protect Indians from hostile settlers and to prevent Indians from escaping. After the closures of forts Yamhill, Hoskins and Umpqua, Indians generally could leave Siletz and Grand Ronde freely. See Barth; Beckham (1917a); Hoop; and J. G. Lewis.

Administration of the new reservations was unsatisfactory, as Rogue leader George Harney told a government inspector in 1873:

"Agents have often promised many things but never performed their *promises*. I want the President to give us a mill. I want the whites to stop troubling us about our land and removing us. What have we done? All that is sorry in my heart I tell you. I want to tell President that the Indians desire to remain here. We do not want to be driven away. We were driven here, and now this is our home, and we want to stay. The most of our people have never been paid for their lands. Now they want to be paid. We want schools for our children. *We do not want blankets and tobacco and shirts sent here*. We can buy such things. We want teams, tools, Wagons, & c., sent here—something to work with. We want plows, harness, &c. instead of tobacco, blankets, shirts and other goods as are sent here" (U.S. Senate 1874).

Off the Reservations

Western Oregon's non-reservation Indians have had a strained and ambiguous relationship with the United States. Some were forced off the reservations, while others never moved there. See Bakken; Beckham (1977); Heckert; Taylor & Suphan; Ruby & Brown (1976); Coos-Lower Umpqua-Siuslaw Tribe; and Cow Creek Band of Umpquas.

were not the same isolated lands that had supported them in generations past.

Allotment policy (*see* discussions on pp. 73-74, 95) caused the next drastic reduction when surplus lands not parceled out to individuals at Siletz and Grand Ronde were reluctantly ceded to the United States in 1892 and 1901. The tribes lost over 230,000 acres of land in this process and received incredibly low payments in return (84 cents an acre at Siletz). Inheritance complications on their allotments, tax sales and basic poverty in the following decades forced many people to sell their 80- or 160-acre tracts. By 1954, western Oregon Indians owned little more than their remaining reservation allotments, small tribal reserves and a few thousand acres of public-domain allotments that had been issued to some of the forgotten non-reservation people during the 1890s.

Congress terminated the federal status of all western Oregon Indian tribes in 1954 (*see* pp. 134-35 for more background on this policy). Although termination meant that all historic ties between the United States and tribal governments would end, many Indians had no say in this decision and others were misled about its impact. The last tribal lands at Siletz and Grand Ronde were sold and members received only a few hundred dollars after deductions were made for various government services. Up and down the coast, people with limited incomes were now required to pay taxes on their allotments and many lost even these last lands. Federal services, already sharply reduced since the 1940s, ended with the closure of the reservations in 1956. The consequences of termination were deeply felt in the following years. Increasing numbers of people could not keep their allotted lands and moved away from their tribal centers. Having fewer educational and job advantages than the non-Indian population, they faced difficulties in the cities and often experienced much discrimination.

Although termination ended the legal relationship between these tribes and the federal government, individual Indians have kept their groups' concerns and traditions alive during the long years since 1954. Efforts to reorganize tribes in the late 1960s and early 1970s produced a new tribalism for Indians of western Oregon.

Tribal groups and councils are active in Portland and the Willamette Valley towns of Eugene, Salem and Springfield and in many coastal areas such as Siletz, Coos Bay, Coquille, Myrtle Point and Brookings. Their activities span a broad range of issues which are described in Part Three.

Among the notable achievements of western Oregon Indians are their many educational programs and manpower projects. They continue to assert their cultural and political separateness and maintain their reverence for the land. Burial sites are being preserved, including the Coos Bay ancestral cemetery, which was closed to the tribe for 111 years. At Siletz and Grand Ronde, the tribal councils began to reorganize, seeking out the people in their communities as well as those who left the reservation areas after termination.

During the 1890s, under the fourth section of the General Allotment Act, 5,406 acres of public-domain lands in southwestern Oregon were allotted to non-reservation Indians. In 1937, on 6.1 acres donated to the Indians in Empire/Coos Bay, the Bureau of Indian Affairs built a hall for the Coos-Lower Umpqua-Siuslaw Tribe. Some non-reservation Indians were able to send their children to the federal Indian school at Chemawa and, over the years, obtained limited services through different Roseburg, Salem and Portland BIA offices.

Termination in Western Oregon

The context of national termination policies is discussed on pp. 134-35 and in accompanying source notes. For *all* western Oregon Indians (reservation and non-reservation), termination legislation, passed on August 13, 1954, took effect in 1956. The number of people this act affected is undetermined, since tribal rolls in 1954 did not include non-reservation Indians. Consult the U.S. Senate & House hearings (1954) for legislative history. *See also* Beckham (1977); Washburn (1971); and AIPRC *Final Report of Task Force Ten* (1976) (chap. 4). The AIPRC concludes that in western Oregon, "the vast majority of Indians neither understood nor participated in the process that resulted in the loss of their land and means of livelihood, the disbanding of tribal government, and the loss of important welfare, educational and health services. Termination was intended to have a positive effect on the lives of Oregon Indians, yet no evidence was found which supported this conclusion" (p. 18).

Renewed Tribalism in Western Oregon Today

Consult local newspapers and Indian people for accurate information on

Without a doubt, the most encouraging development of the last decade was the 1977 federal restoration of the Siletz Tribe. Tribal members, in reorganizing their group and lobbying Congress, demonstrated their commitment to a tribal future that had been severely harmed by the termination act of 1954. As a federally recognized tribe, the Siletz are now entitled to all normal Indian health, education and economic development benefits, and have begun plans for the establishment of their new reservation. The title of a 1976 movie about the Siletz Tribe proclaims their energy and pride: "The People Are Dancing Again!"

recent events. An Indian program in Coos Bay publishes *Indian Education* on a monthly basis. The film, "The People Are Dancing Again" was made in 1976. *See also* Confederated Tribes of Siletz (1977); Beckham (1977); and profiles included in this book.

Siletz Restoration

The act restoring the legal status of the Confederated Tribes of Siletz was signed into law on November 18, 1977 after several years of energetic work by tribal members. Records of the restoration hearings (U.S. Senate 1976) contain excellent background and the personal testimony of many Siletz people.

PHOTOGRAPH:
Coastal family gathering oysters. (OHS neg. 36647)

# Indian Claims Commission Cases

| TRIBES & ICC DOCKET NO. | CLAIMS | ICC DECISION |
|---|---|---|
| CHINOOK TRIBE & BANDS #234 | To recover $30 million for 1850 value of Washington & Oregon lands; small 1912 payments were an unconscionable amount | Recovery allowed for 76,630 acres taken after 1851 unratified treaties, pending valuation, & less offsets of earlier payments. |
| KALAPUYA & GRAND RONDE COMMUNITY #238 | To recover value of 26,000 "surplus" acres ceded to U.S.; 1904 payment of $28,500 an unconscionable consideration | |
| CONFEDERATED SILETZ TRIBES #239 | To recover $10.1 million for value of 191,798 "surplus" acres ceded to U.S.; 1894 payment of $142,600 an unconscionable amount | Recovery allowed pending valuation & less earlier payment as offset |
| TILLAMOOK & NEHALEM BANDS OF TILLAMOOKS #240 | To recover value of lands taken by unratified 1851 treaties; payments in 1897 & 1912 an unconscionable amount | Recovery allowed for 233,750 acres taken 1851 less offsets of earlier payment |
| NEZ PERCE† #175 | To recover value of lands taken in Idaho, Oregon & Washington by 1855 treaty; paid an unconscionable consideration | COMPROMISE SETTLEMENT |

| VALUATION DIFFERENCES*<br>(price/acre) | FINAL AWARD & OFFSETS | |
|---|---|---|
| | | |
| Tribe: $9.00 (plaintiff)<br>U.S.: .33 (defendant)<br>ICC: .98 (final ruling) | $75,000<br>− 26,000 (paid in 1912)<br>− 6,441 (legal expenses)<br>$42,251 | |
| Tribe: $52.65<br>U.S.: .82<br>ICC: 3.00 | $416,240<br>− 48,269 (legal expenses)<br>$367,971 | *Land valuations are based on the date of taking. Deciding value is usually the second phase of a land claims case, after tribes prove that they had title to the land in question. Each party employs expert appraisers to determine the acreages involved & their value; these findings are submitted to the commission, who then makes a final determination on value. Compromise settlements do not have a valuation phase. |
| Tribe: $2.19<br>U.S.: .22<br>ICC: .85 | $190,187<br>− 21,000 (offsets)<br>− 38,472 (legal expenses)<br>$130,715 | |
| | $3,550,000<br>− 355,000 (legal expenses)<br>$3,195,000 | †Note: Other Nez Perce claims not listed here (#175-B, #179, #180, #180-A) involving alleged mismanagement of trust funds & property at Colville (Washington) & Lapwai (Idaho) reservations. |

# Indian Claims Commission Cases

| TRIBES & ICC DOCKET NO. | CLAIMS | ICC DECISION |
|---|---|---|
| #175-A | To recover value of lands ceded in 1863 treaty; paid an unconscionable amount; also alleges unfair & dishonorable dealings in acquisition of these lands | Allows recovery for 6,932,270 acres, pending valuation; a compromise agreement on offsets & earlier payments |
| SNAKE OR PAIUTE INDIANS OF FORMER MALHEUR RESERVATION #17 | To recover $3,500,000 for taking of former reservation in 1881; alternative claim: for unfair & dishonorable dealings in 1868 unratified treaty | Recovery allowed for 1,449,304 acres taken 1879; alternative claim dismissed |
| NORTHERN PAIUTE‡ #87 (Oregon tract) | To recover value of lands taken in southeastern Oregon and corners of northeast & northwest Nevada | Recovery allowed for certain lands north of 41°—part of a large settlement with numerous Paiute groups of Nevada & California; acreages defined but portions conflicting with other claims disallowed |
| COOS, LOWER UMPQUA & SIUSLAW #265 | To recover value of lands taken in unratified 1855 treaty | DISMISSED (Summary judgment on *res judicata*—tribes previously lost their 1938 Court of Claims suit on same claim; *see* 87 Ct Cl. & 143) |
| CONFEDERATED TRIBES OF WARM SPRINGS #198 | To recover $9.8 million for lands ceded in 1855; treaty paid unconscionable amount while tribes held over 10 million acres by Indian title | COMPROMISE SETTLEMENT<br>• after first ICC title findings contested<br>• no acreages or boundaries defined<br>• settlement not admissable as precedent in other cases<br>• no appeals for either party |
| #198-A | To recover compensation for fishing rights impaired by fraudulent 1865 treaty & the destruction of fishing sites | DISMISSED<br>• without prejudice, at tribes' request, 1970 |

| VALUATION DIFFERENCES* (price/acre) | FINAL AWARD & OFFSETS | |
|---|---|---|
| Tribe: $2.63<br>U.S.: .06<br>ICC: .67 | $4,650,000<br>− 492,394 (offsets)<br>− 415,760 (legal expenses)<br>$3,741,846 | |
| Tribe: $2.07<br>U.S.: .27<br>ICC: .40 | $579,722<br>− 90,451 (legal expenses)<br>$489,271 | |
| | $3,650,000 | |
| | $1,225,000<br>− 122,500 (legal expenses)<br>$1,102,500 | ‡Note: Docket #87 also had claims covering two large areas to the south of the "Oregon tract"; these claims decided separately. |

# Indian Claims Commission Cases

| TRIBES & ICC DOCKET NO. | CLAIMS | ICC DECISION |
| --- | --- | --- |
| CONFEDERATED UMATILLA TRIBES #264 | To recover value of lands ceded 1855—treaty paid an unconscionable amount; also compensation for other aboriginal lands taken in addition to 1855 treaty cession | COMPROMISE SETTLEMENT • for all claims in #264, #264-A, & 264-B after first ICC title finding disputed • no findings on acreage or boundaries • not admissable as precedent • no appeals |
| #264-A | For loss of fish & water due to dam construction in Umatilla River & U.S. failure to adjudicate treaty fishing rights | |
| #264-B | To recover value of 85 square miles excluded from reservation by faulty 1871 survey | |
| KLAMATH, MODOC & YAHOOSKIN SNAKES #100 | To recover value of lands ceded in 1864 treaty; paid an unconscionable consideration | COMPROMISE SETTLEMENT • no findings on title since area of "Yahooskin" problematic & certain to be disputed |
| #100-A | To recover additional compensation for 621,824 acres excluded from reservation by faulty surveys; paid an unconscionable consideration of 86 cents/acre in 1906 | Recovery allowed pending valuation & less offsets of 1906 payment |
| #100-C | For mismanagement concerning grazing and right-of-way issues in reservation | COMPROMISE SETTLEMENT |
| #100-B-1 | For mismanagement of tribal funds & other (non-forest) property | COMPROMISE SETTLEMENT |
| #100-B-2 | For mismanagment of the Klamath Forest, including: 1) timber sales claim 2) harvest claim (undercutting) 3) sawmill claim 4) insect infestation control 5) fire protection | COMPROMISE SETTLEMENT |

| VALUATION DIFFERENCES* (price/acre) | FINAL AWARD & OFFSETS | |
|---|---|---|
| | $2,450,000<br>−  245,000 (legal expenses)<br>$2,205,000 | |
| | $2,500,000<br>−  215,000 (legal expenses)<br>$2,285,000 | |
| Tribe:  $10.48<br>U.S.:    3.87<br>ICC:    7.56 | $4,700,000<br>−  537,007 (offsets)<br>−  374,669 (legal expenses)<br>$3,788,324 | |
| | $785,000<br>−  70,650 (legal expenses)<br>$714,350 | |
| | $18,000,000 | |
| | | SOURCES<br>Native American Rights Fund, *Decisions of the Indian Claims Commission*;<br>*Decisions of the Indian Claims Commission*;<br>Expert Testimony in Indian Claims Commission Cases (on microfiche, Lewis & Clark Law School, Portland, OR). |

CLAIMS CASES
Claims Before 1946

The U.S. Court of Claims was established in 1863, but it was not until the Act of May 20, 1924 that claims based on treaty violations were brought under Court of Claims jurisdiction. Narrow language and unclear relief provisions of the separate congressional acts for each claim made litigation slow and costly; by the 1940s, only 142 such acts had been passed. According to one authority on early claims cases, 71 suits were dismissed while only $20 million in compensation (about 1.3 percent of the total compensation requested in all claims) had been recovered by Indian tribes (see U.S. House, 1945, p. 98). Discussion of aboriginal title and land claims are in Cohen (1947); and Sutton (pp. 92-113; this source also includes an excellent bibliography).

Indian Claims Commission Act

Congress created the ICC on August 13, 1946. Five years were allowed for the filing of tribal claims. (Claims arising after 1946 are heard by the Court of Claims.) Due to the complex litigation, the commission, originally composed of three members, was expanded to five. The extensive hearings that preceded passage of the Claims Commission Act are in U.S. House, 1945; see also Lurie; and Wilkinson.

Claims Results and Obstacles

Incisive critiques of the procedural delays and other problems with the claims cases are in Deloria (1974, pp. 207-28); Coulter (pp. 9-11); and Iowa Law Review (1972, pp. 1300-19). O. C. Stewart (1966, p. 1195) discusses the uneven payments for native lands in southern Oregon. A lively exchange between Claims Commissioner Brantley Blue and a symposium of tribal leaders was transcribed

# CLAIMS CASES

The history of Oregon Indians after 1800 reveals that the tribes had numerous reasons for suits against the federal government. Many people never received payment for their lands while others were paid too little for their treaty cessions. Other claims arose from illegal reductions of reservation lands or the mismanagement of tribal funds and properties. Yet Indian tribes did not always have the right to present their grievance claims to a judicial tribunal. Under an 1863 law, a tribe could not sue in the United States Court of Claims unless it first obtained a special jurisdictional act from Congress. In effect, this discriminatory practice meant that Indian people had to argue their cases twice, once in Congress and again in court.

Those few tribes that did receive permission to sue in the Court of Claims encountered further difficulties. Sometimes the acts allowing them to bring suit limited the kinds of claims they could present and the type of relief available. Some Oregon tribes had their cases dismissed because of such jurisdictional problems. Another impediment stemmed from the practice of offsetting the supposedly gratuitous expenditures that the government had made for tribal welfare against the damage awards a tribe was entitled to receive. Thus after the Confederated Warm Springs Tribes won a 1941 case for land excluded from their reservation, federal deductions for past services turned out to be greater than the final award and so the tribes received no payments at all.

Dissatisfaction with such a grievance system increased. Only one Court of Claims judgement ever reimbursed an Oregon group for federal taking of aboriginal lands. This was the famous Alsea Band of Tillamooks v. United States case (1945) in which Tututni, Chetco, Coquille and some Tillamook bands were belatedly paid for the lands they had ceded in the unratified 1855 Coast Treaty. The Coos, Lower Umpqua and Siuslaw people had signed the same 1855 treaty but due to legal technicalities they never gained a favorable judgement on their claim. To this day these tribes have not received payment for their original lands (see claims map, p. 124 and claims chart, pp. 116-21).

The inconsistencies common in the early Court of Claims cases eventually led to the creation of a special forum for the determination of Indian claims. In 1946 Congress authorized the new Indian Claims Commission to consider a wide variety of claims against the government, including moral questions not usually "recognized by any existing rule of law and equity."

Although the commission was set up as a temporary administrative agency to deal with the unusual legal issues of tribal claims, it generally acted much like a court by employing most of the mechanisms developed during the previous Indian cases in the Court of Claims. The commission was supposed to streamline procedures with an investigative division but this unit was not set up until 1968 and then a personnel freeze in government allowed only one person

by the Indian Historian Press (1974, pp. 214-44; the quote on p. 126 comes from p. 233 of this source). *See also* Gamino; and Washburn.

Land Returns and Alternatives to the Claims System

Most claims based on historical wrongs have been litigated although a few cases remain under consideration by the U.S. Court of Claims. Increasingly, tribes are turning to other solutions for loss of essential land and resources. These include not only legislative land restorations (such as the return of the McQuinn Strip to Warm Springs or Mt. Adams to the Yakima) but also administrative actions permitting Indian entry and use of other federal lands and "surplus" sites. In short, besides payment for lands lost, tribes are also seeking some kind of assurance, "that a way of life that was nearly lost be protected from further depredations" (Deloria 1974, p. 228).

The claims system compensates only partially for an injury in the past and cannot address the more complex social and economic difficulties which Indians encounter today. As stated in the *Iowa Law Review* (1972): "The resolution of these problems will require considerable effort and American society would err in assuming that the Indian Claims Commission is coping with them" (p. 319). Reviews of alternative land restorations or protective actions are found in *American Indian Journal* (1978, pp. 45-48); *Congressional Record* (vol. 116, pp. 39586-610, 1970); and *NYU Law Review* (1972, pp. 1107-49). Richard A. Nielsen, discussing several recent land returns, comments on the difficulties of determining which claims warrant return and what lands should be returned. *See also* R. A. Hodge.

to be employed in this capacity. Tribes, typically handicapped by inadequate funds for good legal resources, again found themselves in strict adversarial proceedings before the Indian Claims Commission, arguing and rearguing every detail of their claims, sometimes with the delay of proving that they were "identifiable" groups of American Indians. Appeals of the commission's decisions were frequent, adding years to the already lengthy proceedings. Typical cases have run from eight to fifteen years.

Congress had envisioned that the commission would be able to hear and settle all of its claims in ten years, beginning in 1951. Due to the numerous and complicated cases, the life of the commission had to be extended five times. Out of the original petitions involving Oregon Indian groups, the Klamath Tribe still had an accounting claim pending before the Indian Claims Commission when its congressional authorization expired on September 30, 1978. This Klamath claim, other unfinished cases and any new tribal claims arising after 1946 have all been transferred to the Court of Claims.

How have Oregon tribes fared in their claims against the government? The claims map (p. 124) shows only those awards based on the illegal taking of native lands or for unconscionably low treaty payments while the claims chart (pp. 116-21) lists all tribal claims before the commission, for both land and other unfair dealings. Both the claims map and chart reflect sketchy results in this latest attempt to render justice to Oregon Indians.

Resolution of land claims in Oregon and elsewhere has been difficult for several reasons. Various groups of experts, including attorneys, anthropologists, historians and land appraisers, have had to prepare much technical evidence for the plaintiff tribes and the defendant United States government to prove or disprove the validity of numerous claims. Difficulty in procuring evidence, misinterpretations of historical records and certain inherent biases of the American legal system have sometimes led to unfavorable and much-disputed judgements.

One of the major stumbling blocks undoubtedly arises from the fundamental differences between Indian and non-Indian land-holding practices. When the final decision about who controlled how much land and its value one or two centuries ago is underlain by Euro-American property concepts, proving the validity of a tribe's claim is not easy. Frequently, historical records contain factual inaccuracies (such as geographical mistakes by explorers or incorrect descriptions of Indian life) that further complicate claims cases.

The dominant American property system does not easily incorporate alternative land use concepts of hunting, fishing and gathering peoples. The United States legal system requires that one Indian group prove that it always used and occupied all of its territory to the complete exclusion of all other Indian people. Such a standard is often at odds with the traditions and seasonal usage of land by many Indian peoples, and as a result the tribes receive less and less compensation for what they have lost. There is no payment for areas of "shared occupancy," for example. Commission findings in some

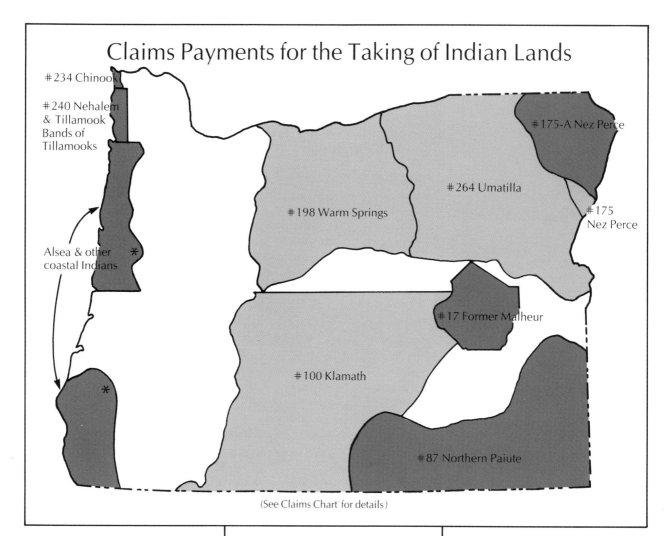

# Claims Payments for the Taking of Indian Lands

#234 Chinook

#240 Nehalem & Tillamook Bands of Tillamooks

Alsea & other coastal Indians

#198 Warm Springs

#264 Umatilla

#175-A Nez Perce

#175 Nez Perce

#17 Former Malheur

#100 Klamath

#87 Northern Paiute

(See Claims Chart for details)

KEY

▮ Claims Payments
▢ Compromise Payments
☐ No Payments
#000 Indian Claims Commission Docket Number
✳ Court of Claims, 1945

MAP: CLAIMS PAYMENTS FOR THE TAKING OF INDIAN LANDS
Chart: Indian Claims Commission Cases (pp. 116-21)

All data were obtained from the judgements on claims brought by Oregon tribes. The ICC decisions are available in printed form (Native American Rights Fund) and on microfiche (indexed by N. A. Ross, 1973a). Expert testimony and land appraisals are also available; see Ross (1973b); the Garland Publishing Company series of selected testimony, edited by Herbert C. Taylor, Jr., and Robert J. Suphan; and *Oregon Indians I* and *II* (the latter volume containing Robert J. Suphan's report on middle Oregon Indians, for example). To obtain further information on the ICC, write to the U.S. Court of Claims, Washington, D.C.

parts of Oregon (such as the John Day drainage or the Lower Columbia) were so confused that the commissioners refused to pay any group or drastically reduced the territory for which awards might have been allowed. Sometimes the long proceedings and appeals to the Court of Claims led to compromise settlements in the land claims cases. These compromises frequently occurred when the commission was apt to draw extremely reduced boundaries for the native territory in question. No final boundary determinations were made in the Klamath, Warm Springs and Umatilla land cases (Dockets Nos. 100, 198, 264) and so the map on page 124 illustrates only the areas these tribes alleged were theirs before United States acquisition.

Although the 1946 Indian Claims Commission Act did not specify what type of compensation tribes should receive, the commission has limited relief to monetary awards. Any payments that Oregon tribes received on their claims did not, of course, alter their basic rights or status as Indians, and no amount of money can make up for the loss of tribal homelands, as was remarked over 100 years ago by a Walla Walla leader: "Goods and the earth are not equal." Monetary judgements have seldom altered the poverty plaguing many Indian communities. The descendants of the Malheur Paiutes, for example, received only $743 each for the confiscation of their 1.8 million-acre reservation in the 1880s.

Not only did rulings minimizing the extent of tribal territories contribute to reduced awards, but the valuation of Indian lands at the date of taking (usually in the last century) has been very low: Nez Perce lands in 1863 were valued at only 67 cents an acre. (See claims chart on pp. 116-21 for wide differences in proposed valuations during land claims cases.) Moreover, the awards pay interest only on a small class of claims.

Inconsistencies in law and justice are apparent throughout the history of U.S. Indian claims cases. A few Oregon tribes were not allowed to present their claims to the commission and sometimes one tribe profited at the expense of another. Groups whose claims were tried later, benefited from improved legal advice as well as from the failed claims of less fortunate tribes.

But while the court cases grind on, and what was once landmark legislation creating the Indian Claims Commission fades with its uneven results, Indian people continue to seek resolutions for their problems. Besides pursuing their legitimate claims in court, they continue to struggle to obtain secure land bases for themselves and their children. Several land restorations, based on varied claims and legal grounds, have taken place in recent years: in New Mexico, Taos Blue Lake, 1970; in Oregon, the Paiute land title transfer of 1972 and the Warm Springs McQuinn Strip restoration of 1972; in Washington, Yakima's Mount Adams restoration; in Rhode Island, the innovative federal-state-tribal arrangement creating the 1,800-acre Narragansett Reservation in 1978; in Maine, the 1980 Penobscot-Passamaquoddy land settlement act.

Indian tribes continue to work toward a time when the mechanisms of all federal law and policy will be fully used to assist their communities. Perhaps one leader best summarized the current intricacies of people, land and law at a 1974 Indian symposium on the claims commission:

Indeed there must be another method of justice. What this method is, I cannot explore now, but certainly paying 47 cents an acre, 27 cents, or one dollar and twenty-five cents an acre does not mete out justice to the Indian people. Once that's recognized, the continued existence of the Indian Claims Commission is questionable. Our position is that the quickest and best action must come and will come if it comes at all, from Congress. You in the Indian Claims Commission have got the law. That's your framework. It constitutes your rule of operations. That's the law. You have to stand on it. There's very little else you can do, no matter how much heart is in the right place and direction. You're working within the framework of the law. But in this society, today, the law is going to have to stretch, or the people will make it stretch.

# OREGON INDIANS

## PART THREE

### CONTEMPORARY

PHOTOGRAPH:
Warm Springs representatives signing the Celilo Fishing Rights Settlement, 1952. (OHS neg. 44181)

# RECENT U.S. INDIAN POLICY

GENERAL SOURCES

Federal Indian policy is an expansive topic, encompassing nothing less than the long and complex history of relations between Indian tribes and the U.S. government. Some general introductions can be found in Debo; Deloria (1971); Getches, Rosenfelt & Wilkinson (chaps. 1, 2); Lieberman; McNickle; Prucha (1975); Washburn (1975); and AIPRC *Final Report* (1977). Lyman Tyler presents a historical outline of policy developments; and Prucha (1977) provides an annotated bibliography. Federal policy is discussed in the "Early U.S. Indian Policy in Oregon" and "Treaty-Making in Oregon" sections of this book.

Policy decisions and federal-tribal relations are shrouded in the details of federal Indian law. The fact that this specialized legal field exists reveals the impact that Congress and the courts have had on American Indian life. The basic reference on Indian law remains the monumental treatise written by Felix Cohen in 1942 (reprinted in 1971). Monroe Price prepared the first casebook in 1973; and Getches, Rosenfelt & Wilkinson have edited an ex-

The intent of most early federal Indian policies was to reduce and isolate tribal territories, and then force assimilation of Indian people into the mainstream of American culture. In the last few decades many Americans have been surprised to learn that Indian tribes, and Indian rights, have not simply faded away. A widespread misconception about American Indians has been that they are a vanishing race—a notion far from the truth. The American Indian population has actually grown since the late 1800s, nearly regaining the level estimated prior to European contact. Not only is there a growing Indian population, there are still more than 51 million acres of Indian trust lands in the United States; more than 650,000 acres of that is in Oregon.

Over 100 different tribes are represented in Oregon today, including many of the original tribes and bands of the region. Other Indian people affiliated with tribes all across the continent have moved here over the years. In addition to those Oregon tribes that have reservation lands in the state today, past policies and events have led to the creation of several other categories of tribes and tribal organizations. Many "landless" and "non-federally recognized" tribes were either left out of treaty signings or were later forgotten through historical errors. During the 1950s, through the policy of termination, some tribes lost their lands and federal recognition. These disruptions have contributed to the increasing number of Indian people moving to the cities, and nearly half of the state's Indian population now lives in urban areas of the Willamette Valley.

Since the 1960s there has been a resurgence of tribalism around the country. Many tribes have reorganized after years of inactivity, and a variety of organizations have formed to work on the special issues confronting Indian people—Indian education, health care, economic development and job training, all essential concerns.

cellent assemblage of major court decisions and seminal articles.

Current information on Indian law and policy developments can be found in the *Manual of Indian Law* (edited by Mary West); and in monthly issues of the *Indian Law Reporter*, both sources compiled by staff of the American Indian Lawyer Training Program (1712 N Street NW, Washington, D.C., 20556). Specific information on many Oregon Indian issues can be found in the official minutes and annual reports of the Oregon State Commission on Indian Services (454 State Capitol Building, Salem, Oregon 97310).

## SOVEREIGNTY AND THE TRUST RELATIONSHIP

Indian law is based on the concepts of tribal sovereignty and federal trust responsibility; these provide a backdrop against which policy decisions are viewed. Yet controversy surrounds the nature and evolution of these principles, and the limits of sovereignty and trust are often weighed against each other. Although some persons question whether tribes can be independently self governing while involved in a federal trust relationship, this conflict is not unresolvable. General sources include Cohen (1971, especially chaps. 1, 5, 7); Getches, Rosenfelt & Wilkinson (chaps. 4-6); and M. West (sect. A). The legal foundations of sovereignty and trust are analyzed in Burke's excellent article on the Cherokee cases. *Also see* Green & Work on sovereignty. Background to the development and expression of the trust relationship can be found in AIPRC *Final Report of Task Force One*; and in Chambers (1970, 1975). A thorough review of the history of trust obligations, in the form of a letter to Attorney General Griffin Bell (signed by numerous national Indian

Treaty rights continue to be a central issue, as they involve questions of reservation land and resource use, and tribal hunting and fishing privileges. Tribal governments are continuing to expand as they exercise their special jurisdictional status. All around the state and the country, Indian tribes and Indian organizations are working for the basic necessities and rights of Indian people, and they are attempting to do so in a manner consistent with the traditions and heritage of the past.

Relations with Indian tribes have been an important concern to the federal government since its inception. The United States Constitution itself (along with many other treaties and laws) established the principle that the federal government, and not the states, was responsible for all transactions with Indian tribes. The resultant federal-tribal relationship is unique and complex, and the legal status of Indian people today is unlike that of any other group in America.

Although Indian tribes today often work closely with state, county and local governments, the federal government still has the primary role in Indian affairs, and federal Indian policy is extremely important to tribes. Policies are simply general goals and guidelines that influence present and future decisions. A policy is an evolving thing—it changes. As U.S. Indian policy has changed over the years, tribes have experienced greatly differing treatment by the federal government. Indian people have felt the impact of policy changes in the form of removals, displacements to reservations, loss of tribal lands, unrequested reforms, termination of the federal relationship and relocation to urban areas. The present direction of federal Indian policy is one of self-determination for Indian people, and it is a refreshing and encouraging attitude. It remains to be seen how consistently this direction will be followed.

No single item can be said to determine Indian policy; it is a combination of past and present legislation, court decisions, administrative attitudes and historical happenstance. Recent policy here refers to events occurring since the 1950s, but decisions made in the past two centuries continue to influence current affairs.

## SOVEREIGNTY AND THE TRUST RELATIONSHIP

Two of the most central concepts that have evolved in federal-Indian relations, and which continue to underly policy directions today, are that Indian tribes have sovereign rights, and that there is a special trust relationship between Indian tribes and the federal government. The statement that tribes have sovereign rights is simple, but very important. It means that Indian tribes have separate governments from those of the United States. Tribes have the power to make their own laws, keep their own forms of court and council, determine the use of their land and property and exercise the many other rights of an independent government.

Yet the sovereignty of Indian tribes is not quite like that of other nations or the states. Tribal sovereignty was most clearly defined

leaders), is in the *Indian Law Reporter* 5 (Sept., 1978) pp. M45-M56.

## FEDERAL RECOGNITION

It is important to note that requirements for gaining federal recognition remain unspecified, and that the benefits of recognition continue to be both inconsistent and insecure. Bills concerning the establishment of specific procedures through which the existence of all Indian tribes would be acknowledged have been introduced to Congress several times. As of this writing, none have passed, but the issue will certainly not disappear.

more than 150 years ago when the Supreme Court referred to American Indian tribes as "distinct, independent, political communities," that have the right to govern their own affairs. Through treaties and agreements, many tribes relinquished their external powers of sovereignty—powers to act as completely separate nations—but they retained the right to be independently self-governing.

The trust relationship refers to the federal obligation to protect and enhance the people, the lands and the self-government of Indian tribes. The basis of the relationship is political, not racial; trust is the result of legal agreements and treaty obligations made by the United States over many years. During the treaty-making period the government began providing services in exchange for lands ceded by tribes. This eventually led to a general policy of assisting Indian tribes in their efforts to rebuild tribal governments and economies. The essence of the trust responsibility is the federal government's assistance in protecting tribal property and tribal rights. Many important services and programs are extended to tribes through this trust responsibility, but there is a problem: only federally recognized Indian tribes are included in the relationship.

## FEDERAL RECOGNITION

Federal recognition is one of the most troublesome issues affecting American Indian tribes today. Tribes that are officially recognized by the federal government are eligible for the benefits of the federal-Indian trust relationship; the government assists them in many ways and acknowledges their rights of self-government. Not all Indian tribes are federally recognized, however, and there is no uniform process to gain recognition.

In the past, the most common way to gain tribal recognition was through the establishment of reservations. A ratified treaty (as with the Tribes of Middle Oregon), an executive order (as with the Malheur Reservation), or an act of Congress granted formal recognition to the tribes involved, as part of a reservation agreement. But many groups that signed treaties did not receive official recognition; some treaties were never ratified, and in other instances records of treaty agreements were misinterpreted or lost. Tribes and bands that were not party to any treaty signings or reservation agreements later found it difficult to obtain recognition.

In addition, some tribes were denied recognition though the treaties they signed were ratified. The Cow Creek Band of Umpquas, for example, signed an 1853 treaty that was ratified, but the band was then split into two groups. One segment of the Cow Creeks was displaced to the Grand Ronde Reservation while the other remained in southwestern Oregon. Federal recognition was extended to the Grande Ronde Cow Creeks but it was denied to the other group until 1982.

A number of tribes that were once federally recognized have lost that status. As an example, the Malheur Reservation was closed in 1883 after the Bannock War, and the Paiute people there were not recognized again until 1968. In more recent years, tribes have lost federal recognition through termination legislation. More than 100 tribes and bands were affected by termination policy nationwide, but only two groups have since regained their recognized status: the Menominee in Wisconsin and the Confederated Tribes of Siletz in Oregon.

Of the organized tribes in Oregon today, only five are federally recognized. Of the more than 400 tribes still in existence across the nation, only some 290 are recognized. The Constitution of the United States, the Federal Trade and Intercourse acts and many other major federal documents that direct policy contain no reference to recognition of specific groups; they speak only of Indian tribes. But because of historical errors and an inconsistent Indian policy, the federal government presently limits the number of people that it will include in its trust relationships.

The simple act of recognition itself is one of the most important reasons why federal recognition is desirable; it is an acknowledgement of the special status and rights of an Indian tribe. Education and health programs, resource management, employment opportunities and legal aid are extremely important aspects of recognition. Although Indian people are eligible for all public services (since being granted United States citizenship in 1924), the federal government has a unique and continuing responsibility to them. Bureau of Indian Affairs and Indian Health Service programs are primarily available only to federally recognized tribes, though, and there are few additional services offering special assistance to non-federally recognized Indians. State agencies are often not prepared to work with the special needs of Indian people, and the confusion over federal recognition and the services it makes available sometimes leads to a situation where local public programs offer less assistance to Indians than to other citizens.

A major limit to full recognition of all tribes has been that many administrators believe the trust relationship is with the land, not the people, of Indian tribes. Tribes that have lost all their land frequently find themselves excluded from other important benefits of the trust responsibility. In order to place any regained land under trust status, or to acquire new land, a tribe must be federally recognized. Yet, at present, federal recognition is difficult to secure without a land trust! Even members of federally recognized tribes have a difficult time obtaining benefits of federal recognition if they move away from their trust lands.

In 1978 legislation was introduced to establish specific procedures for the recognition of all Indian tribes. Disagreements on the requirements for recognition temporarily stalled that bill, but the issue is certain to appear again.

## BUREAU OF INDIAN AFFAIRS TODAY

For general information, *see* Cahn & Hearne; Getches, Rosenfelt & Wilkinson (chap. 3); and AIPRC *Final Report* (1977). Some historical background can be found in Schmeckebier; and in Jackson & Galli.

Since the mid-1970s there have been repeated efforts to reorganize the bureau. Several hearings on "the proposed reorganization of the BIA" have been held by the U.S. Senate Select Committee on Indian Affairs (1976-77). Minutes of these hearings help illuminate some of the problems within the bureau. The quote on this page is from Getches, Rosenfelt & Wilkinson (p. 123).

## BUREAU OF INDIAN AFFAIRS TODAY

The Bureau of Indian Affairs is the primary agent responsible for administering the federal-Indian trust relationship. Congress, not the BIA, retains the ultimate authority over Indian affairs, and there are many other departments and agencies that offer assistance to Indian people (Health and Human Services, Housing and Urban Development, the Department of Agriculture and others). Yet the BIA is by far the most involved, providing a variety of services in the areas of education, employment assistance, resource use and the like. Although many programs are available, the BIA currently extends service only to those members of federally recognized tribes who are living on or near reservations.

As a part of the Department of the Interior, the BIA is headed by an assistant secretary of the Interior for Indian Affairs (this position was occupied by the commissioner of Indian Affairs prior to 1978). There are today 12 area offices in the country (the Portland office oversees Oregon, Washington and Idaho Indian matters), and 82 agencies (such as those on the Warm Springs and Umatilla reservations). There are nine major sections, and many divisions within each section, at every level of the bureau's organization (national, area and agency).

The BIA is one of the oldest bureaucracies in the federal government, and its structure has become complex and cumbersome. Since 1953, 75 different studies of the BIA have been completed, and all of them have confirmed and documented internal problems. The most recent study noted that between 78 and 90 percent of all funds Congress appropriates to the BIA go to internal administrative and management costs. Reorganization of the bureau is now in progress, but it will probably be some time before major changes take place.

Despite the many organizational problems and the limits to who is allowed to receive services, the BIA is important to Indian tribes as a realization of the federal government's obligation to uphold its trust committments. Some people believe that a poorly run bureau administering the trust responsibility is preferable to *no* bureau and the possibility of *no* trust committment. The BIA has had a vital role in the lives of American Indians for well over a century, and it will likely continue to be influential. As a recent book on federal Indian law points out: "It is no exaggeration to say that the Bureau of Indian Affairs' presence in Indian policy is a dominant force rivaled only by the State Department's presence in foreign policy."

## IMPACT OF TERMINATION

For historical background *see* AIPRC *Final Report of Task Force Ten* (sect. 4); Orfield; and Wilkinson & Biggs. Revealing information concerning the development of termination legislation is in Graham; and in U.S. House, H. reports 2503 and 2680. The author of House Concurrent Resolution 108 outlines his intentions in Watkins.

The impact of termination has not been fully documented. Some of the effects are reflected in Trulove & Bunting (re. Klamath); Sayers & Volkman (re. Siletz); and Beckham (1977, re. western Oregon groups). *Also see* AIPRC *Final Report of Task Force Ten* (sect. 2); and consult the discussion and notes regarding termination in Part Two of this volume.

## IMPACT OF TERMINATION

Federal Indian policy has been influenced by changes in the national political climate. In the 1950s there was widespread distrust of excessive government control and un-American customs or lifestyles. In light of this mood, tribalism, the reservation system and the trust relationship all became highly suspect. The reform era of the Indian Reorganization Act effectively ended when John Collier resigned, under pressure, as commissioner of Indian Affairs in 1945. Then in the late 1940s and the early 1950s Congress undertook several studies to determine how to rid itself of the "Indian problem" once and for all.

On August 1, 1953, House Concurrent Resolution 108 was passed, declaring it to be "the sense of Congress that ... [Indian tribes] ... should be freed from Federal supervision and control and from all disabilities and limitations specially applicable to Indians." This seemingly benign statement of policy was to have devastating effects. At the request of Congress, the BIA had developed criteria by which tribes were to be judged ready for their termination of federal supervision. HCR 108 authorized specific acts of legislation to accomplish its objectives. Between 1954 and 1962 thirteen termination bills were passed, affecting more than 100 tribes and bands in eight different states.

Congress passed two termination bills in 1954 regarding the Klamath and all western Oregon tribes. Federal services to these groups ended and 864,820 acres of Indian trust land were sold. The Grand Ronde and Siletz reservations were officially closed in 1956 and the Klamath Reservation in 1961. Altogether, more than 4,000 Oregon Indians were affected by the passage of these bills, nearly half of the state's estimated Indian population at that time. The Western Oregon Act terminated 61 different groups; some of these had never been federally recognized, but they were included in the termination list to avoid any future claims.

As people moved away from the reservations and temporarily lost contact with one another, tribal councils were forced to disband. Many Indians went to cities to look for work, and the unfamiliar environment made it even more difficult to maintain cultural ties. In many cases, Indians involved in the termination process were exploited by businessmen, lawyers and others who sought to profit from the troubled and confused situation.

A good deal of public attention was focused on the distribution of money to tribal members when reservation lands were sold after termination. The money was actually insufficient compensation for what was lost, and tribal economic bases were destroyed. On the Klamath Reservation, for example, tribal members had been receiving a yearly income from the sale of reservation timber since 1910. After termination, tribal timber sales ended, and all tribal economic activity ceased.

Some 25 years after termination, the impact is still felt. Recent surveys have again shown that Oregon Indian people were not fully

## NEW POLICY DIRECTIONS

Termination had its opponents from the start, but it was several years before they affected national policy. By 1958 Secretary Seaton called the whole process "unthinkable" (*see* Prucha 1975, p. 240). His successor, Stewart Udall, also denounced termination, suggesting in 1961 that HCR 108, being only a concurrent resolution, died with the Congress that passed it (*see* Sclar, p. 223). In 1968 President Johnson addressed Congress in a special message entitled "The Forgotten American." This was the first time a president had delivered such a message concerning American Indians. Then in 1970 President Nixon gave Congress his "Recommendations for Indian Policy," outlining the "self-determination without termination" approach that continues to guide federal Indian policy today. On some of the implications of the self-determination era, *see* Israel; and H. Johnson.

### American Indian Policy Review Commission (AIPRC)

The AIPRC was envisioned as a thoroughly comprehensive review of Indian policy that would, through specific recommendations, draw increased congressional attention and spark action regarding Indian affairs. The commission's study was indeed comprehensive and information contained in its various reports is worth reading (*see* bibliography). Its basic recommendations were not seized upon by Congress, however. In part, this was due to a "backlash" that developed in the late 1970s, directed against long-standing Indian rights. Most indicative of the decline in legislative activity is the threatened dissolution of the Senate Select Committee on Indian Affairs.

consulted about the legislation, and that tribal consent was not obtained. The general health and employment levels of those involved have declined sharply since the 1950s. Termination created great hardships for many Oregon Indians, and it did nothing to improve the lives of the people it affected.

There were other infringements on Indian rights in the 1950s, such as the transfer of jurisdiction over Indian Country (*see* p. 156-59), and urban relocation programs (*see* p. 144-45).

## NEW POLICY DIRECTIONS

By the late 1950s strong objections to the termination policy were already being raised. With the advent of the Kennedy administration in 1960, new attitudes toward federal-Indian relations developed. A new direction for Indian policy became visible in 1964, as "War on Poverty" legislation made special programs available to Indian tribes and communities. The Office of Economic Opportunity sponsored Indian Community Action programs, contracting services to tribes themselves, something that had never been done before. Programs such as Head Start, Job Corps and Vista aided many Indian groups in the 1960s. Other federal agencies opened special Indian desks, and new arrangements made it possible for Indian tribes and organizations to design and administer their own programs. This new approach was given support by both President Johnson in 1968 and President Nixon in 1970 when they directed Congress to establish a goal for federal-Indian policy that would work for "self-determination without termination." The new policy direction followed a general resurgence of tribal activities around the country, and it attempted to respond to the needs of Indian people who desired to maintain cultural values while building a place in the modern world.

In 1975, as part of an effort to develop a more coherent direction for Indian policy, Congress created the American Indian Policy Review Commission. Indian-staffed, this commission was directed to conduct "a comprehensive review of the historical and legal developments underlying the Indian's unique relationship with the federal government in order to determine the nature and scope of necessary revisions in the formulation of policies and programs for the benefit of Indians." The commission was the first major effort to review Indian affairs since the Meriam Report in 1928, which had led to the 1930s reforms. The American Indian Policy Review Commission ended in 1977, bringing many recommendations before Congress, some of which have already been implemented.

Also created in 1975 was the Oregon State Commission on Indian Services, designed to monitor services for Oregon's Indian population and recommend legislative or administrative changes. The commission was established to represent all Oregon Indian people, and several far-reaching state laws have been passed with its assistance.

SELF DETERMINATION IN OREGON
The Indian Self-Determination and
Education Assistance Act

PL 93-638 (The Indian Self-Determination and Education Assistance
Act) was a significant piece of legislation for Indians in that it encouraged
freedom from government or bureau
control in developing and administering tribal activities. It did not end
legally bound federal services to tribes
or cut back fundings; rather, it directed government agencies to make contracts with tribes themselves for the
delivery of services. Although welcome, PL 93-638 did not receive total
approval by tribes; some felt that the
contracting went too slowly, and that
its application was limited and fragmented. Some viewed certain aspects
of self-determination as possible
veiled attempts at termination. *See*
U.S. Senate, Select Committee on Indian Affairs: Hearings on Implementation of PL 93-638 (1977); and the
Hearings to Amend the Indian Self-
Determination and Education Assistance Act (1978).

Oregon Tribal Developments
Tribal gains and reorganizations did
not immediately occur upon introduction of the "self-determination" policy. The national policy direction toward self-determination did coincide
with a mood of revitalization among
Indian groups. It did not create that
mood, however. The struggle for Indian rights, though not historically popular or well publicized, has been long.
Return of the McQuinn Strip, for example, was effected only after many
decades of effort (*see* text and notes
concerning Warm Springs in Part Two,
pp. 97-99).

For further information on Oregon
tribal developments, 1960-80, *see* the
text and notes to the reservation histories in Part Two and the profiles. The
tribes themselves are the best source:

As policy direction changed through the 1960s and 1970s, many
new events took place, especially in the areas of self-determination,
economic development and the restoration of Indian tribes.

## SELF DETERMINATION IN OREGON

The programs of the new Indian policy that had begun in the
1960s had a marked impact in Oregon, where many tribes initiated
long-range planning and some tribal councils reorganized. The new
policy direction allowed the three remaining Oregon reservations to
assume greater control than ever before in determining the services
extended to them by the trust relationship. After many years of
uncertain standing, the Burns Paiute Colony was again recognized
in 1968, and the Burns Reservation was established in 1972. The
Umatilla Reservation began rapidly expanding its tribal government
and tribal programs in 1966, and it is continuing to work on consoli-
dating reservation lands. The Confederated Tribes of Warm Springs
regained former lands in the return of the McQuinn Strip (*see* map,
p. 99); that and many other developments have made the Warm
Springs Reservation nationally known.

In the late 1960s and the 1970s non-reservation tribes also became active. The Siletz Tribal Council formed again in 1973 and the
Grand Ronde Tribal Council in 1975. The Coos-Lower Umpqua-
Siuslaw Tribal Council used its reopened tribal hall to continue activities and several new Indian programs developed around Coos Bay.
In Klamath Falls, the Klamath Tribal Council and other groups
worked to overcome the damage caused by termination policy. The
Klamath Tribe began reasserting its rights in several ways, most notably in a landmark court case regarding tribal hunting privileges on
former reservation lands.

Other important developments took place around the state under
the new policy of self-determination. The Portland and Eugene Urban Indian centers were established in the early 1970s, providing
vital services for those Indian people living in urban areas of the
Willamette Valley. Indian health care facilities and services improved, with new clinics like the Yellowhawk Center on the Umatilla
Reservation controlled and directed by the people served. Education
was one of the primary areas of revitalization of Oregon Indian life,
as innovative programs and educators began to address the special
educational needs of Indian students.

In 1975, the Indian Self-Determination and Education Assistance
Act was passed, articulating the policy that had been evolving since
the 1960s. The law formalized national support for self-determination, and it directed all agencies to allow Indian tribes and organizations to contract for, and administer themselves, those federal services and funds that were available to them.

planning reports and tribal studies are usually available to the public. There are also several excellent Indian newspapers published in Oregon. *See* the annual *Directory* distributed by Oregon Commission on Indian Services, Salem, for names and addresses of tribes and publications.

## ECONOMIC DEVELOPMENT
*See* AIPRC *Final Report of Task Force Seven*; Israel; Levitan & Johnson; J. V. White; and Sorkin.

## INDIAN EDUCATION
Education has been a special concern to Indian communities since the late 1960s. Statistically, Indian students were doing poorly, having a much lower percentage of high school and college graduates than their non Indian counterparts. Prior to 1972, the primary source of assistance for any Indian education program was the Johnson-O'Malley Act of 1934, but its funds were restricted to federally recognized students residing on or near reservations. The Indian Education Act of 1972 (Title IV) provided assistance to a broader range of students, including non-federally recognized and urban Indians. Title IV programs expanded to assist early childhood and adult education, cultural, curriculum and career development projects. The Self-Determination and Education Assistance Act of 1975 gave Indian communities even more control over these programs and funds. More recent legislation, such as the Tribally Controlled Community Colleges Assistance Act (P.L. 95-47), reflect the continuing concern for Indian education; P.L. 95-47 is most remarkable in that it was drafted not by Congress or a government agency, but by tribal organizations.

## ECONOMIC DEVELOPMENT

Throughout the 1960s and 1970s, American Indian tribes sought to broaden their financial bases and provide adequate standards of living for their members. The remaining Indian lands across the country today contain vast reserves of natural wealth, in the form of timber, minerals, water and energy. Tribes have long been aware of the potential of their lands and people, but they have attempted to guide economic development with consideration for cultural values. Funding for tribal and community development programs has not always been easy to find. Some tribes have been able to finance economic developments with capital from claims payments or other settlements. Other tribes and groups have found assistance in Indian revolving loan funds (aided by the Indian Financing Act of 1974) and a variety of other federal programs.

In Oregon, the Confederated Tribes of Warm Springs bought a privately owned sawmill on reservation land in 1967, in order to process their own reservation timber. Ten years after its beginnings, the tribally owned Warm Springs Forest Products Industries brought in more than $1.8 million a year in net income. In 1977 the tribes purchased a power plant for the mill, fueled by waste wood products, allowing the mill to be self-sufficient. Additional revenue was generated by selling surplus electricity to other utilities. In 1972 the Kah-Nee-Ta hot springs resort and convention center was opened on the reservation, also on land that the tribes had bought back from an outsider. These and other tribal enterprises are sources of community pride as well as employment.

There has not been as much capital available on the Umatilla Reservation as at Warm Springs, but the Confederated Tribes of Umatilla have begun several successful ventures. A tribally owned gas station and market were opened in 1976, and there are several small businesses that are Indian owned and operated. The tribes have also opened for public use the Indian Lake Campground and Recreation Area on tribal land. A fragmented landbase creates many problems, but as reservation land consolidation continues, the feasibility of agricultural—and other—development improves.

The Burns Paiute Reservation is just beginning to establish economic programs, and the first step there has been to construct adequate housing and secure jobs for tribal members. An Overall Economic Development Plan was prepared by tribal members in 1973, analyzing future needs and potential of the reservation. A small industry or business is expected to locate on the reservation soon, and some tribal land has been irrigated and is already in agricultural use.

One frequently misunderstood issue regarding reservation economic development is that of the income produced from Indian lands. Many Indian people earn money by renting their allotted land or by sharing in profits from tribally owned resources. Tribal governments and businesses function like any corporation that generates profits for its continuance and pays dividends to its shareholders. Profits from tribal lands, because they are administered through the

PHOTOGRAPH:
Drummers at tribal gathering. (OHS neg. 36833)

federal trust relationship, are issued on United States Treasury checks. But these checks are earnings from Indian land and are not payments from the government. Indians earn their land-related income just like anyone who makes money from their own property. They do not receive this money simply because they are Indians, as is often believed.

The tax-exempt status of Indian tribes is another situation that is frequently misunderstood. Indian trust lands, and Indian income produced on them, are not subject to federal, state or local taxes, for these lands belong to separate governments, and their status is protected through the trust relationship. Indian lands and incomes not in trust status are subject to the same taxes as any citizen's earnings.

PHOTOGRAPH:
Women at Grand Ronde celebration.
(photo Claire Stock)

There has also been much off-reservation Indian economic development in Oregon. Groups such as the Eugene Urban Indian Center and the Portland Urban Indian Center, the United Tribal People and Organization for the Forgotten American in Klamath Falls, the Willow River Indian Benevolent Association in Coos Bay and others, operate a variety of programs to help Indian people find jobs or acquire the training and education necessary for desired employment. These programs make available GED and adult basic education classes, on-the-job training, placements and counseling advice on how to secure financial aid for further education or training. Off-reservation legal aid projects also monitor reports of job discrimination. Special CETA and Manpower programs have been created around the state to help people find meaningful work, and to provide counseling on cultural differences to employers and employees.

RESTORATION OF INDIAN TRIBES

The many changes that accompanied the developing policy of self-determination were given their strongest confirmation in 1973, when Congress restored federal recognition and most reservation lands to the Menominee Tribe in Wisconsin (the first group terminated in 1954). Encouraged by this and other events, the Confederated Tribes of Siletz began working that same year to regain their federal recognition. Tribal members and supporters worked long and hard, several times traveling to Washington, D.C. to present testimony about the problems caused by termination. Finally, in 1977, Congress passed the Siletz Restoration Act, returning recognition and the essential services that had been denied for 23 years. The Siletz Restoration was a bright moment in recent Oregon Indian history, and the effort behind it indicated the continuing dedication of Oregon Indian people to preserve their traditions, and their rights, in contemporary society. Since 1977, other terminated Oregon tribes have actively begun to seek restoration.

Although the efforts made in the past two decades have achieved much for Indian people, the struggle is not over. Indian affairs and history have been brought to the public's attention increasingly in recent years, but the basis for tribal rights is not yet widely understood. In the late 1970s, the many Indian gains made in Congress and the courts aroused opposition from some powerful non-Indian groups. Certain non-Indians living on or near reservations, and corporations near reservations with economic interests in tribal resources, were all involved. The result has been a temporary decline in congressional legislative action; revival will require renewed efforts by everyone concerned.

The continuing acknowledgement of tribal sovereignty and the support for self-determination is a policy approach that rests solidly on the most basic points of Indian and United States legal history, and it holds much promise for the future. It may be that now, after more than two centuries, the right of Indian people to live their own lives, and determine their own destiny, will finally be respected.

GENERAL SOURCES

Information included in this section of the text came from numerous meetings with Oregon tribes and tribal organizations from February, 1978 to May, 1979. Other lists of contemporary Oregon tribes can be found in the Oregon Commission on Indian Services annual reports; the BIA Tribal Directory; AIPRC *Final Report of Task Force Ten* (1977); and the Economic Development Administration's 1971 Handbook.

General information on tribal activities can be found in newspapers, annual reports and council minutes of each tribe. Tribal planning reports are also helpful. Additional descriptions of some current tribal activities can be found in Beckham (1977); and Ruby & Brown (1976). McNickle (1973) gives a good description of tribal renewals in the United States.

The *Directory of American Indian Resources*, published by Oregon Commission on Indian Services, lists many Oregon tribal, intertribal and regional organizations and provides brief descriptions of their activities. The *Directory* also contains an annual calendar of Native American events for the Oregon area.

# TRIBES OF CONTEMPORARY OREGON

## TRIBAL AFFILIATIONS

More than 100 Indian tribes are represented in Oregon's Indian population today. In addition to the Oregon reservation tribes discussed in Part Two, there are several "landless" tribes who either never had reservations or had them taken away. A third group of people consists of those associated with tribes outside the state.

The chart on page 141 shows the general distribution of tribal affiliations among Oregon's Indian population. Affiliation covers a broad range of relationships between individuals and tribes. For some people, affiliation means a deep commitment and day-to-day participation in tribal affairs. For others, affiliation is recognition of a shared heritage. Some people are affiliated with more than one tribe because their parents or grandparents came from different groups. Not everyone affiliated with a tribe is officially enrolled; some affiliates live far away from tribal centers and do not maintain active contacts, while others may not qualify for enrollment even though they are descendants of tribal members.

The following pages contain a description of the tribes represented in Oregon today, with a map of the major Oregon tribal organizations (p. 145), another map (p. 142) depicting some of the non-Oregon tribes represented in the state, and a short discussion of intertribal organizations. Statements prepared by tribes themselves, discussing their activities, are included elsewhere in this book.

## ORGANIZED TRIBES

There are nine major organized tribes in Oregon today, representing many of the original tribes and bands of the area. Most of the tribes are confederated, which means that several smaller groups have joined together to form a larger political unit. Many of these confederations were formed in the early treaty-making years, when different groups were placed together on the same reservation. Other tribes have confederated more recently. Nearly 90 percent of all individual tribes in the United States today have less than 1,500 members, and confederation into larger groups is an effective way for people in the same area to work on common problems.

Differing histories and relationships with the federal government have resulted in several categories of tribes. The Confederated Tribes of Warm Springs, the Confederated Tribes of Umatilla and the Burns Paiute are all federally recognized tribes that have reservations. The Confederated Tribes of Grand Ronde and the Klamath Tribe had their reservation lands sold in the 1950s, and their federal recognition terminated. The Confederated Tribes of Siletz were also terminated in 1954, but their federally recognized status was restored in 1977 and they have now reestablished their reservation. The Cow Creek Band of Umpquas were federally recognized for the

This chart represents an approximate distribution of Oregon's Indian population in 1970. This general distribution has remained fairly constant since then. Information came from the 1970 U.S. Census Report; the Census's unpublished "Documentation for America Indian Tabulation;" BIA service populations estimates; Siletz enrollment figures and enrollment reports, or estimates from non-federally recognized Oregon tribes. Problems with U.S. Census undercounting are noted on page 151. BIA figures included individuals enrolled in Oregon tribes but residing elsewhere. The "landless" and "non-Oregon" categories are *minimum* estimates. Individuals affiliated with more than one tribe usually report the tribe they are enrolled in or associated with, although not all people reported affiliations.

Precise figures are unavailable, but the following approximated distribution has been considered sufficiently accurate by reviewers: Oregon Tribes on Reservations, 20 percent; "Landless" Oregon Tribes, 25 percent; Non-Oregon Tribal Affiliations, 35 percent; unknown, 20 percent.

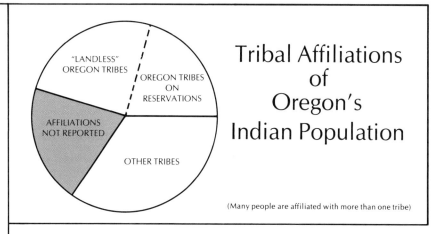

Tribal Affiliations
of
Oregon's
Indian Population

(Many people are affiliated with more than one tribe)

first time in 1982. The Coos-Lower Umpqua-Siuslaw Indian Tribe and the Chinook Tribe have not been federally recognized and have not had reservations due to inconsistencies in the treaty-making process or difficulties encountered in the settlement years.

In addition to those listed on page 142, other tribes have had or are now forming tribal organizations. There is no complete, final list of Oregon Indian tribes, and there could never be one; the tribes of Oregon have never been static, and they are certainly not so today. Groups such as the Chetco, the Coquille and the Tututni have many active members, and we can expect to hear more from these groups, and others, in the future.

Many diverse political factions exist within most contemporary tribes, with differing concerns and opinions. The Chinook present an interesting picture of the diversity of tribal organizations today. Because Chinookan-speaking Indians were displaced to so many areas, there are now many organizations that include their descendants. In addition to the Chinook Tribe described in their profile, Chinook descendants include some members of the Confederated Tribes of Grand Ronde, the Confederated Tribes of Warm Springs, and Siletz, as well as a number of smaller organizations such as the Konniac Tchinoucks (who were displaced to the Klamath Reservation in the 1870s), and the Western Chinooks (who are scattered throughout southwestern Oregon).

Among Oregon's tribes, many differences are evident. Tribal governments, resources and the range of available community services all vary greatly. Some tribes (such as the Burns Paiute and the Konniac Tchinouck) have less than 300 enrolled members, while others (such as the Confederated Tribes of Warm Springs, the Confederated Tribes of Umatilla and the Klamath) have nearly 2,000 each. Each tribe has a different jurisdictional capacity. Several have specific important rights, reserved through treaty provisions (such as tribal hunting and fishing in traditionally used areas). A number of the tribes have extensive education, health and housing programs. These programs have been developed not only by the recognized tribes, but by non-federally recognized groups as well, such as the Coos-Lower Umpqua-Siuslaw.

# Other Tribes Represented in Oregon

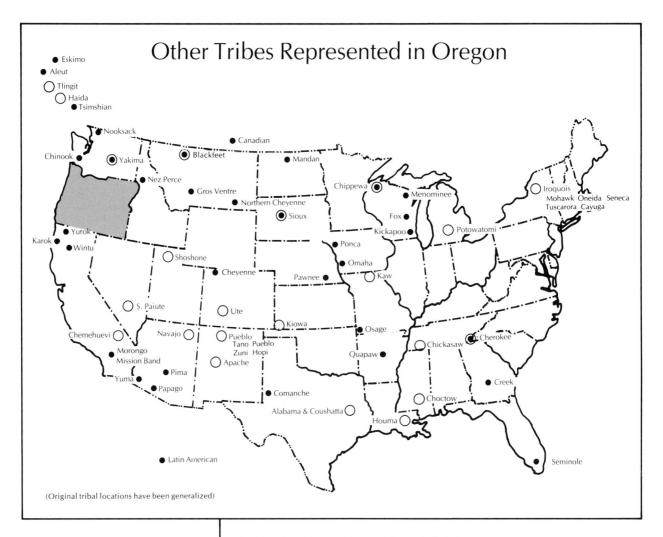

(Original tribal locations have been generalized)

KEY

◉ Tribes with over 250 members living in Oregon

○ Tribes with over 25 members living in Oregon

• Tribes with some members living in Oregon (no estimate available)

## OTHER TRIBES REPRESENTED IN OREGON

A large percentage of Oregon's Indian population today is comprised of individuals affiliated with non-Oregon tribes. In many cases these people have lived here all of their lives and they have contributed much to Oregon Indian life. The tribes they are associated with generally fall into the same categories that apply to Oregon tribes: some are federally recognized and some are not, some are terminated and some have been restored.

Many members of neighboring states' tribes live and work in Oregon. In addition to the Chinooks, several other Washington groups have members here, including the Yakima Indian Nation, the Confederated Tribes of Colville and many of the smaller tribes of western Washington. Tribes from Idaho, Utah and Nevada, such as the Lapwai Nez Perce, the Shoshone-Bannock and the Southern Paiute, are represented in Oregon, as well as many California tribes, including the Yurok and Karok.

Other Indians have come to Oregon from distant tribes. There are nearly 1,000 of Cherokee descent, and more than 500 people from

both Sioux and Chippewa tribes reside in the state. Chemawa
School has brought a diverse group of Indian people to Oregon
including many Alaskan natives. Several thousand more Oregon
residents have come from tribes as far away as Maine and Florida.

Some of these people are Oregon-born, their parents or grandparents having moved to the state years ago. Others have arrived
more recently. Within the past few decades, Indians throughout the
country have been on the move more than ever before. This trend is
partly associated with the increasing shift of Indian population toward the cities. But affiliates of non-Oregon tribes do not necessarily
live in the state's urban areas. Many live on or near Oregon's reservations, and others reside in rural communities. Involvement with
Oregon tribal activities is common.

## INTERTRIBAL AND REGIONAL ORGANIZATIONS

Each of the different tribes represented in Oregon today has its
special history and concerns, but there is also a common, shared
history. Intertribal organizations deal with the special interests and
issues that concern all Indian people; a number of these organizations have been formed in Oregon. Urban Indians, Indians concerned with fishing rights and Indians involved in health care and
education have formed separate cross-tribal groups to work on
these issues. Indian women concerned with their role in Indian and
in non-Indian society have formed groups such as the United Indian
Women and the North American Indian Women's Association.

Several intertribal organizations are active on the statewide level.
The Oregon Commission on Indian Services is the only state legislative commission in the United States specifically devoted to Indian
issues. The Oregon Indian Education Association is another statewide body that brings together people from many tribes.

Regionally, there are three principal intertribal groups, the Affiliated Tribes of Northwest Indians distributes valuable information to
area tribes and represents them in many regionally and nationally
important issues. The Seattle-based United Indians of All Tribes
Foundation provides a variety of technical assistance and planning
support to Northwest tribes, primarily in the field of education. The
Portland-based Northwest Laboratory's Indian Reading and Language Development Program is a third regional organization that
works with almost 20 tribes to produce Indian-oriented curriculum.

State and regional organizations are only one facet of intertribal
activity. The summer pow-wow circuit also keeps members of different tribes in touch with one another, as do sporting events such as
Indian gambling matches, basketball games and rodeos. A conference circuit of tribal leaders, planners and educators leads to a cross-
tribal exchange of ideas. Intertribal organizations do not seek to
negate the cultural and political differences between tribes; rather,
they work to share traditions and present a unified stand on common concerns.

GENERAL SOURCES

*See* AIPRC *Final Report of Task Force Eight*; DeRosier; Waddell & Watson; and Levine & Lurie. Most Oregon urban Indian centers regularly publish newsletters and/or papers. *See* the *Directory of American Indian Resources* for publications and addresses (published annually by the Commission on Indian Services, 454 State Capitol Bldg., Salem, Oregon 97310).

Urban Migration

As early as 1928 the federal government anticipated a shift of Indian population toward urban areas: "General social and economic forces will inevitably operate to accelerate the migration of Indians from the reservations to industrial communities" (Brookings Institution, p. 667). Yet no preparation was made for Indian migrants, and nothing was done to alleviate the "social and economic forces" that caused many people to leave their reservations in search of better living conditions. The development of reservation resources was ignored.

Relocation

Despite predictions to the contrary, the vast majority of Indians did not seem eager to leave their homelands. But by the early 1950s the American public widely assumed that reservations were overcrowded, and this led to some misdirected legislation.

DeRosier describes the evolution and impact of the relocation program. Neils outlines some aspects of migration during the relocation years. Indian education policies also contributed to urban migration. *See* AIPRC *Final Report* (1977, p. 429 *et passim*).

# URBAN INDIANS

Most Indian people historically have lived on their reservation lands or in rural areas. During the last four decades, however, a large population shift toward the cities has occurred, and today nearly 50 percent of all American Indians live in urban areas. In Oregon they live in Portland, Eugene and other cities of the Willamette Valley, as well as other towns around the state such as Klamath Falls, The Dalles and Coos Bay. While urban Indian people are now involved in diverse fields of activity within these cities, they have also endeavored to maintain traditional ties. For many, the move from reservations and tribal life to urban society has proved difficult. Community-based urban Indian centers have been set up to ease the transition by providing access to urban services and opportunities, and, at the same time, support maintenance of cultural ties.

## MIGRATIONS, TERMINATION AND RELOCATION

The reduction of land bases and displacement of tribal groups over two centuries greatly disrupted Indian societies and economies. The continuing impact of this disruption is reflected in the poor social and economic conditions still experienced by many reservation Indians. For decades the unemployment rate on many reservations has been several times the national average, and reservation health, housing and education levels are among the lowest in the United States. Although today conditions are generally improving, in the past 40 years numerous Indian people were forced to leave their reservation homes and seek better opportunities in the cities.

In 1940 less than 10 percent of the Indian population was urban, but during World War II many Indians left reservations and rural areas to join the military or to work in war-related industries. After the war, a number of them stayed in the cities. Others moved to join friends and family, or to find new jobs. Quite a few alternated between living on the reservations and in the cities, working for a while and then returning home. By 1950, increasing numbers of American Indians had become involved in urban life.

Although many Indians moved to the cities on their own initiative during the 1950s, several unwelcome incentives increased that migration. Passage of the termination acts abruptly left many without jobs, income or tribal land. Residents of the Klamath, Grand Ronde and Siletz reservations witnessed their tribal lands being sold and their tribal incomes and all federal services ended. Many, their future uncertain, went to the cities to find new means of existence. Few were prepared to deal with the changes involved in moving from a reservation community to an urban environment, and for most the years after termination were a time of great hardship.

Another aspect of the termination era was a federal program developed in 1952 known as "Voluntary Relocation." The idea behind relocation was to remove more Indian people from reservation

# Tribes & Urban Indian Communites 1980

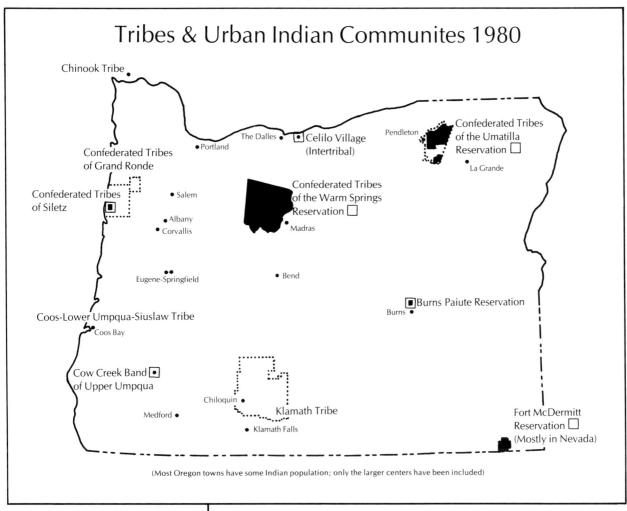

Chinook Tribe •

• Portland

The Dalles • □ • Celilo Village (Intertribal)

Pendleton • Confederated Tribes of the Umatilla Reservation □

• La Grande

Confederated Tribes of Grand Ronde

Confederated Tribes of Siletz

• Salem

• Albany
• Corvallis

Confederated Tribes of the Warm Springs Reservation □

• Madras

Eugene-Springfield • •

• Bend

□ Burns Paiute Reservation
Burns •

Coos-Lower Umpqua-Siuslaw Tribe

Coos Bay •

Cow Creek Band □ of Upper Umpqua

Chiloquin •

Klamath Tribe

Medford •

• Klamath Falls

Fort McDermitt Reservation □ (Mostly in Nevada)

(Most Oregon towns have some Indian population; only the larger centers have been included)

KEY
■ Reservations
⋮⋮ Former Reservations
(Boundaries at termination)
□ Federally Recognized

MAP: TRIBES & URBAN INDIAN COMMUNITIES 1980

This map does not include a comprehensive listing of Indian groups; its selection is based on the suggestions of all organizations contacted and does not reflect any formal recognition or lack thereof.

lands, which at the same time would remove them from the trust relationship. The program was administered through the Bureau of Indian Affairs, and relocation offices set up on reservations throughout the country encouraged Indians to take part in the program by telling of a better life waiting in the cities. In the early years of the program, relocation officers spent little time preparing prospective urban migrants for the shock that lay before them. Usually less than two months passed between the moment a family or individual expressed interest in relocation and the date of their move. Jobs were arranged, but the positions were rarely secure. The program placed Oregon Indians as far away as Los Angeles, Chicago and Denver, with few contacts to help them find work or public assistance. Over 35,000 Indian people across the country moved to urban areas between 1953 and 1960 through the relocation program, but more than one-third eventually returned to their reservations. The program changed significantly in the late 1950s, to emphasize employment assistance rather than migration. The BIA's Employment Assistance Program continues today, but its orientation is markedly different than that of the earlier version. The BIA now assists people

CHART: URBAN AND RURAL
POPULATION
    Data from U.S. Census reports,
1940-70.


Federal Services to Urban Indians
    Lee Sclar describes the BIA and Indi-
an Health Service programs available
to off-reservation Indians, and proposes a broader scope of assistance.
K. C. Davis analyzes the *Morton* v.
*Ruiz* case that challenged the BIA's interpretation of service boundaries.
*See also* Getches, Rosenfelt & Wilkinson (pp. 132-36).


Urban Indian Programs
    Lyndon Bohanen has written a
good description of the history and
operations of Portland's Urban Indian
Center, from its club beginnings in the
1940s to the large organization today.

# Oregon Urban & Rural Population

(Data from U.S. Census)

in obtaining vocational training or education, and it attempts to secure desirable and permanent jobs, both off- and on-reservation.

## URBAN ASSISTANCE PROGRAMS

There are not many federal services available specifically to Indi-ans in the cities at present. Virtually no services are extended to members of non-federally recognized or terminated tribes. Mem-bers of federally recognized tribes also receive little assistance once they leave their reservation. The BIA has long considered the bulk of its trust obligations to end at reservation boundaries, although Bu-reau programs have included people residing "near" reservations. The "on or near" eligibility requirement has been so loosely defined as to include the entire states of Alaska and Oklahoma, but not the major urban concentrations of Indian population. The Indian Health Service has recently set aside special funds for urban Indian Health care, but most federal assistance programs for Indians still exclude urban residents.

Encouraged by the government to become urban residents, but denied federal assistance once they do, American Indians in the cit-ies have had to struggle to establish themselves. Urban Indian peo-ple from widely varying backgrounds have found common ties and concerns, and they have worked to support one another. Communi-ty-based programs aimed at enhancing urban Indian life have devel-oped all around the United States. The Portland American Indian Center held its first meeting in 1959, and other Portland Indian-op-

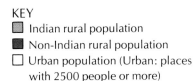
# U.S. Urban & Rural Population

16.3%

83.7%

27.8%

72.2%

44.9%

55.1%

1950

1960

1970

35.9%

64.1%

30.0%

70.0%

26.4%

73.6%

(Data from U.S. Census)

erated groups, such as the Bow and Arrow Club, organized in the 1960s. The Portland Urban Indian Council evolved from these and other groups by 1972. Elsewhere in the state, the Organization of the Forgotten American, founded in 1969, serves Indian people in Klamath Falls and Klamath County. The United Tribal People also developed programs for Indians in Klamath Falls. The Fort Dalles Urban Indians organization was incorporated in 1975, to assist people in The Dalles and surrounding counties. The Eugene Indian Center also began operations in 1975, and it now has satellite offices in Roseburg and Medford. In Coos Bay, the Willow River Indian Benevolent Association and the Coos Bay Rural-Urban Indian Program provide services.

The urban Indian programs in Oregon today offer a variety of services and activities. Each program is unique, but basic to all of them is the desire to provide Indians with a sense of community and support. One of the main concerns of urban Indian programs is to assist Indians seeking job advancement and opportunity. Vocational training, General Equivalency Degree programs, college financial aid counseling and job placement services are provided in all Oregon cities. Most urban Indian programs also serve as resource centers giving access to health care, legal services, youth and senior citizen projects as well as alcohol and drug abuse counseling. A third important function is preservation of cultural bonds. Many urban Indians, especially children, find it difficult to maintain cultural ties in the cities. Through arts and crafts programs, dancing and drumming groups and classes in traditional culture, urban Indian programs en-

147

courage retention of that heritage. Media projects such as urban Indian newsletters and television and radio programs also provide cultural support. Cultural programs are organized sometimes by groups with similar tribal backgrounds and sometimes by inter-tribal groups. The latter emphasize the common concerns of all Indians and work to share diverse cultural traditions.

QUESTIONS FOR THE FUTURE

The fact that the Indian population today is almost equally split between urban and rural residence does raise some important issues. Some people remaining on the reservations question whether tribal members living in the cities should be allowed to participate in reservation matters. On the other hand, urban Indians often wish to maintain contacts with their tribe or their reservation, considering tribal or reservation lands to be their real homes. There is a move underway at present to increase reservation lands and create more jobs, housing and services for those people who wish to return to reservations. Those involved believe that Indian people must be allowed to live where they freely choose, and that the services and opportunities they need must be made available to them.

GENERAL SOURCES

Stephen Langone has reviewed the problems of an accurate population count in his 1974 statistical profile. Other sources to consult include Washburn (1971, part 4); AIPRC *Final Report of Task Force Ten* (part 3); and Meister.

Different estimates and descriptions of the Indian population are found in U.S. Dept. of Commerce (1975); T. Taylor; and the Economic Development Administration Handbook; as well as in various BIA and Indian Health Service reports. Some additional data on Oregon Indians is in Valde & Coppedge; and in Migrant and Indian Coalition.

# INDIAN POPULATION

The American Indian population has grown rapidly since the turn of the century, and it has now nearly regained the numbers it had prior to European contact. Some studies have suggested that the original population may have been much higher than the generally accepted estimate of 890,000, but then the 1970 U.S. Census estimate of 792,730 was likewise considered to be notoriously low. Whatever the exact figures may be, it is clear that the Indian population has experienced a significant regrowth in the last 100 years. The survival that this growth represents is remarkable, after the devastations of the wars and epidemics and the policies of isolation and disintegration that were directed toward American Indian communities. The survival has been one of more than numbers—the traditions, beliefs and Indian ways of life are still very much alive.

Many Indian individuals and programs are working to preserve the traditions and history of their people today, helping youth to learn the value of the old ways and the contributions that have been made through the years. Population statistics and demographics do not tell much about this qualitative growth, but they do partially reflect it. There are serious problems with census data and other statistics about Indian people, and it must be emphasized that accurate and complete information is simply not available. Enough information does exist, however, to show that American Indians are far from "vanishing"; this fact is clear even in the midst of uncertain statistics.

## OREGON INDIAN POPULATION

The Indian population in Oregon has increased at a rate similar to that of the U.S. Indian population. Unlike the national figures, however, Oregon's Indian population is still far below the pre-contact estimate of 45,000 people for this area. Considering that about 40 percent of the state's current Indian population is affiliated with non-Oregon tribes, it may be that the effects of epidemics and displacements were more critical here than in other parts of the country.

The age distribution charts (p. 150) show that the Indian population is much younger than the non-Indian, both in Oregon and the United States. A high percentage of young people is typical in developing and growing societies, while a more even age distribution indicates an established group. As the current youth reach adulthood and begin raising families, the population will grow even more. It has been projected that the Indian population in Oregon will continue to increase at a rate much greater than the non-Indian population at least until the year 2000. Tribes and local organizations are actively planning for this continued growth. Federal and state governments must also take the growing population into ac-

# Age Distribution of Indian & Total Populations 1970

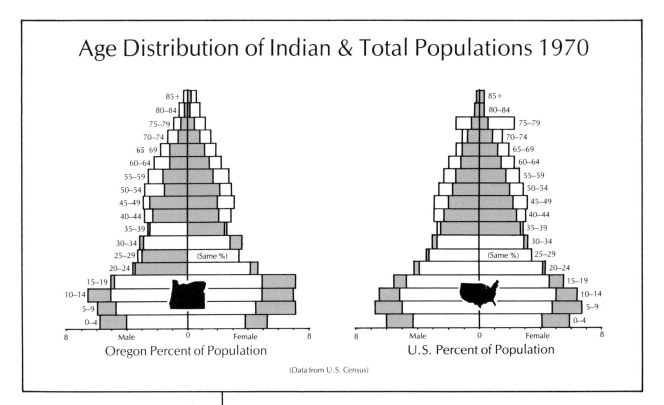

Oregon Percent of Population

U.S. Percent of Population

(Data from U.S. Census)

KEY

▨ Indian Population
☐ Total Population

Median Age of Population (1970)

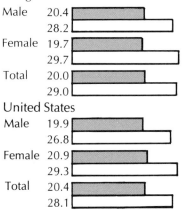

Oregon

| | | |
|---|---|---|
| Male | 20.4 | |
| | 28.2 | |
| Female | 19.7 | |
| | 29.7 | |
| Total | 20.0 | |
| | 29.0 | |

United States

| | | |
|---|---|---|
| Male | 19.9 | |
| | 26.8 | |
| Female | 20.9 | |
| | 29.3 | |
| Total | 20.4 | |
| | 28.1 | |

count in their planning and development of Indian programs and services.

The map of Oregon's Indian population by county (1890–1970), shows that the original reservations have remained important centers of Indian population throughout the years. Klamath and Umatilla counties, the north and south coasts, Warm Springs, Celilo, Burns and Chemawa have all had many Indian residents since 1890. Indian people have also moved into the Portland and Willamette Valley areas, especially since 1940. As the 1970 census map shows, Indian people are now living throughout the state. The selected age profiles for Oregon counties underscores the fact that every community is different.

Some movements shown on the population maps are not easy to understand. Looking at the south coast, for example, the population seems to have disappeared and reappeared several times in the last 90 years, although the people have been there all the while. What this shows is not a movement of the people, but inconsistencies in censuses, and it indicates some of the problems associated with census information about Indians.

## UNRELIABILITY OF U.S. CENSUS DATA

The official Census Bureau count of the Indian population has been, like so many federal Indian policies and programs, contradictory and inconsistent over the years. Census methods, techniques and definitions of who to count as Indian have all changed many times. The first U.S. Census was taken in 1790, but Indian people

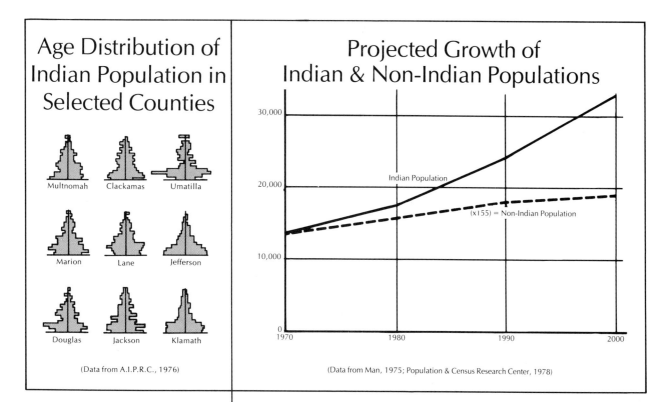

(Data from A.I.P.R.C., 1976)

## Age Distribution of Indian Population in Selected Counties

Multnomah    Clackamas    Umatilla

Marion    Lane    Jefferson

Douglas    Jackson    Klamath

## Projected Growth of Indian & Non-Indian Populations

30,000

20,000

Indian Population

(x 155) = Non-Indian Population

10,000

0

1970    1980    1990    2000

(Data from Man, 1975; Population & Census Research Center, 1978)

CHARTS: AGE DISTRIBUTION/PRO-JECTED GROWTH

This chart and accompanying illustrative material are based on 1970 U.S. Census Report; AIPRC *Final Report of Task Force Ten* (part 3); Man; and Portland State University's Center for Population Research and Census (by personal communication).

Unreliability of U.S. Census Data

Considerable protest regarding the counting of the Indian population prompted the Bureau of the Census to attempt a more complete counting in 1980. The enumeration was to be based on self-identification.

The final report of the 1980 census (PC80) somewhat surprisingly noted a 72 percent increase of the 1980 Indian population over 1970. The Bureau attributed this to the "result of natural increase and overall improvements in census procedures, including . . . the use of self-identification." The fact

were not included until 1860. From then until 1890 only "Indians taxed" were counted; in other words, those confined to reservations were not considered part of the U.S. population.

Since 1890 the Census Bureau has attempted to count the entire Indian population. Its attempts have met with varying degrees of success. Special efforts were made to enumerate the Indian population in 1910 and 1930, and as might be expected, those years show relatively higher population counts than immediately preceding or following censuses. For several reasons, however, most of the U.S. censuses to date do not contain very complete or accurate information about the Indian population. It has not always been very popular or advantageous to be identified as Indian, and this has affected the "visibility" of Indian people during different periods of history. Also, census takers have often neglected to travel to remote places where many Indian people have lived.

Finally, it was not until 1960 that the Census Bureau asked people themselves about their ancestry (even then it was not done in all cases). Before this, people were counted as Indian only if they were recognized as such by the visiting census taker. This accounted for

that such a large increase was recorded throughout all areas of the country would seem to reflect changes in census procedure more than actual population growth.

It is encouraging that the 1980 census "found" Indian people in every Oregon county and in every major Oregon city.

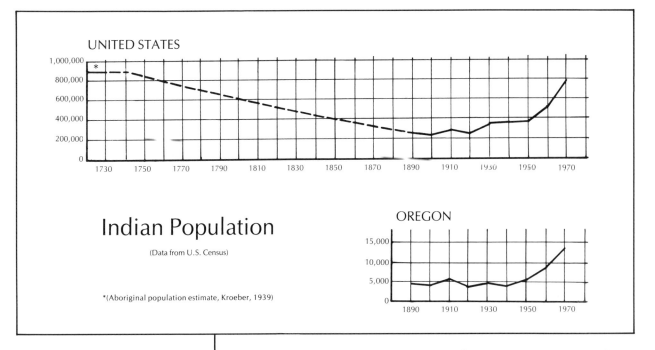

## Indian Population

(Data from U.S. Census)

*(Aboriginal population estimate, Kroeber, 1939)

some very arbitrary estimates of the Indian population, especially in areas away from reservations.

Census figures about the Indian population are incomplete, inconsistent and sometimes simply inaccurate. Unfortunately, however, census data is the primary available source of statistical information about the contemporary Indian population and its social conditions. It is somewhat incredible that there is less information available today about the Indian population than there was 100 years ago, when the annual reports of the commissioner of Indian Affairs published detailed summaries of all reservation communities in the country.

The lack of good statistical information causes serious problems for tribal and federal planners. It also limits the extent to which health, education and other programs can assess Indian needs and evaluate the effectiveness of the programs designed to serve those needs. Most information used in planning today is gathered on a local or tribal level, a time-consuming process, and the information obtained is hard to compare to other areas. The American Indian Policy Review Commission recommended in 1977 that the secretary of the Interior initiate a comprehensive plan for collecting and maintaining accurate data on the Indian population, but this proposal has yet to be realized.

# Differing Estimates of Oregon's Indian Population
## The Problem of Defining Indian Identity

| SOURCE OF ESTIMATE | POPULATION ESTIMATE | BASIS OF ESTIMATE |
| --- | --- | --- |
| Bureau of Indian Affairs | 5,009 | Service population as of May 1978, including estimate of Siletz enrollment. |
| Indian Health Service | 8,616 | Service population estimate for 1978 based on number of 1975-1977 users; does not include Portland and Eugene contract programs. |
| US Census | 26,591 | US Census data, 1980. |
| Migrant and Indian Coalition (Survey/Census) | 28,000 | Estimate of Census Survey, 1980. |

DIFFERING ESTIMATES OF OREGON'S INDIAN POPULATION

Agency definitions and service populations change frequently. Agency data base is not comparable from year to year. *See* Lee Sclar.

Defining Indian identity determines who is eligible for tribal enrollments as well as federal and state programs. It is an important individual and tribal concern. In an interesting article, the National Advisory Council on Indian Education addressed the problem in 1976, concluding that "failure to come up with an acceptable and workable definition soon, will lead to more confusion and discord among the Indian communities to a point that serious division would threaten the very heritage that the Indian people are trying so hard to preserve for present and future generations."

## DIFFERING ESTIMATES OF OREGON'S INDIAN POPULATION

United States Census estimates are often unreliable, but to confuse matters further, there are other agencies and programs that also compile information and prepare estimates about the Indian population, and all of these figures vary. This inconsistency often creates serious problems for the people who are supposed to be served by the agencies making the estimates.

The problems of defining Indian identity involve many legal, political, tribal and personal questions. The fact that many people are affiliated with more than one tribe, along with the limits of recognition that the federal government applies to Indian people, makes a single definition of Indian impossible. The best way to understand the discrepancies among estimates is to look at the basis for some of the different definitions (*see* chart, p. 153).

Service population estimates are not intended to be total counts of Indian population. Yet these estimates are frequently and erroneously used to refer to the entire Indian population of the state. They are not complete counts and they are limited in who they serve. The Bureau of Indian Affairs includes in its service population estimate only enrolled members of federally recognized tribes within Oregon. Tribes determine their own membership rolls, but the BIA requires federally recognized tribes to verify at least one-fourth blood heritage for all tribal members. Even some full-blood Indians may not be recognized if they have less than the required blood quantum of one particular tribe. The BIA service population estimate does not make distinctions between people presently living on or off the reservation, people living in urban or rural areas or those who are

# Indian Population by County 1890-1970

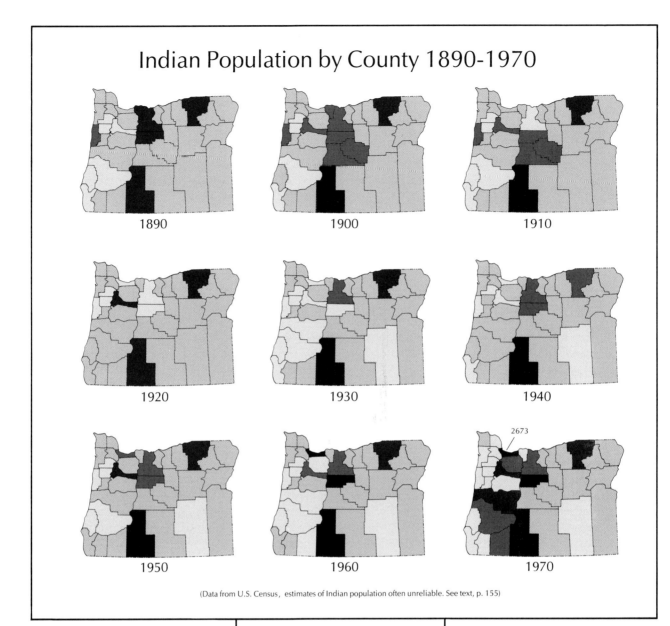

2673

(Data from U.S. Census, estimates of Indian population often unreliable. See text, p. 155)

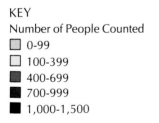

KEY
Number of People Counted
- 0-99
- 100-399
- 400-699
- 700-999
- 1,000-1,500

MAP: INDIAN POPULATION BY COUNTY, 1890-1970
    These are based on U.S. Census reports.

no longer residents of the state. Although the service population estimate includes all the above categories, actual services are essentially limited to on-reservation residents.

The Indian Health Service population estimate includes people enrolled in federally recognized tribes that make use of IHS programs over a three-year period. No distinction is made about people's current residence when preparing the estimate, although there are priorities and limitations placed on the services available, depending on whether people are living on or near reservations.

The Migrant and Indian Coalition survey-census estimate is considerably higher than any other estimates of service populations. The survey was designed and carried out by Indian people, and many observers feel that it is the most accurate census of Oregon Indians to date.

A number of other agencies have their own estimates of Indian population, based on combinations of the above or on other variables. A Title IV census of Indian students enrolled in public schools identified more than 5,000 Indian children in Oregon in 1973. Several organizations have used that census to develop estimates of local or total state Indian population levels, taking into account cultural differences in family size.

Combined tribal enrollments of all Oregon tribes would not give an accurate or complete estimate of the state's Indian population, since not all people are enrolled in tribes, and not all enrolled members are living in Oregon. Also, as previously mentioned, many people in Oregon are affiliated with tribes elsewhere.

Although it may be possible in the years ahead to gather more accurate and complete information about the Indian population, it is unlikely that there will be any fewer problems associated with defining Indian identity. Only the tribes and communities themselves can decide upon their membership, and as such there cannot be any uniform definition of Indian useful to all groups, tribes and agencies.

GENERAL SOURCES

Basic sources of information are: AIPRC final reports of Task Force Two and Four; Clinton; Indian Civil Rights Task Force; Getches, Rosenfelt & Wilkinson (chap. 7); P. S. Taylor; and Vollman (1974). Valuable background information can be found in Cohen (1971, chaps. 5-7, 18, 19). Additional information and perspective came from Norma Smith (Warm Springs Tribal Court Clerk); Doug Nash (Tribal Attorney for the Confederated Tribes of the Umatilla Indian Reservation); and Charles Wilkinson (University of Oregon Law School).

*"Indian Country" is that area where tribal jurisdiction applies. When first defined by Congress in 1834, Indian Country was said to be "all lands west of the Mississippi River, not within Missouri, Louisiana, or Arkansas, and all land east of the Mississippi still under Indian title." This definition was abandoned in 1883, and for more than half a century Indian Country was variously defined by the courts as cases came before them. In 1948 Indian Country was again interpreted by Congress, and this definition is the one in effect today: all lands within the boundaries of any Indian reservation, all allotted lands under Indian title, and all dependent Indian communities.

## TRIBAL POWERS IN INDIAN COUNTRY

Tribal sovereignty is confronted head-on in jurisdictional disputes. The famous nineteenth century Supreme Court decisions regarding Cherokee sovereignty were in response to a question of jurisdiction. The basis of tribal powers is discussed in Cohen (1971, chap. 7); W. R. West (1976);

# JURISDICTION OVER INDIAN COUNTRY*

*Our history and culture is unique and different from yours. Certain of our civil laws will reflect those differences so that longstanding customs, familiar to our people, can be perpetuated. In order to govern our people fully and well, criminal and civil jurisdiction is essential.*
   *—Leslie Minthorn, Chairman of the Umatilla Board of Trustees, before the U.S. Senate Committee on the Judiciary, 14 Jan. 1975.*

A crucial question for all tribal governments today is how much jurisdiction the tribe has over questions that affect its land and people, questions that involve nearly all aspects of contemporary tribal life, from matters of law and order to resource rights, zoning and land use regulations, taxation, child welfare and many other issues. Tribal self-government is a basic right that has long been acknowledged by Congress and the courts, but it has been seriously limited over the years. Responsibility for governing Indian activities has become divided among tribal, federal and state authorities. The unit of government with jurisdiction in any particular instance depends upon what issue is at stake, where it took place, and who is involved. Yet there are no clear guidelines to this division of responsibility, and as a result jurisdiction over Indian Country is often a confusing and entangling matter.

## TRIBAL POWERS IN INDIAN COUNTRY

American Indian tribes governed themselves long before any foreign settlers arrived. This original autonomy is the basis for tribal powers that exist today. Even after tribes were displaced to reservations, they retained control over their internal affairs. Congress has in some instances granted additional powers to tribes, but the right to be self-governing was inherent.

The range of powers that tribes have within Indian Country is extensive. The tribes can choose their own form of government, determine their own membership, tax property, regulate commerce and govern the conduct of members and non-members on Indian lands. One of the basic principles of federal Indian law and policy is that an Indian tribe possesses full powers of a separate government

and Getches, Rosenfelt & Wilkinson (chaps. 4-6). *Also see* the references concerning tribal sovereignty in the Early and Recent Federal Indian Policy notes.

Robert Clinton traces the develop-

ment of Indian Country from a geographical to a legal concept. *Also see* the Indian Country Statute (18 USC 1151).

LIMITS TO TRIBAL AUTHORITY

Several writers have referred to the myriad of laws and decisions regarding jurisdiction in Indian Country as a "maze" or "crazy-quilt." The situation has become so complex that each case must be examined independently in order to determine what laws apply.

The more prominent legislative limits are, as mentioned in the text, the Major Crimes Act (18 USC 1153, 3242); the Assimilative Crimes Act (18 USC 13); and the General Crimes Act (18 USC 1152). *See,* generally, the Corpus Juris Secundum 42:75.

Getches, Rosenfelt & Wilkinson (pp. 367-70) discuss the McBratney-Draper-Martin line of cases. The Oliphant decision has aroused much opposition in Indian Country. Many observers feel the ruling differs from previous Indian law and policy. *See* Kays; Smith; and W. R. West (1978).

PUBLIC LAW 83-280

Carole E. Goldberg presents an excellent and comprehensive analysis of PL 83-280. *Also see* Ackerman; and M. West. Bishop argues against the attitude that tribal jurisdiction is a "granted" and "developed" reality secondary to states' rights.

except where limited by act of Congress. Although many limitations have been placed on tribes over the years, it is generally agreed that potential tribal powers are even more extensive than those exercised at present.

## LIMITS TO TRIBAL AUTHORITY

Changing definitions of Indian Country reflected the fact that Indian lands were fast decreasing. Years of treaty-making and reservation policy left tribes as "island" governments, but full tribal jurisdiction continued intact within what lands remained.

Then in the late 1800s Congress began to pass legislation that limited the *kinds* of crimes or actions tribes had jurisdiction over. One of the first such limits came in 1885 with the passage of the Major Crimes Act. This law specified that certain crimes committed by an Indian in Indian Country came under federal jurisdiction (crimes such as murder, burglary and rape). The act originally named seven crimes, but more have been added, and today it lists fourteen.

Limits of the Major Crimes Act were followed with other laws that further reduced tribal authority by placing additional crimes or situations outside the realm of tribal jurisdiction. The Assimilative Crimes Act, for example, allows the federal government to apply some state laws to Indian Country. Individuals tried under such laws must be brought before federal courts with federal prosecutors, however.

Some limitations to tribal powers have not been expressly defined at all, but have come instead in the form of court decisions interpreting congressional intent. Such is the series of decisions that form the basis for claiming state jurisdiction over all crimes committed by non-Indians against non-Indians in Indian Country (the McBratney-Draper-Martin trilogy of cases). A more recent Supreme Court decision (*Oliphant* v. *Suquamish Indian Tribe*, 1978) has expressed the opinion that tribes have no jurisdiction over any non-Indian offenses committed in Indian Country. This does not, however, mean that the states do.

Exclusive tribal jurisdiction over Indian lands has—like the land itself—been gradually taken away. Federal and state governments now have jurisdiction over many crimes and actions. The situation is complicated by the sheer bulk of jurisdictional laws and decisions in existence. Some of these actions are contradictory, and many of them refer only to specific tribes. This makes it difficult to determine just what limits are applicable in each new situation. All of these restrictions have interfered with the operation of tribal governments, and they have created a maze of conflicting responsibility.

## PUBLIC LAW 83-280

In 1953 many quick solutions were being offered to complex problems in Indian affairs. Two weeks after Congress declared its policy of termination (*see* p. 134), a law intended to simplify the jurisdictional situation in Indian Country was passed. Public Law

157

Indian Civil Rights Act of 1968

This act did more than require tribal consent before any state assumed further jurisdiction under PL 83-280. Especially controversial has been Title 1 of the act, which provided an unrequested "Indian Bill of Rights" that effectively weakened tribal courts and governments. *See* the act itself (PL 90-284; 82 Stat. 79); and 25 USCA 1321-1326.

For background *see* Getches, Rosenfelt & Wilkinson (pp. 334-46); and Burnett. Price considers some of the effects of the act after its first test case, *Dodge* v. *Nakai*, ruled against a tribal government. *See also* Ziontz; and Werhan.

## JURISDICTION IN OREGON

The pre-contact political organization of Oregon tribes is discussed on pages 13-14. In the late 1800s Indian courts and police were established on several Oregon reservations, including Umatilla and Klamath. Early tribal courts and police were sometimes more a measure of assimilation than tribal autonomy, but after the 1930s tribes began to regain greater control and determination of their governing systems.

By the late 1970s more than 120 tribal courts were operating in the United States. *See* the American Indian Lawyer Training Program; Collins; Johnson & Perkins; and Hagan.

The Warm Springs case referred to in the text is *Red Fox* v. *Red Fox* (23 Or. App. 393; 542 P. 2nd 918). *See* Getches, Rosenfelt & Wilkinson (pp. 324-28). The Burns Paiute case questioning state jurisdiction was *Hoodie* v. *Kennedy*.

*Also see* Oregon Commission on Indian Services (1978, chap. 2).

83-280 transferred criminal and civil jurisdiction from tribal and federal authorities to the states. It was one of the most drastic limits to tribal self-government to date. The law initially applied to five states, of which Oregon was one, but all other states were given the option to assume jurisdiction at a later time.

Indian people did not support Public Law 280. The jurisdictional transfer infringed upon the unique status of tribes and it failed to fund states for the additional workload. Most distressing of all, the act did not require tribal consultation or consent.

In Oregon, the Warm Springs Reservation requested and obtained exemption from the transfer, as it had a tribal court in operation and it feared discrimination in state courts. Other reservations in Oregon were placed under state jurisdiction, although Klamath, Siletz and Grand Ronde were terminated shortly thereafter. At Umatilla, the tribal police force that had been organized since 1881 was disbanded, and state and local officers assumed law and order authority.

In 1968 the Indian Civil Rights Act included an amendment to Public Law 280, requiring tribal consent before any state could assume jurisdiction in the future. It also provided for state- or federally initiated return of jurisdiction to those tribes who were affected by P.L. 280. These changes, although 15 years late, have lessened P.L. 280's impact. Ironically though, the Indian Civil Rights Act itself limits tribal authority in several ways.

Public Law 280 did not end tribal governments. Courts have ruled that the act did not affect the trust status of Indian lands, nor did it affect tribal water rights or any treaty rights concerning hunting or fishing. It has also been ruled that P.L. 280 did not grant states the right to tax Indian lands or reservation income.

## JURISDICTION IN OREGON

The issue of jurisdiction in Indian Country has affected all American Indian tribes, but in Oregon it has been of especial concern. Being in a mandatory Public Law 280 state, most Oregon tribes have had to deal with the added complexities of state intervention in their governing powers. Termination has further affected the jurisdictional status of several tribes.

Since each Oregon reservation and tribe has a unique history and each has been subjected to different limitations on their governing powers, the state's tribes today do not all have exactly the same jurisdictional capacities.

The Tribal Court of the Warm Springs Reservation, with three judges and a staff of thirteen, hears more than 2,000 cases a year. It retains jurisdiction over appropriate matters occurring between Indians within the reservation boundaries, but has voluntarily chosen not to extend its jurisdiction to non-Indians, except for zoning and land use. Tribal policemen are cross-deputized with local law enforcement officials, however, in order to maintain peace on the reservation at all times. State and federal courts have upheld recent tribal court rulings, acknowledging the validity of the tribal court's decisions.

At Umatilla, the Oregon reservation most affected by Public Law 280, there is today close cooperation with state and local governments, but there is also a strong desire to have jurisdiction returned to the Confederated Tribes. Several bills have been drafted regarding the retrocession of jurisdiction to the tribes, but none has yet been passed. County and local officials have added their support to tribal jurisdiction, agreeing that the Umatilla Tribal Government is capable of and best suited to overseeing reservation matters. There is a tribal court in operation for use by tribal members, and an active Law and Order Committee. The Confederated Tribes have already made great strides in enacting cooperative zoning and land use plans, central to their aims of tribal land consolidation.

The Burns Paiute Reservation implemented a law and order system soon after the reservation was officially established in 1972. Tribal police now coordinate with county and state jurisdictions. There has been some dispute over whether state jurisdiction, under Public Law 280, should apply to the Burns Reservation. The Portland area solicitor for the Bureau of Indian Affairs affirmed tribal jurisdiction in a 1975 opinion, but a recent court decision favored state authority. The issue now appears to be settled, as the governor has acknowledged tribal and federal jurisdiction with an executive order.

Other tribal governments around the state possess varying degrees of jurisdictional authority. Celilo Village is presently within state jurisdiction. The Klamath Tribe maintains limited jurisdiction through its Wildlife Management Plan, overseeing Indian hunting and trapping on former reservation lands (see p. 162). Lack of federal recognition or trust land limits the jurisdictional reach of other tribes in the state.

Recent actions continue to support tribal autonomy. Laws such as the 1975 Indian Self-Determination and Education Assistance Act and the 1978 Indian Child Welfare Act allow tribes greater control over their affairs. Although many jurisdictional issues remain undecided, the extent of recognized tribal powers is increasing. Land encroachments have made the scope of tribal jurisdiction more situational than territorial, but Indian Country is still a separate area in this nation, where different values and customs are in force.

Doug Nash, attorney for the Confederated Tribes of the Umatilla Indian
Reservation, has written a comprehensive chapter on hunting and fishing law for Mary West's *Manual of Indian Law*. David McDonald has
compiled an annotated bibliography
on Indian hunting and fishing rights.
*Also see* Getches, Rosenfelt & Wilkinson (chap. 11).

For background to these and other
treaty rights *see* AIPRC *Final Report
of Task Force One*; and Wilkinson &
Volkman.

Hunting, fishing and gathering
rights are a rapidly developing area of
Indian law. Recent court decisions and
interpretations are analyzed in various
issues of the *Indian Law Reporter*
(offices at 1712 N Street NW, Washington, D.C., 20556).

PROBLEMS DUE TO DIMINISHED
RESERVATION RIGHTS

Citation and review of the relevant
cases relating to the Umatilla Indian
Reservation are in Nash.

# HUNTING, FISHING & GATHERING RIGHTS

Indian people of the Oregon area traditionally made use of a wide
variety of food resources. Salmon and other seafoods, elk, deer,
small game and many different kinds of plants and berries were all
sought in their appropriate season. Fishing, hunting and gathering
were an integral part of life, interwoven with social activities and
religious ceremonies. The importance of these activities continues
for Oregon Indians today. They provide vital food and income for
many Indian families. They are also a form of traditional expression,
and an essential link with the Indian heritage.

When treaties were signed in the Northwest, many tribes insisted
that their fishing and hunting rights expressly be reserved. Maintenance of these rights has survived the years since treaty times, but
not without some struggle. Competition for fish and wildlife from
other user groups has created a great deal of controversy over the
basis, and extent, of Indian fishing and hunting rights. As a result,
many courts have had to consider and interpret tribal resource
rights. With the notable exception of the Columbia River off-reservation Indian fishery (*see* pp. 165-72), most of the court rulings
regarding Indian hunting, fishing and gathering in Oregon have
addressed the use of reservation lands. As the status of some reservations has changed over the years due to termination or the reduction of tribally owned lands, tribal use of resources has come under
attack. A major controversy has been state versus tribal regulation,
and conservation is frequently the battlecry issue.

## ON RESERVATION RIGHTS

Tribes have exclusive rights to the use of their reservation lands.
On-reservation hunting, fishing and gathering are supposedly free
of state controls. A number of Oregon Indian treaties specifically
recognized these exclusive tribal rights, but even without specific
treaty provisions, exclusive tribal use of reservation land is guaranteed as an extension of original use.

On the Warm Springs Reservation where nearly all of the land is
tribally owned or under Indian title, hunting and fishing is monitored
and controlled by the Confederated Tribes. The tribal government
approves seasons and limits, and it issues licenses to both Indian and
non-Indian users. Tribal fish and wildlife officers and tribal biologists
work to maintain and enhance reservation fish and game resources.

## PROBLEMS DUE TO DIMINISHED RESERVATION LANDS

Tribal hunting and fishing rights on reservation lands have rarely
been contested, but some questions have arisen when a large part of
the land within a reservation has passed into non-Indian ownership.

When presented with this situation most courts have referred to Congress's clear description of Indian Country as "all land within the limit of any Indian reservation . . . . notwithstanding the issuance of any patent, and, including rights-of-way running through the reservation," and ruled that a tribe's right to hunt and fish on a reservation is not determined by the amount of land the tribe has official title to.

Another question here is the extent to which tribal resource rights exist in areas historically held by the tribe, but which no longer lie within tribal control or reservation boundaries. Several Oregon Indian treaties specifically stated that tribes could continue to use "open and unclaimed lands" for hunting and gathering purposes. This phrase was included in the treaties to guarantee tribes the right to use lands "not occupied by settlers." It has been interpreted by contemporary courts to mean National Forest lands near a reservation, and other public and private lands where hunting and fishing are allowed.

The Confederated Tribes of the Umatilla Indian Reservation have had to confront several of these issues over the years. The Umatilla Reservation is largely checkerboarded with Indian and non-Indian ownership (*see* map, p. 100), and an 1885 reduction of the reservation has left some tribal lands outside of the present boundary. Despite these problems, the tribes' various resource rights have been repeatedly upheld. The Law and Order Committee currently enforces the Tribal Fish and Game Code, establishing hunting and trapping seasons for tribal members. Three different court rulings since 1963 have underscored the Confederated Tribes' right to hunt and fish on unclaimed lands outside the reservation. Umatilla and Warm Springs Indians are also part of the Columbia River treaty Indian fishery (discussed on pp. 165-72).

## EFFECTS OF TERMINATION

The Klamath Termination Act passed in 1954 included a provision stating that nothing in the act was to abrogate water or fishing rights or other privileges that the tribe or its members enjoyed under federal treaty. Even with this direct statement, many Klamath people found it difficult to exercise their treaty rights to hunt and fish in the years following termination. In 1973, five Klamath Indians filed a suit in federal district court to have their rights upheld (*Kimball* v. *Callahan*). That case, which stretched on through a series of decisions and appeals, concluded upon the following points:

> Klamath treaty rights to hunt, fish and trap survived termination.

> These rights belong to all members of the Klamath Tribe who were on the final roll at termination, and to their descendants.

> Klamath Indians may hunt, fish and trap on lands of the former reservation including all National Forest land and

EFFECTS OF TERMINATION

For the Klamath Indians the *Kimball et al* v. *Callahan et al* case has been important in terms of hunting and fishing law and has further defined the rights of terminated tribes. *See* the *Indian Law Reporter* 6 (12 March 1979), pp. D 22-D-27; and Pearson.

those privately owned lands where hunting, fishing or trapping are permitted.

The state of Oregon can regulate Klamath hunting, fishing and trapping for purposes of conservation, but it should do so in consultation with the tribe.

In April, 1979 this case was remanded back to District Court to develop mutually agreeable management regulations. The Klamath General Council has approved a Tribal Wildlife Management Plan, and is working with the state on its implementation.

The Klamaths recognize that they no longer have exclusive rights to hunt and fish on their ancestral grounds. What they do claim is a nonexclusive right to use the land as they have in the past, free from unnecessary controls or interference.

OTHER ISSUES

Tribal hunting and fishing rights were the focus of much debate during the Siletz restoration hearings in 1976 and 1977. The Oregon Fish and Wildlife Commission opposed the return of federal recognition to Siletz on the grounds that such action might give the tribes some "procedural advantage" in possible future hunting and fishing disputes. The Siletz Indians made it clear that their concern was to reestablish essential health and education services and not exploit fish or wildlife resources because they did not want restoration to hinge upon the fishing or hunting issue. The final result was that the restoration act did "not grant or restore any hunting, trapping, or fishing rights."

Only a few of Oregon's tribes have been involved in major litigation over hunting, fishing and gathering rights, but the issue is important to all tribes in the state. To date, however, there have been no clear court rulings on the extent of other tribes' rights.

Opponents of Indian rights have long claimed that tribal hunting and fishing activities, beyond state regulation, would result in the wholesale depletion of wildlife resources. As time has shown, this is not the case. Tribal hunting, fishing and gathering activities—under tribal regulations—have been carried on with restraint and with respect for those resources that for so long have sustained Indian people.

The social and religious aspects of Indian hunting, fishing and gathering are not mere remnants of the past; they have a deep significance today. In the following statement, Joe Coburn, Vice-Chairman of the Klamath Tribe, describes what hunting means to him:

## THE IMPORTANCE OF HUNTING TO KLAMATH PEOPLE

Hunting and fishing mean many things to many people. Most sportsmen look on them as recreational activities. Many attempt to save money on their food bills by supplementing their larders with game. Economically, the businessman reaps the greatest profit. The suppliers of equipment, gas, lodging and other necessities see hunting and fishing as a boon to their annual sales. One of the great come-ons in real estate pitches is the hunting and fishing available in the area.

Hunting and fishing means something entirely different to a Klamath Indian.

I will attempt to show this difference by taking a look at deer hunting, which is of prime importance to us at the present time. I'm not sure my people will approve of what I am about to say. To the best of my knowledge it has not been said in public before, but I feel the issue at hand is important enough for me to take it upon myself to do so.

Boys begin hunting with their fathers at a very early age. They spend a long, exacting apprenticeship. During this time they are learning how, where and when to hunt; the deer's habits; how to care for the carcass; et cetera.

They are also learning moral lessons. For instance, they learn that the *Ga gon as* (little people who live in the Klamath country) observe them whenever they are in the field. If they should abuse game, such as fail to track a crippled deer down, or should waste game, the *Ga gon as* will go ahead of them in the future and scare game away from them. They will never become successful hunters.

They usually receive their own, or the use of, a .22 at an early age, say eight or nine. It isn't long before they hunt with these without supervision. They learn not to shoot animals that they do not intend to eat or give to someone who will make use of the meat. They are restricted more or less to varmint type hunting. When we had rabbits, they would hunt these, but rabbits seem to have gone the way of the buffalo, at least in Klamath County.

Eventually, the boy becomes adept at shooting. He is usually given a large caliber rifle or the use of one at this stage, about 12 to 14 years of age. He finally gets to hunt deer.

Klamaths place high status on hunting ability and marksmanship so there is tremendous pressure on the youngsters. Chances are pretty good that he will miss several deer before he finally hits one. His father, who is also very anxious, will explain what the boy did wrong when he misses. When a Klamath boy finally makes his first kill it is one of the greatest moments he will ever experience.

He must distribute his first kill to other people—usually elders, widows, favorite relatives, et cetera. He will receive a great deal of praise from each. They refer to him as a hunter, but he still has a long time to go as an apprentice.

They will usually give him some gift in return for the meat; a knife, some bullets, et cetera. At first it is very difficult for the boy to face giving away his first kill, as he is so proud of it, but the purpose of giving away the meat is so that he will learn to share his good fortunes with those that are less fortunate. The indescribably good feeling that he gets through this procedure of being able to help someone, becomes a very strong part of his personality.

The boy is allowed to eat the liver. Through this act he will gain some attributes directly from the deer, Powers, if you will. The boy will gain speed, stamina, alertness and other favorable attributes from his deer which will help him to become a better hunter in the future.

The father is extremely proud of the boy and will have the boy repeat step by step, his story of his first kill to other adults.

Almost visibly, you can observe the status gained by the boy with his peers. For a time, at least, he is number one among them.

Now the boy begins hunting alone, or with his peers, but he will still spend much time hunting with his father. He gets more and more proficient at hunting. He often will kill several deer on a hunt. This meat is not wasted, but is distributed as was taught him, a practice he will continue the rest of his life.

He will begin receiving invitations to hunt with some of the better hunters. Now he is "big time," as this means that he is beginning to be recognized for his abilities as a hunter.

Eventually, established hunters will begin soliciting his opinions about hunting, and he will be welcomed to tell some of his favorite hunting experiences during "bull sessions." Younger males will seek his advice. He has achieved status, he is a hunter.

The hunting "code" the boy has learned is reinforced by peer pressure, usually in the form of ridicule. An example would be if a poor shot is made, his peers will laugh at him and tease him. The result is that the next time he will ensure a "clean" kill. This brief description is not a cut and dried procedure. It varies from individual to individual and from family to family. The results are nearly the same no matter what procedure is followed. Klamath hunters, in general, have a completely different outlook toward wild game. I'm not saying that our treatment of game is any better, or any worse than others. I'm saying that that's what we believe in and we wish to continue doing so, as is guaranteed us by treaty with the United States government.

Exploitation of game by sportsmen and businessmen over the past 14 years has proven to be disastrous from our viewpoint. Hunting to us is a social institution, an institution that is vital to our lives and it is very much threatened by the policies of game management demonstrated to us by the state of Oregon.

(Submitted by Joseph Coburn, Vice Chairman, the Klamath Tribe)

Background information is presented in Chaney; Beiningen; and BIA (1977). McDonald lists many basic references in an annotated bibliography concerning treaty Indian hunting and fishing rights. A good introduction to the subject is *Uncommon Controversy*, by the American Friends Service Committee. The Columbia River Intertribal Fish Commission has distributed a newsletter; and several other fishery organizations issue pamphlets and publications (*see* the *Oregon Directory of American Indian Resources* compiled by the Oregon Commission on Indian Services). The Northwest Resource Information Center (P.O. Box 427, Eagle, Idaho, 83616) reports on the status of Columbia Basin salmon and steelhead.

The Confederated Tribes of the Umatilla and the Warm Springs reservations have established fishing regulations. Both have also sponsored various fishery studies and reports, many of which are available to the public.

The comments and suggestions of reviewers were extremely helpful in the preparation of this section, especially those of Don Wharton (Oregon Legal Services); Dennis Karnopp (Tribal Attorney, Confederated Tribes of Warm Springs); and Kirk Beiningen (Oregon Dept. of Fish and Wildlife).

BASIS FOR INDIAN FISHING RIGHTS

For the history of Indian and non-Indian fisheries in the Columbia *see* Craig & Hacker; Swindell; and Schoning et al. William L. Robinson describes the recent status of the ceremonial catch.

Sol Tax presents the minutes of a late 1960's open fishing rights conference held in Washington state. The basic anti-treaty fishing rights arguments can be found in Williams & Neubrech.

# COLUMBIA RIVER FISHING CONTROVERSY

Salmon was traditionally the major food resource for many Oregon Indians. The Indian trade network at Celilo Falls distributed preserved fish to tribes that lived as far away from the river as California, Nevada and Canada (see pp. 42-44). Salmon also had great religious significance, as evidenced by its role in mythology and its use in such ceremonies as the First Salmon rites.

When Indians signed treaties that displaced them to reservations farther from the river, they made certain specific provisions were included allowing them to continue to fish at traditional locations. In the years following the treaty-signings, non-Indian settlers and fishermen moved into the original area in increasing numbers competing for the river's resources. As the river's available catch decreased, conflicts between Indian and non-Indian fishermen multiplied. Violent confrontations and far-reaching court decisions, especially in the last decade, have attracted much public attention to this controversy.

Many Oregon Indian people continue to fish for subsistence and ceremonial needs today, and commercial Indian fishermen still depend on fishing for their livelihood.

## BASIS FOR INDIAN FISHING RIGHTS

The tribes that signed treaties granted settlers rights to land, and rights to hunt and fish—it was not the other way around. Treaties with a number of tribes (the Tribes of Middle Oregon; the Walla Walla, Cayuse and Umatilla; the Nez Perce; and the Yakima) were almost identical in their wording of a provision reserving fishing rights: "the exclusive right of taking fish in the streams running through and bordering said reservation is hereby secured to said Indians, and at all other usual and accustomed places in common with citizens of the United States, and of erecting suitable buildings for curing the same" (Treaty with the Nez Perces, 1855).

On-reservation fishing rights have long been honored, but the concept of off-reservation fishing rights is frequently misunderstood. The latter rights are the result of specific political and legal agreements; they are not granted simply on the basis of race. By signing treaties, Indian tribes agreed to give up exclusive rights to fish on aboriginal territory outside their reservations, and to share wildlife resources in the same area with non-Indians. But the tribes were careful to protect their fishing activities at traditional locations. Only the four above-mentioned treaty tribes are currently part of the off-reservation Indian fishery in the Columbia, but the issue is of concern to many Indian people.

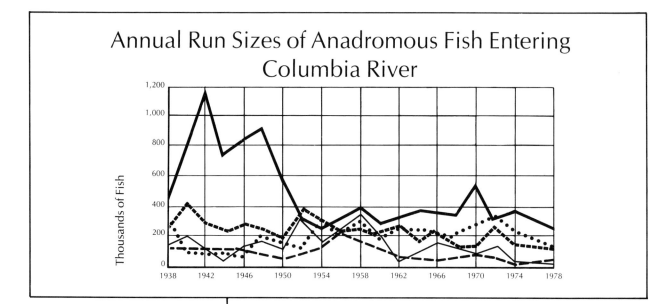

# Annual Run Sizes of Anadromous Fish Entering Columbia River

Thousands of Fish

1,200
1,000
800
600
400
200
0

1938  1942  1946  1950  1954  1958  1962  1966  1970  1974  1978

KEY
━━━ Fall Chinook
▬▬▪ Summer Steelhead
•••• Spring Chinook
──── Sockeye Salmon
•▬ ▬ Summer Chinook

DECLINING FISH RUNS

*See* Pacific Northwest Regional Commission; Oregon Fish Commission & Washington Department of Fisheries; Oregon Department of Fish and Wildlife & Washington Department of Fisheries; and Pacific Northwest River Basin Commission (appendix 14).

## DECLINING FISH RUNS

Salmon and steelhead are anadromous fish; they are born in freshwater streams and then travel to the ocean where they live for several years before returning to spawn in their original waters. Indians of the Columbia Basin originally fished in virtually all major streams and tributaries that were used by anadromous fish. In their upstream migrations fish would slow down and congregate at rapids and natural obstacles such as Celilo, Willamette and Kettle falls, and these places were important fishing centers. It has been estimated that at least 18 million pounds of fish were taken annually by Indian fishermen on the Columbia.

The first white explorers and settlers who entered the Columbia Basin and the Oregon area quickly became interested in the large amount of fish available. At first many of them only traded for fish or fished for their own use, but before long they were catching large numbers to sell. In 1830 Columbia River salmon began to be commercially exported abroad. Non-Indian commercial fishing grew rapidly, and in 1866 the first salmon cannery on the river was built at Eagle Cliff, Washington. The amount of fish taken from the Columbia continued to increase, and in 1883 the catch was nearly 43 million pounds. The choice spring and summer chinook salmon runs had already begun to decline, and fishermen shifted their attention to other runs and other species in order to maintain a large catch. By 1919, the largest remaining run was that of upriver fall chinook. This run continues to be the primary fishery target today, and it provides nearly 90 percent of the treaty Indian catch.

Overfishing was not the only reason for declining fish runs. Logging, mining, urban growth, irrigation and hydroelectric projects have all reduced the amount of habitat suitable for fish. After the gasoline engine was invented, ocean trolling for salmon began to account for a large percentage of the catch of Columbia River fish.

# Fishing Rights: Treaty Indian Catch in Relation to Other Fisheries

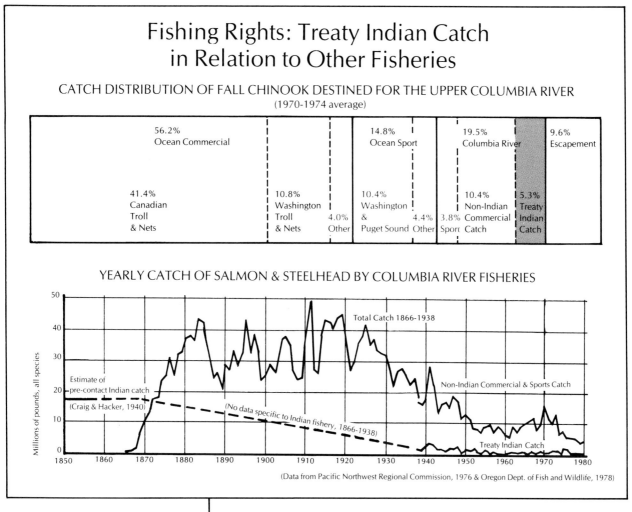

## CATCH DISTRIBUTION OF FALL CHINOOK DESTINED FOR THE UPPER COLUMBIA RIVER
### (1970-1974 average)

| 56.2% Ocean Commercial | | | 14.8% Ocean Sport | | 19.5% Columbia River | | 9.6% Escapement |
|---|---|---|---|---|---|---|---|
| 41.4% Canadian Troll & Nets | 10.8% Washington Troll & Nets | 4.0% Other | 10.4% Washington & Puget Sound | 4.4% Other | 10.4% Non-Indian Commercial / 3.8% Sport | 5.3% Treaty Indian Catch | |

### YEARLY CATCH OF SALMON & STEELHEAD BY COLUMBIA RIVER FISHERIES

Millions of pounds, all species

Estimate of pre-contact Indian catch
(Craig & Hacker, 1940)

Total Catch 1866-1938

(No data specific to Indian fishery, 1866-1938)

Non-Indian Commercial & Sports Catch

Treaty Indian Catch

(Data from Pacific Northwest Regional Commission, 1976 & Oregon Dept. of Fish and Wildlife, 1978)

---

CHART: FISHING RIGHTS: TREATY INDIAN CATCH IN RELATION TO OTHER FISHERIES
Catch data from 1975-80 supplied by Oregon Dept. of Fish and Wildlife.

Kirk Beiningen has pointed out that the treaty Indian catch on the bottom chart cannot rise in a corresponding manner to the Indian population level charted on page 151. The fish runs have been too severely depleted and different user groups are well established.

Some fish from the Columbia go as far north as Alaska before returning to spawn in the stream where they were born. Since the 1920s the ocean catch of fish destined for the Columbia has seriously reduced the number of fish available for in-river fisheries.

## DAMS ON THE COLUMBIA

Dam construction in the Columbia Basin had a devastating effect on the already declining fish runs. More than 20 large dams have been constructed on the river since 1910 and many smaller dams on its tributaries. Some, such as the Grand Coulee, were built without fish ladders, creating total blocks to the migrating fish. Dams also destroyed spawning grounds by covering ideal gravel riffles with water too deep for use by fish. Even the dams that have fish passage facilities are serious obstacles to migratory fish. It has been estimated that 15-20 percent of all fish reaching each major dam are killed as they attempt to pass it, in both their up and downstream travel.

The dams also flooded numerous fishing grounds and stations that for centuries had been used by Indian fishermen. After Bon-

167

MAP: DECLINING FISH RUNS IN
THE COLUMBIA BASIN

These have been compiled from information produced by the Pacific
Northwest Regional Commission,
1976.

# Declining Fish Runs
# in the Columbia Basin

neville Dam was completed in 1938, some efforts were made to
provide "in lieu" (replacement) fishing sites for the Indian fishery,
but these sites could not accommodate many people, and they were
slow to be established. When The Dalles Dam was completed in
1957, the reservoir it formed flooded Celilo Falls and Five Mile Rapids, destroying the largest and perhaps oldest Indian fishery in the
Pacific Northwest. Up to that time, Indian fishermen made most of
their catch in a traditional manner with dipnets from rocks or wood-
en platforms near the falls. The treaty tribes received a cash settlement as compensation for the loss of Celilo Falls and rapids but the
damage was incalculable. Significantly, however, the settlement still
affirmed treaty rights, as only the falls were taken and not the right
to fish.

Before 1957 Indian and non-Indian commercial fishermen fished
anywhere in the river up to the mouth of the Deschutes. After The
Dalles Dam was completed, non-Indian commercial fishing was restricted to the river below Bonneville Dam, and treaty Indian commercial fishing was confined to the area between Bonneville and
McNary dams.

For four years after the completion of The Dalles Dam in 1957 there was almost no Indian fishing in the Columbia. Then treaty fishermen resumed fishing with set gill nets, and the fishery slowly grew again. By 1966, tribal governments at the Warm Springs, Umatilla and Nez Perce reservations specified formal off-reservation fishing regulations and seasons for their members, as the Yakima tribal council had done in 1962. The states of Washington and Oregon did not agree with the idea of tribal regulation of fisheries, however, and state intervention severely reduced Indian fishing in 1966.

By 1967 it was obvious that court hearings would be necessary to sort out the various legal issues involved. Less fish were being sought by more and more fishermen, and regulatory control of the fisheries was inadequate and unclear. The Indian fishery was in the worst position of any group, as Canadian and U.S. ocean fishermen and Columbia River commercial and sport fishermen all had prior access to fish runs destined for the Indian fishery above Bonneville Dam. By the late 1960s, the river's first fishermen had become the last to have a chance to catch what remained of the once-abundant fish.

## COURT DECISIONS AND MANAGEMENT

COURT DECISIONS AND MANAGEMENT

*See* Getches, Rosenfelt & Wilkinson (chap. 11b); BIA (1977); M. West (appendix C); and R. W. Johnson. Much background and current information concerning Columbia River Fishing cases is in the issues of the *Indian Law Reporter*.

Numerous court cases arose to determine the extent and limits of Indian fishing rights. In 1968 the Supreme Court held that Washington state had the right to regulate Indian fisheries, but only for the purpose of "necessary and reasonable conservation." Following this decision, a group of Columbia River treaty fishermen brought suit against the Oregon Fish Commission to have their rights, and the state's authority, more precisely defined. The federal government then brought suit against the state of Oregon as part of its trust responsibility, and the four treaty tribes quickly entered the case. Judge Belloni's decision in the U.S. District Court of Oregon a year later allowed for state regulation of the Indian fishery, but it placed strict limitations on state powers and it required that Indian fishermen be guaranteed a "fair and equitable share of all harvestable fish."

A similar case regarding off-reservation fishing rights was brought before the Washington District Court of Judge Boldt in 1970, whose 1974 decision interpreted the treaty phrase "to fish in common with" to mean that the treaty tribes had the right to an opportunity to take up to 50 percent of the harvestable catch of fish. Judge Belloni then amended his 1969 decision to apply this same allocation to the Columbia River, and the decision was upheld by the Ninth Circuit Court of Appeals in 1975.

The Columbia River treaty tribes agreed to a trial five-year management plan with Oregon and Washington in 1977. Fishing seasons and formulae for sharing the available catch were specified for each run according to estimated run sizes and escapement needs. The tribes and the states also agreed to work cooperatively for the enhancement of the river's fish, and the states and the federal government agreed to seek a reduction of the devastating ocean harvest. During the first year of the plan, Indian fishermen did not have the opportunity to catch their allocated number of fish, but adjustments on future runs were made to compensate as necessary.

## THE "50 PERCENT ALLOCATION"

The 50 Percent Allocation ruling has caused much misunderstanding. One of the most important points of the allocation plan is its definition of "harvestable fish." Harvestable fish are considered to be those that actually return to the Columbia River and are destined for spawning locations above Bonneville Dam. At present, ocean fisheries account for more than 50 percent of the catch of all Columbia River fish. These fisheries are difficult to regulate due to conflicting authority and mixed stocks of fish in the open sea. Also, not all fish that do manage to return to the river head to locations above Bonneville Dam. Many of them enter the Willamette River or other downstream tributaries. Of those that do pass Bonneville, some must be allowed to survive in order to provide adequate spawning for the future. After these deductions, it is only those runs that are abundant enough when they enter the river, and that are headed above Bonneville Dam, that are considered as the harvestable fish to be shared equally between Indian and non-Indian fishermen. The actual catch by Columbia River treaty fishermen is thus much less than 50 percent of all fish caught in-river, and only about 5 percent of the total catch of fish that originate in the river. (*See* chart on p. 167.)

A frequently raised objection to the allocation plan is that treaty Indians comprise a very small segment of the area's total population (less than .03 percent), yet they are permitted to catch up to half of the harvestable fish. Less frequently heard is the fact that non-Indian commercial fishermen—who are allowed to catch the other half of the harvestable fish—also comprise less than .03 percent of the area's population.

The allocation to treaty fishermen must also be viewed in light of the basic tenets of treaty rights, the years of declining fish runs and the continual encroachments on the Indian fishery.

## FUTURE OF THE INDIAN FISHERY

Although many legal questions have been raised by all sides since the important 1969 and 1974 court decisions, the basic point continues to be that Indian treaty fishing rights are legally correct and clearly understandable. The major difficulty lies in the implementation of these rights. Depending on how the management plan works out, the agreement may be renegotiated in coming years. Certain inequities in the enforcement of the plan concern Indian fishermen, as they are the last to fish and therefore the most closely regulated. They must also bear the penalty of any illegal non-Indian downriver

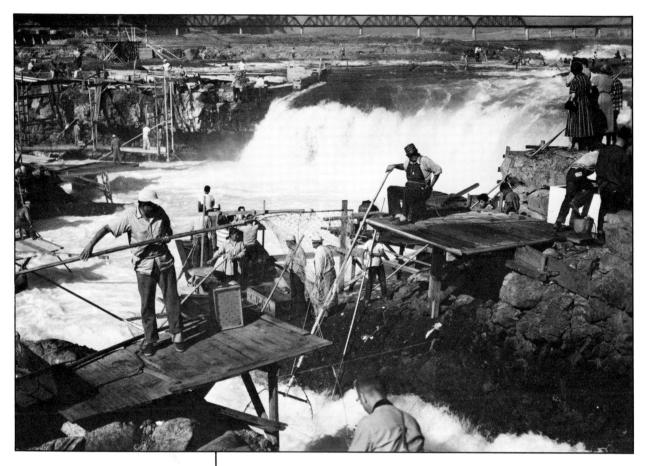

PHOTOGRAPH:
Indian fishing grounds at Celilo Falls prior to construction of Bonneville Dam. (OHS neg. 42690)

catch. Indian fishermen have experienced many instances of harassment and interference in recent years, making for a tense situation on the river.

Despite all the past difficulties, the Columbia River Indian fishery today is very much alive. Celilo Village is more active than it has been in years, and a new longhouse has been built there. Recently formed organizations such as the Columbia River Inter-Tribal Fish Commission and the United Indian Fish Committee continue to work for Indian fishing rights. A major goal at present is greater regional control of fish and river resources, so that regulation and conservation efforts will not conflict with other interests. Increasing demands for the river's resources by its various users will further limit fisheries in the future. As more people desire water, power and fish from the Columbia, treaty fishing rights will need continual protection.

The court-directed concern for conservation of fish resources is something that was not a part of treaty language. It was not foreseen in 1855 that the huge fish runs you could "walk across the river on" would ever become so diminished as to be endangered. Indians have always been concerned with the protection of this resource, as it signifies much more to them than just economic livelihood. Today more than half of all river fish are hatchery produced, and Indian fish hatcheries such as the one on the Warm Springs Reservation contribute to these fish enhancement programs. Other tribal projects and Indian fisheries biologists are working to restore wild anadromous fish habitats where possible.

It is ironic that although the treaties did not foresee or provide for fishery conservation, they may be one of the best means of ensuring it. Treaty rights simply acknowledged Indian rights and activities that had existed for thousands of years. Indians were not responsible for the damage done to Columbia River fish runs, but the determination to protect their heritage may be one of the strongest forces behind the preservation of the river's fish.

# CHRONOLOGY

# CHRONOLOGY

This chronology is a selective list of events that have affected Indians in Oregon and the United States over the past 250 years. It summarizes local and national occurrences, legislation and court rulings.

It also serves as a reference guide, providing readers with legal citations for all treaties, laws, executive orders and court cases discussed in Part Two and Part Three of this volume, and in the accompanying notes. Documents and secondary sources cited here are available in most public and college libraries.

A word about the legal citations and their abbreviations:

FEDERAL LAWS AND INDIAN TREATIES

These are recorded in the *United States Statutes at Large*, abbreviated here as "Stat." For example, the citation for the Indian Allotment Act, "Feb. 8, 1887, 24 Stat. 388," locates this act in volume 24 of the *Statutes at Large*, beginning on page 388. Public Law (P.L.) numbers assigned (assigned since 1950) identify which Congress passed particular bills into law: P.L. 90-284 was passed by the 90th Congress. Public Law numbers are handy for locating more interpretive sources concerning legislation. For example, knowing that the Act of Restoration for the Siletz Tribe (91 Stat. 1415) is also referenced as "P.L. 95-159" enables one to use helpful publications such as the *Congressional Record*. CIS (Congressional Information Service) and USCCAN (U.S. Code, Congressional and Administrative News), sources which document political reaction, debate, amendments, competing bills, public hearings and committee reports detailing an act's journey through the legislative process.

## OREGON LAWS

Oregon Laws are cited as "ORS" (Oregon Revised Statutes). ORS uses a decimal system to identify chapters and sections of the state's legal code: the number to the left of the decimal point identifies the chapter in which the law is codified (classified by subject) while the number to the right refers to the sections within the chapter where the law is found.

## COURT CASES

These are also identified for reference by volume, page and year. The Supreme Court case, *Alcea* v. *U.S.*, is cited as "341 U.S. 48 (1951)" and thus can be found in the 341st volume of the United States Supreme Court Reports, beginning on page 48. Cases heard in U.S. district courts are found in the volumes of the Federal Supplement ("F. Supp.") reporter: *Confederated Tribes of the Umatilla Reservation* v. *Maison* is cited "262 F. Supp. 871 (1966)." Appeal cases heard in the U.S. appellate courts (federal circuits) appear in the Federal 2nd ("F. 2nd") reporter volumes, for example, *Callahan* v. *Kimball*, 590 F.2d 768 (1979).

## EXECUTIVE ORDERS OF THE PRESIDENT

Presidential executive orders concerning Indians and reservations are compiled in a five-volume series of *Indian Laws and Treaties* by Charles Kappler. In the following chronology, the orders are identified as "Kappler." For example, the June 30, 1857 executive order creating the Grand Ronde Reservation is referenced here as "1 Kappler 886," and can be found on page 886 of Kappler's first volume.

## CHRONOLOGY OF HISTORICAL EVENTS, MAJOR FEDERAL AND STATE LAWS AND IMPORTANT COURT CASES (1643-1979)*

1643     First treaty between an Indian nation and a foreign government; Mohawk and Dutch sign in New York.

1778     First U.S.-Indian treaty; signed with Delawares. Sept. 17, 7 Stat. 13.

1787     "Utmost Good Faith" provision of the Northwest Ordinance; Congress declares Indian land title unalterable without a treaty.

1789     War Department begins to administer Indian Affairs. Act of Aug. 7, 1 Stat. 49.

1790     First Trade & Intercourse Act with Indian tribes; sale of Indian lands possible only under public treaty to U.S. government (not directly available to private citizens). July 22, 1 Stat. 137.

1793     1790 Trade & Intercourse Act amended. March 1, 1 Stat. 329.

1794     Treaty with Oneidas, Tuscaroras, Stockbridges; first to provide for education of Indian people. Dec. 2, 7 Stat. 47.

1795     Indian Intercourse Act. Mar. 3, 1 Stat. 443.

1796     Indian Trade & Intercourse Act; "to preserve peace on the frontiers," contains first statutory description of Indian Country based on boundaries established by treaties (redefined by Congress to conform with new treaties in later years). May 19, 1 Stat. 469.

1799     Indian Intercourse Act. Mar. 3, 1 Stat. 743.

1800     Indian Intercourse Act. Apr. 22, 2 Stat. 39.

1802     Indian Trade & Intercourse Act. Mar. 30, 2 Stat. 139.

1819     $10,000 annual federal appropriation passed for Indian "civilization" and education. Mar. 3, 3 Stat. 516.

1823     *Johnson* v. *McIntosh*; first case recognizing "aboriginal" Indian land title for use and occupancy. 21 U.S. (8 Wheat) 543.

| 1824 | Office of Indian Affairs (BIA) established in War Department. |
|---|---|
| 1827 | Cherokee Nation adopts own constitution; ignored by state of Georgia. |
| 1830 | Indian Removal Act; Eastern tribes sent to Indian Territory (Oklahoma). May 28, 4 Stat. 411. |
| 1831 | *Cherokee Nation* v. *Georgia*. 30 U.S. (5 Pet.) 1. |
| 1832 | *Worcester* v. *Georgia*. 31 U.S. (5 Pet.) 515. |
| | Office of Commissioner of Indian Affairs established in War Department. Act of July 9, 4 Stat. 564. |
| 1834 | Final Indian Trade & Intercourse Act; redefines Indian Country; also allows U.S. Army to quarantine Indians to facilitate assimilation. (Also called ''Reorganization Act of 1834,'' ''Organic Act'' of the BIA, setting up agency and field force system.) June 30, 4 Stat. 729. |
| 1835 | Treaty of New Echota (Cherokee Removal). Dec. 29, 7 Stat. 478. |
| 1842 | First U.S. Indian Agent in Northwest begins work; Dr. Elijah White. |
| 1846 | Oregon Treaty of 1846; Great Britain and U.S. divide Northwest Indian lands. |
| 1848 | Organic Act creates Oregon Territory; U.S. obligated to make treaties: ''Nothing in this act contained shall be construed to impair the rights of person or property now pertaining to Indians in said Territory, so long as such rights shall remain unextinguished by treaty between the United States and such Indians.'' Aug. 14, 9 Stat. 323. |
| | Cayuse War begins. |
| 1849 | Oregon's first governor and superintendent of Indian Affairs arrives; Joseph Lane. |
| | Indian Affairs transferred from War Department to Department of Interior. Mar. 3, 9 Stat. 395. |
| 1850 | Five Cayuse men (accused of 1843 Whitman massacre) tried and hanged at Oregon City, June 3. |

Act creates three-member treaty commission to obtain agreements from western Oregon tribes for removal to east side of Cascades ("Thurston Bill"). June 5, 9 Stat. 437.

Donation Land Act awards free land to Oregon's early non-Indian settlers. Sept. 27, 9 Stat. 496.

1851    Oregon Treaty Commission makes six treaties with Willamette Valley tribes at Champoeg (never ratified by Congress and commission abolished). Act of Feb. 27, 9 Stat. 547.

New Oregon Indian superintendent takes office; Anson Dart.

Ten Tansey Point treaties concluded between tribes and Dart (never ratified). Two Port Orford treaties concluded between southwestern coast tribes and Dart (never ratified). Treaty between Clackamas Tribe and Dart (never ratified). (See B and D on map, p. 83.)

1853    Dart resigns as Indian superintendent; Joel Palmer takes office.

First ratified treaty in Oregon; treaty with Rogue River. Sept. 10, 10 Stat. 1018.

Treaty with Cow Creek Umpquas. Sept. 19, 10 Stat. 1027.

1853–56 Southwest Oregon Indian conflicts ("Rogue" Indian Wars).

1854    Act appropriates money for Indian Affairs, assigns Palmer to negotiate treaties. July 31, 10 Stat. 315, 330.

Treaty with Tualatins (never ratified). (See E on map, p. 83)

Treaty; U.S.-Umpqua and Kalapuya. Nov. 29, 10 Stat. 1125.

1855    Treaty; U.S.-Kalapuya and Confederated Bands of Willamette Valley. Jan. 22, 10 Stat. 1143.

Treaty; U.S.-Walla Walla, Cayuses and Umatillas. June 9, 12 Stat. 945.

Treaty; U.S.-Nez Perce. June 11, 12 Stat. 957.

Treaty; U.S.-Tribes of Middle Oregon (Warm Springs). June 25, 12 Stat. 963.

Coast Treaty cedes 11 million acres (never ratified).

Executive order creates Siletz (Coast) Reservation. Nov. 9, 1 Kappler 890.

Treaty; U.S.-Molallas. Dec. 21, 12 Stat. 981.

Yakima War; Congress reacts by delaying until 1859 ratification of many Oregon treaties.

| | |
|---|---|
| 1855–60 | Warm Springs Reservation settled. |
| 1856 | Final southwestern Oregon conflict (Big Bend of Rogue River), June 20. Military removals of western Oregon Indians to Grand Ronde and Siletz reservations. |
| 1857 | Executive order creates Grand Ronde Reservation. June 30, 1 Kappler 886. |
| 1858 | Act extends public land laws to area east of Cascades; opens Indian land to settlers before Plateau treaties ratified. May 29, 11 Stat. 293. |
| 1859 | U.S. Senate ratifies 1855 Plateau treaties. |
| | Oregon statehood. Act of Feb. 14, 11 Stat. 383. |
| 1861 | Failed promises create suffering at Siletz when 257 people have ratified treaties while 1,176 do not. |
| | Executive order removes Yaquina tract from Siletz Reservation under pressure from non-Indian settlers. Dec. 21, 1 Kappler 891. |
| 1863 | Treaty with Nez Perce (Lapwai, Idaho); cedes Wallowa Valley. June 9, 14 Stat. 647. |
| | U.S. Court of Claims created; Indian claims *not* allowed. Mar. 3, 12 Stat. 765. |
| 1864 | Act appropriates $20,000 to negotiate treaties with southern Oregon Indian tribes. Mar. 25, 13 Stat. 37. |
| | Unauthorized Steele Treaty with Modocs in northern California; pledges Indian retention of Tule Lake (never ratified). |

|      | Treaty with Klamaths, Modocs and Yahooskin Snakes (modified by 1869 treaty). Oct. 14, 16 Stat. 707. |
|------|------|
| 1865 | Treaty with Snakes. Aug. 12, 14 Stat. 683. |
|      | Second treaty with the Tribes of Middle Oregon; restricts travel and fishing rights of Warm Springs tribes. Nov. 15, 14 Stat. 751. |
| 1868 | Final treaty with Nez Perce in Idaho. Aug. 13, 15 Stat. 693. |
|      | Paiute "Peace" Treaty, Fort Harney (never ratified). Dec. 10. |
| 1869 | Act creates Board of Indian Commissioners to advise on national policy and correct mismanagement in purchase of Indian supplies (in effect until 1933). April 10, 16 Stat. 13. |
|      | U.S.-Paiute post-treaty council, Fort Harney; most Paiutes demand separate reservation in southeastern Oregon; two bands agree to settle at Klamath Reservation. |
| 1870 | Subagency set up at Yainax, Klamath Reservation. |
| 1871 | Act terminates treaty-making between U.S. and Indian tribes; all earlier treaties remain in effect. Mar. 3, 16 Stat. 544, 570. |
| 1872 | Executive order creates Malheur Reservation. Sept. 12, 1 Kappler 888. |
| 1872–73 | Modoc War (southern Oregon and northern California); many Modocs sent to Oklahoma afterwards. |
| 1873 | *U.S.* v. *Cook*; Supreme Court rules tribes cannot sell reservation timber for profit but only use it to satisfy their own needs (later reversed). 19 Wall. 591. |
|      | Executive order creates "Wallowa Reserve for Roaming Nez Perce." June 16, 1 Kappler 894. |
| 1874 | Oregon Legislature petitions Congress for land sale from Umatilla tribes. |
| 1875 | Act reduces Siletz Reservation; residents displaced. Mar. 3, 18 Stat. 420, 446. |

Executive order alters Malheur Reservation boundary. May 15, 1 Kappler 888.

Executive order annuls Nez Perce Wallowa Reserve of 1873. June 10, 1 Kappler 895.

Indian Homestead Act; permits Indian people to obtain public domain allotments. Mar. 3, 18 Stat. 402.

1876    Executive order alters Malheur Reservation boundary. Jan. 28, 1 Kappler 889.

1877    Nez Perce War; Chief Joseph's people removed to Kansas and Oklahoma.

1878    Klamath Reservation tribal police force organized.

Bannock War (southern Idaho and Southeastern Oregon); Paiutes flee Malheur Reservation, and U.S. Army occupies it.

1879    Five hundred Paiutes marched to Yakima Reservation.

1881    Umatilla Reservation tribal police force organized.

1882    Indian Industrial Schools Act. July 31, 22 Stat. 181.

Act ratifies sale of 640 acres by Umatilla tribes for town of Pendleton. Aug. 5, 22 Stat. 297.

1883    Umatilla Reservation Indian court established.

Executive order closes all but 320 acres of Malheur Indian Reservation (Fort Harney). May 21, 1 Kappler 890.

1885    Slater Allotment Act; divides and reduces Umatilla Reservation. Mar. 3, 23 Stat. 340.

1887    Indian Allotment (also called "Dawes," "Severalty" or "General Allotment") Act; allows individual parceling of tribal lands and sale of surplus to non-Indians. Feb. 8, 24 Stat. 388.

1888    Secretary of Interior order reduces Umatilla Reservation, permits sale of surplus land to outsiders. Dec. 4, 1 Kappler 891.

1889    Act permits tribes to sell dead or down timber on their reservation to outside parties. Feb. 16, 25 Stat. 673.

Executive order closes Malheur Reservation; returns last 320 acres of Fort Harney to public domain. Mar. 2, 1 Kappler 890.

1891    Indian Reservation Leasing Act; allows leasing of Indian allotments for farming and grazing to non-Indians. Feb. 28, 26 Stat. 794.

1893    *U.S. v. California and Oregon Land Co.*; unsuccessful suit by federal government to regain southern Oregon road land patents, some of which cross Klamath tribal lands. 148 U.S. 31.

1894    Act ratifies 1892 agreement ceding 191,798 surplus tribal acres of Siletz Reservation to the federal government. Aug. 15, 28 Stat. 286, 323.

1896    115 Paiute people obtain 160-acre or smaller public domain allotments in the Burns area.

1897    Klamath Boundary Commission determines that 617,490 acres were excluded from reservation by faulty surveys.

Act pays Nehalem Tillamooks small sums for lands taken by 1851 unratified treaty. June 7, 30 Stat. 62.

1904    *U.S. v. California and Oregon Land Co.*; second unsuccessful suit to recover road grants running through Klamath Reservation. 192 U.S. 325.

Act ratifies 1901 agreements ceding 26,111 unallotted acres on Grand Ronde Reservation to U.S. April 28, 33 Stat. 567.

1906    Act ratifies agreement to cede disputed Klamath boundary lands to U.S.; road grant sections inside Klamath Reservation restored to tribe while land company compensated with 87,000 acres elsewhere on reserved Klamath lands (Yamsay Mountain). June 21, 24 Stat. 325, 367.

Burke Act amends Dawes Act; sets standard of competency for issuing fee patents on Indian allotments. May 8, 34 Stat. 182.

*Winans v. U.S.*, Supreme Court rules that treaties are grants *from* (not to) Indians; tribes reserved all rights not expressly granted; tribal access to off-reservatin fishing sites can not be impeded. 198 U.S. 371.

| 1908 | *Winters* v. *U.S.*; affirms tribal reserved rights to waters arising from or flowing through reservation lands. 207 U.S. 564. |
| | Indian Reservation Timber Cutting Act. Mar. 28, 35 Stat. 51. |
| | Act awards Klamaths small sum for 1906 loss of 87,000 acres. April 30, 35 Stat. 70, 92. |
| 1908–10 | Allotment occurs on Klamath Reservation. |
| 1910 | Indian Trust Allotment Act. June 25, 36 Stat. 855. |
| 1912 | Act awards small payments to northern coast and Chinook bands for lands taken by 1851 unratified treaties. Aug. 24, 37 Stat. 518, 535. |
| 1913 | *U.S.* v. *Sandoval*; landmark ruling on extent of trust protections extended to Indian tribes. 231 U.S. 28. |
| 1919 | Indian Reservation (Mineral Lands) Leasing Act. June 30, 41 Stat. 3. |
| 1921 | Indian Appropriations Expenditures (Snyder) Act; directs Bureau of Indian Affairs to use its funds to benefit all Indians; regardless of degree of blood or enrollment status in federally recognized tribes. Nov. 2, 42 Stat. 208. |
| 1924 | Indian Citizenship Act. June 2, 43 Stat. 253. |
| | Indian Health Division established in BIA. |
| | Indian Reservation (Oil and Gas) Leasing Act. May 29, 43 Stat. 244. |
| 1925 | Egan Land Co. donates ten acres to Burns Paiutes; site of "Indian Village." |
| 1926 | Act provides for construction of a school for Burns Paiute Indian children. June 23, 44 Stat. 761. |
| 1927 | Amendment to Indian Reservation Oil and Gas Leasing Act. Mar. 3, 44 Stat. 1347. |
| 1928 | Meriam Report calls for reforms in federal Indian policy. |
| 1933 | Executive order abolishes Board of Indian Commissioners; all affairs now completely under secretary of Interior. May 25, 1 Kappler 6145. |

Federal Emergency Relief Act (FERA); authorizes provision of subsistence homesteads to landless Indian tribes. April 8, 49 Stat. 115.

National Industrial Recovery Act (NIRA); authorizes provision of submarginal land to Indian tribes and other rural people. June 16, 48 Stat. 200.

1934 Indian Welfare (Johnson O'Malley) Act; authorizes secretary of Interior to contract with states for Indian education, health and welfare. April 16, 48 Stat. 596.

Indian Reorganization (Wheeler-Howard) Act (IRA); ends allotment and encourages tribal self government. June 18, 48 Stat. 984.

Pacific Northwest Conference on the IRA (Chemawa School, March 8-9); tribes present express uncertainty about this legislation.

*Duwamish et al Indian* v. *U.S.*; disappointing claims case ruling on value of lands lost by Chinooks and other western Washington tribes. 79 Ct. Cl. 530.

1935 Burns Paiutes obtain some homestead and submarginal lands but trust title not transferred to tribe.

Deficiency Appropriations Act; requires Court of Claims to subtract ("offset") gratuitous and other voluntary expenditures by U.S. on behalf of tribes from legal awards due tribes in claims cases. Aug. 12, 49 Stat. 571, 596.

*Klamath and Moadoc Tribes et al* v. *U.S.*; unsuccessful first attempt by tribes to obtain adequate reimbursement for 87,000 acres lost in 1906. 296 U.S. 244.

1936 Grand Ronde Indian Community, Inc. formed (under terms of Indian Reorganization Act), May 18.

National Indian Arts and Crafts Board established.

1934 Indian Welfare Act amended. June 4, 49 Stat. 1458.

1937 Burns Paiute Colony Business Committee organized.

Executive order transfers Burns subsistence homesteads (purchased in 1935) from Dept. of Agriculture to Interior. Tribe does not possess trust title to its lands. Feb. 1, 5 Kappler 643.

| 1938 | *U.S.* v. *Brookfield Fisheries*; Umatilla and Yakima tribes guaranteed access to Celilo Falls fishing grounds. 24 F. Supp. 712. |
| | Warm Springs Tribes adopt a constitution, accept IRA and incorporate. |
| | *Klamath and Moadoc et al* v. *U.S.*; Supreme Court reverses 1935 Yamsay Mountain decision; rules that Klamath received inadequate compensation for 87,000 acres lost in 1908. 304 U.S. 119. |
| | *U.S.* v. *Shoshoni Tribe* rules that tribes own timber and minerals on reserved lands. 304 U.S. 111. |
| | Executive order transfers "Burns Colony Project" submarginal lands. April 5, 5 Kappler 644, 652. |
| | *Klamath and Moadoc et al* v. *U.S.*; Klamath suit for compensation for lands lost in previous century boundary disputes dismissed. 86 Ct. Cl. 614. |
| 1939 | Act restores to Umatilla Reservation 14,000 acres of lands excluded in 1888. Aug. 10, 53 Stat. 1351. |
| | Coos-Lower Umpqua and Siuslaw tribal hall built. |
| | *U.S.* v. *Walker Irrigation District*; finds trust lands set aside by executive order also reserved river water for Indian use. 104 F.2d 334. |
| 1940 | *Klamath et al* v. *U.S.*; Klamath sues U.S. for accounting and nonfulfillment of 1864 treaty (dismissed). 90 Ct.Cl. 681. |
| 1941 | *Confederated Tribes of Warm Springs* v. *U.S.*; Warm Springs people ruled owners of McQuinn Strip (78,611 acres taken by faulty surveys in 1871). 95 Ct.Cl. 23. |
| | *Nez Perce* v. *U.S.*; suit to recover value of gold taken from Nez Perce Tribe (dismissed because government offsets exceeded compensation due). 96 Ct.Cl. 606. |
| | *Nez Perce* v. *U.S.*; suit for land taking and general accounting (dismissed). 95 Ct.Cl. 11. |
| 1945 | *Confederated Tribes of Warm Springs* v. *U.S.*; tribes awarded $241,084 for loss of McQuinn Strip (dismissed when federal offset resulted in no award to tribe). 103 C.Cl. 741. |

|      | *Alcea Band of Tillamooks et al* v. *U.S.*; some coastal people win suit for "aboriginal Indian title" to lands taken by unratified 1855 treaty. 103 Ct.Cl. 494 |
| --- | --- |
| 1946 | Act creates Indian Claims Commission. Aug. 13, 60 Stat. 1049. |
|      | Senate Bill 845; unsuccessful attempt to restore McQuinn Strip lands to Warm Springs. |
|      | 1945 Lower court *Alcea* decision affirmed by Supreme Court. 329 U.S. 40. |
| 1948 | Act authorizes Warm Springs tribes to receive timber profits from, but not ownership of, excluded McQuinn Strip. July 3, 62 Stat. 1237. |
| 1949 | Umatilla Indian Reservation adopts constitution and by-laws; delegation travels to Washington, D.C. to obtain better rental fees (cropshares) for allotted lands leased to non-Indians. |
| 1950 | *Alcea et al* v. *U.S.*; awards compensation for value of coast lands in 1855 plus interest since that date (following 1945 court case). 87 F. Supp. 938. |
| 1951 | *Alcea et al* v. *U.S.*; Supreme Court reverses 1950 ruling on interest payment; allows compensation for 1885 land value only. 341 U.S. 48. |
| 1953 | House Concurrent Resolution 108; declares congressional intent to end federal trust relationship with Indian tribes. Aug. 1, 67 Stat. B. 132. |
|      | Public Law 280; act confers state jurisdiction over tribes in California, Minnesota, Nebraska, Wisconsin and Oregon (excluding Warm Springs). Aug. 15, P.L. 83-280, 67 Stat. 588. |
|      | BIA begins Volunteer Relocation Program in effort to move Indian people to cities. |
|      | *Snake or Paiute Indians* v. *U.S.*; descendants of Malheur Paiutes win appeal against federal government for taking of their reservation without compensation in 1882. 112 F. Supp. 543. |
| 1954 | Act terminates Klamath Tribe. Aug. 13, P.L. 83-587, 68 Stat. 718. |

Act terminates all western Oregon Indians, Siletz and Grand Ronde tribes. Aug. 13, P.L. 83-538, 68 Stat. 724.

1956    Chairman of Coos-Lower Umpqua and Siuslaw Tribal Council petitions United Nations for assistance.

Grand Ronde and Siletz reservations closed.

1957    Completed Dalles Dam destroys Celilo Falls Indian fishery; some monetary compensation later paid to tribes.

Amendment to 1954 Klamath Termination Act provides management specialists and defers sale of tribal property. Aug. 14, P.L. 85-132, 71 Stat. 347.

Act conveys federal land at McNary Dam townsite to Umatilla Reservation, to stimulate industrial development. Aug. 28, P.L. 85-186, 71 Stat. 468.

1958    Amendment to 1954 Klamath Termination Act provides for sales of Klamath Forest and Marsh to private or federal parties. Aug. 23, P.L. 85-731, 72 Stat. 816.

1959    Act provides revolving loan fund for Klamath people withdrawing from tribe. June 11, P.L. 86-40, 73 Stat. 70.

Amendment to 1954 Klamath Termination Act provides for sale of Klamath Forest and Marsh. Sept. 9, P.L. 86-247, 73 Stat. 477.

Act permits tax exempt status for Celilo Falls settlement payments to Yakima, Warm Springs, Umatilla and Nez Perce tribes. July 31, P.L. 86-125, 73 Stat. 271.

1960    Act holds Fort McDermitt Indian lands in trust. April 4, P.L. 86-401, 74 Stat. 12.

*Confederated Tribes of Umatilla Indian Reservation* v. *Maison*; Umatilla off-reservation fishing rights in Columbia and Snake tributaries upheld. 186 F.Supp. 519.

Federal Housing Assistance programs opened to Indian people.

1963    *Maison* v. *Confederated Tribes of Umatilla Indian Reservation*; State appeals 1960 Umatilla fishing rights ruling but tribal rights are affirmed. 314 F.2nd 169.

1964    Economic Opportunity Act (EOA) programs open to Indians.

Act awards descendants of Malheur Paiutes Indian Claims Commission payment for illegal taking of their reservation in the 1880s. Aug. 20, P.L. 88-464, 78 Stat. 563.

Amendment to 1954 Housing Act makes housing and planning grants more available to Indian tribes. Sept. 2, P.L. 88-560, 78 Stat. 769.

| | |
|---|---|
| 1965 | Remaining tribal members vote on Klamath termination. |

1966    *Confederated Tribes of Umatilla Indian Reservation* v. *Maison*; upholds treaty rights to hunt on unclaimed land in Umatilla and Wallowa-Whitman national forests without restriction by Oregon Game Commission. 262 F.Supp. 871.

1968    Executive order creates National Council on Indian Opportunity. Aug. 11, Order No. 115551.

Indian Civil Rights Act; guarantees constitutional rights of Indian people. April 11, P.L. 90-284, 82 Stat. 77.

Secretary of Interior recognizes Burns Paiute Colony.

1968–69 Five Indian students form Native American Student Union at University of Oregon, Eugene.

1969    Remaining Klamath reservation members vote to dissolve trust arrangement with U.S. National Bank of Oregon.

*U.S.* v. *Oregon* (*Sohappy* v. *Smith*, also called the "Belloni Decision"); rules that state regulation of Columbia River anadromous fisheries must respect treaty tribes' right to fish "in usual and accustomed places." 302 F.Supp. 899.

1970    *Choctaw Nation* v. *Oklahoma*; affirms that treaties promising displaced Choctaws and Cherokees fee simple patents on their Oklahoma lands also reserved Indian ownership of river beds. 397 U.S. 620.

1970–80 Many non-federally recognized or terminated Oregon tribes reorganize during this decade.

1972    Portland Urban Indian Council (UIC) organizes and incorporates.

Willow River Indian Benevolent Association (WRIBA) incorporates.

Indian Education Act amends 1950 Education Act; creates Title IV Apparatus for new Indian programs in local schools. June 23, P.L. 92-318, 86 Stat. 235, 334.

Warm Springs Inheritance Act; preserves trust status of inherited allotments. Aug. 10, P.L. 92-377, 86 Stat. 530.

Act restores McQuinn Strip to Warm Springs. Sept. 21, P.L. 92-427, 86 Stat. 719.

Act creates Burns Paiute Reservation; transfers 1935 lands trust title to tribe. Oct. 13, P.L. 92-488, 86 Stat. 719.

Native American Rights Fund and U.S. Federal Trade Commission investigate exploitation of Klamath people since termination era.

1973     Confederated Tribes of Siletz form new tribal council.

Act authorizes U.S. purchase of Klamath Tribe's last assets; land added to Winema National Forest and federal wildlife refuge. Aug. 16, P.L. 93-102, 87 Stat. 349.

1974     Native American Programs Act (passed Jan. 4, 1975). P.L. 93-644, 88 Stat. 2291.

Cow Creek Umpquas incorporate.

*Kimball* v. *Callahan*; reverses lower court judgement, affirms hunting rights on former reservation for Klamath members who withdrew under 1954 Termination Act. 493 F.2d 564.

1975     American Indian Policy Review Commission (AIPRC) established; first comprehensive examination of federal Indian policy since 1928 Meriam Report.

Eugene Indian Center incorporates.

Grand Ronde Tribal Council reorganizes.

Klamath Game Commission formed following *Kimball* v. *Callahan* decision.

Indian Self-Determination & Education Assistance Act. Jan. 4, P.L. 93-638, 88 Stat. 2203.

Klamath Tribe Executive Group forms.

| 1976 | Indian Health Care Improvement Act. Sept. 30, P.L. 94-437, 90 Stat. 1400. |
|---|---|
| 1977 | Bill to aid consolidation of Umatilla tribal lands introduced in U.S. House; withdrawn a year later. HR 2539. |
|  | Oregon Legislature act prohibits disturbance, destruction or removal of Indian burial sites. Reinterment provisions under supervision of appropriate Indian organization also established. ORS 97.740-97.750. |
|  | Act restores Confederated Tribes of Siletz with federal recognition of tribal status. Nov. 18, P.L. 95-195, 91 Stat. 1415. |
|  | *Confederated Tribes of Umatilla* v. *Alexander*; prevents dam construction on Catherine Creek which would have infringed on treaty fishing rights. 440 F.Supp. 553. |
| 1978 | Umatilla Inheritance Act; preserves trust status of inherited allotments. April 18, P.L. 95-264, 92 Stat. 202. |
|  | Native American Indian Religious Freedom Act. Aug. 11, P.L. 95-341, 92 Stat. 469. |
| 1978 | Indian Claims Commission ends; unfinished cases go to U.S. Tenure of Court of Claims. |
| 1979 | *Washington* v. *Washington State Commerical Fisheries*, etc.; Supreme Court affirms district court orders implementing Boldt decision in U.S. Washington; 1855 treaties did reserve Indian rights to harvest specific share of Puget Sound fishery resources. July 2, 99 S.Ct. 3055. |
|  | Archeological Resources Protection Act (ARPA) of 1979 becomes law. July, P.L. 96-95. |
|  | Tribal-State Compact Act of 1979; would allow mutual compacts to resolve tribal and state jurisdictional problems in Indian Country. Introduced: H.R. 11489, S. 2502. |
|  | *Callahan* v. *Kimball*; appeals court rules Klamath Tribe is entitled to hunt, trap and fish within ancestral (former) reservation free from state regulation, despite termination. 590 F.2d. 768. |
|  | Bill permitting Cow Creek Band of Umpquas to sue in U.S. court of claims. S. 668 passes Senate in October. H.R. 2822 pending in House. |

Bill to Create Siletz Reservation (3,666 acres) introduced. Nov. 28, S. 2055.

# BIBLIOGRAPHY

# BIBLIOGRAPHY

The following selected abbreviations have been used in the Bibliography:

| | |
|---|---|
| *AA* | *American Anthropologist* |
| *BBAE* | *Bulletin of the Bureau of American Ethnology* |
| *CA* | *Current Anthropology* |
| *CUCA* | *Columbia University Contributions to American Anthropology* |
| *ICAES* | *International Congress of the Anthropological and Ethnological Sciences* |
| *IH* | *Indian Historian* |
| *IJAL* | *International Journal of American Linguistics* |
| *JAFL* | *Journal of American Folklore* |
| *LR* | *Law Review* (Name of particular institution precedes each) |
| *NWARN* | *Northwest Anthropological Research Notes* |
| *OHQ* | *Oregon Historical Quarterly* |
| *PNQ* | *Pacific Northwest Quarterly* |
| *SWJA* | *Southwestern Journal of Anthropology* |
| *UCAR* | *University of California Anthropological Records* |
| *UCASR* | *University of California Archaeological Survey Reports* |
| *UCPAAE* | *University of California Publications in American Archaeology and Ethnology* |
| *UWPA* | *University of Washington Publications in Anthropology* |

Ackerman, David. 1975. "Background Report on PL 280 for Committee on Interior and Insular Affairs." U.S. Senate. Report No. 442-11. Washington, D.C.

Aikens, C. Melvin, ed.

1971. "Great Basin Anthropological Conference 1970." *University of Oregon Anthropological Papers*, no. 1. Eugene.

1975. "Archaeological Studies in the Willamette Valley, Oregon." *University of Oregon Anthropological Papers*, no. 8. Eugene.

American Friends Service Committee. 1970. *Uncommon Controversy: Fishing Rights of the Muckleshoot, Puyallup, and Nisqually Indians.* Seattle.

American Indian Journal. 1978. "Indian Land Claims in Maine and Elsewhere: A Long Costly Path." *American Indian Journal* 4, no. 12: 45-48.

American Indian Lawyer Training Program. 1975. *Indian Tribes as Governments*. Oakland.

American Indian Policy Review Commission. (All reports published in Washington, D.C.)

1976. *Final Report of Task Force One: On Trust Responsibilities and the Federal-Indian Relationship, Including Treaty Review.*

1976. *Final Report of Task Force Two: On Tribal Government.*

1976. *Final Report of Task Force Three: On Federal Administration and Structure of Indian Affairs.*

1976. *Final Report of Task Force Four: On Federal, State and Tribal Jurisdiction.*

1976. *Final Report of Task Force Five: On Indian Education.*

1976. *Final Report of Task Force Six: On Indian Health.*

1976. *Final Report of Task Force Seven: On Reservation Resource Development and Protection.*

1976. *Final Report of Task Force Eight: On Urban and Rural Non-Reservation Indians.*

1976. *Final Report of Task Force Nine: On Law Consolidation, Revision and Codification.*

1976. *Final Report of Task Force Ten: On Terminated and Non-Federally Recognized Tribes.*

1976. *Final Report of Task Force Eleven: On Alcohol and Drug Abuse.*

1976. *Special Joint Task Force Report on Alaskan Native Issues.*

1977. *Final Report of the AIPRC.*

Anastasio, Angelo. 1972. "The Southern Plateau: An Ecological Analysis of Intergroup Relations." *NWARN* 6., no. 2:109-229. (Reprint. University of Idaho Laboratory of Anthropology. Moscow, ID, 1975.)

Aoki, Haruo.

1966. "Nez Perce and Proto-Sahaptin Kinship Terms." *IJAL* 32: 357-68.

1967. "'Chopunnish' and 'Green Wood Indians': A Note on Nez Perce Tribal Synonymy." *AA* 69: 505-06.

1970. "Usage of Referential Kin Terms in Nez Perce." In *Languages and Cultures of Western North America*, edited by Earl H. Swanson, Jr. Pocatello, ID.

Bailey, Robert G. 1943. *Nez Perce Indians*. Lewiston, ID.

Bakken, Lavola. 1973. *Land of the North Umpquas: Peaceful Indians of the West*. Grants Pass, OR.

Barnett, Homer G.

1937. "Culture Element Distributions: Oregon Coast." *UCAR* 1, no. 7: 155-204.

1957. *Indian Shakers: A Messianic Cult of the Pacific Northwest.* Carbondale, Ill.

Barrett, S. A. 1910. "The Material Culture of the Klamath Lake and Modoc Indians of Northeast California and Southern Oregon." *UCPAAE* 5, no. 4.

Barth, Gunther, ed. 1959. *All Quiet on the Yamhill: The Civil War in Oregon.* Eugene.

Baumhoff, Martin. 1963. "Ecological Determinants of Aboriginal California Populations." *UCPAAE* 49, no. 2.

Beal, Merrill A. 1963. *I Will Fight No More Forever: Chief Joseph and the Nez Perce War.* Seattle.

Beckham, Stephen Dow.

1971a. "Lonely Outpost: The Army's Fort Umpqua." *OHQ* 72: 233-58.

1971b. *Requiem for a People.* Norman, OK.

1977. *The Indians of Western Oregon: This Land was Theirs.* Coos Bay, OR.

Beeson, John. 1858. *A Plea for the Indians: With Facts and Features of the Late War in Oregon.* New York.

Beiningen, Kirk T. 1976. "Indian Fishery." In *Investigative Reports of Columbia River Fisheries Project*, sect. P. Vancouver, WA.

Benson, Robert. 1973. "Map of Indian Languages." In *An Historical Atlas of Early Oregon*, edited by Judith A. Farmer and Kenneth Holmes. Portland.

Bergquist, James. 1957. "The Oregon Donation Act and the National Land Policy." *OHQ* 58: 17-35.

Berreman, Joel. 1937. "Tribal Distribution in Oregon." *Memoirs of the American Anthropological Association* 47 (1937).

Billard, Jules B., ed. 1974. *World of the American Indian.* Washington, D.C.

Bischoff, William N. 1945. *The Jesuits in Old Oregon.* Caldwell, ID.

Bishop, Bruce. "The State and Indian Jurisdiction: Another Approach." *State Government* 51: 4, 230-34.

Blanchet, Rev. Francis N. 1878. *Historical Sketches of the Catholic Church in Oregon During the Past Forty Years (1838-1878).* Portland.

Blinderman, Abraham. 1978. "Congressional Social Darwinism and the American Indian." *IH* 11: 2, 15-17.

Blyth, Beatrice. 1938. "Northern Paiute Bands in Oregon." *AA* 40: 402-405.

Boas, Franz.

1893. "Doctrine of Souls Among the Chinook Indians." *JAFL* 6: 20, 37-43.

1898. "Traditions of the Tillamook Indians." *JAFL* 11: 23-38, 133-50.

1923. "Notes on the Tillamook." *UCPAAE* 20.

Bohanen, Lyndon. 1974. "The Urban Indian Program in Portland, Oregon." MSW thesis, Portland State University.

Bowen, William A. 1978. *The Willamette Valley: Migration and Settlement on the Oregon Frontier.* Seattle.

Boyd, Robert. 1975. "Another Look at the 'Fever and Ague' of Western Oregon in the Early 1930s." (Paper presented at Northwest Anthropological Conference.)

Bright, Jane O., and Bright, William. 1965. "Semantic Structures in Northwest California and the Sapir-Whorf Hypothesis." (In "Formal Semantic Analysis," edited by E. A. Hummel.) *Society for American Archaeology Special Publications*. no. 67, part 2.

Brimlow, George F.
1938. *The Bannock Indian War of 1878*. Caldwell, ID.
1951. *Harney County, Oregon, and Its Range Land*. Portland.
1967. "Two Cavalrymen's Diaries of the Bannock War, 1878." *OHQ* 68: 221-57, 293-316.

Brink, Pamela. 1971. "Paviotso Child Training: Notes." *IH* 4: 1, 47-50, 66.

Brookings Institution. 1928. *The Problem of Indian Administration (The Meriam Report)*. Washington, D.C. (Reprint, 1971).

Brophy, William, and Aberle, Sophie D., eds. 1966. *The Indian: America's Business*. Norman, OK.

Bunting, David, and Trulove, W. T. 1970. "Some Experiences with Guaranteed Incomes and Lump Sum Payments: The Case of the Klamath Indians." (Paper presented at the 137th meeting of the American Association for Advancement of Science. Chicago.)

Bureau of Indian Affairs. n.d. *Tribal Directory*. Washington, D.C.

Bureau of Indian Affairs Planning Support Group.
1974. *The Burns Paiute Colony, Its Resources and Development Potential*. Billings, MT.
1977. *Background Information of Indian Fishing Rights in the Pacific Northwest*. Portland.

Bureau of Land Management. 1974. "Burns, Oregon" (map). Washington, D.C.

Burke, M. 1969. "The Cherokee Cases: A Study in Law, Politics and Morality." *Stanford LR* 21: 500.

Burnett, Lee.
1968. "The Indian Bill of Rights and the Status of Tribal Governments." *Harvard LR* 82: 1343.
1972. "An Historical Analysis of the 1968 Indian Civil Rights Act." *Harvard Journal on Legislation*. 9: 557.

Burns Paiute Indian Reservation. 1975. *Burns Paiute Reservation Short Range Planning 1975-1978*. Burns.

Burns, Robert I. 1966. *The Jesuits and the Indian Wars of the Northwest*. New Haven.

Cahn, Edgar S., ed. 1969. *Our Brother's Keeper: The Indian in White America*. Washington, D.C.

Carey, C. A. 1971. *General History of Oregon*. Portland.

Chalfant, Stuart A. 1974. *Aboriginal Territory of the Nez Perce Indians*. New York.

Chambers, Reid P.
1970. "Discharge of the Federal Trust Responsibility to Enforce Legal Claims of Indian Tribes: Case Studies of Bureaucratic Conflict of Interest." In U.S. Congress, Senate, Committee on the Judiciary. *Study of Administrative Conflicts of Interest*. Washington D.C.

1975. "Judicial Enforcement of the Federal Trust Responsibility to Indians." *Stanford LR* 27: 1213-48.

Chaney, Ed. 1978. *A Question of Balance: Water, Energy, Salmon and Steelhead Production in the Upper Columbia River Basin. Summary Report*. Eagle, ID.

Chief Joseph (the Younger).

   1879. "An Indian's Views of Indian Affairs." *North American Review* 128: 412-33.

   1968. *Chief Joseph's Own Story* (facsimile reproduction). Seattle.

Chittenden, Hiram. 1902. *The History of the Fur Trade of the Far West*. 3 vols. New York.

Chittenden, Hiram M., and Richardson, Alfred T., eds. 1905. *Letters and Travels of Father Pierre-Jean De Smet, S. J., 1801-1873*. New York.

Clark, Ella E. 1953. *Indian Legends of the Pacific Northwest*. Berkeley.

Clark, Robert C. 1927. *History of the Willamette Valley, Oregon*. Chicago.

Clearwater Publishing Company. n.d. *Expert Testimony in Indian Claims Commission Cases*. Clearwater, ID.

Clinton, Robert. 1976. "Criminal Jurisdiction Over Indian Lands: A Journey Through a Jurisdictional Maze." *Arizona LR* 18: 503.

Coale, George L. 1958. "Notes on the Guardian Spirit Concept Among the Nez Perce." *National Archives of Ethnography Publications*, no. 48.

Coan, C. F.

   1921. "The First Stage of Federal Indian Policy in the Pacific Northwest, 1849-1852." *OHQ* 22: 46-89.

   1922. "The Adoption of the Reservation Policy in the Pacific Northwest, 1853-1855." *OHQ* 23: 1-38.

Cohen, Felix S.

   1947. "Original Indian Title." *Minnesota LR* 32: 28-59.

   1953. "The Erosion of Indian Rights, 1950-1953: A Case Study in Bureaucracy." *Yale Law Journal* 62: 348-90.

   1971. *Federal Indian Law*. Albuquerque.

Collins, Lloyd. 1951. "The Cultural Position of the Kalapuya in the Pacific Northwest." MA thesis, University of Oregon.

Collins, Richard; Johnson, Ralph; and Perkins, Kathy. 1977. "American Indian Courts and Tribal Self-Government." *American Bar Association Journal* 63: 808.

Colville, Frederick V.

   1897. "Notes on the Plants used by the Klamath Indians." *Contributions From U.S. National Herbarium* 5, pt. 2: 87-108.

   1902. "Wocas, A Primitive Food of the Klamath Indians." *U.S. National Museum Report* (1902): 725-39.

Commission on Indian Services.

   1978. "First Annual Report: Submitted to Members of the 59th Legislative Assembly and the Governor of the State of Oregon." Salem.

   n.d. *Oregon Directory of Native American Resources*.

Commission on Rights and Responsibilities. 1956. *The Rights and Liberties of the American Indians*. Eugene.

Confederated Tribes of Siletz. 1977. *First Annual Siletz Restoration Days (November Commemoration Publication)*, edited by Bob Tom. Siletz, OR.

Confederated Tribes of Siletz and Center for Urban Education, with assistance of KOIN Television. 1976. ''The People Are Dancing Again'' (Film). Portland.

Confederated Tribes of the Umatilla Indian Reservation. 1957. *Constitution and Bylaws*. Washington, D.C.

Confederated Tribes of Warm Springs Reservation.

    1966. *Confederated Tribes of the Warm Springs Reservation* v. *United States*. Appellant's Brief from the Judgement of the Indian Claims Commission, Appeals Docket 2-64. Washington, D.C.

    1972. *A History of the McQuinn Strip*. Warm Springs, OR.

    n.d. *A Short History of the Confederated Tribes of the Warm Springs Reservation* (pamphlet). Warm Springs, OR.

Cook, Sherborn F.

    1955. ''The Epidemic of 1830-33 in California and Oregon.'' *UCPAAE* 43: 303-25.

    1956. ''The Aboriginal Population of the North Coast of California.'' *UCAR* 16: 81-130.

Corlett, William Thomas. 1935. *The Medicine Man of the American Indian and his Cultural Background*. Baltimore.

Corning, Howard McKinley. 1956. *Dictionary of Oregon History*. Portland.

Coues, Elliott. 1893. *History of the Lewis and Clark Expedition*. New York.

Courts, Barbara. 1965. ''A History of the Warm Springs Indian Reservation and its Land Claims.'' A thesis, Reed College.

Cox, Ross. 1883. *Adventures on the Columbia River*. 2 vols. London. (Republished as *The Columbia River*, edited by Edgar I. Stewart and Jane R. Stewart. Norman, OK, 1957.)

Cow Creek Band of Umpquas. n.d. *History of the Cow Creek Band of Umpqua Tribe of Indians* (pamphlet).

Craig, Joseph, and Hacker, Robert L. 1940. ''The History and Development of the Fisheries of the Columbia River.'' *U.S. Bureau of Fisheries Bulletin* 49, no. 32.

Cressman, Luther S.

    1962. *The Sandal and the Cave*. Portland. (Reprint. Corvallis, 1981.)

    1977. *Prehistory of the Far West: Homes of Vanished Peoples*. Salt Lake City.

Curtis, Edward S. 1907. *The North American Indian*, edited by F. W. Hodge. 20 vols. Seattle, 1907.

Cutsforth, T. D., and Young, K. 1928. ''Hunting Superstitions in the Cow Creek Region.'' *JAFL* 41: 293-95.

Dale, H. E., ed. 1918. *The Ashley-Smith Explorations and the Discoveries of a Central Route to the Pacific*. Cleveland.

Davies, K. G., ed. 1961. *Ogden's Snake Country Journal, 1826-27*. London.

Davis, James T. 1961. ''Trade Routes and Economic Exchange Among the Indians of California.'' *UCASR* 54.

Davis, Kenneth Culp. 1975. ''Administrative Law Surprises in the Ruiz Case.'' *Colorado LR* 75: 823.

Day, Ronnie.

    1975a. ''The Dissident Chief.'' In *Forked Tongues and Broken Treaties*, edited by Donald E. Worcester. Caldwell, ID.

1975b. "Thief Treaties and Lie-Talk Councils." In *Forked Tongues and Broken Treaties*, edited by Donald E. Worcester. Caldwell, ID.

D'Azevedo, Warren L., ed. 1966.
"The Current Status of Anthropological Research in the Great Basin: 1964." *Technical Report Series S-H, Social Sciences and Humanities Publications* no. 1 (reprint). Reno.

Debo, Augie. 1970. *A History of the Indians of the United States*. Norman, OK.

Deloria, Vine, Jr.
1969. *Custer Died for Your Sins; An Indian Manifesto*. New York.
1970. *We Talk, You Listen: New Tribes, New Turf*. New York.
1971. *Of Utmost Good Faith*. San Francisco.
1974. *Behind the Trail of Broken Treaties*. New York.
1977. *Indians of the Pacific Northwest*. Garden City, NY.

Dennis, Elsie F. 1930. "Indian Slavery in Pacific Northwest." *OHQ* 31: 69-81, 181-95, 285-96.

De Rosier, Arthur, Jr. 1975. "The Past Continues: Indian Relations in the 1950s." In *Forked Tongues and Broken Treaties*, edited by Donald E. Worcester. Caldwell, ID.

De Smet, Pierre Jean. 1906. "De Smet's Letters and Sketches, 1841-1842." In *Early Western Travels, 1748-1846*, edited by R. G. Thwaites. Vol. 27, pp. 123-411. Cleveland. (Reprint of original English edition, Philadelphia, 1843.)

De Voto, Bernard. 1955. *The Journals of Lewis and Clark*. Boston.

Dixon, Roland B.
1905. "The Shasta-Achomawi." *AA* n.s. 7: 213-17.
1907. "The Shasta." *Bulletin of the American Museum of Natural History* 17: 381-498.

Dobyns, Henry F. "Estimating Aboriginal American Populations: An Appraisal of Techniques With a New Hemispheric Estimate." *CA* 7, part 4: 395-416.

Dorsey, J. Owen.
1884. *Siletz Notes of 1884*. Office of Anthropology Archives, Smithsonian Institution.
1889. "The Indians of Siletz Reservation." *AA* 2:55-60.
1890. "The Gentile System of the Siletz Tribes." *JAFL* 3: 227-37.

Drew, C. S. "Official Report of the Owyhee Reconaissance Made by Lieut. Colonel C. S. Drew." Erminie Wheeler-Voegelin, ed. *Ethnohistory* 2: 146-82.

Driver, Harold E.
1939. "Culture Area Distribution: Northwest California." *AA* 1: 297-433.
1961. *Indians of North America*. Chicago.

Driver, Harold, and Coffin, James. "Classification and Development of North American Indian Cultures: A Statistical Analysis of the Driver-Massey Sample." *Transactions of the American Philosophical Society* 65, part 3: 5-120.

Drucker, Philip.
1937. *The Tolowa and Their Southeast Oregon Kin*. Berkeley.

1939. "Land, Wealth and Kinship in Northwest Coast Society." *AA* 41: 55-64.

Drury, Clifford M.
1936a. *Nez Perce Indian Missions*. Caldwell, ID.
1936b. *Pioneer of Old Oregon: Henry Harmon Spalding*. Caldwell, ID.

DuBois, Cora.
1932. "Tolowa Notes." *AA* n.s. 34: 248-62.
1936. "The Wealth Concept as an Integrative Factor in Tolowa-Tututni Culture." In *Essays in Anthropology Presented to A. L. Kroeber*. Berkeley.
1938. "The Feather Cult of the Middle Columbia." *General Series in Anthropology*, no. 7. Edward L. Spier, ed.

Dunn. J. P. 1958. *Massacres of the Mountains: A History of the Indian Wars of the Far West*. New York. (Reprint of 1886 edition.)

Dunn, Lynn P. 1975. *American Indians: A Study Guide and Sourcebook*. San Francisco.

Economic Development Administration. 1971. *Federal and State Indian Reservations: An EDA Handbook*. Washington, D.C.

Eells, Myron.
1881. *History of the Congregational Association of Oregon and Washington Territory*. Portland.
1894. *Father Eells*. Boston.

Egan, Ferol. 1972. *Sand in a Whirlwind: The Paiute Indian War of 1860*. Garden City, NY.

Egerton, John. 1973. "How to Eradicate an Indian Tribe." *Race Relations Reporter* 4, no. 21: 26-30.

Eggleston, Dale Clarence. 1970. "Harney County, Oregon: Some Aspects of Sequent Occupancy and Land Use." MA thesis, University of Oregon.

Elmendorf, William W.
1962. "Relations of Oregon Salish as Evidenced in Numerical Stems." *Anthropological Linguistics* 4, no. 2: 1-16.
1971. "Coast Salish Family and Intergroup Ties." *SWJA* 27, no. 4: 353-80.

Engel, Bruce. 1961. "Oregon Coast Indian Reserve: Establishment and Reduction, 1855-1875." BA thesis, Reed College.

Erikson, Erik Homburger. "Observations on the Yurok: Childhood and World Image." *UCPAAE* 35: 10.

Ernst and Ernst. 1969. *A Program for Economic Development for the Umatilla Indian Reservation, Pendleton, Oregon*. Washington, D.C.

Farmer, Judith A., and Holmes, Kenneth. 1973. *An Historical Atlas of Early Oregon*. Portland.

Farmer, Judith A., and Karnes, Daniel B. n.d. "Mapping Indian Epidemics in Washington and Oregon in 1775-1850: A Preliminary Analysis." Unpublished ms. from authors.

Farrand, Livingston.
1901. "Notes on the Alsea Indians." *AA* n.s. 2: 239-47.
1921. "Notes on the Nez Perce Indians." *AA* n.s. 23: 244-46.

Ferrell, John Samuel.
1973a. "Indians and Criminal Justice in Early Oregon, 1842-59." MA thesis, Portland State University.

1973b. "Preliminary Inventory of BIA Records of the Umatilla Indian Agency." NARS RG 75.

Foreman, Grant.

1932. *Indian Removal: The Emigration of the Five Civilized Tribes*. Norman, OK.

1946. *The Last Trek of the Indians*. Chicago.

1953. *Indian Removal*. Norman, OK.

Frachtenberg, Leo J. 1916. "Ethnological Researches Among the Kalapuya Indians." *Smithsonian Miscellaneous Collections* 65, pt. 6: 85-89.

Frachtenberg, Leo J., and St. Clair, Henry. 1909. "Traditions of the Coos Indians." *JAFL* 22: 25-41.

Franchere, Gabriel. 1906. "Narrative of a Voyage to the Northwest Coast of America in the Years 1811, 1812, 1813 and 1814." In *Early Western Travels, 1748-1846*, edited by R. G. Thwaites. Vol. 6, pp. 167-410. Cleveland. (Reprint of original English edition, New York, 1854.)

Franchere, Hoyt C. 1967. *Adventure at Astoria 1810-1814*. Norman, OK.

Fremont, John C. 1846. *Narrative of the Exploring Expedition to the Rocky Mountains in the Year 1842 and to Oregon and California in 1843-44*. London.

French, David H.

1956. "An Exploration of Wasco Ethnoscience." In *Yearbook of the American Philosophical Society*.

1958. "Cultural Matrices of Chinookan Non-Casual Language." *IJAL* 24: 258-63.

1960. "Review of *Indian Uses of Native Plants*, by E. von Allen Murphey." *Economic Botany* 14, no. 2: 164-65.

1961. "Wasco-Wishram." In *Perspectives in American Indian Culture Change*, edited by Edward Spicer. Chicago.

1965. "Ethnobotany of the Pacific Northwest Indians." *Economic Botany* 19, no. 4: 378-82.

1979. "The Columbia-Fraser Plateau: A Little-Known Part of the World." (Paper presented at 32nd annual Northwest Conference, Eugene.)

French, Katherine, and French, David. 1955. "The Warm Springs Community," *American Indian* 8:3-17.

Gamino, John. 1976. "Indian Claims Commission: Discretion and Limitation in the Allowance of Attorneys' Fees." *American Indian LR* 3: 115-35.

Garth, Thomas R. 1964. "Early Nineteenth Century Tribal Relations in the Columbia Plateau." *SWJA* 20: 43-57.

Gatchet, Albert S.

1880. "The Numerical Adjective in the Klamath Language." *American Antiquarian and Oriental Journal* 2: 210-17.

1890. "The Klamath Indians of Southwestern Oregon." *Contributions to North American Ethnology* 2. (Extract reprinted. Seattle, 1966.)

Getches, D. H.; Rosenfelt, D. M.; and Wilkinson, C. F. 1979. *Federal Indian Law: Cases and Materials*. St. Paul.

Gibbs, George.

1877. "Tribes of Western Washington and Northwestern Oregon."

*Contributions to North American Ethnology* 1, pt. 2.
1967. *Indian Tribes of Washington Territory*. Fairfield, WA.

Glassley, Ray Moard. 1972. *Indian Wars of the Pacific Northwest*. Portland.

Goldberg, Carole E. 1975. "Public Law 280: The Limits of State Jurisdiction Over Reservation Indians." *UCLA LR* 22: 535-94.

Goldsmidt, Walter Rochs. 1940. "The Hupa White Deerskin Dance." *UCPAAE* 35: 8.

Gould, Richard. 1966. "The Wealth Quest Among the Tolowa Indians of Northwestern California." *Proceedings of the American Philosophical Society* 110: 67-89.

Graham, George, ed. 1949. *Commission on the Organization of the Executive Branch of the Government-Indian Affairs: A Report to Congress*. Washington, D.C.

Green, Jessie D., and Work, Susan. 1976. "Comment: Inherent Indian Sovereignty." *American Indian LR* 4: 311-42.

Gunther, Erna.
1926. "An Analysis of the First Salmon Ceremony." *AA* n.s. 28: 605-17.
1928. "A Further Analysis of the First Salmon Ceremony." *UWPA* 2, no. 5.
1945. "Ethnobotany of Western Washington." *UWPA* 10, no. 1. (Reprint, 1973.)
1949. "The Shaker Religion of the Northwest." *CUCA* 36: 37-76.
1972. *Indian Life on the Northwest Coast of North America As Seen by the Early Explorers and Fur Traders During the Last Decades of the Eighteenth Century*. Chicago.

Hagan, William T. 1966. *Indian Police and Judges: Experiments in Acculturation and Control*. New Haven.

Haines, Francis.
1938a. "Northward Spread of Horses to the Plains Indians." *AA* 40: 429-37.
1938b. "Where Did the Plains Indians Get Their Horses?" *AA* 40: 112-17.
1950. "Problems of Indian Policy." *PNQ* 41: 203-12.
1954. "Chief Joseph and the Nez Perce Warriors." *PNQ* 45: 1-7.
1955. *The Nez Perce Tribesmen of the Columbia Plateau*. Norman, OK.

Haines, Francis; Hatley, George B.; and Peckinpah, Robert. 1950. *The Appaloosa Horse*. Lewiston, ID.

Hale, Horatio. 1846. *Ethnography and Philology*. Ridgewood, NJ.

Hall, Gilbert L. 1979. *The Federal-Indian Trust Relationship*. Washington, D.C.

Harger, Jane Marie. 1972. "The History of the Siletz Reservation, 1856-1877." MA thesis, University of Oregon.

Harmon, Ray. 1971. "Indian Shaker Church: The Dalles." *OHQ* 72: 148-58.

Harvison, Robert G. 1970. "The Indian Reorganization Act of 1934 and the Indians of Oregon and Their Land." MA thesis, University of Oregon.

Head, Harlow Z.
1969. "The Oregon Donation Acts: Background, Development and Ap-

plication." MA thesis, University of Oregon.

    1971. "The Oregon Donation Claims and Their Patterns." Ph.D. diss., University of Oregon.

Heckert, Elizabeth. 1977. *The People of the River: A History of the Indians of the Upper Rogue Valley*. Ashland, OR.

Heizer, Robert F., and Hester, Thomas R. 1970. "Shasta Villages and Territory." In *Papers on California Ethnography*, pp. 119-58. Berkeley.

Hill, Edward E.

    1972. *Records in the General Archives Division Relating to American Indians*. NARS. Washington, D.C.

    1974. *The Office of Indian Affairs, 1824-1880: Historical Sketches*. Clearwater, ID.

Hilliard, Sam B. 1971. "Indian Land Cessions West of the Mississippi." *Journal of the West* 10: 493-510.

Hines, Gustavus. 1881. *Wild Life in Oregon. . . .* New York.

Hirst, Kenneth F. 1973. *Preliminary Inventory of BIA Records of the Warm Springs Indian Agency, 1861-1952*. NARS RG 75. Washington, D.C.

Hobbs, Richard (comp.). 1977. *Guide to the Seattle Archives Branch*. NARS. Seattle.

Hodge, Felicia S. 1977. *Need Assessment for a Northwest Indian Hospital*. Portland.

Hodge, Frederick Webb, ed. 1907-10. "Handbook of American Indians, North of Mexico." *BBAE* 30.

Hodge, Ronald A. 1973. "Getting Back the Land: How Native Americans Can Acquire Excess and Surplus Federal Property." *North Dakota LR* 49: 333-42.

Hoijer, Harry. 1962. "Linguistic Sub-Groupings by Glottochronology . . . Athapascan." *Lingua* 11: 192-98.

Holford, David M. 1975. "The Subversion of the Indian Land Allotment System, 1887-1934." *IH* 8: 11-21.

Holman, Frederick V. 1912. "A Brief History of the Oregon Provisional Government and What Caused its Formation." *OHQ* 13: 89-139.

Holt, Catherine. 1946. "Shasta Ethnography." *UCAR* 3, no. 4: 299-349.

Hood, Susan. 1972. "Termination of the Klamath Indian Tribe of Oregon." *Ethnohistory* 19: 379-92.

Hoop, Oscar Winslow. 1929. "History of Fort Hoskins: 1856-65." *OHQ* 30: 346-61.

Hopkins, Nicholas A. 1965. "Great Basin Prehistory and Uto-Aztecan." *American Antiquity* 31: 48-60.

Hopkins, Sarah Winnemucca. 1883. *Life Among the Piutes: Their Wrongs and Claims*. Edited by Mrs. Horace Mann. Boston. (Reprint, with pref. by M. R. Harrington, Bishop, CA, 1969.)

Howard, Oliver O. 1881. *Nez Perce Joseph: An Account of His Ancestors, His Lands, His Confederates, His Enemies, His Murders, His War, His Pursuit and Capture*. Boston. (Reprint, New York, 1972.)

Howe, Carrol B. 1968. *Ancient Tribes of the Klamath Country*. Portland.

Hunt, Jack. 1970. "Land Tenure and Economic Development on the Warm Springs Reservation." *Journal of the West* 9: 93-109.

Hussey, John. 1967. *Champoeg: Place of Transition*. Portland.

Hymes, Dell H.

1957. "Some Penutian Elements and the Penutian Hypothesis." *SWJA* 13: 69-87.

1960a. "Lexicostatistics So Far." *CA* 1: (3)-426.

1960b. "More on Lexicostatistics." *CA* 1: (3)-33.

1964. "'Hail' and 'Bead': Two Penutian Etymologies." In *Studies in California Linguistics*, edited by William Bright. Berkeley.

1966. "Some Points of Siuslaw Phonology." *IJAL* 32: 328-42.

Hymes, Dell, and Hymes, Virginia. 1972. "Chinook Jargon as 'Mother's Tongue'." *IJAL* 38: (3)-207.

Indian Civial Rights Task Force. 1974. "Development of Tripartite Jurisdiction in Indian Country." *Kansas LR* 22: 351.

*Indian Voices: The Native American Today*. 1974. San Francisco.

Institute for the Development of Indian Law. n.d. *Treaties of the Pacific Northwest*. Washington, D.C.

Isherwood, J. 1976. "Indian Fishing Rights in the Pacific Northwest: Impact of the Fishery Conversation Management Act." *Environmental Law* 8: 101-31.

Israel, Daniel. 1976. "The Reemergence of Tribal Nationalism and its Impact on Reservation Resource Development." *Colorado LR* 47: 617-29.

Jackson, Curtis, and Galli, Marcie. 1977. *A History of the Bureau of Indian Affairs and its Activities Among Indians*. San Francisco.

Jacobs, Melville.

1932. "Northern Sahaptin Kinship Terms." *AA* 34: 688-93.

1937. "Historic Perspectives in Indian Language of Oregon and Washington." *PNQ* 28: 56.

1939. "Coos Narrative and Ethnologic Texts." *UWPA* 8, pt. 1.

1941. "Survey of Pacific Northwest Anthropological Research, 1930-40." *PNQ* 32: 9-106.

1945. "Santiam Kalapuya Ethnologic Texts." *UWPA* 11: 3-81.

1954. "The Areal Spread of Sound Features in the Languages North of California." (Papers from the Symposium on American Indian Linguistics.) *University of California Publications in Linguistics* 10: 46-56.

1955. "A Few Observations on the World View of the Clackamas Chinook Indians." *JAFL* 68: 283-89.

1958. "The Romantic Role of Older Women in a Culture of the Pacific Northwest." *Kroeber Anthropological Society Publications* 18: 79-86.

Jacobs, Melville, and Jacobs, Elizabeth Derr. *Nehalem Tillamook Tales*. Eugene, 1959.

Jacobs, Wilbur R. 1972. *Dispossessing the American Indian: Indians and Whites on the Colonial Frontier*. New York.

James, George Wharton. 1972. *Indian Basketry*. New York.

Jennings, Jesse. 1968. *Prehistory of North America*. New York.

Jensen, Vernon H., ed. 1976. *Ump-Sa-Qua: Studies of the Upper Indians*. Roseburg.

Jessett, Thomas Edwin. 1969. *The Indian Side of the Whitman Massacre*. Fairfield, WA.

Johansen, Dorothy O., and Gates, Charles M. 1957. *Empire of the Columbia*. New York.

Johnson, Helen. 1975. *American Indians in Transition*. Washington, D.C.

Johnson, Leroy, Jr., and Cole, David L. 1969. *A Bibliographic Guide to the Archaeology of Oregon*. Eugene.

Johnson, O. H. 1927. "The History of the Klamath Indian Reservation." MS thesis, University of Oregon.

Johnson, Ralph W. 1972. "The States versus Indian Off-Reservation Fishing: A U.S. Supreme Court Error." *Washington LR* 47: 207-36.

Jones, Ray F. 1972. *Wappato Indians of the Lower Columbia River Valley*. Vancouver, WA.

Josephy, Alvin M.
1965. *The Nez Perce Indians and the Opening of the Northwest*. New Haven.

Josephy, Alvin M., ed. 1968. *The Indian Heritage of America*. New York.

Kappler, Charles J. 1904. *Indian Affairs, U.S. Laws and Treaties*. 5 vols. Washington, D.C.

Kelly, Isabel T. 1932. "Ethnography of the Surprise Valley Paiute." *UCPAAE* 31, no. 3: 67-210.

Kelsay, Laura E. 1977. *Cartographic Records of the Bureau of Indian Affairs*. NARS Special List B. Washington, D.C.

Kennedy, James B. 1977. "The Umatilla Indian Reservation, 1855-1975: Factors Contributing to a Diminished Land Resource Base." MA thesis, Oregon State University.

Kent, William Eugene. 1973. "The Siletz Indian Reservation, 1855-1900." MST thesis, Portland State University.

Kephart, George S. 1941. "Forestry on the Klamath Indian Reservation." *Journal of Forestry* 39: 896-99.

Keys, John R., Jr. 1978. "Some Early Comments on the Meaning of Oliphant." *Indian Law Reporter* 5: M-20.

Kickingbird, Kirke; and Ducheneaux, Karen. 1973. *One Hundred Million Acres*. New York.

Kickingbird, Kirke, and Kickingbird, Lynn. 1977. *Indians and the U.S. Government*. Washington, D.C.

Kickingbird, Kirke; Kickingbird, Lynn; Chibitty, Charles J.; and Berkey, Curtis. 1977. *Indian Sovereignty*. Washington D.C.

Kinney, J. P. 1937. *A Continent Lost—A Civilization Won: Indian Land Tenure in America*. Baltimore.

Kip, Lawrence. 1855. *The Indian Council in the Valley of the Walla Walla*. San Francisco.

Krauss, Michael E. 1970. "Na-Dene." In *Current Trends in Linguistics*, edited by T. A. Sebeok. The Hague.

Kroeber, Alfred Louis.
1937. "Athapascan Kin Term Systems." *AA* 39: 602-09.
1939. "Cultural and Natural Areas of Native North America." *UCPAAE* 38. (Reprint, Berkeley, 1947.)
1957. "Coefficients of Cultural Similarity of Northern Paiute Bands." *UCPAAE* 47: 209-214.

Kroeber, Alfred Louis, and Barrett, S. A. 1962. "Fishing Among the Indians of Northwestern California." *UCAR* 21:1.

Langone, Stephen. 1974. "A Statistical Profile of the Indian: The Lack of Numbers." In National Advisory Council on Indian Education, *First Annual Report to the U.S. Congress*. Washington, D.C.

Large, Donald W. 1973. "This Land Is Whose Land? Changing Concepts of Land as Property." *Wisconsin LR* no. 4: 1039-83.

Lattimore, Owen. 1962. "On the Wickedness of Being Nomads." In *Studies in Frontier History*. Oxford.

Lavender, David, ed. 1972. *The Oregon Journals of David Douglas ... During the Years 1825, 1826 and 1827*. Ashland, OR.

Lee, Daniel, and Frost, Joseph. 1968. *Ten Years in Oregon*. Fairfield, WA.

Lee, Jason. 1916. "Diary of Reverend Jason Lee." *OHQ* 17: 116-46, 240-66, 397-430.

Lee, Shirley. 1967. "A Survey of Acculturation in the Intermountain Area of the United States." *Museum of Idaho State University Occasional Papers*, no. 19.

Levine, Stuart, and Lurie, Nancy O., eds. 1968. *The American Indian Today*. Delaware, FL.

Levitan, Sam, and Johnston, William. 1975. *Indian Giving: Federal Programs for Native Americans*. Baltimore.

Lewis, Albert Buell. 1906. "Tribes of the Columbia Valley and Coast of Oregon and Washington." *Memoirs of the American Anthropological Association* 1, pt. 2.

Lewis, Henry T. 1973. "Patterns of Indian Burying in California: Ecology and Ethnohistory." *Ballena Press Anthropological Papers*, no. 1. Ramona, CA.

Lewis, John G. 1911. *History of the Grand Ronde Military Block House*. Dayton, OR.

Lieberman, Joan. 1976. *American Indians: Their Need for Legal Services*. Washington, D.C.

Lowie, Robert H. 1923. "The Cultural Connection of Californian and Plateau Shoshonean Tribes." *UCPAAE* 20: 145-56.

Loy, William G. 1976. *Atlas of Oregon*. Eugene.

Lundsgaarde, Henry P. 1967. "Structural Analysis of Nez Perce Kinship." *Washington State College Research Studies* 35: 48-77.

Lurie, Nancy O. 1957. "The Indian Claims Commission Act." *Annals of the American Academy of Political and Social Science* 311: 56-70.

Lyman, H. S. 1900. "Indian Names." *OHQ* 1: 316-27.

McArthur, Lewis A. 1974. *Oregon Geographic Names*. 5th ed., revised and enlarged by Lewis L. McArthur. Portland.

McChesney, Charles E. 1969. *The Rolls of Certain Indian Tribes in Oregon and Washington*. Fairfield, WA.

McDonald, David. 1978. "Native American Fishing and Hunting Rights: An Annotated Bibliography." *IH* 11, no. 4: 57-67.

McFeat, Tom, ed. 1966. *Indians of the North Pacific Coast*. Seattle.

McGreehan, Albert. 1973. *Burns Paiute Indian Reservation Resource Development Survey*. Western Interstate Commission for Higher Education and Burns Paiute Reservation. Boulder, CO.

McLoughlin, John. 1941-44. *McLoughlin's Fort Vancouver Letters*. Hudson's Bay Series nos. 4, 5, 6. London.

McNickle, D'Arcy.
1973. *Native American Tribalism: Survivalism and Renewals*. New York.
1975. *They Came Here First*. New York.

McNickle, D'Arcy, and Fey, H. E. 1959. *Indians and Other Americans: Two Ways of Life Meet*. New York.

Mackey, Harold.
  1972. "New Light on the Molalla Indians." *OHQ* 73: 63-65.
  1974. *The Kalapuyans: A Sourcebook on the Indians of the Willamette Valley*. Salem.

Man, Peter. 1975. *Northwest Indian Population Projection*. Center for Population Research and Census. Portland.

Marchington, Stanley Eugene. 1955. "Organization of the Klamath Adult Special Education and Training Program for the Klamath Reservation." MA thesis, Willamette University.

Martin, L. F. 1969. "A History of the Modoc Indian: An Acculturation Study." *Chronicles of Oklahoma* 47: 398-446.

Martone, Frederick J. 1976. "American Indian Tribal Self-Government in the Federal System: Inherent Right or Congressional License." *Notre Dame LR* 51: 600.

Mason, Otis T. 1902. *Aboriginal American Basketry*. Report of U.S. National Museum. Washington, D.C. (Reprint. Glorieta, NM, 1970.)

Meilleur, Brian A. 1977. "The All Purpose Germs: Comatium as Protein Producer." Paper presented at the 32nd Annual Northwest Anthropological Conference. Eugene.

Meister, Cary. 1978. "The Misleading Nature of Data in the Bureau of the Census Subject Report on 1970 American Indian Population." *IH* 11, no. 4: 20-29.

Merk, Frederick, ed. 1931. *Fur Trade and Empire: George Simpson's Journal*. Cambridge, MA.

Migrant and Indian Coalition, Inc. 1979. *State Wide Oregon Indian Needs Assessment*. Hood River, OR.

Miller, Gerald R. 1957. "Indians, Water, and the Arid Western States—Prelude to the Pelton Dam Decision." *Utah LR* 5: 495-510.

Miller, Wick R.; Tanner, James L.; and Foley, Lawrence P. 1971. "A Lexicostatistical Study of Shoshoni Dialects." *AL* 13: 142-64.

Minor, Rick, and Pecor, Audrey. 1977. "Cultural Resource Overview of the Willamette National Forest, Western Oregon." *University of Oregon Anthropological Papers*, no. 12.

Minto, John. 1900. "The Number and Condition of the Native Race in Oregon When First Seen by White Men." *OHQ* 1 (1900): 296-395.

"Missionaries vs. Native Americans in the Northwest: A Bibliography for Re-evaluation." *IH* 5, no. 2 (1972): 46-48.

Mooney, James.
  1910. "Population." (In *Handbook of American Indians North of Mexico*, edited by F. W. Hodge.) *BBAE* 30: 286-87.
  1928. "The Aboriginal Population of America North of Mexico." *Smithsonian Miscellaneous Collections* 80, pt. 7: 1-40.

Moore, John T. 1963. "The Early Days of Pharmacy in the West." *Journal of the American Pharmaceutical Association* 25: 705-15.

Movious, James Gilbert. 1968. "Sagebrush War: White-Paiute Conflicts, 1825-1868." MA thesis, University of Oregon.

Murdock, George Peter.
  1938. "Notes on the Tenino, Molala, and Paiute of Oregon." *AA* 40

(1938): 384-415.

    1958. "Social Organization of the Tenino." In *Miscellanea Paul Rivet: Octogenario Dicata*. Mexico City.

    1965. "Tenino Shamanism." *Ethnology* 4: 165-71.

Murray, Keith. 1959. *The Modocs and Their War*. Norman, OK.

Nash, Douglas. 1976. "A Summary of Indian Hunting and Fishing Law." In *Manual of Indian Law*, edited by M. B. West. Washington, D.C.

Nash, Philleo. 1955. "The Place of Religious Revivalism in the Formation of the Intercultural Community on the Klamath Reservation." In *Social Anthropology of North American Indian Tribes*, edited by Fred Eggan. Chicago.

National Advisory Council on Indian Education. 1976. *Third Annual Report to the Congress of the United States*, pt. 4. Washington, D.C.

    National Coalition to Support Indian Treaties. n.d. *Questions and Answers on Treaty Rights* (pamphlet). Seattle.

Native American Rights Fund. 1973. *Indian Claims Commission Decisions*. 30 vols. Washington, D.C.

Neils, Elaine. 1971. *Reservation to City: Indian Migration and Federal Relocation*. Chicago.

Neilsen, Richard A. 1973. "American Indian Land Claims: Land Versus Money as a Remedy." *University of Florida LR* 25: 308-26.

"Note: Systematic Discrimination in the Indian Claims Commission: The Burden of Proof in Redressing Historical Wrongs." *Iowa LR* 57 (1972): 1300-19.

"Note: Toward a New System for the Resolution on Indian Resource Claims." *NYU LR* 47 (1972): 1107-49.

O'Callaghan, Jerry A.

    1951a. "The Disposition of the Public Domain in Oregon." Ph.D. dissertation, Stanford University.

    1951b. "Extinguishing Indian Titles on the Oregon Coast." *OHQ* 52: 139-44.

    1960. *Disposition of the Public Domain in Oregon*. Washington, D.C.

Ogden, Peter Skene. 1909-10. "The Peter Skene Ogden Journals." T. C. Elliott, ed. *OHQ* 10: 331-65; 11: 201-22, 355-97.

Oliphant, J. Orin. 1950. "Encroachments of Cattlemen on Indian Reservations in the Pacific Northwest, 1870-1890." *Agricultural History* 24: 1-4.

Olson, Ronald LeRoy. 1927. "Adze, Canoe and House Types of the Northwest Coast." *UWPA* 2:1-38.

Oregon Department of Fish and Wildlife and Washington Department of Fisheries. 1977. *Columbia River Fish Runs and Fisheries: 1957-76*. Salem.

Oregon Historical Society. n.d. "Manuscript Holdings of Records, Siletz Indian Reservation." OHS Mss. 442. Portland.

Oregon State College. 1960. *Warm Springs Research Project Final Report*. 5 vols. Corvallis.

Orfield, Gary. 1966. *A Study of Termination Policy*. Washington, D.C.

Owens, David W., comp. n.d. "Preliminary Inventory of the Records of the Grand Ronde-Siletz Indian Agency, 1863-1947." NARS RG 75. Seattle.

Pacific Northwest Regional Commission. 1976. *Investigative Reports of the Columbia River Fisheries Project*. Vancouver, WA.

Pacific Northwest River Basins Commission. 1971. *Columbia North Pacific Comprehensive Framework Study*. Vancouver, WA.

Palmer, Joel. 1906. *Journals and Travels Over the Rocky Mountains 1845-46*. Cleveland.

Park, Willard Z. 1937. "Paviatso Polyandry." *AA* n.s. 39: 366-68.

Parker, Samuel. 1838. *Journal of an Exploring Tour Beyond the Rocky Mountains Under the Direction of the ABCFM Performed in the Years 1835, '36 and '37*. Ithaca, NY.

Pearsall, Marion. 1950. "Klamath Childhood and Education." *UCAR* 9, no. 5: 339-51.

Pearson, Mary. 1976. "Hunting Rights: Retention of Treaty Rights After Termination—*Kimball* v. *Callahan*." *American Indian LR* 4: 121-33.

Peterson, Ethel M. 1939. "Oregon Indians and Indian Policy, 1849-1871." *Oregon University Thesis Series*, no. 3. Eugene.

Pierce, Joe E.

1964a. "The Field Situation in Oregon, 1964." *Canadian Journal of Linguistics* 10: 120-28.

1964b. "The Status of Athapaskan Research in Oregon." *IJAL* 30: 137-43.

1966. "Genetic Comparisons and Hanis, Miluk, Alsea, Siuslaw and Takelma." *IJAL* 32: 379-87.

Plummer, Norman B. 1955. "Appraisal Report of Unallotted Lands of Siletz Reservation Ceded Under the Agreement of October 31, 1982 by the Tillamook Tribe." U.S. Expert Witness Testimony in Indian Claims Commission Docket No. 239, *Tillamook* v. *U.S.* Washington, D.C.

Price, Monroe.

1969. "Lawyers on the Reservation: Some Implications for the Legal Profession." *Law and the Social Order* 161.

1973. *Law and the American Indian*. Indianapolis.

Prucha, Francis Paul.

1962. *American Indian Policy in the Formative Years*. Cambridge, MA.

1975. *Documents of the United States Indian Policy*. Lincoln, NE.

1976. *American Indian Policy in Crisis: Christian Reformers and the Indian, 1865-1900*. Norman, OK.

Prucha, Francis Paul, ed. 1973. *Americanizing the American Indians—Writings by the "Friends of the Indian" 1880-1900*. Cambridge, MA.

Ramsey, Jarold, ed. 1977. *Coyote Was Going There: Indian Literature of the Oregon Country*. Seattle.

Ratcliff, James L. 1973. "What Happend to the Kalapuya? A Study of the Depletion of their Economic Base." *IH* 6, no. 3: 27-33.

Ray, Verne F.

1936. "Native Villages and Groupings of the Columbia Basin." *PNQ* 27: 99-152.

1937a. "The Bluejay Character in the Plateau Spirit Dance." *AA* 39: 593-601.

1937b. "The Historical Position of the Lower Chinook in the Native Culture of the Northwest." *PNQ* 28: 363-72.

1938. "Lower Chinook Ethnographic Notes." *UWPA* 9, no. 1.

1939. *Cultural Relations in the Plateau of Northwestern America*. Los Angeles.

1942. "Culture Element Distribution: Plateau." *UCAR* 7, no. 22: 99-258.

1960. "The Columbia Indian Confederacy: A League of Central Plateau Tribes." In *Culture in History*, edited by Stanley Diamond. New York.

1963. *Primitive Pragmatists*. Seattle.

1974. *Ethnohistory of the Joseph Band of Nez Perce Indians: 1805-1905*. New York.

Ray, Verne F.; Murdock, George P., and Blyth, Beatrice. 1938. "Tribal Distribution in Eastern Oregon and Adjacent Regions." *AA* 40: 384-415.

Relander, Click. 1956. *Drummers and Dreamers: The Story of Smohala the Prophet*. Caldwell, ID.

Rich, E. E., ed.

1941. *McLoughlin's Fort Vancouver Letters, 1st series, 1825-1838*. Toronto.

1943. *McLoughlin's Fort Vancouver Letters, 2nd series, 1839-1844*. Toronto.

1944. *McLoughlin's Fort Vancouver Letters, 3rd series, 1844-1846*. Toronto.

1950. *Peter Skene Ogden's Snake Country Journals, 1824-25 and 1825-26*. Hudson's Bay Record Society Publications, no. 13. London.

Riddle, George W. 1953. *Early Days in Oregon: A History of the Riddle Valley*. Riddle, OR.

Riddle, Jeff C. 1914. *The Indian History of the Modoc War*. San Francisco. (Reprint. Medford, 1973.)

Rigsby, Bruce J.

1966. "On Cayuse-Molalla Relatability." *IJAL* 32: 369-78.

1969. "The Waillatpuan Problem." *NWARN* 3: 68-146.

Rivers, Theodore John. 1978. "The Nez Perce Laws (1842): The Introduction of Laws Foreign to an Independent People." *IH* 2, no. 3: 15-24.

Robbins, William G. 1974. "Extinguishing Indian Land Title in Western Oregon." *IH* 7, no. 2: 10-14.

Robinson, William L. 1978. "Columbia River Treaty Ceremonial Fishing 1977." Oregon Dept. of Fish and Wildlife Informational Reports, no.

Roe, Frank G. n.d. *The Indian and the Horse*. Norman, OK.

Ross, Alexander.

1923. *Adventures of the First Settlers on the Columbia River*. Chicago.

1924. *The Fur Hunters of the Far West*. M. M. Quaife, ed. Chicago.

Ross, Norman A., ed.

1973a. *Index to the Decisions of the Indian Claims Commission*. New York.

1973b. *Index to the Expert Testimony Before the Indian Claims Commission*. New York.

Royce, Charles C. 1900. "Indian Land Cessions in the United States." In U.S. Bureau of Ethnology, *18th Annual Report, 1896-97*. Washington, D.C.

Ruby, Robert H. 1966. "A Healing Service in the Shaker Church." *OHQ* 67: 347-55.

Ruby, Robert H., and Brown, John A.

1965. *Half-Sun on the Columbia*. Norman, OK.

1972. *The Cayuse Indian, Imperial Tribes—Men of Old Oregon*. Norman, OK.

1976. *The Chinook Indians: Traders of the Lower Columbia River*. Norman, OK.

Rumberger, J. P., Jr. 1949. "Ethnolinguistic Observations Based on Kalapuya Texts." *IJAL* 15: 158-62.

Sacket, Lee. 1973. "The Siletz Indian Shaker Church." *PNQ* 64: 120-ff.

Sapir, Edward.

1907a. "Notes on the Takelma Indians of Southwest Oregon." *AA* n.s. 9: 251-75.

1907b. "Religious Ideas of the Takelma Indians of Southwest Oregon." *JAFL* 20: 33-49.

1921. "A Characteristic Penutian Form of Stem." *IJAL* 2: 58-67.

Sauter, John, and Johnson, Bruce. 1974. *Tillamook Indians of the Oregon Coast*. Portland.

Sayers, Jerome, and Volkman, John. 1976. *A Statistical Profile of the Confederated Tribes of Siletz Indians*. Portland.

Schaeffer, Claude E. 1959. "Indian Tribes and Languages of the Old Oregon Country." *OHQ* 60: 129-33.

Schmeckebier, L. F. 1971. *The Office of Indian Affairs: Its History, Activities and Organizatons*. New York.

Schoning, R. W. 1951. "The Indian Dip Net Fishery at Celilo Falls on the Columbia River." *Oregon Fish Commission Contributions*, no. 17.

Schwede, Madge. 1970. "The Relationship of Aboriginal Nez Perce Settlement Patterns to Physical Environ and to Generalized Distribution of Food Resources." *NWARN* 4, no. 2: 129-35.

Sclar, Lee. 1972. "Participation of Off-Reservation Indians in Programs of the BIA and IHS." *Montana LR* 33: 191-232.

Scott, Leslie M.

1928. "Indian Diseases as Aids to Pacific Northwest Settlement." *OHQ* 29: 144-61.

1941. "Indian Women as Food Providers and Tribal Counselors." *OHQ* 42: 208-19.

Silverstein, Michael. 1972. "Chinook Jargon: Language Contact and the Probelm of Multi-Level Generative Systems." *Language* 48: 378-406, 596-625.

Simpson, George. 1931. *Fur Trade and Empire: George Simpson's Journal*, edited by Frederick Merk. Cambridge, MA.

Slacum, W. A. 1912. "Slacum's Report on Oregon, 1836-7." *OHQ* 13: 175-224.

Slickpoo, Allen P., Sr. 1973. *Noon-Nee-Me-Poo (We the Nez Perces)*. Lapwai, ID.

Smith, Kyle B. 1978. "*Oliphant* v. *Squamish Indian Tribe:* A Restriction of Tribal Sovereignty." *Willamette LR* 15: 127-42.

Sorkin, Alan. 1971. *American Indians and Federal Aid*. Washington, D.C.

Spaid, Stanley S.

1950. "Joel Palmer and Indian Affairs in Oregon." Ph.D. dissertation, University of Oregon.

1954. "The Later Life and Activities of General Joel Palmer." *OHQ* 55: 311-32.

Spalding, Henry Harmon. 1958. *The Diaries and Letters of H. H. Spalding and Asa Browen Smith Relating to the Nez Perce Mission, 1838-1842*, edited by Clifford M. Drury. Glendale, CA.

Spier, Leslie.

    1927a. "The Ghost Dance of 1870 Among the Klamath of Oregon." *UWPA* 2: 43-55.

    1927b. "Tribal Distribution in Southwestern Oregon." *OHQ* 28: 358-65.

    1930. "Klamath Ethnography." *UCPAAE* 30.

    1935. "The Prophet Dance in the Northwest and Its Derivatives: The Source of the Ghost Dance." *General Series in Anthropology*, no. 1. Menasha, WI.

Spier, Leslie, and Sapir, Edward. 1930. *Wishram Ethnography. UWPA* 3, no. 3.

Spinden, Herbert J. 1908. "The Nez Perce Indians." *Memoirs of the American Anthropological Association* 2, pt. 3.

Steffon, Frederick J. 1978. "The Irony of Termination: 1943-1958." *IH* 11, no. 3: 3-17.

Stern, Theodore.

    1956. "The Klamath Indians and the Treaty of 1864." *OHQ* 57: 229-73.

    1960. "A Umatilla Prophet Cult." *Acts of the ICAES* 5: 346-50.

    1953. "Trends in Culture Change, Taking as a Universe the Community of Indians Resident on the Umatilla Reservation, Oregon," *Yearbook of the American Philosophical Society*: 219-20.

    1964. "Review of Primitive Pragmatists." *AA* 66: 676.

    1966. *The Klamath Tribe: A People and Their Reservation*. Seattle.

    1972. "Livelihood and Tribal Government on the Klamath Indian Reservation. In *The Emergent Native American: A Reader in Culture Contact*, edited by Deward Walker, Jr. Boston.

Stern, Theodore, and Boggs, James P. 1971. "White and Indian Farmers of the Umatilla Indian Reservation." In *The Emergent Native American: A Reader in Culture Contact*, edited by Deward Walker, Jr. Boston.

Stevens, Isaac I. 1855. House Executive Document 56: *Narrative and Final Report of Explorations for a Route for a Pacific Railroad*. 36th Cong., 1st sess. (Vol. 12, Book 1 of *Pacific Railroad Reports*.) Washington, D.C., 1860.

Steward, Julian H.

    1934. *Two Paiute Biographies*. Berkeley.

    1938. "Basin-Plateau Aboriginal Sociopolitical Groups." *BBAE* 120.

    1939. "Some Observations on Shoshonean Distributions." *AA* 41: 261-65.

Steward, Julian H., and Wheeler-Voegelin, Erminie. 1974. *The Northern Paiute Indians*. New York.

Stewart, Hilary. 1977. *Indian Fishing*. Seattle.

Stewart, Omer C.

    1938. "Northern Paiute." *AA* 40: 405-407.

    1939. "The Northern Paiute Bands." *UCAR* 2, no. 3.

1941. "Culture Element Distributions XIV: Northern Paiute." *UCAR* 4, no. 3.

1955. "Forest and Grass Burning in the Mountain West." *Southwestern Lore* 21: 5-9.

1956. "Tribal Distribution and Boundaries in the Great Basin." In *Current Status of Anthropological Research in the Great Basin*, edited by W. L. D'Azevedo et al. Reno.

Stowell, Cynthia. 1978. "Warm Springs Treaties." *Spilyay Tymoo*.

Suphan, Robert J. 1974. *Oregon Indians II*. New York.

Sutherland, Johnnie Davis. 1973. "Umatilla Agricultural Landscapes, 1700-1793: An Historical Geography of a Region in the Oregon Country." MA thesis, University of Oregon.

Suttles, Wayne.

1968a. "Coping with Abundance." In *Man the Hunter*, edited by R. Lee and I. DeVore. Chicago.

1968b. "Variation in Habitat and Culture on the Northwest Coast." in *Man in Adaptation, Vol. 2: The Cultural Present*, edited by Y. A. Cohen. Chicago.

1973. "Native Languages of the North Pacific Coast of North America" (map). Portland.

n.d. "Classification of Northwest Indian Languages." Mimeo. (Available from author.)

Suttles, Wayne, ed. (forthcoming). *Handbook of American Indians: The Northwest Coast*.

Sutton, Dorothy. 1969. *Indian Wars of the Rogue River*. Grants Pass, OR.

Sutton, Imre. 1975. *Indian Land Tenure: Bibliographical Essays and a Guide to the Literature*. New York.

Swadesh, Morris.

1949. "The Linguistic Approach to Salish Prehistory." In *Indians of the Urban Northwest*, edited by M. W. Smith. New York.

1954. "On the Penutian Vocabulary Survey." *IJAL* 20: 123-33.

1965. "Kalapuya and Takelma." *IJAL* 31: 237-40.

Swan, James G. 1857. *The Northwest Coast, Or Three Years' Residence in Washington Territory*. New York.

Swanton, John R. 1953. "The Indian Tribes of North America." *BBAE* 145.

Swartz, B. K., Jr. 1960. "A Bibliography of Klamath Basin Anthropology, with Excerpts and Annotations." *Klamath County Museum Research Papers*, no. 3. Klamath Falls, OR.

Swindell, Edward G. 1942. *Report on Source, Nature, and Extent of the Fishing, Hunting and Miscellaneous Related Rights of Certain Indian Tribes in Washington and Oregon, Together with Locations of a Number of Usual and Accustomed Fishing Grounds and Stations*. U.S. Office of Indian Affairs. Los Angeles.

Tax, Sol. 1968. "American Anthropological Association Symposium on American Indian Fishing and Hunting Rights." *NWARN* 2, no. 2: 1-43.

Taylor, Herbert C., Jr.

1962. "The Utilization of Archeological and Ethnohistorical Data in Estimating Aboriginal Population." *Bulletin of the Texas Archeological Society* 32.

1969. "Aboriginal Populations of the Lower Northwest Coast." In *Rolls of Certain Indian Tribes in Oregon and Washington*, edited by Charles E. McChesney. Fairfield, WA.

Taylor, Herbert C., Jr., ed. 1974. *Oregon Indians I*. New York.

Taylor, Herbert C., Jr., and Hoaglin, Lester L. 1962. "The 'Intermittent Fever' Epidemic of the 1830's on the Lower Columbia River." *Ethnohistory* 9, no. 2.

Taylor, Peter S. 1976. "Criminal Jurisdiction." In *Manual of Indian Law*, edited by M. B. West. Washington, D.C.

Taylor, Theodore. 1972. *The States and Their Indian Citizens*. Washington, D.C.

Teit, James A. 1928. "The Middle Columbia Salish." *UWPA* 2, no. 4.

Thompson, David. 1916. *Narrative of Explorations in Western America, 1784-1812*. J. B. Tyrrell, ed. Toronto.

Thompson, Erwin N.
1971. *Modoc War: Its Military History and Topography*. Sacramento.
1973. *Shallow Grave at Wailatpu: The Sager's West*. Rev. ed. Portland.

Thompson, Laurence C. 1970. "The Northwest." In *Current Trends in Linguistics*, edited by Thomas A. Sebeok. The Hague.

Thompson, Morris. 1976. "A Treaty is a Treaty is a Treaty." *Seattle Post Intelligencer*. 17 November.

Thwaites, Reuben Gold, ed.
1896-1901. *The Jesuit Relations and Allied Documents, 1610-1791*. Cleveland.
1904. *Original Journals of the Lewis and Clark Expedition, 1804-1806*. 7 vols., atlas. New York. (Reprint. New York, 1959.)
1904-1907. *Early Western Travels, 1853-1913*. Cleveland.

Trager, George L., and Harber, F. E. 1958. "North American Indian Languages—Classification and Maps Studies in Linguistics." *Department of Anthropology Occasional Papers*, no. 5. Buffalo.

Trulove, William Thomas. 1973. "Economics of Paternalism: Federal Policy and Indians." Ph.D. dissertation, University of Oregon.

Trulove, W. T., and Bunting, David. 1971. "The Economic Impact of Federal Policy: Incentives and Response to the Klamath Indians." Unpublished paper, Eastern Washington University.

Tyler, Lyman. 1973. *A History of Indian Policy*. Washington, D.C.

Underhill, Ruth. 1944. *Indians of the Pacific Northwest*. Washington, D.C.

U.S. Congress.
House, Committee on Indian Affairs, *Hearing on H.R. 1198 and H.R. 1341, to Create an Indian Claims Commission*, 79th Cong., 1st sess., 1945.
House, Committee on Interior and Insular Affairs, *An Investigation of the Bureau of Indian Affairs, Pursuant to H. Res. 698*, 82d Cong., 2d sess., 1952, H. Rept. 2503.
House, Committee on Interior and Insular Affairs, *Providing for Termination of Federal Supervision Over Property of Klamath Tribe of Indians Located in Oregon and Individual Members Thereof: Report to Accompany S. 2745*, 83d Cong., 2d sess., July 23, 1954, H. Rept. 2483.

House, Committee on Interior and Insular Affairs, *Providing for Termination of Federal Supervision Over Property of Certain Tribes and Bands of Indians Located in Western Oregon and Individual Members Thereof: Report to Accompany S. 2746*, 83d Cong., 2d sess., July 26, 1954, H. Rept. 2492.

House, Committee on Interior and Insular Affairs, *An Investigation of the Bureau of Indian Affairs Pursuant to H. Res. 89*, 83d Cong., 2d sess., Sept. 20, 1954, H. Rept. 2680.

House, Committee on Interior and Insular Affairs, *Amending the Act Terminating Federal Supervision Over the Klamath Indian Tribe by Providing in the Alternative For Private or Federal Acquisition of the Part of the Tribal Forest That Must Be Sold: Report to Accompany S. 3051*, 85th Cong., 2d sess., 1958, H. Rept. 2278.

House, *Message from the President of the United States Transmitting Recommendations for Indian Policy*, 91st Cong., 2d sess., 1970, H.R. Doc. 363.

House, Committee on Interior and Insular Affairs, *Declaring that Certain Federally Owned Lands Shall Be Held by the United States In Trust for the Burns Indian Colony, Oregon, and for Other Purposes: Report to Accompany H.R. 6318*, 92d Cong., 2d sess., Sept. 5, 1972, H. Rept. 1370.

House, Committee on Interior and Insular Affairs, *History of Indian Health Care, part 1*, 94th Cong., 2d sess., April 9, 1976. H. Rept. 1026.

House, Committee on Interior and Insular Affairs, *Land Consolidation and Development on the Umatilla Indian Reservation*, 95th Cong., 1st sess., Nov. 22, 1977, H. Rept. 819.

U.S. Congress.

Senate, *Minutes of Siletz Reservation Council:* Senate Misc. Doc. 65, 43d Cong., 1st sess., 1874.

Senate, *Letter From the Secretary of the Interior Transmitting Copies of Treaties Between the United States and Certain Indians In Oregon:* Senate Exec. Doc. 25, 53d Cong., 1st sess., 1893.

Senate, *Report of Klamath Boundary Commission of 1896:* Senate Doc. 93, 54th Cong., 2d sess., 1897.

Senate, Subcommittees of Committees on Interior and Insular Affairs, *Termination of Federal Supervision Over Certain Tribes of Indians Joint Hearings, Pt. 4, Klamath Indians, Oregon*, 83d Cong., 2d sess., Feb. 23 and 24, 1954.

Senate, Subcommittees of Committees on Interior and Insular Affairs, *Termination of Federal Supervision Over Certain Tribes of Indians, Joint Hearings, Pt. 4-A, Klamath Indians, Oregon, and Klamath Agency, Oregon*, 83d Cong., 2d sess., April 19, 1954.

Senate, Committee on Interior and Insular Affairs, *Termination of Federal Supervision Over Property of Certain Indians in Western Oregon: Report to Accompany S. 2746*, 83d Cong., 2d sess., May 12, 1954, S. Rept. 1325.

Senate, Committee on Interior and Insular Affairs, *Termination of Federal Supervision Over Property of Klamath Tribe, Oregon: Report to Accompany S. 2745*, 83d Cong., 2d sess., June 25, 1954, S. Rept. 1631.

Senate, Committee on Interior and Insular Affairs, *Klamath Indian Tribe: Termination of Federal Supervision, Hearings*, 84th Cong., 2d sess., May 21 and Oct. 18, 1956.

Senate, Subcommittee on Indian Affairs of the Committee on Interior and Insular Affairs, *Review Appraisal—Klamath Indian Assets, Hearing*, 86th Cong., 1st sess., March 23, 1959.

Senate, Committee on Interior and Insular Affairs, *Lands Held In Trust for Burns Indian Colony, Oregon*, 92d Cong., 2d sess., 1972, S. Rept. 1257.

Senate, Committee on Interior and Insular Affairs, *Pertaining to the Inheritance of Enrolled Members of Confederated Tribes of Warm Springs Reservation of Oregon: Report to Accompany H.R. 5721*, 92d Cong., 2d sess., May 22, 1972, S. Rept. 998.

Senate, Committee on Interior and Insular Affairs, *Lands Held In Trust for Confederated Tribes, Warm Springs Reservation, Oregon*, 92d Cong., 2d sess., May 22, 1972, S. Rept. 999.

Senate, Subcommittee on Public Lands of the Committee on Interior and Insular Affairs, *Klamath Indian Forest, Hearing on S. 3594*, 92d Cong., 2d sess., June 16, 1972.

Senate, Committee on Interior and Insular Affairs, *Indian Health Care Improvement Act*, 94th Cong., 1st sess., May 13, 1975, S. Rept. 133.

Senate, Subcommittee on Indian Affairs of the Committee on Interior and Insular Affairs, *Siletz Restoration Act, Hearings on S. 2801*, 94th Cong., 2d sess., March 30 and 31, 1976.

Senate, Select Committee on Indian Affairs, *Hearings on Implementation of P.L. 93-638, Indian Self-Determination and Education Assistance Act*, 95th Cong., 1st sess., June 7 and 24, 1977.

Senate, Select Committee on Indian Affairs, *Umatilla Indian Reservation Land Consolidation, Development and Inheritance of Trust, Hearing on S. 470 and S. 471*, 95th Cong., 1st sess., July 5, 1977.

Senate, Select Committee on Indian Affairs, *Siletz Indian Restoration, Hearing on S. 1560*, 95th Cong., 1st sess., July 13, 1977.

Senate, Select Committee on Indian Affairs, *Bureau of Indian Affairs Organization, Hearings*, 95th Cong., 1st sess., July 13 and Aug. 1, 1977.

Senate, Select Committee on Indian Affairs, *Federal Domestic Assistance Programs, Hearing on Oversight on the Problems and Barriers Attendant to Indian Tribal and Organizational Participation in Federal Domestic Assistance Programs*, 95th Cong., 1st sess., Sept. 8, 1977.

Senate, Select Committee on Indian Affairs, *Indian Child Welfare Act of 1977*, 95th Cong., 1st sess., Nov. 3, 1977, S. Rept. 597.

Senate, Select Committee on Indian Affairs, *Status of the Bureau of Indian Affairs Reorganization, Hearing*, 95th Cong., 2d sess., Aug. 16, 1978.

Senate, Select Committee on Indian Affairs, *Establishment of A Siletz Indian Reservation, Hearing on S. 2055*, 96th Cong., 1st sess., Jan. 30, 1980.

U.S., Dept. of Commerce. *Federal State and Indian Reservations*. Washington, D.C., 1975.

_____, Bureau of the Census. *1970 Census of the Population.* Washington, D.C., 1973.

_____, Bureau of the Census. "Documentation for American Indian Tabulation." Unpublished, 1970.

U.S., Federal Trade Commission. *Consumer Problems of the Klamath Indians—A Call for Action.* Seattle, 1974.

Valde, Gary, and Coppedge, Robert. 1972. *Income and Poverty Data for Racial Groups: A Compiliation for Oregon Census County Divisions Special Report 367.* Oregon State University Extension Service. Corvallis.

Vastokas, Joan Marie. 1967. "Architecture of the Northwest Coast Indians of America." *Dissertation Abstracts* 28: 563A, UM 67-844.

Vattel, Emmerich de. 1916. *Le Droit de gens; ou Principes de la loi Naturelle appliques a la conduite et au affaires des nations et souverains.* (Reprint of 1758 edition.) Washington, D.C.

Vaughan, Thomas., ed. 1971. *Paul Kane, Columbia Wanderer 1846-47: Sketches and Paintings and His Lecture "The Chinooks."* Portland.

Vayda, Andrew P. 1961. "A Re-Examination of Northwest Coast Economic Systems." *Transactions of the New York Academy of Sciences*, 2d.s. 23: 618-24.

Victor, Frances. 1894. *The Early Indian Wars of Oregon Compiled from the Oregon Archives and Other Original Sources.* Salem.

Voegelin, Carl F., and Wheeler-Voegelin, Erminie. 1944. "Map of North American Indian Languages." *American Ethnological Society Publications*, no. 20.

Vogel, Virgil J. 1970. *American Indian Medicine.* Norman, OK.

Vollman, Timothy. 1974. "Criminal Jurisdiction in Indian Country: Tribal Sovereignty and Defendant's Rights in Conflict." *Kansas LR* 22: 387.

Waddell, Jack O., and Watson, Michael, eds. 1971. *The American Indian in Urban Society.* Boston.

Walker, Deward E., Jr.

1967a. "Mutual Cross-Utilization of Economic Resources in the Plateau: An Example from Aboriginal Nez Perce Fishing Practices." *Washington State University Laboratory of Anthropology Report of Investigations*, no. 41.

1967b. "Nez Perce Sorcery." *Ethnology* 6: 66-96.

1969. "New Light on the Prophet Dance Controversy." *Ethnohistory* 16: 245-55.

1978. *Indians of Idaho.* Moscow, Idaho.

Warm Springs Indian Agency. 1977. "Branch Realty Report." Warm Springs. Unpublished report.

Warm Springs Research Project. 1960. *Final Report.* 5 vols. Corvallis.

Washburn, Wilcomb E.

1971. *Red Man's Land/White Man's Law: A Study of the Past and Present Status of the American Indian.* New York.

1975. *The Indian in America.* New York.

Washington, State of. 1973. *The People Speak: Will You Listen?* Report of the Governor's Indian Affairs Task Force: Urban and Landless Tribes Committees. Olympia.

Wasson, John. 1970. "The Nimipu War." *IH* 3, no. 4: 5-9.

Watkins, Arthur. 1957. "Termination of Federal Supervision: The Removal of Restrictions over Indian Property and Persons." In *American Indians and American Life*, edited by George Simpson and J. Milton Yinger. Philadelphia.

Werhan, Keith M. 1978. "The Indian Civil Rights Act After *Santa Clara Pueblo* v. *Martinez*." *Indian Law Reporter* 5: M-31.

West, Mary Beth. 1976. "Public Law 280." In *Manual of Indian Law*, edited by M. B. West. Washington, D.C.

West, Mary Beth, ed. 1976. *Manual of Indian Law*. Washington, D.C.

West, W. Richard.
1976. "Tribal Powers." In *Manual of Indian Law*, edited by M. B. West. Washington, D.C.
1978. "A Response to *Oliphant* v. *Squamish Tribe*." *Indian Law Reporter* 5: M-20.

Whalen, Sue. 1971. "The Nez Perces' Relationship to Their Land." *IH* 4, no. 3: 30-33.

Wheat, Margaret M. 1967. *Survival Arts of the Primitive Paiutes*. Reno.

Wheeler-Voegelin, Erminie.
1942. "Culture Element Distribution: Northeast California." *UCAR* 7: 47-252.
1955-56. "The Northern Paiute of Central Oregon: A Chapter in Treaty Making." *Ethnohistory* 2: 95-132, 241-72; 3: 1-10.

White, Elijah. 1848. *Ten Years in Oregon: Travels and Adventures of Doctor E. White and Lady West of the Rocky Mountains*. Ithaca.

White, Jay Vincent. 1972. *Taxing Those They Found Here: An Examination of the Tax Exempt Status of the American Indian*. Albuquerque.

Whiting, Beatrice Blyth. 1950. *Paiute Sorcery*. New York. (Reprint. New York, 1970.)

Wilkes, Charles W.
1845. *Narrative of the United States Exploring Expedition During the Years 1838, 1841, 1842*. Philadelphia.
1911. "Report on the Territory of Oregon [1838-42]." *OHQ* 12: 269-99.

Wilkinson, C. F., and Biggs, Eric R.
1976. "A Summary of the Law of American Indian Treaties." In *Manual of Indian Law*, edited by M. B. West. Washington, D.C.
1977. "The Evolution of the Termination Policy." *American Indian LR* 5:139-54.

Wilkinson, C. F., and Volkman, J. M. "Judicial Review of Indian Treaty Abrogation: 'As Long as Water Flows or Grass Grows Upon the Earth'—How Long a Time is That?" *California LR* 63: 601-61.

Wilkinson, Glen A. 1972. "Indian Tribal Claims Before the Court of Claims." In *The Western American Indian: Case Studies in Tribal History*, edited by R. N. Ellis. Lincoln, NE.

Williams, C., and Neubrech, W. 1976. *Indian Treaties: America's Nightmare*. Seattle.

Winnemucca, Sarah. 1960. "An Ethnographic Sketch of the Paviotso in 1882." R. F. Heizer, ed. (In "Papers on Anthropology of the Great Basin.'') *Columbia University Archaeological Research Facility Contributions 7*.

Wissler, Clark. 1950. *The American Indian: An Introduction to the Anthropology of the New World*. New York.

Worcester, Donald E., ed. 1975. *Forked Tongues and Broken Treaties*. Caldwell, ID.

Work, John.
1923. *The Journal of John Work*. William S. Lewis and Paul C. Phillip, eds. Cleveland.
1971. *The Snake Country Expedition of 1830-1831*. Francis D. Haines, Jr., ed. Norman, OK.

Work, S., and Native American Rights Fund. 1975. *Memorandum for Native American Rights Fund Attorneys, re. Siletz Indian Reservation History*. Boulder.

Wyeth, Nathaniel J. 1897. *The Correspondence and Journals of Captain Nathaniel J. Wyeth*, edited by F. G. Young. Eugene, OR.

Zakoji, Hiroto. 1953. ''Klamath Culture Change.'' MA thesis, University of Oregon.

Zakoji, Hiroto, comp. 1961. *Termination and the Klamath Indian Education Program, 1955-1961*. Oregon State Department of Education. Salem.

Zimmerman, William, Jr. 1972. ''The Role of the Bureau of Indian Affairs Since 1933.'' In *The Western American Indian: Case Studies in Tribal History*, edited by R. N. Ellis. Lincoln, NE.

Ziontz, Alvin. 1975. ''In Defense of Tribal Sovereignty: An Analysis of Judicial Error in Construction of the Indian Civil Rights Act.'' *South Dakota LR* 20: 1.

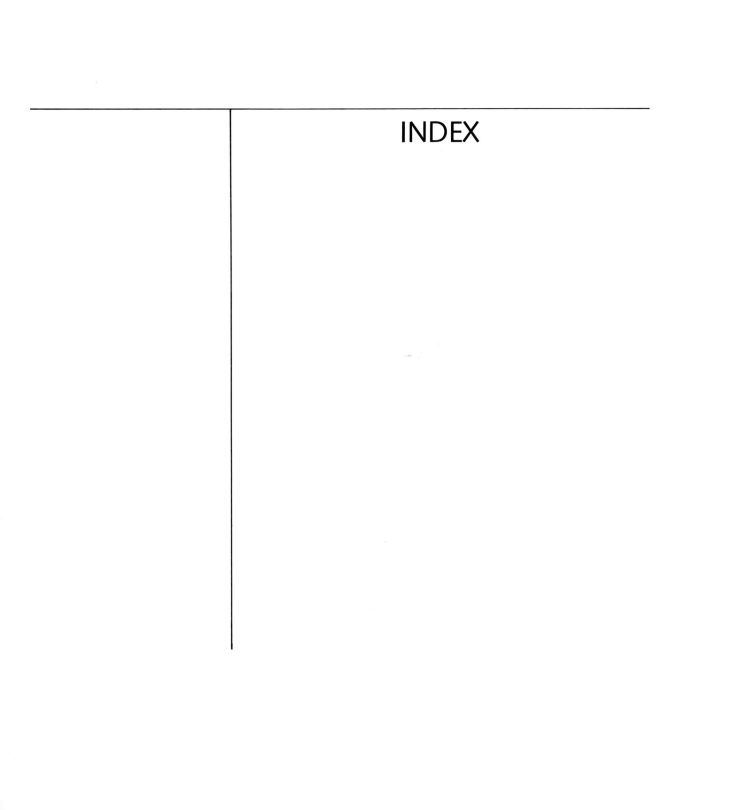

# INDEX

c = inside front cover

Achomawi, 11
Afiliated Tribes of Northwest Indians, 143
Agaidika, c, 9
Agaipanina, c, 9
Agriculture, 21
Ahantchuyuk, c, 9
*Alcea Band of Tillamooks et al* v. *U.S.* (1945, 1950, 1951), 187
Alcohol and drug treatment, 40
Allotment, 97
    Benefits for non-Indians, 74, 182
    Definition, 73, 95
    Klamath Indian Reservation, 110, 184
    Public domain, 103, 105, 114-15, 182, 183
    Trust restrictions on, 95-96, 184
    Umatilla Indian Reservation, 74, 101
Alsea, c, 9, 29, 57, 113
*Alsea Band of Tillamooks* v. *U.S.* (1945), 122
American Indian Policy Review Commission, 77-78, 135, 190
Applegate, Jesse, 59
Applegate Creek, c, 9, 10, 13
Archaeology, 3
Architecture, 36, 37, 38, 40
    *See also* Technology
Armed conflicts
    *See* Conflicts
Art:
    Basketry, 19, 21, 23-25, 42, 45-47
    Leatherwork, 27, 45-47
    Stoneworking, 18, 26, 43
    Woodworking, 15-20, 35-40, 45-47
Assimilation, 71, 78, 107
Atfalati, c
Athapascan, 6, 10, 35, 57
Aukckni, c
Backlash against Indian rights, 135, 139
Bannock, 11-12, 62-63, 90
Basketry
    *See* Art

Big Camas Prairie, Idaho, 103
Blackfoot, 46, 47
Blanchet, Father Francis N., 59
Boldt decision, 169
Brownsville, c
Bureau of Indian Affairs, 72-74, 77, 84-85, 133, 178, 184
    ''On or near'' reservation requirements, 146, 153-55
Burns Paiute, 76, 103-06, 125, 137, 159
    Federal recognition of, 105-06, 131-32, 189
    ''Indian village,'' 105, 184
Burns Paiute Indian Reservation, 53, 93-96, 190
    Creation, 79, 105-06
Calapooia, c
*Callahan* v. *Kimball* (1979), 191
Camp Harney, 103
Camp Stevens Council, 87-88
Captain Jack, 62-63
Cascades, c, 9
Cathlamet, c, 8, 9
Cayuse, c, 9, 11, 12, 46, 47, 59, 62-63, 82, 87
Celilo Falls, 166
    Loss to tribes, 98, 102, 188
Celilo Village, 159, 171
Census, U.S.:
    Unreliability of, 150-52
Ceremonies
    *See* Religion
Champoeg treaty commission, 84
Chelamela, c, 9
Chemawa Indian School, 115, 143
Chepenafa, c, 9
Cherokee, 70, 142, 178
*Cherokee Nation* v. *Georgia* (1831), 70, 178
Chetco, c, 9, 10, 84, 113, 122
Chetleschantunni, c
Chief Joseph the Elder, 66
Chief Joseph the Younger (Hinmah-tooyahlatkekht), 62, 66, 93
Child-rearing
    *See* Family organization
Chinook, c, 6, 8, 9, 32, 42, 54, 75, 84-85, 94, 107, 116-17, 141

Bands, 97, 113
Chinook jargon, 90
Chippewa, 142-43
Chocktote, 105
*Choctaw Nation* v. *Oklahoma* (1970), 91, 189
Chowwatnanee, 103
Chronology, 173-92
Clackamas, c, 9
Clatskanie, c, 9, 10, 32
Clatsop, c, 8, 9, 56, 113
Clowwewalla, c, 9
Coast Area:
    Environment, 6
    Ethnographies, 57
    Social organization, 56
    Tribal distribution, c, 9-10
Coast Reservation
    *See* Siletz Indian Reservation
Coeur D'Alene, 46
Cohen, Felix, 129
Collier, John, 76, 77
Columbia River fishing controversy, 165-72
Columbia River Intertribal Fish Commission, 171
Confederated Tribes of Grand Ronde, 76-78, 114-15, 140-41, 190
Confederated Tribes of Siletz, 114-17, 168, 190
    Restoration, 78, 115, 136, 139, 191
    Termination, 77-78
    *See also* Siletz Indian Reservation
Confederated Tribes of Umatilla, 74, 79, 100-02, 137, 159, 169, 188
    Hunting and fishing rights, 160-61 169
    Indian Claims Commission cases, 118-21, 125
    *See also* Umatilla Indian Reservation
*Confederated Tribes of Umatilla* v. *Maison* (1960, 1963), 188
*Confederated Tribes of the Umatilla Indian Reservation* v. *Alexander* (1977), 102, 191
Confederated Tribes of Warm Springs, 13, 74-76, 79, 93, 97-99,

137, 158, 169, 186
Hunting and fishing rights on reservation, 81, 160
Indian Claims Commission cases, 118-19, 125
*See also* Warm Springs Indian Reservation
*Confederated Tribes of Warm Springs v. U.S.* (1941, 1945, 1966), 97, 99, 186
Confederations, 13
Conflicts, 12, 46, 62-64, 81, 84, 85, 87, 178, 181
Bannock Wars, 103, 106, 182
Modoc War, 93, 107, 181
Nez Perce War, 103, 106, 182
Yakima War, 87, 180
Cooniac, c, 9
Coos, c, 9, 57, 113
*Coos et al* v. *U.S.* (1938), 113
Coos–Lower Umpqua–Siuslaw Tribe, 75, 76, 118-19, 122, 188
Contemporary affairs, 136, 141
Displacement, 93-94, 113-14
Tribal hall, 114, 186
Coquille, 113, 122, 141
Cow Creek Band of Upper Umpquas, c, 9, 86, 114, 190, 191
Federal recognition, 131, 140-41
Cow Creek-Umpqua Reservation, 81
Crook, George, 103
Cultural areas, 2, 3-7
Dakubetede, c, 13
Dart, Anson, 84, 179
Delaware, 177
Dentalium, 25
Discovery theory, 81
*See also* Indian lands
Displacement, 93-94, 103, 113-14
*See also* Removal policy
Dockspus, c
Dog River, c
Donation Land Act, 82, 84, 179
Dreamer Movement, 106
Duck Valley Reservation, 106
Dukwakni, c
*Duwamish et al Indians* v. *U.S.* (1934), 90
Economic development, 137, 188

Ehagant (Egan), 103
Elders, 41
Environment, 47
Epidemics, 60
Euchre Creek, c
Eugene Urban Indian Center, 139, 147, 190
Euskni, c
Euro-Americans, 44
Exploration and settlement, 58-60
First contacts, 3-5
Perception of Indians, 13, 29, 53, 60-62
Executive orders, 81, 103, 176
Exploration of Oregon
*See* Euro-Americans
Factions in contemporary tribes, 141
Family organization, 35-41, 48, 54-57, 61
Federal Emergency Relief Act (FERA), 76, 106, 185
Federal Indian law, 91, 122-23, 125-26, 129-30, 175-76
Federal Indian policy, 67-78, 91, 93, 175, 184
Assimilation, 68, 71, 73, 77-78
Extended to Oregon, 82, 84, 178
*Federal Power Commission* v. *U.S.* (1955), 98
Federal recognition, 75, 78, 105-06, 115, 131-32, 146, 191
Fee patent allotment, 95
Fishing, 15-20, 42
Fishing rights, 165-72
Five Civilized Tribes, 70
Flathead, 46
Food resources, 5, 15-28, 61
Fort Dalles Urban Indians, 147
Fort Harney, 89, 181, 182
Fort Hoskins, 114
Fort McDermitt, Nevada, 105, 106, 188
Fort Umpqua, 114
Fort Yamhill, 114
Galice Creek, c, 9, 10
General Allotment Act (Dawes Act), 73, 101, 182
*See also* Allotment
Gididika, c, 9

Government
*See* Social organization
Goyatikadu, c
Grand Ronde, 116-17
*See also* Confederated Tribes of Grand Ronde
Grand Ronde Indian Reservation, 50, 53, 85, 87, 112-15, 180, 185
Displacement, 93, 113-14
Land base after allotment, 74, 183
*See also* Confederated Tribes of Grand Ronde
Grant, Ulysses S., 89, 103
Great Basin Area:
Environment, 7
Ethnographies, 57
Social organization, 56
Tribal distribution, c, 11-12
Great Basin–Plateau border, 7, 12
Gshanee, 103
Gumbotkni, c
Gwinidiba, 9
Haida, 45
Hanis Coos, 9
*See also* Coos
Harney, George, 114
Hinmahtooyahlatkekht
*See* Chief Joseph the Younger
Hines, Gustavus, 61
Horses, 12, 34, 46-47
Housing, 5, 35-40
Hunibuidika, c, 9
Hunting, 26-28
Hunting, fishing and gathering rights, 160-62
Huntington, J.W.P., 89, 105
Imnaha Band of Nez Perce, c, 11
Indian Appropriations Expenditures Act, 184
Indian Child Welfare Act, 159
Indian Citizenship Act, 75, 184
Indian Civil Rights Act, 158, 189
Indian claims, 109-11, 113, 116-25
Chinook, 116-17, 185
Land valuation, 117, 125-26
Nez Perce, 116-19, 186
Northern Paiute, 103, 106, 118-19, 187, 188
Offsets reducing awards, 97-98,

122, 185
U.S. Court of Claims, 122, 180
Indian Claims Commission, 116-26,
    187, 191
Indian Country, 77, 96
    Definition, 79-81, 156
Indian education, 137, 177, 190
Indian Education Act, 137, 190
Indian Health Care Improvement Act
    191
Indian Health Service, 146, 155, 184
Indian Homestead Act, 182
Indian identity, 153, 155
Indian Lake Campground, 101
Indian lands, 66-68, 75-76, 89-90,
    96
    Federal obligations, 70-72
    Loss of, 74-75, 82, 95-96, 107-09,
        112-14, 181, 182
    Oregon Indian views, 67-68, 96
    Restorations, 101-02, 123, 125,
        186, 190
    Surplus after restoration, 74, 96
    Title, 67, 81, 82, 122, 123, 125,
        177
    Trust, 70, 95
Indian New Deal, 76, 106, 185
Indian Reorganization Act (IRA), 75,
    76, 97, 106, 185
Indian Reservation Leasing Act, 184
Indian Self-Determination and Educa
    tion Assistance Act, 136, 159, 190
Indian Trade and Intercourse acts, 68
    178
Indian Trust Allotment Act, 184
Inland Valleys Area:
    Environment, 7
    Ethnographies, 57
    Social organization, 56
    Tribal distribution, c, 10
Intertribal Organizations, 143
Jefferson, Thomas, 58
John Day Indians, c, 9, 11, 12, 97
Johnson-O'Malley Act, 76, 137, 185
Johnson v. McIntosh (1823), 81, 177
Joseph, The Elder
    See Chief Joseph the Elder
Joseph, The Younger
    See Chief Joseph the Younger

Joseph Band of Nez Perce, 11
Joshua, c
Jurisdiction over Indian Country, 156-
    59, 191
Kah-Nee-Tah, 98
Kalapuya, c, 6, 9, 10, 13, 29, 57, 81,
    84, 116-17
Kalawatset, c
Kamiakin, 87
Karok, 10
Kathlamet, 113
Khustenete, c
Kimball v. Callaghan (1969, 1974,
    1979), 78, 111, 190
Kinship
    See Family organization
Klamath & Moadoc Tribes et al v.
    U.S. (1935, 1938), 109, 110, 185,
    186
Klamath Indian Reservation, 53, 63,
    89, 107-11, 181
    Boundary disputes, 90, 107-09
    Displacement, 93, 103
    See also Klamath Indians
Klamath Indians, c, 6, 9, 11, 12, 20,
    21, 26, 35, 36, 39, 42, 43, 52, 54,
    59, 74, 88, 107-11, 159, 190
    Boundary disputes, 75, 183
    Hunting and fishing rights, 161-62
    Importance of hunting, 163-64
    Indian Claims Commission cases,
        120-21, 125
    Termination, 77-78, 110-11, 187
    See also Klamath Indian Reservation
Klamath Lakes Area:
    Environment, 6-7
    Ethnographies, 57
    Social organization, 56
    Tribal distribution, c, 11
Kokikwas, c
Koniac Tchinouck, 141
Kowacdikni, c
Kuitsch, c
Kwakiutl, 45
Kwalhioqua, 10
Kwatami, 9
Kwikwulit, c
Land ownership, 14
Lane, Joseph, 84

Languages, 48-53
Lapwai Reservation, 63
Latgawa, c, 9, 10
"Lawyer," 62
Leatherwork
    See Art
Lee, Jason, 59
Lewis and Clark, 32, 58-60
Lohim, 12
Long Tom River, c
Louisiana Purchase, 81
Lower Columbia Area:
    Environment, 6
    Ethnographies, 57
    Social organization, 56
    Tribal distribution, c, 8-9
Lower Coquille, c
Lower Deschutes, c
Lower Umpqua, c, 9
Luckiamute, c, 9
McQuinn Strip, 97-98, 123, 125, 190
Maison v. Confederated Tribes of
    Umatilla Reservation (1963), 102
Malheur Indian Reservation, 75, 89,
    94, 103-04, 182
    Closure, 106, 182
    See also Burns Paiute and Paiute
Marriage
    See Family organization
Marshall, John, 68
Mary's River, c
Meek, Joseph, 59
Menominee, 78
Meriam Report, 75-76, 135, 184
Meyer, Dillon, 77
Migrant and Indian Coalition, 155
Mikonotunne, c
Miluk, 9
    See also Coos
Mishikwutmetunne, c
Missionaries, 59-62
Mix (Indian commissioner), 88
Modoc, c, 6, 9, 11, 20, 42, 43, 62-63,
    88, 93, 107
Mohawk, 177
Molalla, c, 9, 10-12, 14, 36, 57, 107
Mukluks Hemeunga (newspaper),
    111
Multnomah, c, 9

Myths
    *See* Oral literature
Nahankuotana, c
Narragansett Indian Reservation, 125
Natches, 105
National Industrial Recovery Act
    (NIRA), 76, 106, 185
Native American Indian Religious
    Freedom Act, 191
Natural areas
    *See* Cultural areas
Nee-Me-Poo, c
Nehalem, c, 9, 113, 183
Nestucca, c, 9
Nez Perce, c, 9, 11-14, 34, 46, 47,
    52, 58-60, 62-63, 93, 142, 165,
    182
    Indian Claims Commission cases,
        116-19, 125
    Treaties, 87-88
Nicht Yow Way Village Community
    Center, 102
Nimipu, 13-14
Nootka, 45
North American Indian Women's
    Association, 143
Northern Paiute
    *See* Burns Paiute, Malheur Indian
        Reservation and Paiute
Northwest Laboratory, 143
Northwest Ordinance of 1787, 82,
    177
Ocheo, 105
Ogden, Peter S., 59
Oneida, 177
Oral literature, 29-30, 42, 54, 56
Oregon Central Military Road, 107-
    09
    *See also* Klamath Indian Reserva-
        tion and Yamsay Mountain case
Oregon Revised Statutes, 176
Oregon State Commission on Indian
    Services, 135, 143
Oregon Territory:
    Creation of, 72, 82, 178
Oregon Treaty of 1846, 82, 178
Organization for the Forgotten
    American, 139, 147
Ornaments, 25, 42-44

Owhi, 89
Owits (Otis, Oitz), 103
Paiute, c, 9, 11-14, 21, 24, 26, 29,
    31, 59, 97, 107
    Burns Paiute Indian Reservation,
        93-96
    Conflicts, 62-63
    Displacement, 93-94
    Indian Claims Commissions cases,
        118-19, 125
    Population and settlement, 32-34
    Transportation, 46, 47
    Treaties, 88-90
    *See also* Burns Paiute Indian
        Reservation
Palmer, Joel, 85, 87, 179
Panaina, 64, 88
Paskankwas, c
Patihichidika, c, 9
Paviotso, c
Pendleton, 100, 182
Penobscot-Passamaquoddy, 125
Penutian, 113
Peopeopmoxmox, 87
Pistol River, c
Pit River Indians, 42, 107
Plaikni, c
Plains Indians, 13, 40, 46
Plant gathering, 21-24, 43
Plateau Area:
    Environment, 7
    Ethnographies, 57
    Social organization, 56
    Tribal distribution, c, 11
Plateau tribes, 85, 87-88
Political organization, 32
Ponee, 103
Population, 74
    Aboriginal, 5, 32-34
    Contemporary, 149-52
        Age distribution, 149-50
        Differing estimates, 153, 155
Portland Urban Indian Council, 139,
    146-47, 189
Port Orford treaties (1851), 179
Pow-wow circuit, 143
Prehistory, 3
Preservation of resources, 17
Public Law 83-280, 77, 98, 157

Pudding River, c
Quinault Indian Reservation,
    Washington, 93
Ratified treaties, 87-88
Religion, 4, 14, 15, 29-30, 40, 42, 44,
    54, 56, 61
Relocation, 77
    To urban areas, 144-45
Removal policy, 70, 93-94, 178, 180
Reservations, 72-74, 93-94, 96
    As means to gain federal recog-
        nition, 131-32
    Creation, 69, 79, 81, 91
    *See also* specific reservations
Restoration of terminated tribes, 78,
    115, 139, 191
Rinehart, W. V., 106
Rogue River, 10, 13, 57, 62-63
Roosevelt, Franklin D., 76
Sahaptian, 11, 12, 35
Salmon River, c, 9, 113
Santiam, c, 9
Schonchin, 62
Seafood and shellfish, 25
Seasonal cycles, 29-32
Seasonal movements, 5
Self-determination, 76, 78, 135, 136
Settlement patterns, 32-34
Shamanism
    *See* religion
Shasta, c, 6, 9, 10, 42, 57, 107
Shasta-Costa, c, 9, 10
Shellfish gathering, 25
Shoalwater Chinook, 8
Shoalwater Indian Reservation, 93
Shoshoni, 11, 12
Siletz, c, 9, 113
    *See also* Confederated Tribes of
        Siletz
Siletz Agency, 113
Siletz Indian Reservation, 50, 53, 87,
    89, 112-15, 180, 192
    Displacement, 93, 113-14
    Land base, 74, 75, 183
    Yachats subagency, 93, 113
    *See also* Confederated Tribes of
        Siletz
Sioux, 142-43
Siuslaw, c, 9, 113

Sixes River, c
Skilloot, c, 8
Slater Allotment Act, 101, 182
Slavery, 42, 55-56
Smackshop, c
Snake, c, 13
    See also Malheur Indian Reserva-
        tion and Paiute
Snake or Paiute Indians v. U.S.
    (1953), 89
Social organization, 5, 54-57,
    See also Family organization, Tribal
        organization, Women's role in
        Indian society
Sohappy v. Smith (1966), 97
Sovereignty, 68, 70, 77-78, 96, 130-
    31
Spalding, Eliza, 59
Spalding, Henry, 59
Spiritual beliefs
    See Religion
Stevens, Isaac I., 87
Stockbridges, 177
Stoneworking
    See Art
Surprise Valley Paiute, c
Sweatlodges, 40
Table Rock Reservation, 81, 86
Tagudika, c, 9
Takelma, c, 9, 10, 35, 41, 57, 84, 86
Taltushtuntude, c
Tansey Point treaties (1851), 178
Taos, New Mexico, 125
Tashego, 103
Tax-exempt status of Indian tribes,
    138
Technology:
    Architecture, 35-41
    Fishing, 15-20
    Hunting, 26-28
    Plant gathering, 21-24
Tekopa, c
Tenino, c, 9, 11, 97
Termination, 132
    Abandoned as policy, 78, 135
    Grand Ronde Indian Reservation,
        77-78
    Impact of, 77-78, 110-11, 114-15,
        134-35, 190

Klamath Indians, 77-78, 110-11,
    190
    Legislation and resolutions, 77, 187
    Western Oregon tribes, 77-78,
        114-15, 190
    See also Public Law 83-280
Thiel, William, 107
Tillamook, c, 9, 36, 52, 57, 58, 75,
    84-85, 113, 116-17, 122, 183
Title IV, 137, 155
Tolowa, c, 9, 10
Tools
    See Technology
Trade, 42-44, 58, 61
Traditional culture, 73, 91, 191
    Contemporary survival, 67, 149
    In urban communities, 114, 147-
        48
    Specific tribes, 98, 102, 105-06,
        111, 114-15
Transportation, 5, 14, 45-47
Treaties, 81-92
    Congressional end to, 88, 103, 181
    Definition of, 69, 79
    Effects of, 68, 90-91
    Federal recognition, 131-32
    Public Law 83-280, 158
    Ratified, 80-81, 113
        Klamath, 88, 107, 181
        Middle Oregon tribes, 81, 88,
            97, 180, 181
        Modoc, 88, 181
        Nez Perce, 87-88, 180, 181
        Plateau tribes, 87-88, 180
        Rogue River (Takelma), 81, 180
        Snake, 88, 181
        Warm Springs
            See Middle Oregon tribes
        Western Oregon tribes, 85, 113
    Reserved rights, 69, 71, 79, 91,
        111, 165, 183
    Reserving hunting and fishing
        rights, 88, 165, 191
    U.S. Constitution, 69, 71
    Unratified, 71, 84-85, 178
        Coast treaty (1855), 85, 87, 113,
            122, 180
        Effects of, 81, 113-14
        Modoc, 88, 180

Paiute peace and friendship trea-
    ty (1868), 88-89, 103, 181
    Tualatin, 85, 179
    Western Oregon, 84, 183
Tribal affiliations, 140, 142, 145
Tribal courts, 158-59, 182
Tribal distribution, c, 8-14
Tribal names, 8-14
Tribal organization, 8-14
Tribal powers, 156, 157
Tribally Controlled Community
    Colleges Assistance Act, 137
Tribes:
    Landless, 75-76, 94, 103-05, 111,
        114-15
    See also specific tribes
Tribes of contemporary Oregon, 140-
    43, 145
Trust relationship, 70-71, 77-78, 81,
    91, 130-31
    Federal recognition, 75, 132
Tsitsiadi, c
Tualatin, c, 9, 85
Tule Lake, 88
Tuscaroras, 177
Tututni, c, 9, 84, 113, 122, 141
Tygh, c, 9, 11, 97
Umatilla Indian Reservation, 53, 93,
    100-02, 182, 190
    Inheritance legislation, 102, 191
    See also Confederated Tribes of
        Umatilla
Umatillas, c, 9, 11, 14, 87
    See also Confederated Tribes of
        Umatilla
Umpquas, 57, 81, 86, 113
United Indian Fish Committee, 171
United Indian Women, 143
United Indians of All Tribes, 143
United States Citizenship for
    American Indians, 132
United States Indian policy, 67-78
    Recent, 127-39
United States Statutes at Large, 175
United States Treasury checks, 137-
    38
U.S. v. California and Oregon Land
    Co. (1893, 1904), 110, 183
U.S. v. Cook (1873), 181

*U.S.* v. *Klamath & Moadoc Tribes et al* (1938), 110
*U.S.* v. *Oregon* (*Sohappy* v. *Smith*) (1969), 97, 189
*U.S.* v. *Sandoval* (1913), 184
*U.S.* v. *Shoshoni Tribe* (1938), 186
*U.S.* v. *Walker Irrigation District* (1939), 91
*U.S.* v. *Washington* (1974), 90
U.S. National Bank of Oregon, 110-11, 189
United Tribal People, 139, 147
Upper Coquille, c, 9, 10
Upper Deschutes, c
Upper Umpqua, c, 9, 10
Urban Indians, 144-48
    Population shifts, 146-47
    References, 144, 146
    *See also* Eugene Urban Indian Center and Portland Urban Indian Council
Wadadika Paiute, c, 9, 12, 32-33
Waiilatpu, c
Walla Walla, c, 11
Walla Walla Council (Camp Stevens Council), 87-88
Walla Walla treaty (1855), 87
Wallowa, c
Walpapi Paiute, c, 9, 11
Walula, c
Wappato, c

Wardship:
    *See* Trust relationship
Warm Springs, c, 11, 13, 59, 87-88, 97
    *See also* Confederated Tribes of Warm Springs
Warm Springs Agency, 105
Warm Springs Indian Reservation, 50, 53, 93, 97-99
    Inheritance legislation, 98, 190
    McQuinn Strip, 90, 97-98, 123, 125, 190
    *See also* Confederated Tribes of Warm Springs
Wars
    *See* Conflicts
Wasco, c, 6, 8, 9, 13, 32-33, 42, 44, 52, 58
Wasco Council, 87-88
Wasco treaty (1855), 87-88
Watihichidika, c, 9
Wayampam, c, 11
Western Chinook, 141
Wetouwewa, 103
White, Elijah, 59, 84, 178
Whitman massacre, 82
Whitman Mission, 59, 63
Willamette Tumwater, c
Willow River Indian Benevolent Association, 139, 147, 189
*Winans* v. *U.S.* (1906), 69, 183
Winema National Forest, 110, 190

Winnemucca, 62, 105, 106
Winnemucca, Sarah, 62
*Winters* v. *U.S.* (1908), 69, 91, 184
Wishram, 6, 8
Woll-Pah-Pe Snake treaty (1865), 88
Women's role in Indian societies, 17, 21, 26, 41, 54-56
Woodworking
    *See* Art
*Worcester* v. *Georgia* (1832), 68, 70, 178
Wyam, c, 9, 11, 42, 58, 97
Wyeth, Nathaniel, 59
Yahooskin Snake treaty (1864), 88
Yahuskin Paiute, c, 9, 11
Yakima Indian Nation, 142, 165
Yakima Indian Reservation:
    Displacement, 93, 103, 106
    Mt. Adams restoration, 123, 125
Yakimas, 11, 46, 62-63, 87
Yamhill, c, 9
Yamsay Mountain case, 107-10, 183
Yapadika, c, 9
Yaquinas, c, 9, 113
Yellowhawk Medical Clinic, 102
Yoncalla Kalapuya, c, 9, 10
Young, Ewing, 59
Yukichetunne, c
Yulalonkni, c
Yurok, 35
Zimmerman, William, 77